A New Star-Rating System & Other Exciting News from Frommer's!

In our continuing effort to publish the savviest, most up-to-date, and most appealing travel guides available, we've added some great new features.

Frommer's guides now include a new **star-rating system.** Every hotel, restaurant, and attraction is rated from 0 to 3 stars to help you set priorities and organize your time.

We've also added **seven brand-new features** that point you to the great deals, in-the-know advice, and unique experiences that separate travelers from tourists. Throughout the guide, look for:

Finds	Special finds—those places only insiders know about
Fun Fact	Fun facts—details that make travelers more informed and their trips more fun
Kids	Best bets for kids—advice for the whole family
Moments	Special moments—those experiences that memories are made of
Overrated	Places or experiences not worth your time or money
Tips	Insider tips—some great ways to save time and money
Value	Great values—where to get the best deals

We've also added a **"What's New"** section in every guide—a timely crash course in what's hot and what's not in every destination we cover.

Here's what the critics say about Frommer's:

Other Great Guides for Your Trip:

Frommer's Canada
Frommer's Montréal & Québec City
Frommer's Ottawa with Kids
Frommer's Toronto with Kids

Frommer's®

Toronto

2003

by Hilary Davidson

WILEY

Wiley Publishing, Inc.

About the Author

Toronto native **Hilary Davidson** now calls New York City home, thanks to her persuasive Manhattan-born husband, Daniel. She is a contributing editor at *Chatelaine* magazine and writes for *Working Mother, Wedding Bells, Discover, Profit,* and *Pages.* She is also a contributor to *Frommer's Canada.* She can be reached at hcdavidson@excite.com.

Published by:

Wiley Publishing, Inc.

909 Third Ave.
New York, NY 10022

ISBN 0-7645-6698-9
ISSN 1047-7853

Editor: Joel Enos
Production Editor: Suzanna R. Thompson
Cartographer: Nick Trotter
Photo Editor: Richard Fox
Production by Wiley Indianapolis Composition Services

Front cover photo: View of the city skyline and harbor
Back cover photo: Hockey Hall of Fame statue

For information on our other products and services or to obtain technical support, please contact our Customer Care Department within the U.S. at 800-762-2974, outside the U.S. at 317-572-3993 or fax 317-572-4002.

Wiley also publishes its books in a variety of electronic formats. Some content that appears in print may not be available in electronic formats.

Manufactured in the United States of America

5   4   3   2   1

Contents

List of Maps

Acknowledgments

Many thanks to my terrific editors, Myka Carroll and Joel Enos, and to the rest of the Frommer's team, who expertly shepherded this project from manuscript to book. I am also grateful to my mother, Sheila Davidson, who helped me in countless ways with this project. Finally, I owe a heartfelt thanks to my husband, Dan, whose tireless enthusiasm carried me throughout this project.

An Invitation to the Reader

In researching this book, we discovered many wonderful places—hotels, restaurants, shops, and more. We're sure you'll find others. Please tell us about them, so we can share the information with your fellow travelers in upcoming editions. If you were disappointed with a recommendation, we'd love to know that, too. Please write to:

Frommer's Toronto 2003
Wiley Publishing, Inc. • 909 Third Ave. • New York, NY 10022

An Additional Note

Please be advised that travel information is subject to change at any time—and this is especially true of prices. We therefore suggest that you write or call ahead for confirmation when making your travel plans. The authors, editors, and publisher cannot be held responsible for the experiences of readers while traveling. Your safety is important to us, however, so we encourage you to stay alert and be aware of your surroundings. Keep a close eye on cameras, purses, and wallets, all favorite targets of thieves and pickpockets.

New! Frommer's Star Ratings & Icons

Every hotel, restaurant, and attraction listing in this guide has been ranked for quality, value, service, amenities, and special features using a star-rating scale. In country, state, and regional guides, we also rate towns and regions to help you narrow down your choices and budget your time accordingly. Hotels and restaurants in the Very Expensive and Expensive categories are rated on a scale of one (highly recommended) to three stars (exceptional). Those in the Moderate and Inexpensive categories rate from zero (recommended) to two stars (very highly recommended). Attractions, towns, and regions are rated according to the following scale: zero stars (recommended), one star (highly recommended), two stars (very highly recommended), and three stars (must-see).

In addition to the rating system, we also use seven icons to highlight insider information, useful tips, special bargains, hidden gems, memorable experiences, kid-friendly venues, places to avoid, and other useful information:

(Finds (Fun Fact (Kids (Moments (Overrated (Tips (Value

The following abbreviations are used for credit cards:

AE	American Express	DISC	Discover	V	Visa
DC	Diners Club	MC	MasterCard		

FROMMERS.COM

Now that you have the guidebook to a great trip, visit our website at **www.frommers.com** for travel information on nearly 2,500 destinations. With features updated regularly, we give you instant access to the most current trip-planning information available. At Frommers.com, you'll also find the best prices on airfares, accommodations, and car rentals—and you can even book travel online through our travel booking partners. At Frommers.com, you'll also find the following:

- Online updates to our most popular guidebooks
- Vacation sweepstakes and contest giveaways
- Newsletter highlighting the hottest travel trends
- Online travel message boards with featured travel discussions

What's New in Toronto

Toronto—or "Hollywood North," as some wags would have it—is brimming with energy these days. Here's a quick look at what's happening now.

PLANNING YOUR TRIP Air Canada (www.aircanada.ca) is now Canada's only national airline, and it operates direct daily flights from most major U.S. cities and from many smaller ones. Luckily, it also provides service over the pond, since **Virgin Atlantic** has suspended its London-to-Toronto service. Within Canada's borders, Air Canada has launched a new division called **Tango,** a cheaper, no-frills service that operates through Toronto's Pearson International Airport (www.flytango.com). And speaking of the airport, there are major changes afoot: the grand new terminal is almost complete, and when it opens for business it will replace the gloomy terminals 1 and 2. In the meantime, try to ignore the messy rerouting of traffic at the airport.

ACCOMMODATIONS Toronto has a fine selection of hotels, and some of them are breaking new ground in their appeal to travelers. Last year, the trend was for hotels to open day spas; the Stillwater Spa at the **Park Hyatt Toronto,** 4 Avenue Rd. (© **800/ 233-1234**), remains one of the best in the city. This year, hotels are branching out in different directions. Several, including the **Park Hyatt Toronto,** the **Fairmont Royal York, Le Royal Meridien King Edward,** and the **Four Seasons,** are offering glamorous afternoon teas. And some, like the **Fairmont Royal York,** are reaching out to a new four-legged clientele, by creating special programs for guests with pets. See chapter 4, "Where to Stay," for more information.

DINING The biggest change on Toronto's dining scene is something you won't see—namely, smoking at the table. The summer of 2001 brought with it a new law that makes all restaurants smoke-free. Establishments that want to continue to allow smoking have to reclassify themselves as bars, which can't admit anyone under the age of 19. As you can imagine, the regulation is causing quite the food fight.

In other news, there have been some notable openings. The **Mercer Street Grill,** a longstanding favorite, may have closed, but its owner, Simon Bower, has created a dazzling new restaurant called **YYZ,** 345 Adelaide St. W. (© **416/599-3399**). Other new hot spots include the Greek-inspired **Gus,** 1033 Bay St. (© **416/ 923-8159**), and the ultra-modern **Rouge,** 467 Bloor St. W. (© **416/ 413-0713**). And vegetarians, take note: An increasing number of Toronto chefs are creating special meat-free menus. See chapter 5, "Where to Dine," for all the details.

WHAT TO SEE & DO Several Toronto museums, including the **Art Gallery of Ontario,** have recently changed their admission fee structure. While pay-what-you-can was commonplace in the past, almost everyone now has a fixed admission fee in place.

However, they also have some time slots for cut-rate admission or special family passes (see individual reviews for the details). Also, Toronto-bound parents will find lots to keep small fry entertained if they consult a new website: **www.helpwevegotkids.com**. See chapter 6, "What to See & Do," for complete details.

SHOPPING The Canadian dollar might be in the doldrums, but that's a boon to U.S. and overseas shoppers. Not that you should need further inducement to stop in at the unique local shops, including only-in-Toronto spots like **Caban** (for chic housewares), **Peach Berserk** and **Fashion Crimes** (for women's fashions), **Mink** (for jewelry and accessories), and **Mabel's Fables** (for children's books and toys). Budget-minded shoppers will note the opening of the new **Winner's** flagship store (the place to shop for designer clothes and housewares at a discount) at **College Park.** See chapter 8, "Shopping," for complete details.

AFTER DARK Toronto's club scene is ever changing. The classic **El**

Mocambo lounge is closed at the moment, but its owner claims its spirit is alive at the **Tequila Lounge,** 794 Bathurst St. (© 416/536-0346). The gargoyle-clad **Temple,** 469 King St. W. (© 416/598-4050), is the latest hot spot to cut a rug, and the new **Yuk Yuk's Superclub** at 224 Richmond St. W. (© 416/967-6425) is the place to be to catch local and international standup comedians. See chapter 9, "Toronto After Dark," for complete details.

SIDE TRIPS The **Stratford Festival** opened a new theater space in 2002: called the **Studio Theatre,** it's an intimate 278-seat space that will be devoted to new and experimental pieces. The Stratford Festival has also created a new Sunday lecture offering, called the **Celebrated Writers Series,** in which prominent authors discuss their works. Literary luminaries that it has attracted so far include Michael Ondaatje and Joyce Carol Oates. See chapter 10, "Side Trips From Toronto," for complete details.

The Best of Toronto

Chances are that even if you've never set foot in Toronto, you've seen the city a hundred times over. Known for the past decade as "Hollywood North," Toronto has stood in for international centers from European capitals to New York—but rarely does it play itself. Self-deprecating Torontonians embody a paradox: Proud of their city's architectural, cultural, and culinary charms, they are unsure whether it's all up to international snuff.

After spending a single afternoon wandering around Toronto, you might wonder why this is a question at all. The sprawling city boasts lush parks, renowned architecture, and excellent galleries. There's no shortage of skyscrapers, particularly in the downtown core. Still, many visitors marvel at the number of Torontonians who live in houses on tree-lined boulevards that are a walk or a bike ride away from work.

Out-of-towners can see the fun side of the place, but Torontonians aren't so sure. They recall the stuffiness of the city's past. Often called "Toronto the Good," it was a town where you could walk down any street in safety, but you couldn't get a drink on Sunday.

Then a funny thing happened on the way through the 1970s. Canada loosened its immigration policies and welcomed waves of Italians, Greeks, Chinese, Vietnamese, Jamaicans, Indians, Somalians, and others, many of whom settled in Toronto. Political unrest in Quebec drove out Anglophones, many into the waiting arms of Toronto. The city's economy flourished, which in turn gave its cultural side a boost.

Natives and visitors alike enjoy the benefits of this rich cultural mosaic. More than 5,000 restaurants are scattered across the city, serving everything from simple Greek souvlaki to Asian-accented fusion cuisine. Festivals such as Caribana and Caravan draw tremendous crowds to celebrate heritage through music and dance. Its newfound cosmopolitanism has made Toronto a key player on the arts scene, too. The Toronto International Film Festival in September and the International Festival of Authors in October draw top stars of the movie and publishing worlds. The theater scene rivals London's and New York's.

Toronto now ranks at or near the top of any international urban quality-of-life study. The city has accomplished something rare, expanding and developing its daring side while holding on to its traditional strengths. It's a great place to visit, but watch out: You might just end up wanting to live here.

1 Frommer's Favorite Toronto Experiences

- **Horseback Riding in Sunnybrook Park.** One of Toronto's proudest features is its amazing expanse of green. In the 243-hectare (600-acre) Sunnybrook Park system, 20 minutes from downtown, you can explore trails on horseback. See chapter 6.
- **Trend-Setting at a Local Theater.** Toronto likes its blockbuster

Metropolitan Toronto

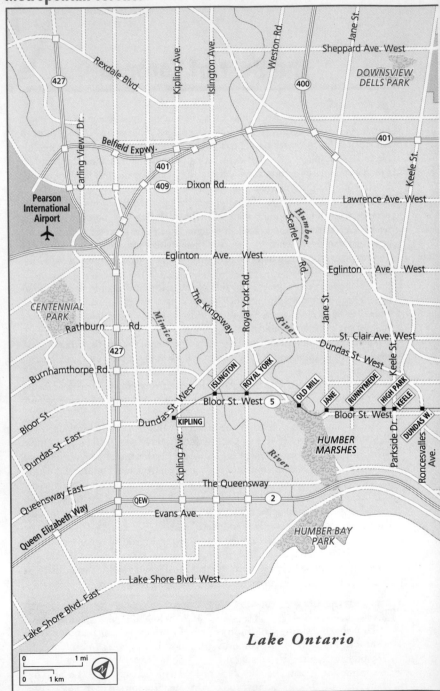

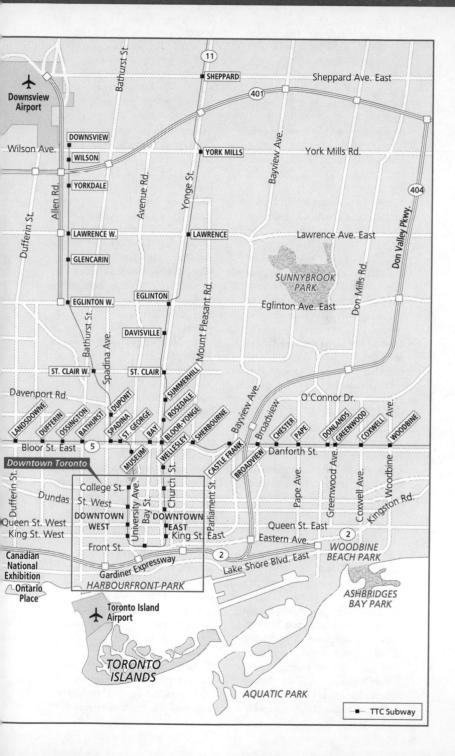

Downsview Airport

Wilson Ave.

11 SHEPPARD

Sheppard Ave. East

401

DOWNSVIEW

WILSON

YORK MILLS

York Mills Rd.

YORKDALE

404

Bayview Ave.

LAWRENCE W.

LAWRENCE

Lawrence Ave. East

GLENCARIN

Don Mills Rd.

Don Valley Pkwy.

EGLINTON W.

EGLINTON

SUNNYBROOK PARK

Eglinton Ave. East

DAVISVILLE

ST. CLAIR W.

ST. CLAIR

Davenport Rd.

O'Connor Dr.

SUMMERHILL

ROSEDALE

Broadview

CHESTER

PAPE

DONLANDS

GREENWOOD

COXWELL

WOODBINE

LANDSDOWNE

DUFFERIN

OSSINGTON

BATHURST

DUPONT

SPADINA

ST. GEORGE

BAY

BLOOR-YONGE

SHERBOURNE

Bayview Ave.

Ave.

Bloor St. East

5

Danforth St.

MUSEUM

WELLESLEY

CHURCH St.

CASTLE FRANK

BROADVIEW

Pape Ave.

Greenwood Ave.

Coxwell Ave.

Woodbine

Kingston Rd.

Downtown Toronto

College St.

St. West

DOWNTOWN WEST

University Ave.

Bay St.

DOWNTOWN EAST

Church St.

Parliament St.

Queen St. East

2

WOODBINE BEACH PARK

Dufferin St.

Dundas

Queen St. West

King St. West

Front St.

King St. East

Eastern Ave.

2

Canadian National Exhibition

Gardiner Expressway

HARBOURFRONT PARK

Lake Shore Blvd. East

ASHBRIDGES BAY PARK

Ontario Place

Toronto Island Airport

TORONTO ISLANDS

AQUATIC PARK

■ TTC Subway

shows: *Show Boat* and *Ragtime* got their start here before heading to Broadway. Offerings from the CanStage Company, the Tarragon Theatre, and the Lorraine Kimsa Theatre for Young People are consistently excellent, too. See chapter 9.

- **Picnicking on Centre Island.** Hop on the ferry and escape to the islands. From across the water, you'll see the city in a whole new light. See chapter 6.
- **Taking In a Game at SkyDome or the Air Canada Centre.** SkyDome is home base for the Toronto Blue Jays baseball team. The Air Canada Centre is where the Maple Leafs (hockey) and the Raptors (basketball) play. Torontonians love their teams and come out to support them in droves. See chapter 6.
- **Staying Up Until the Wee Hours in Greek Tavernas.** No one's saying that Toronto is a city that never sleeps, but you can make such a claim about lively-at-all-hours Greektown. At 4am, upbeat bouzouki music can still be heard along the Danforth. See chapter 5.
- **Busting a Gut at a Comedy Club.** Maybe it's something in the water: Toronto has produced more than its share of top-notch comedians, including the shagadelic Mike Myers, Jim Carrey, Dan Aykroyd, and the late John Candy. Check out local talent or international stand-up stars at one of the many comedy clubs. See chapter 9.
- **Treasure Hunting for Vintage Clothing in Kensington Market.** How can one small area have a dozen vintage-clothing vendors? And how do they keep prices low and quality good? Haphazard Kensington Market is a joy for bargain hunters. See chapters 7 and 8.

- **Watching Kids Explore the Wonders of the World at the Ontario Science Centre.** You don't have to be a tyke to appreciate the amazing interactive displays about biology, ecology, and technology. See chapter 6.
- **Contemplating the Henry Moore Sculptures at the Art Gallery of Ontario.** The British sculptor Henry Moore so loved Toronto that he bestowed his greatest works on this museum. Kids have been known to swing from the gigantic works in front of the gallery. See chapter 6.
- **Wandering Through the Riverdale Farm.** In case you need more proof that Toronto is a very green city, it has a working farm in its midst. Cows, sheep, pigs, goats, and other critters call it home. See p. 141.
- **Cafe Hopping at Trattorias in Little Italy.** Several magazines have zeroed in on this neighborhood as one of the *haute*-est spots in North America. Trendy, yes, but it's also a fun area for stopping by the many cafes and wine bars, and for dining on outstanding food. See chapter 5.
- **Dining Alfresco on One of the City's Endless Patios.** Any piece of sidewalk might be appropriated for open-air dining at any time. If you can't beat 'em, join 'em. See chapter 5.
- **Viewing the World from the Top of the CN Tower.** Most Toronto natives say they've never gone to the top of their most famous landmark. It's a pity, because the view is inspiring. On any reasonably clear day, you can see Niagara Falls. See p. 123.
- **Exploring Harbourfront.** There's always something going on—the International Festival of Authors, art exhibits, cultural celebrations,

Impressions

In the eyes of the rest of the country Toronto is a kind of combination Sodom and Mecca.

—Pierre Berton (1961)

and an antiques market, just to name a few. See chapter 6.

- **Shopping—or Window-Shopping—in Chic Yorkville.** Once home to the city's bohemian community, Yorkville is an enclave of exclusive shops, art galleries, and upscale cafes. See chapter 8.

- **Visiting Niagara-on-the-Lake or Stratford for a Day.** Niagara-on-the-Lake is Ontario's wine country, and home of the Shaw Festival. Picturesque Stratford has its own theater festival. See chapter 10.

2 Best Hotel Bets

- **Best Historic Hotel:** The (gloved) hands-down winner is **Le Royal Meridien King Edward** (© 416/ 863-3131), which was built in 1903 and in the past few years has been restored to its former glory. The lobby, with its pink marble columns and ornate frescoes, has seen the crème de la crème of society trot through over the years. In the 1960s, the Beatles holed up in the King Eddy while 3,000 fans stormed the lobby. See p. 64.

- **Best for a Romantic Rendezvous:** The **Park Hyatt Toronto** (© 800/ 233-1234) has it all: a beautifully renovated Art Deco building, top-notch service, and one of the best views in the city from the rooftop terrace lounge. This is the place to relax and let yourself be pampered. See p. 70

- **Best for Families:** The **Delta Chelsea** (© 800/243-5732) is a longtime family favorite. It offers children's programs, a day-care center, and kid-friendly restaurants. There are two pools, one for tykes and one for adults, and many rooms have refrigerators or kitchenettes. See p. 63.

- **Best for Business Travelers:** The **Metropolitan Hotel** (© 416/ 977-5000) is just a few minutes from the Financial District, and its amenities are competitive with those of its pricier competitors. Features include fax-modem hookups, large work desks, and cordless two-line phones. There is also a 24-hour business center. The restaurants, Hemispheres and Lai Wah Heen, are favorite sites for business lunches. See p. 60.

- **Best Moderately Priced Hotel:** Given the location and amenities, it's hard to beat the **Delta Chelsea** (© 800/243-5732) for price. Close to the Eaton Centre, Chinatown, and the Financial District, double rooms start at C$129 (US$88) per night. See p. 63.

- **Best Budget Accommodations:** **Victoria University** (© 416/585-4524) rents out its student residences from mid-May until late August. It's in an excellent location, with simple rooms and great facilities, including tennis courts and a pool. All this for C$65 (US$44) a night. See p. 72.

- **Best Service:** At **The Sutton Place Hotel** (© 800/268-3790), ask and you shall receive. The high staff-to-guest ratio means that there's always someone around to do your bidding. See p. 71. You won't lack for attention at the **Four Seasons Hotel Toronto** (© 800/268-6282; p. 67) or the **Park Hyatt Toronto** (© 800/233-1234; p. 70), either.

- **Best Hotel Dining:** This is a three-way tie: the Hilton Toronto's very grand dining room, **Tundra** (© 416/860-6800; p. 85), is a treat for all the senses. But so are the Fairmont Royal York's new offering, **Epic** (© 416/860-6949; p. 86) and the Park Hyatt's restaurant, Annona (© 416/924-5471; p. 97).

- **Best Gay-Friendly Hotel:** Everyone comes to the **Howard Johnson Selby Hotel & Suites** (© 800/387-4788). In a Victorian building in a predominantly gay neighborhood, this hotel draws gay, lesbian, and straight travelers with Belle Epoque style and individually decorated rooms. See p. 72.

- **Best for Travelers with Disabilities:** The **Fairmont Royal York** (© 800/441-1414) looks monolithic, but it pays a lot of attention to accessibility. The adaptations accommodate wheelchair users, the visually impaired, and the hearing impaired. See p. 58.

3 Best Dining Bets

- **Best for a Business Lunch:** The always-hopping **Jump Café and Bar,** 1 Wellington St. W. (© 416/363-3400), in the heart of the Financial District, is a longtime favorite for deal-makers and traders; see p. 87. Another sure bet is **Canoe Restaurant & Bar,** in the Toronto Dominion Tower, 66 Wellington St. W. (© 416/364-0054), a see-and-be-seen spot for local and visiting power brokers; see p. 84.

- **Best for a Celebration:** The atmosphere at **Veni Vidi Vici,** 650 College St. (© 416/536-8550), is celebratory every night. The glamorous private dining room at the back provides swank elegance for parties of up to 12. See p. 91.

- **Best for a Romantic Dinner:** The setting, the music, the food—everything caters to your five senses at **Senses,** 15 Bloor St. W. (© 416/935-0400). Relax and let the pampering begin. See p. 101.

- **Best Decor: Monsoon,** 100 Simcoe St. (© 416/979-7172), has an award-winning interior design

by Toronto firm Yabu Pushelberg. The brown-on-black setting steals attention from the impressive kitchen. See p. 84. Upstart **Rain,** 19 Mercer St. (© 416/599-7246), is easy on the eye, but good luck getting in—even pop diva Nelly Furtado couldn't do it; see p. 88.

- **Best View:** The obvious choice is **360 Revolving Restaurant,** in the CN Tower, 301 Front St. W. (© 416/362-5411); see p. 85. **Scaramouche,** 1 Benvenuto Place (© 416/961-8011), offers serious competition, with floor-to-ceiling windows overlooking the downtown skyline; see p. 111.

- **Best Wine List:** The international selection **Centro,** 2472 Yonge St. (© 416/483-2211), is hard to beat. The basement is a wine bar with Italian, Californian, and Australian vintages by the glass; upstairs, the dining room boasts more than 600 bottles from around the world. Prices range from C$32 (US$22) into four figures. See p. 110.

The Best of Toronto Online

How did anyone ever plan a trip without the help of the Internet? It's hard to imagine now, given the wealth of information available online. But not all sites are created equal, so before you get ensnared in the Web, point and click on these gems.

- **Toronto.com** (www.toronto.com) boasts articles on arts and culture as well as a hotel directory, restaurant reviews, community news, and events listings. One of its best features is its extensive use of photographs.

- **City of Toronto** (www.city.toronto.on.ca) is the official municipal guide to Toronto, a straightforward source of practical information peppered with profiles of fun places to visit and announcements of festivals, free concerts, kids' events, and more.

- **Girl Talk Toronto: A Mini City Guide** (www.journeywoman.com/girltalk/toronto.html) runs the gamut from the serious (transit safety) to the frivolously fun (the best places to shop for shoes). This user-friendly site also highlights arty spots, off-the-beaten-path attractions, and the best places for brunch, all from a female perspective.

- **Green Tourism Association** (www.greentourism.on.ca) is an excellent resource for eco-friendly travelers. There's information about car-free transportation, outdoor activities and sports, and healthy dining.

- **Toronto Online** (www.toronto-online.com) is a great tool to put the city in historical and cultural context before your visit. A condensed history lesson covers the 1600s through the present. A neighborhood guide describes the character of each district.

- *Toronto Life* (www.torontolife.com) has extensive restaurant listings, as well as links for events, activities, and nightlife.

- *Toronto Star* (www.thestar.com) includes everything from theater and concert reviews to local news and weather conditions.

- **Best Bistro:** Bistros often do well with comfort foods, but **Biff's,** 4 Front St. E. (© 416/860-0086), serves up modern takes on classic dishes; its setting goes beyond comfortable to luxury. See p. 93.

- **Best Italian: Il Posto Nuovo,** 148 Yorkville Ave. (© 416/968-0469), serves fine modern Italian cuisine in elegant digs—and the efficient, knowledgeable wait staff makes everyone feel at home. See p. 100.

- **Best Portuguese:** Standing alone on Italian-dominated College Street, **Chiado,** 484 College St. (© 416/538-1910), serves modern Portuguese cuisine. The seafood is flown in daily. See p. 86.

- **Best Greek:** The cooking at **Pan on the Danforth,** 516 Danforth Ave. (© 416/466-8158), will convince you that Pan was *really* the god of food. This is Greek cuisine updated with panache; see p. 108. Watch out for the new restaurant **Gus** (© 416/923-8159) as a challenger; see p. 102.

- **Best People Watching:** Across from the Sutton Place Hotel is **Bistro 990,** 990 Bay St. (© 416/921-9990), where everyone in Toronto but me has made a celebrity sighting (I'm too busy enjoying the delicious food). See p. 96.
- **Best Value: Messis,** 97 Harbord St. (© 416/920-2186), has acted as a training ground for some of the best chefs in Toronto. It's a popular, moderately priced spot where you can check out the up-and-comers. See p. 103.
- **Best for Kids: Millie's Bistro,** 1980 Avenue Rd. (© 416/481-1247), is a family favorite with sunny dining rooms and a special children's menu; see p. 111. A more casual choice would be the deli-style **Shopsy's** (© 416/365-3333); see p. 96.
- **Best Steak House: Barberian's,** 7 Elm St. (© 416/597-0335), has boosted the level of protein in Torontonians' diets since 1959. It also serves great martinis and desserts, but what everyone comes here for is the meat. See p. 81.
- **Best Pizza:** A cubbyhole-size eatery in midtown, **Serra,** 378 Bloor St. W. (© 416/922-6999), makes thin-crust pizzas laden with gourmet ingredients. See p. 105.
- **Best Sushi:** There's only one possible answer—**Hiro Sushi,** 171 King St. E. (© 416/304-0550). Chef Hiro Yoshida offers up classically prepared sushi as well as a few unique specialties. See p. 93.
- **Best Afternoon Tea:** For tea with all the finger sandwiches, pastries, and clotted cream you can handle, head to the **Annona at the Park Hyatt,** 21 Avenue Rd. (© 416/924-5471). The lavender-and-rose-infused Rooibos Provence tea alone is incredible. See p. 97.
- **Best Alfresco Dining:** The lovely patio at **Biff's,** 4 Front St. E. (© 416/860-0086), is just about perfect—set well back from the street, it affords terrific people-watching possibilities. See p. 93.
- **Best If You Have Only One Meal in Toronto and Price Is No Object:** While I hate to go along with the crowd, the common wisdom is on the money with **North 44,** 2537 Yonge St. (© 416/487-4897). Great food, great staff, great setting. See p. 110.
- **Best If You Have Only One Meal in Toronto and Price *Is* an Object:** Look no further than **Goldfish,** 372 Bloor St. W. (© 416/513-0077). The minimalist Scandinavian design might not be to everyone's taste, but the inspired cooking and attentive service hit the mark every time. See p. 101.
- **Best Chinese: Lai Wah Heen,** at the Metropolitan Hotel, 110 Chestnut St. (© 416/977-9899), serves deluxe Cantonese and Sichuan specialties, including a variety of shark's-fin soups and abalone dishes. It features several good-value prix-fixe specials at lunch and dinner. See p. 87.
- **Best Brunch:** Who needs bacon and eggs when you can have *torta rustica* with layers of ricotta, mozzarella, leeks, peas, and smoked trout? This and other glamorous offerings are available at **Agora,** at the Art Gallery of Ontario, 317 Dundas St. W. (© 416/977-0414). See p. 85.
- **Best Desserts:** Dufflet Rosenberg (p. 214) bakes up a storm at **Dufflet Pastries,** 787 Queen St. W. (© 416/504-2870). You'll find her name on the dessert list at some of the city's top restaurants. See p. 214.

Planning Your Trip to Toronto

Whether you're traveling on a whim or charting your course months in advance, it's important to do some planning to make the most of your trip. You may already be asking how you'll get there and how much it will cost. There are many different sides of Toronto, so you'll need to figure out what kind of trip you want. This chapter will help you find the answers.

1 Visitor Information

VISITOR INFORMATION

FROM NORTH AMERICA The best source for Toronto-specific information is **Tourism Toronto, Metro Toronto Convention & Visitors Association,** 207 Queen's Quay W., Suite 590, Toronto, ON M5J 1A7 (© **800/363-1990** from North America, or 416/203-2600; www.toronto tourism.com). Call before you leave and ask for the free information package, which includes sections on accommodations, sights, and dining. Better yet, visit the website, which includes all of the above plus up-to-the-minute events information.

Also check out the terrific travel-planning sites listed in "Planning Your Trip Online," later in this chapter.

For information about traveling in the province of Ontario, contact **Tourism Ontario,** P.O. Box 104, Toronto, ON M5B 2H1 (© **800/ ONTARIO** or 416/314-0944; www. travelinx.com), or visit the travel center in the Eaton Centre on Level 1 at Yonge and Dundas streets. It's open Monday to Friday from 10am to 9pm, Saturday from 9:30am to 6pm, and Sunday from noon to 5pm.

Canadian consulates in the United States do not provide tourist information. They will refer you to the offices above. Consular offices in Buffalo, Detroit, Los Angeles, New York, Seattle, and Washington, D.C., deal with visas and other political and immigration issues.

FROM ABROAD The following consulates can provide information or refer you to the appropriate offices. Consult Tourism Toronto (see "From North America," above) for general information. For a list of Canadian consular offices around the world, visit www.dfait-maeci.gc.ca/english/missions/rep-can1e.htm.

U.K. and Ireland: The **Canadian High Commission,** MacDonald House, 1 Grosvenor Sq., London W1X 0AB (© **0207/258-6600;** fax 0207/258-6333).

Australia: The **Canadian High Commission,** Commonwealth Avenue, Canberra, ACT 2600 (© **02/ 6273-3844**), or the **Consulate General of Canada,** Level 5, Quay West, 111 Harrington St., Sydney, NSW 2000 (© **02/9364-3000**). The consulate general also has offices in Melbourne and Perth.

New Zealand: The **Canadian High Commission,** 3rd floor, 61 Molesworth St., Thomdon, Wellington (© **04/473-9577**).

South Africa: The **Canadian High Commission,** 1103 Arcadia St., Hatfield 0083, Pretoria (© 012/ 422-3000). The commission also has offices in Cape Town and Johannesburg.

2 Entry Requirements & Customs

ENTRY REQUIREMENTS

Safeguard your passport in an inconspicuous, inaccessible place like a money belt and keep a copy of the critical pages with your passport number in a separate place. If you lose your passport, visit the nearest consulate of your native country as soon as possible for a replacement. Passport applications are downloadable from the websites listed below.

FOR RESIDENTS OF THE UNITED STATES

If you're applying for a first-time passport, you need to do it in person at a U.S. passport office; a federal, state, or probate court; or a major post office (though not all post offices accept applications; call the number below to find the ones that do). You need to present a certified birth certificate as proof of citizenship, and it's wise to bring along your driver's license, state or military ID, and social security card as well. You also need two identical passport-size photos (2 in. by 2 in.), taken at any corner photo shop (not one of the strip photos, however, from a photo-vending machine).

For people over 15, a passport is valid for 10 years and costs $85; for those 15 and under, it's valid for 5 years and costs $70. If you have a valid passport that was issued within the past 15 years (and you were over age 16 when it was issued) and in your current name, you can renew it by mail for $55; otherwise, you must renew your passport in person. Whether you're applying in person or by mail, you can download passport applications from the U.S. State Department website at **http://travel. state.gov.** Allow plenty of time before

your trip to apply; processing normally takes 3 weeks but can take longer during busy periods (especially spring). For general information, call the **National Passport Agency** (© 202/647-0518). To find your regional passport office, either check the U.S. State Department website or call the **National Passport Information Center** (© 900/225-5674); the fee is 55¢ per minute for automated information and $1.50 per minute for operator-assisted calls.

American Passport Express (© 800/841-6778; www.american passport.com) will process your first-time passport application for you in 5 to 8 business days for $145, plus a $60 service fee; for renewals, it's $115 plus a $60 service fee. If you need the passport in 3 to 5 business days, the service fee is $100, and for a $150 service fee, you can receive your passport in 24 hours.

FOR RESIDENTS OF THE UNITED KINGDOM

To pick up an application for a standard 10-year passport (or 5-yr. passport for children under 16), visit your nearest passport office, major post office, or travel agency. You can also contact the **United Kingdom Passport Service** at © 0870/571-0410 or search its website at www.ukpa.gov.uk. Passports are £30 for adults and £16 for children under 16. Processing takes about 2 weeks.

FOR RESIDENTS OF IRELAND

You can apply for a 10-year passport, costing €57 at the **Passport Office,** Setanta Centre, Molesworth Street, Dublin 2 (© 01/671-1633; www.irl gov.ie/iveagh). Those under age 18 and over 65 must apply for a 3-year passport, costing €12. You can also apply at 1A South Mall, Cork (© 021/272-525) or over the counter at most main post offices.

FOR RESIDENTS OF AUSTRALIA

You can pick up a passport application at your local post office or any branch of Passports Australia, but you must schedule an interview at the passport office to present your application materials. Call the **Australian Passport Information Service** at © **131-232,** or visit the government website at www.passports.gov.au. Passports cost A$144 for adults and A$72 for those under 18.

FOR RESIDENTS OF NEW ZEALAND

You can pick up a passport application at any New Zealand Passports Office or download it from the website. Contact the **Passports Office** at © **0800/ 225-050** in New Zealand or 04/ 474-8100, or log on to www.passports.govt.nz. Passports are NZ$80 for adults and NZ$40 for those under 16.

CUSTOMS
WHAT YOU CAN BRING INTO CANADA

Most customs regulations are generous, but they get complicated when it comes to firearms, plants, meat, and pets. Fishing tackle poses no problem (provided the lures are not made of restricted materials—specific feathers, for example), but the bearer must possess a nonresident license for the province or territory where he or she plans to use it. You can bring in free of duty up to 50 cigars, 200 cigarettes, and 200 grams of tobacco, provided you're at least 18 years of age. You are also allowed 40 ounces (1.14ml) of liquor or 1.5L of wine as long as you're of age in the province you're visiting (19 in Ontario). There are no restrictions on what you can take out. But if

you're thinking of bringing Cuban cigars back to the United States, beware—they can be confiscated, and you could face a fine.

For a clear summary of **Canadian** rules, write for the booklet *I Declare,* issued by the **Canada Customs and Revenue Agency** (© **800/461-9999** in Canada, or 204/983-3500; www.ccra-adrc.gc.ca).

WHAT YOU CAN TAKE HOME

Returning **U.S. citizens** who have been away for at least 48 hours are allowed to bring back, once every 30 days, $400 worth of merchandise duty-free. You'll be charged a flat rate of 4% duty on the next $1,000 worth of purchases. Be sure to have your receipts handy. On mailed gifts, the duty-free limit is $100. You cannot bring fresh foodstuffs into the United States; tinned foods, however, are allowed. For more information, contact the **U.S. Customs Service,** 1300 Pennsylvania Ave., NW, Washington, DC 20229 (© **877/287-8867**) and request the free pamphlet *Know Before You Go.* It's also available on the Web at www.customs.gov. (Click on "Traveler Information" then "Know Before You Go.")

U.K. citizens returning from a non-EU country have a customs allowance of 200 cigarettes; 50 cigars; 250g of smoking tobacco; 2 liters of still table wine; 1 liter of spirits or strong liqueurs (over 22% volume); 2 liters of fortified wine, sparkling wine or other liqueurs; 60cc (ml) perfume; 250cc (ml) of toilet water; and £145 worth of all other goods, including gifts and souvenirs. People under 17 cannot have the tobacco or alcohol allowance. For more information, contact **HM Customs & Excise** at © **0845/010-9000** (020/8929-0152 from outside the U.K.), or consult the website at www.hmce.gov.uk.

The duty-free allowance in **Australia** is A$400 or, for those under 18, A$200. Upon returning to Australia, citizens can bring in 250 cigarettes or 250 grams of loose tobacco and 1,125 milliliters of alcohol. If you're returning with valuable goods you already own, such as foreign-made cameras, you should file form B263. A helpful brochure, available from Australian consulates or Customs offices, is *Know Before You Go*. For more information, call the **Australian Customs Services** at ✆ **1300/363-263** in Australia; 202/797-3189 in the U.S.), or go to www.customs.gov.au.

The duty-free allowance for **New Zealand** is NZ$700. Citizens over 17 can bring in 200 cigarettes, or 50 cigars, or 250 grams of tobacco (or a mixture of all three if their combined weight doesn't exceed 250g); plus 4.5 liters of wine and beer, or 1.125 liters of liquor. New Zealand currency does not carry import or export restrictions. Fill out a certificate of export, listing the valuables you are taking out of the country; that way, you can bring them back without paying duty. Most questions are answered in a free pamphlet available at New Zealand consulates and Customs offices: *New Zealand*

 Destination Toronto: Red Alert Checklist

- If you have you heart set on dining in one of the hot spots mentioned in chapter 5, such as YYZ, Rain, or Susur, you'd be well advised to make the reservation before you arrive in Toronto. It's also a good idea to book theater tickets for the big shows (*Lion King*, I'm talking about you) in advance. Ditto for hockey tickets.
- Did you make sure your favorite attraction is open? Many of Toronto's museums are closed Monday. Call ahead for opening and closing hours (the information in this book is a guideline, and subject to change).
- If you purchased traveler's checks, have you recorded the check numbers, and stored the documentation separately from the checks?
- Did you pack your camera and an extra set of camera batteries and purchase enough film? If you packed film in your checked baggage, did you invest in protective pouches to shield film from airport x-rays?
- Do you have a safe, accessible place to store money?
- Did you bring your ID cards that could entitle you to discounts such as AAA and AARP cards, student IDs, etc.?
- Did you bring emergency drug prescriptions and extra glasses and/or contact lenses?
- Do you have your credit card pin numbers?
- If you have an E-ticket, do you have documentation?
- Did you leave a copy of your itinerary with someone at home?
- Did you check to see if any travel advisories have been issued by the U.S. State Department (http://travel.state.gov/travel_warnings.html) regarding your destination?
- Do you have the address and phone number of your country's embassy with you?

Customs Guide for Travellers, Notice no. 4. For more information, contact **New Zealand Customs,** The Customhouse, 17–21 Whitmore St., Box 2218, Wellington (© 04/473-6099 or 0800/ 428-786; www.customs.govt.nz).

3 Money

CURRENCY

Canadians use **dollars** and **cents,** but with a distinct advantage for U.S. visitors—the Canadian dollar has been fluctuating between 65 and 68¢ in U.S. money, give or take a couple of points' daily variation. In effect, your American money gets you 32% more the moment you exchange it for local currency, and because the nominal prices of many goods are roughly on par with those in the United States, the difference is real, not imaginary. Sales taxes are higher, though you should be able to recoup at least part of them (see "Taxes" under "Fast Facts," in chapter 3).

Paper currency comes in $5, $10, $20, $50, and $100 denominations. (The $1,000 bill is being phased out.) Coins come in 1-, 5-, 10-, and 25-cent, and 1- and 2-dollar denominations. The gold-colored $1 coin is a "loonie"—it sports a loon on its "tails" side—and the large gold-and-silver-colored $2 coin is a "toonie." If you find these names somewhat, ah, colorful, just remember that there's no swifter way to reveal that you're a tourist than to say "one-dollar coin."

It's a good idea to exchange at least some money—just enough to cover airport incidentals and transportation to your hotel—before you leave home, so you can avoid the less-favorable rates you'll get at airport currency exchange desks. Check with your local American Express or Thomas Cook office or your bank. American Express cardholders can order foreign currency over the phone at © 800/807-6233.

It's best to exchange currency or traveler's checks at a bank, not a currency exchange, hotel, or shop.

ATMS

ATMs are linked to a network that most likely includes your bank at home. **Cirrus** (© 800/424-7787; www.mastercard.com) and **PLUS** (© 800/843-7587; www.visa.com) are the two most popular networks in the U.S.; call or check online for ATM locations at your destination. Be sure you know your four-digit PIN access number before you leave home and be sure to find out your daily withdrawal limit before you depart. You can also get cash advances on your credit card at an ATM. Keep in mind that credit card companies try to protect themselves from theft by limiting the funds someone can withdraw away from home. It's therefore best to call your credit card company before you leave and let them know where you're going and how much you plan to spend. You'll get the best exchange rate if you withdraw money from an ATM, but keep in mind that many banks impose a fee every time a card is used at an ATM in a different city or bank. On top of this, the bank from which you withdraw cash may charge its own fee.

Tips Small Change

When you change money, ask for some small bills or loose change. Petty cash will come in handy for tipping and public transportation. Consider keeping the change separate from your larger bills, so it's readily accessible and you'll be less of a target for theft.

What Things Cost in Toronto	US$
Taxi from the airport to downtown	24.50
Subway/bus from the airport to downtown	6.80
Local telephone call	17¢
Double at the Park Hyatt (very expensive)	153.00–339.00
Double at the Delta Chelsea (moderate)	88.00–245.00
Double at Victoria University (inexpensive)	44.20
Two-course lunch for one at Stork on the Roof (moderate)*	15.00
Two-course lunch for one at Kalendar (inexpensive)*	10.60
Three-course dinner for one at North 44 (very expensive)*	50.40
Three-course dinner for one at Goldfish (moderate)*	28.30
Three-course dinner for one at the Rivoli (inexpensive)*	16.30
Pint of beer	3.50
Coca-Cola	1.00
Cup of coffee	1.00
Roll of ASA 1100 Kodacolor film, 36 exposures	5.40
Admission to the Royal Ontario Museum	8.20
Movie ticket at a Silver City multiplex	7.50
Ticket for the Royal Alexandra Theatre	17.00–85.00
* Includes tax and tip, but not wine.	

TRAVELER'S CHECKS

Traveler's checks are something of an anachronism from the days before the ATM made cash accessible at any time. Traveler's checks used to be the only sound alternative to traveling with dangerously large amounts of cash. They were as reliable as currency, but, unlike cash, could be replaced if lost or stolen.

These days, traveler's checks seem less necessary because most cities have 24-hour ATMs that allow you to withdraw small amounts of cash as needed. However, keep in mind that you will likely be charged an ATM withdrawal fee if the bank is not your own, so if you're withdrawing money every day, you might be better off with traveler's checks—provided that you don't mind showing identification every time you want to cash one.

You can get traveler's checks at almost any bank. **American Express** offers denominations of $20, $50, $100, $500, and (for cardholders only) $1,000. You'll pay a service charge ranging from 1% to 4%. You can also get American Express traveler's checks over the phone by calling ℭ **800/221-7282;** Amex gold and platinum cardholders who use this number are exempt from the 1% fee. AAA members can obtain checks without a fee at most AAA offices.

Visa offers traveler's checks at Citibank locations nationwide, as well as at several other banks. The service charge ranges between 1.5% and 2%; checks come in denominations of $20, $50, $100, $500, and $1,000. Call ℂ **800/732-1322** for information. **MasterCard** also offers traveler's checks. Call ℂ **800/223-9920** for a location near you.

CREDIT CARDS

Credit cards are invaluable when traveling. They are a safe way to carry money and provide a convenient record of all your expenses. You can also withdraw cash advances from your credit cards at any bank (though you'll start paying hefty interest on the advance the moment you receive the cash.) At most banks, you don't even need to go to a teller; you can get a cash advance at the ATM if you know your PIN access number. If you've forgotten yours, or didn't even know you had one, call the number on the back of your credit card and ask the bank to send it to you. It usually takes 5 to 7 business days, though some banks will provide the number over the phone if you tell them your mother's maiden name or pass some other security clearance.

WHAT TO DO IF YOUR WALLET IS LOST OR STOLEN

Be sure to block charges against your account the minute you discover a credit card has been lost or stolen. Almost every credit card company has an emergency toll-free number to call if your card is stolen. They may be able to wire you a cash advance off your credit card immediately, and in many places, they can deliver an emergency credit card in a day or two. The issuing bank's toll-free number is usually on the back of your credit card—though of course, if your card has been stolen, that won't help you unless you recorded the number elsewhere.

Citicorp Visa's U.S. emergency number is ℂ **800/336-8472.** American Express cardholders and traveler's check holders should call ℂ **800/221-7282.** MasterCard holders should call ℂ **800/307-7309.** Otherwise, call the toll-free number directory at ℂ **800/555-1212.**

After you've contacted your credit-card company, be sure to file a police report. Odds are that if your wallet is gone, the police won't be able to recover it for you. However, it's still worth informing the authorities. Your credit card company or insurer may require a police report number or record of the theft.

If you choose to carry traveler's checks, be sure to keep a record of their serial numbers separate from your checks. You'll get a refund faster if you know the numbers.

If you need emergency cash over the weekend when all banks and American Express offices are closed, you can have money wired to you from **Western Union** (ℂ **800/325-6000;** www.westernunion.com). You must present valid ID to pick up the cash at the Western Union office.

⌐ *Tips* **Spending American Cash**

If you spend American money at Canadian establishments, you should understand how the conversion is calculated. Many times, especially in downtown Toronto, you'll see a sign at the cash register that reads U.S. CURRENCY 50%. This 50% is the "premium," which means that for every U.S. greenback you hand over, the cashier will consider it $1.50 Canadian. For example, for a $15 tab you need pay only $10 in U.S. currency.

The Canadian Dollar, the U.S. Dollar & the British Pound

The prices quoted in this guide are in Canadian dollars, with the U.S. equivalent in parentheses. The exchange rate we've used is $1.40 Canadian to $1 American. The conversion rate for the British pound is $2.30 Canadian.

Here's a quick table of equivalents:

Canada $	U.S. $	British £
1	68¢	40p
5	3.40	2.10
10	6.80	4.10
20	13.60	8.20
50	34.00	20.50
80	54.40	32.90
100	68.00	41.10

However, in most countries, you can pick up a money transfer even if you don't have valid identification, as long as you can answer a test question provided by the sender. Be sure to let the sender know in advance that you don't have ID. If you need to use a test question instead of ID, the sender must take cash to his or her local Western Union office, rather than transferring the money over the phone or online.

Identity theft or fraud are potential complications of losing your wallet, especially if you've lost your driver's license along with your cash and credit cards. Notify the major credit-reporting bureaus immediately; placing a fraud alert on your records may protect you against liability for criminal activity. The three major U.S. credit-reporting agencies are **Equifax** (© **800/766-0008;** www.equifax. com), **Experian** (© **888/397-3742;** www.experian.com), and **TransUnion** (© **800/680-7289;** www.transunion. com). For more information about identity theft and how to protect yourself, check the Federal Trade Commission's website at **www.ftc.gov** or www.consumer.gov/idtheft.

Finally, if you've lost all forms of photo ID, call your airline and explain the situation; they might allow you to board the plane if you have a copy of your passport or birth certificate and a copy of the police report you've filed.

4 When to Go

THE CLIMATE

Paris may be most delightful in springtime, but Toronto is truly sublime in the fall. It's my favorite time of year for a number of reasons: The climate is brisk but temperate, the skies are sunny, the countless city parks are a riot of color, and the cultural scene is in full swing. Another great time to see the city—if you don't mind some snow—is December, with nonstop holiday festivities. I can also make good arguments for visiting in spring or summer, but I do feel it's my duty to warn you away in January: The temperature can be unbearably cold, and there's less to do.

Never mind what the calendar says; these are Toronto's true seasons: **Spring** runs from late March to mid-May (though occasionally there's snow in mid-Apr); **summer,** mid-May to mid-September; **fall,** mid-September to mid-November; **winter,** mid-November to late March. The highest recorded temperature is

---

Tips Don't Forget the Sunscreen

Because of Canada's image of a land of harsh winters, many travelers don't realize that summer can be scorching. "The UV index goes quite high, between 7 and 10, in Toronto," says Dr. Patricia Agin of the Coppertone Solar Research Center in Memphis. "It's the same as in New York, Boston, Chicago, or Detroit." A UV index reading of 7 can mean a sunburn, so don't forget to pack your sunscreen and a hat, especially if you're planning to enjoy Toronto's many parks and outdoor attractions.

105°F; the lowest, –27°F. The average date of first frost is October 29; the average date of last frost is April 20.

The wind blasts from Lake Ontario can be fierce, even in June. Bring a light jacket or cardigan.

Toronto's Average Temperatures

	Jan	Feb	Mar	Apr	May	June	July	Aug	Sept	Oct	Nov	Dec
High °F	30	31	39	53	64	75	80	79	71	59	46	34
°C	1	1	4	12	18	24	27	26	22	15	8	1
Low °F	18	19	27	38	48	57	62	61	54	45	35	23
°C	8	7	3	3	9	14	17	16	12	7	2	5

HOLIDAYS

Toronto celebrates the following holidays: New Year's Day (Jan 1), Good Friday and Easter Monday (Mar or Apr), Victoria Day (Mon following the third weekend in May), Canada Day (July 1), Civic Holiday (first Mon in Aug), Labour Day (first Mon in Sept), Thanksgiving (second Mon in Oct), Remembrance Day (Nov 11), Christmas Day (Dec 25), and Boxing Day (Dec 26).

On Good Friday and Easter Monday, schools and government offices close; most corporations close on one or the other, and a few close on both. Only banks and government offices close on Remembrance Day (Nov 11).

TORONTO CALENDAR OF EVENTS

January, February, March, and April are dominated by trade shows, such as the International Boat and Automobile shows, Metro Home Show, Outdoor Adventure Sport Show, and more. For information, call **Tourism Toronto** (✆ **800/363-1990** or 416/203-2600; www.torontotourism.com).

February

Chinese New Year Celebrations, downtown. 2003 is the year of the goat. Festivities include traditional and contemporary performances of Chinese opera, dancing, music, and more. For **Harbourfront** celebration information, call ✆ **416/ 973-3000** (www.harbourfront.on. ca); for **SkyDome,** call ✆ **877/ 666-3838** (www.skydome.com). The new year starts on February 1.

Winterfest, Nathan Phillips Square, Yonge and Eglinton, and Mel Lastman Square. This 3-day celebration spreads over three neighborhoods. It features ice-skating shows, snow play, midway rides, performances, ice sculpting, arts-and-crafts shows, and more. For information, call ✆ **416/338-0338** (www.city.toronto.on.ca). Usually around Valentine's Day.

Toronto Festival of Storytelling, Harbourfront. Now in its 25th year, this event celebrates international folklore, with 60 storytellers imparting legends and fables from around the world. For information, call ℂ 416/973-3000 (www. harbourfront.on.ca). Last weekend of February.

March

Canada Blooms, Metro Toronto Convention Centre. At this time of year, any glimpse of greenery is welcome. There are 2.5 hectares (6 acres) of indoor garden and flower displays, seminars with green-thumb experts, and competitions. For information, call ℂ 416/593-0223 (www.canadablooms.com). Usually the second week of March.

St. Patrick's Day Parade, downtown. Toronto's own version of the classic Irish celebration. For information, call ℂ 416/487-1566. March 17.

April

Blue Jays Season Opener, Sky-Dome. Turn out to root for your home-away-from-home team. For information, call ℂ 416/341-1000 (www.bluejays.ca); for tickets, which usually aren't too hard to get, call ℂ 888/654-6529. Mid-April.

The Shaw Festival, Niagara-on-the-Lake, Ontario. This festival presents the plays of George Bernard Shaw and his contemporaries. (For more information, see chapter 10.) Call ℂ 416/690-7301 or 905/468-2172 (www.shawfest. com). Mid-April through October.

Sante—The Bloor-Yorkville Wine Festival, Yorkville. This 4-day gourmet event brings together award-winning Ontario vintages, food by top-rated chefs, and live jazz. For information, call ℂ 416/504-3977. Last weekend in April.

May

Milk International Children's Festival, Harbourfront. This is a 9-day celebration of the arts for kids—from theater and music to dance, comedy, and storytelling.

For information, call ℂ 416/973-3000 (www.harbourfront.on.ca). Usually starts on Mother's Day (second Sun in May).

The Stratford Festival, Stratford, Ontario. Featuring a wide range of contemporary and classic plays, this festival always includes several works by Shakespeare. (For more information, see chapter 10.) Call ℂ 800/567-1600 or 416/364-8355 (www.stratford-festival.on.ca). Early May through October.

June

Harbourfront Reading Series, Harbourfront. Now in its 29th year, this festival celebrates the best of Canadian literature. Top writers such as Timothy Findley, Anne Michaels, and Barbara Gowdy read from their latest works. For information, call Harbourfront (ℂ 416/973-3000); for tickets, call ℂ 416/973-4000 (www.harbourfront.on. ca). Readings go on through most of June.

North by Northeast Festival, city-wide. Known in the music biz as NXNE, the 3-day event features rock and indie bands at 28 venues. For information, call ℂ 416/469-0986 (www.nxne.com). Second weekend in June.

Toronto International Festival Caravan, citywide. This popular 9-day event is North America's largest international festival. It features more than 40 themed pavilions, craft demonstrations, authentic cuisine, and traditional dance performances by 100 cultural groups. For information, call ℂ 416/977-0466. Usually the third and fourth weekends of June.

Benson & Hedges Symphony of Fire, Ontario Place. This international fireworks competition is set to music and draws two million people to the waterfront. Six shows take place, on several Saturdays and Wednesdays. For information, call ℂ 416/442-3667; for tickets for waterfront seating, call ℂ 416/870-8000. Mid-June to July.

Taste of Little Italy, College Street between Euclid and Shaw streets. Restaurants, craftspeople, musicians, and other performers put on displays during this 2-day festival for the whole family. For information, call ℂ 416/531-9991. Mid-June.

International Dragon Boat Festival, Centre Island. More than 160 teams of dragon-boaters compete in the 2-day event, which commemorates the death of the Chinese philosopher and poet Qu Yuan. For information, call ℂ 416/598-8945 (www.dragonboat.com). Third weekend in June.

Gay & Lesbian Pride Celebration, citywide. A week of events, performances, symposiums, and parties culminates in an extravagant Sunday parade. For information, call ℂ 416/92-PRIDE or 416/927-7433 (www.pridetoronto.com). Late June.

Du Maurier Downtown Jazz Festival, citywide. Going strong since 1987, this 10-day festival showcases more than 2,000 international artists playing every jazz style—blues, gospel, Latin, African, traditional—at 60 venues. For information, call ℂ 416/363-8717 (www.tojazz.com). Late June.

July

Canada Day Celebrations, citywide. July 1, 2003, marks the nation's 136th birthday. Street parties, fireworks, and other special events celebrate the day. For information, call Tourism Toronto (ℂ 800/363-1990 or 416/203-2600; www.torontotourism.com). Weekend of July 1.

The Fringe—Toronto's Theatre Festival, citywide. More than 90 troupes participate in this 10-day festival of contemporary and experimental theater. Shows last no more than an hour. For information, call ℂ 416/534-5919 (www.fringe toronto.com). First week of July.

Great Canadian Blues Festival, Harbourfront Centre. Toronto shows that it's got soul in this 3-day festival of Canada's best blues musicians. In case the rhythm isn't enough to catch you, the Blues Festival coincides with a lip-smacking BBQ fest, also at Harbourfront. For information, call Harbourfront (ℂ 416/973-3000); for tickets, call ℂ 416/973-4000 (www.harbour front.on.ca). Second weekend in July.

Molson Indy, the Exhibition Place Street circuit. One of Canada's major races on the IndyCar circuit. Away from the track, you'll find live music and beer gardens. For information, call ℂ 416/922-7477 (www.molsonindy.com). Third weekend in July.

Caribana, citywide. Toronto's version of Carnival transforms the city. It's complete with traditional foods from the Caribbean and Latin America, ferry cruises, picnics, children's events, concerts, and arts-and-crafts exhibits. Call ℂ 416/465-4884 for more information (www.toronto.com/caribana). Late July to early August.

August

Festival of Beer, Fort York. More than 70 major Ontario breweries and microbreweries turn out for this celebration of suds. There's also a wide selection of food from local restaurants and live music of the blues, swing, and jazz persuasions. For information, call ℂ 416/698-7206. First weekend in August.

Canadian National Exhibition, Exhibition Place. One of the world's largest exhibitions, this 18-day extravaganza features midway rides, display buildings, free shows, and grandstand performers. The 3-day Canadian International Air Show (first staged in 1878) is a bonus. Call © **416/393-6000** for information (www.theex.com). Mid-August to Labour Day.

Du Maurier Ltd. Open, National Tennis Centre at York University. Canada's international tennis championship is an important stop on the pro tennis tour. It attracts players such as Sampras, Agassi, Seles, and Sanchez-Vicario. The Open runs in conjunction with a tournament in Montreal. In 2003, the women play in Toronto and the men in Montreal. In 2004, they'll alternate. For information, call © **416/665-9777** (www.tennis canada.com). Mid- to late August.

September

Toronto International Film Festival, citywide. The stars come out for the second-largest film festival in the world. More than 250 films from 70 countries are shown over 10 days. For information, call © **416/968-FILM** or log on to www.e.bell.ca/filmfest. Early September.

PGA Tour Canadian Open, Glen Abbey Golf Club, Oakville. Canada's national golf tournament (© **905/844-1800**) has featured the likes of Greg Norman and Tiger Woods in recent years. It's almost always held at Glen Abbey, though Montreal played host in 1997. First or second weekend of September.

Word on the Street, Queen Street West between Simcoe Street and Spadina Avenue. This street fair celebrates the written word with readings, discounted books and magazines, and children's events. Other major Canadian cities hold

---

⌒*Moments* **Jump Up!**

One of the undisputed highlights of summer in Toronto is the annual Caribana festival. Created in 1967 as a community heritage celebration to tie in with Canada's centennial, Caribana has become North America's largest street festival, drawing more than a million visitors from North America, Britain, and the Caribbean each year. Originally based on Trinidad's Carnival, the festival now draws on numerous cultures—Jamaican, Guyanese, Brazilian, and Bahamian, to name a few—for its music, food, and events.

During the 2 weeks that it runs, you will see the influence of Caribana around the city. It starts with a bang (literally, as there are steel drums involved) at Nathan Phillips Square in front of Toronto City Hall, with a free concert that features calypso, salsa, and soca music. In the days that follow, there are boat cruises, dances, and concerts; the King and Queen Extravaganza, which showcases some of the most amazing costumes you could hope to see; and an arts festival. The highlight is the Caribana Parade, which brings together masquerade and steel-drum bands, dancers, and floats for a memorable feast for all the senses. This is one party you just can't miss.

similar events on the same weekend. For information, call ✆ **416/504-7241.** Last weekend in September.

October

Oktoberfest, Kitchener–Waterloo, about 1 hour (97km/60 miles) from Toronto. This famed 9-day drinkfest features cultural events plus a pageant and parade. For information, call ✆ **519/570-4267** (www.oktoberfest.ca). Mid-October.

International Festival of Authors, Harbourfront. This renowned 11-day literary festival is the most prestigious in Canada. It draws more than 100 authors from 25 countries to perform readings and on-stage interviews. Among the literary luminaries who have appeared are Salman Rushdie, Margaret Drabble, Thomas Kenneally, Joyce Carol Oates, A. S. Byatt, and Margaret Atwood. For information, call Harbourfront (✆ **416/973-3000**); for tickets, call ✆ **416/973-4000** (www.harbourfront.on.ca). Third weekend of October.

Toronto Maple Leafs Opening Night, Air Canada Centre. Torontonians love their hockey team, so securing a ticket will be a challenge. For information, call ✆ **416/216-1700;** for tickets, call ✆ **416/872-5000** (www.torontomapleleafs.com). Mid-October.

The Old Clothing Show & Sale, Exhibition Place. Everything from Jazz Age flapper frocks to Austin Powers–like '60s suits, all under one roof. For information, call ✆ **416/410-1310.** Third weekend of October.

November

Royal Agricultural Winter Fair and Royal Horse Show, Exhibition Place. The 12-day show is the largest indoor agricultural and equestrian competition in the world. Displays include vegetables and fruits, crafts, farm machinery, livestock, and more. A member of the British royal family traditionally attends the horse show. Call ✆ **416/393-6400** for information (www.royalfair.org). Mid-November.

Santa Claus Parade, downtown. A favorite with kids since 1905, it features marching bands, floats, clowns, and jolly St. Nick. American visitors are usually surprised that the parade's in November, but it's better than watching Santa try to slide through slush. For information, call ✆ **416/249-7833** (www.city.toronto.on.ca). Third Sunday of November.

One-of-a-Kind Craft Show & Sale, Exhibition Place. More than 400 craft artists from across Canada display their unique wares at this 11-day show. For information, call ✆ **416/960-3680** (www.oneofakindshow.com). Last weekend in November through early December.

Cavalcade of Lights, Nathan Phillips Square. During this holiday celebration, lights decorate trees in and around Nathan Phillips Square, parties and performances take over the skating rink, and ice sculptures decorate the square. Visit www.city.toronto.on.ca for more information. Late November through December 31.

Canadian Aboriginal Festival, SkyDome. More than 1,500 Native American dancers, drummers, and singers attend this weekend celebration. There are literary readings, an arts-and-crafts market, and traditional foods. Call ✆ **519/751-0040** (www.canab.com). Last weekend in November.

December

First Night Toronto and New Year's Eve at City Hall. First Night is an alcohol-free family New Year's

Eve celebration. A button (C$8/ US$5) admits you to a variety of musical, theatrical, and dance performances at downtown venues. In Nathan Phillips Square and in Mel Lastman Square in North York, concerts begin at around 10pm to usher in the countdown to the New Year. Visit www.city.toronto.on.ca for more information. December 31.

5 Health & Insurance

HEALTH

While Toronto has excellent doctors and some fine hospitals, it's common sense to prepare for the trip as you would for any other. Be sure to pack an adequate supply of any prescription drugs that you are taking; keep them stored in their original, labeled containers as required by Canada Customs. It's also a good idea to take along a written prescription for any drugs that you take. For conditions like epilepsy, diabetes, or heart problems, wear a Medic Alert Identification Tag (© **800/825-3785;** www. medicalert.org).

TRAVEL INSURANCE AT A GLANCE

Check your existing insurance policies before you buy travel insurance to cover trip cancellation, lost luggage, medical expenses, or car-rental insurance. You're likely to have partial or complete coverage. But if you need some, ask your travel agent about a comprehensive package. The cost of travel insurance varies widely, depending on the cost and length of your trip, your age and overall health, and the type of trip you're taking. Insurance for extreme sports or adventure travel, for example, will cost more than coverage for a cruise. Some insurers provide packages for specialty vacations, such as skiing or backpacking. More dangerous activities may be excluded from basic policies.

And keep in mind that in the aftermath of the World Trade Center attacks, a number of airlines, cruise lines, and insurers no longer cover tour operators. *The bottom line:* Always, always check the fine print before you sign on; more and more policies have built-in exclusions and restrictions that may leave you out in the cold if something does go awry.

For information, contact one of the following popular insurers:

- **Access America** (© 800/284-8300); www.accessamerica.com/)
- **Travel Guard International** (© 800/826-1300; www.travel guard.com)
- **Travel Insured International** (© 800/243-3174; www.travel insured.com)
- **Travelex Insurance Services** (© 800/228-9792; www.travelex-insurance.com)

MEDICAL INSURANCE

Most health insurance policies cover you if you get sick away from home—but check, particularly if an HMO insures you. With the exception of certain HMOs and Medicare/Medicaid, your medical insurance should cover medical treatment—even hospital care—overseas. However, most out-of-country hospitals make you pay your bills up front, and send you a refund after you've returned home and filed the necessary paperwork. Members of **Blue Cross/Blue Shield** can now use their cards at select hospitals in most major cities worldwide (© **800/810-BLUE** or www.blue cares.com for a list of hospitals).

Some credit cards (American Express and certain gold and platinum Visas and MasterCards, for example) offer automatic flight insurance against death or dismemberment in case of an airplane crash if you charged the cost of your ticket.

If you require additional insurance, try one of the following companies:

- **MEDEX International**, 9515 Deereco Rd., Timonium, MD 21093-5375 (✆ **888/MEDEX-00** or 410/453-6300; fax 410/453-6301; www.medexassist.com)
- **Travel Assistance International** (✆ **800/821-2828**; www.travel assistance.com), 9200 Keystone Crossing, Suite 300, Indianapolis, IN 46240 (for general information on services, call the company's Worldwide Assistance Services, Inc., at ✆ **800/777-8710**).

The cost of travel medical insurance varies widely. Check your existing policies before you buy additional coverage. Also, check to see if your medical insurance covers you for emergency medical evacuation: If you have to buy a one-way same-day ticket home and forfeit your nonrefundable roundtrip ticket, you may be out big bucks.

LOST-LUGGAGE INSURANCE

On international flights (including U.S. portions of international trips), baggage is limited to approximately $9.07 per pound, up to approximately $635 per checked bag. If you plan to check items more valuable than the standard liability, you may purchase "excess valuation" coverage from the airline, up to $5,000. Be sure to take any valuables or irreplaceable items with you in your carry-on luggage. If you file a lost luggage claim, be prepared to answer detailed questions about the contents of your baggage, and be sure to file a claim immediately, as most airlines enforce a 21-day deadline. Before you leave home, compile an inventory of all packed items and a rough estimate of the total value to ensure you're properly compensated if your luggage is lost. You will only be reimbursed for what you lost, no more. Once you've filed a complaint, persist in securing your reimbursement; there are no laws governing the length of time it takes for a carrier to reimburse you. If you arrive at a destination without your bags, ask the airline to forward them to your hotel or to your next destination; they will usually comply. If your bag is delayed or lost, the airline may reimburse you for reasonable expenses, such as a toothbrush or a set of clothes, but the airline is under no legal obligation to do so.

Lost luggage may also be covered by your homeowner's or renter's policy. Many platinum and gold credit cards cover you as well. If you choose to purchase additional lost-luggage insurance, be sure not to buy more than you need. Buy in advance from the insurer or a trusted agent (prices will be much higher at the airport).

CAR RENTAL INSURANCE (LOSS/DAMAGE WAIVER OR COLLISION DAMAGE WAIVER)

If you hold a private auto insurance policy, you probably are covered in the U.S., but not abroad, for loss or damage to the car, and liability in case a passenger is injured. The credit card you used to rent the card also may provide some coverage.

Car rental insurance probably does not cover liability if you caused the accident. Check your own auto insurance policy, the rental company policy, and your credit card coverage for the extent of coverage: Is your destination covered? Are other drivers covered? How much liability is covered if a passenger is injured? (If you rely on your credit card for coverage, you may want to bring a second credit card with you, as damages may be charged to your card and you may find yourself stranded with no money.)

Car rental insurance costs about $20 a day.

> **Tips Quick ID**
>
> Tie a colorful ribbon or piece of yarn around your luggage handle, or slap a distinctive sticker on the side of your bag. This makes it less likely that someone will mistakenly appropriate it. And if your luggage gets lost, it will be easier to find.

WHAT TO DO IF YOU GET SICK AWAY FROM HOME

If you worry about getting sick away from home, consider purchasing **medical travel insurance** and carry your ID card in your purse or wallet. In most cases, your existing health plan will provide the coverage you need. See the section on insurance earlier in this chapter for more information.

If you suffer from a chronic illness, consult your doctor before your departure. For conditions like epilepsy, diabetes, or heart problems, wear a **Medic Alert Identification Tag** (© 800/825-3785; www.medic alert.org), which will immediately alert doctors to your condition and give them access to your records through Medic Alert's 24-hour hot line.

Pack **prescription medications** in your carry-on luggage, and carry prescription medications in their original containers. Also bring along copies of your prescriptions in case you lose your pills or run out. Carry the generic name of prescription medicines, in case a local pharmacist is unfamiliar with the brand name.

And don't forget sunglasses and an extra pair of contact lenses or prescription glasses.

Contact the **International Association for Medical Assistance to Travelers (IAMAT)** (© 716/754-4883 or 416/652-0137; www.iamat.org) for tips on travel and health concerns in the countries you're visiting, and lists of local, English-speaking doctors. The United States **Centers for Disease Control and Prevention** (© 800/311-3435; www.cdc.gov) provides up-to-date information on necessary vaccines and health hazards by region or country (Their booklet, *Health Information for International Travel,* is $25 by mail; on the Internet, it's free). Any foreign consulate can provide a list of area doctors who speak English. If you get sick, consider asking your hotel concierge to recommend a local doctor—even his or her own. You can also try the emergency room at a local hospital; many have walk-in clinics for emergency cases that are not life threatening. You may not get immediate attention, but you won't pay the high price of an emergency room visit (usually a minimum of $300 just for signing your name).

6 Tips for Travelers with Special Needs

FOR TRAVELERS WITH DISABILITIES

Toronto is a very accessible city. Curb cuts are well made and common throughout the downtown area; special parking privileges are extended to people with disabilities who have special plates or a pass that allows parking in "No Parking" zones. The subway

and trolleys are not accessible, but the city operates **Wheel-Trans,** a special service for those with disabilities. Visitors can register for this service. For information, call © 416/393-4111 or visit www.city.toronto.on.ca/ttc.

The **Community Information Centre of Metropolitan Toronto,** 425 Adelaide St. W., at Spadina

Avenue, Toronto, ON M5V 3C1 (© **416/392-0505**), may be able to provide limited information and assistance about social service organizations in the city. It does not have specific accessibility information on tourism or hotels. It's available weekdays from 8am to 10pm, and weekends from 10am to 10pm.

The Society for Accessible Travel and Hospitality (© **212/447-7284;** www.sath.org) offers a wealth of travel resources for all types of disabilities and informed recommendations on destinations, access guides, travel agents, tour operators, vehicle rentals, and companion services. Annual membership costs $45 for adults, $30 for seniors and students.

Mobility International USA (© **541/343-1284;** www.miusa.org) publishes *A World of Options*, a 658-page book of resources, covering everything from biking trips to scuba outfitters, and a biannual newsletter, *Over the Rainbow*. Annual membership is $35.

FOR SENIORS

Many city attractions and some hotels grant senior discounts. Bring a form of photo ID.

If you haven't already done so, think about joining the **AARP,** 601 E St. NW, Washington, DC 20049 (© **202/434-2277;** www.aarp.org). Members get discounts on hotels, airfares, and car rentals. AARP offers members a wide range of benefits, including *Modern Maturity* magazine and a monthly newsletter. Anyone over 50 can join.

Also look into the fun courses offered in the Toronto region at incredibly low prices by **Elderhostel** (© **877/426-8056;** www.elderhostel. org). Elderhostel arranges study programs for those 55 and over (and a spouse or companion of any age); many courses include airfare, accommodations in university dormitories or modest inns, meals, and tuition.

For a catalog, write Elderhostel, P.O. Box 1959, Wakefield, MA 01880-5959.

Another great resource is the **Toronto Seniors Community Guide** (www.ageofreason.com/projon toronto.htm). Travelers aged 50 and over will appreciate this guide, which lists accommodations, tours, and events geared toward mature visitors. The discounts section lists special savings and deals.

FAMILY TRAVEL

The family vacation is a rite of passage for many households, one that in a split second can devolve into a *National Lampoon* farce. But in Toronto, a city that boasts a plethora of family-friendly sites, such as the Ontario Science Centre, the Children's Own Museum, and the Toronto Zoo, you'll find that a family trip really can offer something for everyone.

For more suggestions on family and kid-oriented entertainment in Toronto, see "Frommer's Favorite Toronto Experiences" in chapter 1 and "Especially for Kids" in chapter 6, or pick up a copy of *Toronto Life,* a local magazine that has an excellent kid's section and events listing.

Other helpful features in this guide include "Family-Friendly Hotels" (p. 66) and "Family-Friendly Restaurants" (p. 89). The "Shopping" chapter includes great suggestions for children's clothes and toys, and Indigo Books Music & More (p. 176) often offers events for kids.

Familyhostel (© **800/733-9753;** www.learn.unh.edu/familyhostel) takes the whole family on moderately priced domestic and international learning vacations. The program staff handles all trip details, and a team of academics guides lectures, field trips, and sightseeing for kids ages 8 to 15 accompanied by their parents and/or grandparents.

How to Take Great Trips with Your Kids (The Harvard Common Press) is full of good general advice that can apply to travel anywhere. You also might want to check out these two valuable handbooks for traveling with children in Canada: *Frommer's Toronto with Kids* and *Frommer's Ottawa with Kids.*

Family Travel Network (www. familytravelnetwork.com) offers travel tips and reviews of family-friendly destinations, vacation deals, and thoughtful features such as "What to Do When Your Kids Are Afraid to Travel" and "Kid-Style Camping." **Traveling Internationally with Your Children** (www.travelwithyourkids. com) is a comprehensive site offering sound advice for long-distance and international travel with children.

FOR STUDENTS

The key to securing discounts and other special benefits is the **International Student Identity Card (ISIC),** available to any high school or university student. Contact the **Council on International Educational Exchange,** or CIEE, 205 E. 42nd St., New York, NY 10017 (℃ **212/822-2600** or 212/822-2700; www.ciee.com). The card is available at all Council Travel offices and on many U.S. college campuses. To find the office nearest you, call ℃ **888/COUNCIL** (888/268-6245) or 800/GETANID (800/438-2643).

If you'd like to meet other students, you've come to the right place. Toronto has several major colleges in addition to the sprawling **University of Toronto.** The largest university in Canada, with more than 50,000 students (41,000 full-time), the University of Toronto offers many year-round activities and events that any visitor can attend—lectures, seminars, concerts, and more. U of T Day is usually celebrated in the middle of October. The university holds an open

house for the community and celebrates with a children's fair and the annual homecoming football game and parade. Call ℃ **416/978-8342** for more information, call 416/978-5000 for campus tours, or visit www.utoronto.ca.

WOMEN TRAVELERS

Women Welcome Women World Wide (5W) (℃ **203/259-7832;** www. womenwelcomewomen.org.uk) works to foster international friendships by enabling women of different countries to visit one another (men can come along on the trips; they just can't join the club). It's a big, active organization, with more than 3,000 members from all walks of life in some 70 countries.

Safety and Security for Women Who Travel, by Sheila Swan Laufer and Peter Laufer (Travelers' Tales, Inc.), offers commonsense advice and tips on safe travel. **Journeywoman** (www.journeywoman.com) is a lively travel resource, with a "GirlTalk Guide" to Toronto, and a free e-mail newsletter.

FOR GAY & LESBIAN TRAVELERS

Toronto has a large gay population, estimated at about 250,000. Community life is centered north and south of the intersection of Church and Wellesley streets. Gay and lesbian travelers can pick up a copy of the biweekly *Xtra!* It's available free at many bookstores, including the **Glad Day Bookshop,** 598A Yonge St., 2nd floor (℃ **416/961-4161;** www.glad daybookshop.com). It's open Monday to Wednesday from 10am to 6:30pm, Thursday and Friday from 10am to 9pm, Saturday from 10am to 6pm, and Sunday from noon to 6pm. To receive a copy of *Xtra!* ahead of time, write to 491 Church St., Suite 200, Toronto, ON M4Y 2C6 (℃ **416/925-6665;** www.xtra.ca).

For information on upcoming events, call **Tel-Xtra** (© **416/925-9872**). Another resource is **Gay Toronto** (www.gaytoronto.com), which lists gay-friendly restaurants, bars, nightclubs, guesthouses, travel agencies, and other businesses and organizations.

The International Gay & Lesbian Travel Association (IGLTA) (© **800/448-8550** or 954/776-2626; fax 954/776-3303; www.iglta.org) links travelers up with gay-friendly hoteliers, tour operators, and airline and cruise-line representatives. It offers monthly newsletters, marketing mailings, and a membership directory that's updated once a year. Membership is $200 yearly, plus a $100 administration fee for new members.

7 Getting There

BY PLANE

Wherever you're traveling from, always shop the airlines and ask for the lowest fare. You'll have a better chance of landing a deal if you're willing to be flexible about when you arrive and leave.

You may be able to fly for less than the standard advance (APEX) fare by contacting a ticket broker or consolidator. These companies, which buy tickets in bulk and sell them at a discount, advertise in the Sunday travel sections of major city newspapers. You may not be able to get the lowest price they advertise, but you're likely to pay less than the price quoted by the major airlines. Tickets purchased through a consolidator are often nonrefundable. If you change your itinerary after purchase, chances are you'll pay a stiff penalty.

FROM THE U.S. Canada's only national airline, **Air Canada** (© **888/247-2262**; www.aircanada.ca), operates direct flights to Toronto from most major American cities and many smaller ones. It also flies from major cities around the world and operates connecting flights from other U.S. cities.

Among U.S. airlines, **American** (© **800/433-7300**) has daily direct flights from Chicago, Dallas, Miami, and New York. **United** (© **800/241-6522**) has direct flights from Chicago, San Francisco, and Washington (Dulles); it's a code-share partner with Air Canada. **US Airways** (© **800/428-4322**) operates directly into Toronto from a number of U.S. cities, notably Baltimore, Indianapolis, Philadelphia, and Pittsburgh. **Northwest** (© **800/225-2525**) flies direct from Detroit and Minneapolis. **Delta** (© **800/221-1212**) flies direct from Atlanta and Cincinnati.

FROM ABROAD There's frequent service (direct and indirect) to Toronto from around the world.

Several airlines operate from the **United Kingdom. British Airways** (© **0845/773-3377**) and **Air Canada** (© **08705/247-226**) fly direct from London's Heathrow airport. Air Canada also flies direct from Glasgow and Manchester. **Virgin Atlantic** (© **01293/747-245**; www.virginatlantic.com) launched direct flights out of Gatwick airport in June 2001.

In **Australia, Air Canada** (© **9286-8900**) has an agreement with Qantas and flies from Sydney to Toronto, stopping in Honolulu. From **New Zealand, Air Canada** (© **379-3371**) cooperates with Air New Zealand, scheduling on average three flights a week from Auckland to Toronto, via Honolulu, Fiji, or both.

From **Cape Town,** South Africa, **Delta** (© 800/221-1212, or 011/482-4582 in South Africa) operates via New York; **Air Canada** (© 011/875-5800) via Frankfurt; and **South African Airways** (© 021/254-610) via Miami or New York.

Several airlines fly from **Johannesburg,** including **British Airways** (© 011/441-8600) via Heathrow and **South African Airways** (© 011/333-6504) via Miami or New York.

FLYING FOR LESS: TIPS FOR GETTING THE BEST AIRFARE

Passengers within the same airplane cabin are rarely paying the same fare. Business travelers who need to purchase tickets at the last minute, change their itinerary at a moment's notice, or get home for the weekend pay the premium rate. Passengers who can book their ticket long in advance, who can stay over Saturday night, or who are willing to travel on a Tuesday, Wednesday, or Thursday after 7pm, will pay a fraction of the full fare. On many flights, even the shortest hops, the full fare is close to $1,000 or more, while a 7- or 14-day advance purchase ticket may cost less than half that amount. Here are a few other easy ways to save.

- Airlines periodically lower prices on their most popular routes. Check the travel section of your Sunday newspaper for advertised

discounts or call the airlines directly and ask if any **promotional rates** or special fares are available. You'll almost never see a sale during the peak summer vacation months of July and August, or during the Thanksgiving or Christmas seasons; but in periods of low-volume travel, you should pay no more than $400 for a domestic cross-country flight. If your schedule is flexible, say so, and ask if you can secure a cheaper fare by staying an extra day, by flying midweek, or by flying at less-trafficked hours. If you already hold a ticket when a sale breaks, it may even pay to exchange your ticket, which usually incurs a $100 to $150 charge.

Note: The lowest-priced fares are often nonrefundable, require advance purchase of 1 to 3 weeks and a certain length of stay, and carry penalties for changing dates of travel.

- **Consolidators,** also known as bucket shops, are a good place to find low fares. Consolidators buy seats in bulk from the airlines

---

Tips What You Can Carry On—And What You Can't

The Transportation Security Administration (TSA) has devised new restrictions on carry-on baggage, not only to expedite the screening process but also to prevent potential weapons from passing through airport security. Passengers are now limited to bringing one carry-on bag and one personal item onto the aircraft (previous regulations allowed two carry-on bags and one personal item, such as a briefcase or a purse). For more information, visit the TSA website at **www.tsa.gov.** The agency has released a new list of items passengers are not allowed to carry onto an aircraft:

Not permitted: knives and box cutters, corkscrews, straight razors, metal scissors, golf clubs, baseball bats, pool cues, hockey sticks, ski poles, ice picks.

Permitted: nail clippers, tweezers, eyelash curlers, safety razors (including disposable razors), syringes (with documented proof of medical need), walking canes and umbrellas (must be inspected first).

Air Travel Security Measures

In the wake of the terrorist attacks of September 11, 2001, the airline industry implemented sweeping security measures in airports. Expect a lengthier check-in process and possible delays. Although regulations vary from airline to airline, you can expedite the process by taking the following steps:

- **Arrive early.** Arrive at the airport at least 2 hours before your scheduled flight.

- **Try not to drive your car to the airport.** Parking and curbside access to the terminal may be limited. Call ahead and check.

- **Don't count on curbside check-in.** Some airlines and airports have stopped curbside check-in altogether, whereas others offer it on a limited basis. For up-to-date information on specific regulations, check with the individual airline.

- **Be sure to carry plenty of documentation.** A government-issued photo ID (federal, state, or local) is now required. You may need to show this at various checkpoints. With an E-ticket, you may be required to have with you printed confirmation of purchase, and perhaps even the credit card with which you bought your ticket (see "All about E-Ticketing," below). This varies from airline to airline, so call ahead to make sure you have the proper documentation. And be sure that your ID is up-to-date: an expired driver's license, for example, may keep you from boarding the plane altogether.

- **Know what you can carry on—and what you can't.** Travelers in the United States are now limited to one carry-on bag, plus one personal bag (such as a purse or a briefcase). The Transportation Security Administration (TSA) has also issued a list of restricted carry-on items; see "What You Can Carry On—and What You Can't," above.

- **Prepare to be searched.** Expect spot-checks. Electronic items, such as a laptop or cellphone, should be readied for additional screening. Limit the metal items you wear on your person.

- **It's no joke.** When a check-in agent asks if someone other than you packed your bag, don't decide that this is the time to be funny. The agents will not hesitate to call security.

- **No ticket, no gate access.** Only ticketed passengers will be allowed beyond the screener checkpoints, except for those people with specific medical or parental needs.

and then sell them back to the public at prices usually below even the airlines' discounted rates. Their small ads usually run in Sunday newspaper travel sections. And before you pay, request a confirmation number from the consolidator and then call the airline to confirm your seat. Be aware that bucket shop tickets are usually nonrefundable or rigged with stiff cancellation penalties, often as high as 50% to 75% of the ticket price. Protect yourself

> **Tips   All About E-Ticketing**
>
> Until recently, **electronic tickets (E-tickets)** were the fast and easy ticket-free alternative to paper tickets. E-tickets allowed passengers to avoid long lines at airport check-in, all the while saving the airlines money on postage and labor. With the increased security measures in airports, however, an E-ticket no longer guarantees an accelerated check-in. You often can't go straight to the boarding gate, even if you have no bags to check. You'll probably need to show your printed E-ticket receipt or confirmation of purchase, as well as a photo ID, and sometimes even the credit card with which you purchased your E-ticket. That said, buying an E-ticket is still a fast, convenient way to book a flight; instead of having to wait for a paper ticket to come through the mail, you can book your fare by phone or on the computer, and the airline will immediately confirm by fax or e-mail. In addition, airlines often offer frequent flier miles as incentive for electronic bookings.

by paying with a credit card rather than cash. Keep in mind that if there's an airline sale going on, or if it's high season, you can often get the same or better rates by contacting the airlines directly, so do some comparison shopping before you buy. Also check out the name of the airline; you may not want to fly on some obscure Third World airline, even if you're saving $10. And check whether you're flying on a charter or a scheduled airline; the latter is more expensive but more reliable.

Council Travel (© 800/226-8624; www.counciltravel.com) and STA Travel (© 800/781-4040; www.statravel.com) cater especially to young travelers, but their bargain-basement prices are available to people of all ages. **The TravelHUB** (© 888/AIR-FARE; www.travelhub.com) represents nearly 1,000 travel agencies, many of whom offer consolidator and discount fares. Other reliable consolidators include 1-800-FLY-CHEAP (www.1800flycheap.com); TFI Tours International

(© 800/745-8000 or 212/736-1140), which serves as a clearinghouse for unused seats; or "rebators" such as Travel Avenue (© 800/333-3335; www.travelavenue.com) and the Smart Traveller (© 800/448-3338 in the U.S., or 305/448-3338), which rebate part of their commissions to you.

- **Last-minute online specials,** known as "E-savers," such as weekend deals or Internet-only fares, are offered by airlines to fill empty seats. Most of these are announced on Tuesday or Wednesday and must be purchased online. They are only valid for travel that weekend, but some can be booked weeks or months in advance. Air Canada always has specials to Toronto from U.S. and Canadian cities; visit www.air canada.ca to sign up for a weekly e-mail that will let you know where the deals are.
- Join **frequent-flier clubs.** It's best to accrue miles on one program, so you can rack up free flights and achieve elite status faster. But it

makes sense to open as many accounts as possible, no matter how seldom you fly a particular airline. It's free, and you'll get the best choice of seats, faster response to phone inquiries, and prompter service if your luggage is stolen, your flight is canceled or delayed, or if you want to change your seat.

BY TRAIN

Amtrak's "Maple Leaf" service links New York City and Toronto via Albany, Buffalo, and Niagara Falls. It departs daily from Penn Station. The journey takes 11¾ hours. From Chicago, the "International" carries passengers to Toronto via Port Huron, Michigan, a 12½-hour trip. Note that these lengthy schedules allow for extended stops at customs and immigration checkpoints at the border. Both trains arrive in Toronto at Union Station on Front Street, 1 block west of Yonge Street, opposite the Fairmont Royal York Hotel. The station has direct access to the subway.

To secure the lowest round-trip fares, book as far in advance as possible, and try to travel midweek. Seat availability determines price levels; the earlier you book, the more likely you are to land a lower fare. Sample fares (for use as guidelines only), depending on seat availability: from New York, US$65 to $99 one-way or US$130 to $198 round-trip; from Chicago, US$98 one-way, US$108 to $196 round-trip. Prices do not include meals. Always ask about the availability of discounted fares, companion fares, and any other special tickets. Call **Amtrak** at (C) **800/USA-RAIL** or 800/872-7245; www.amtrak.com.

BY BUS

Greyhound ((C) **800/231-2222;** www.greyhound.com) is the only bus company that crosses the U.S. border. You can travel from almost anywhere in the United States. You'll arrive at the Metro Coach Terminal downtown at 610 Bay St., near the corner of Dundas Street.

The bus may be faster and cheaper than the train, and its routes may be more flexible if you want to stop along the way. Bear in mind that it's more cramped, toilet facilities are meager, and meals are taken at somewhat depressing rest stops.

Depending on where you are coming from, check into Greyhound's special unlimited-travel passes and discount fares. It's hard to provide sample fares because bus companies, like airlines, are adopting yield-management strategies, causing prices to change from day to day.

BY CAR

Crossing the border by car gives you a lot of options—the U.S. highway system leads directly into Canada at 13 points. If you're driving from Michigan, you'll enter at Detroit–Windsor (I-75 and the Ambassador Bridge) or Port Huron–Sarnia (I-94 and the Bluewater Bridge). If you're coming from New York, you have more options. On I-190, you can enter at Buffalo–Fort Erie; Niagara Falls, N.Y.–Niagara Falls, ON; or Niagara Falls, N.Y.–Lewiston. On I-81, you'll cross the Canadian border at Hill Island; on Rte. 37, you'll enter at either Ogdensburg–Johnstown or Rooseveltown–Cornwall.

Tips **Cancelled Plans**

If your flight is cancelled, don't book a new fare at the ticket counter. Find the nearest phone and call the airline directly to reschedule. You'll be relaxing while other passengers are still standing in line.

Flying with Film & Video

Never pack unprotected, undeveloped film in checked bags, which may be scanned. The film you carry with you can be damaged by scanners, too. X-ray damage is cumulative; the slower the film, and the more times you put it through a scanner, the more likely the damage. Film under 800 ASA is usually safe for up to five scans. If you're taking your film through additional scans, request a hand inspection. In domestic airports, the Federal Aviation Administration guarantees hand inspections. In international airports, you're at the mercy of airport officials. On international flights, store your film in transparent baggies, so you can remove it easily before you go through scanners. Keep in mind that airports are not the only places where your camera may be scanned: Highly trafficked attractions are X-raying visitors' bags with increasing frequency.

Most photo supply stores sell protective pouches designed to block damaging X-rays. The pouches fit both film and loaded cameras. They should protect your film in checked baggage, but they also may raise alarms and result in a hand inspection.

An organization called **Film Safety for Traveling on Planes, FSTOP** (© **888-301-2665;** www.f-stop.org), can provide additional tips for traveling with film and equipment.

Carry-on scanners will not damage **videotape** in video camera, but the magnetic fields emitted by the walk-through security gateways and handheld inspection wands will. Always place your loaded camcorder on the screening conveyor belt or have it hand-inspected. Be sure your batteries are charged, as you will probably be required to turn the device on to ensure that it's what it appears to be.

From the United States you are most likely to enter Toronto from the west on Hwy. 401 or Hwy. 2 and the Queen Elizabeth Way. If you come from the east via Montreal, you'll also use 401 and 2.

Here are approximate driving distances in kilometers to Toronto: from Boston, 911km (566 miles); Buffalo, 155km (96 miles); Chicago, 859km (534 miles); Cincinnati, 806km (501 miles); Detroit, 379km (236 miles); Minneapolis, 1,564km (972 miles); New York, 797km (495 miles).

Be sure you have your driver's license and car registration if you plan to drive your own vehicle into Canada. It isn't a bad idea to carry proof of automobile liability insurance, either.

If you are a member of the American Automobile Association (AAA), the **Canadian Automobile Association (CAA)** Central Ontario Branch in Toronto (© **416/221-4300;** www.caa.ca) provides emergency road service.

8 Package Deals

Package tours are not the same thing as escorted tours. With a package tour, you travel independently but pay a group rate. Packages usually include airfare, a choice of hotels, and car rentals, and packagers often offer several options at different prices. In many cases, a package that includes airfare, hotel, and transportation to and from the airport will cost you less than just the hotel alone would have, had you booked it yourself. That's because packages are sold in bulk to tour operators—who resell them to the public at a cost that drastically undercuts standard rates.

RECOMMENDED PACKAGE TOUR OPERATORS

One good source of package deals is the airlines themselves. Most major airlines offer air/land packages, including **American Airlines Vacations** (© 800/321-2121; www.aavacations. com), **Delta Vacations** (© 800/221-6666; www.deltavacations.com), and **US Airways Vacations** (© 800/455-0123 or 800/422-3861; www. usairwaysvacations.com), **Continental Airlines Vacations** (© 800/301-3800; www.coolvacations.com), and **United Vacations** (© 888/854-3899; www.unitedvacations.com/)

Online Vacation Mall (© 800/839-9851; www.onlinevacationmall. com) allows you to search for and book packages offered by a number of tour operators and airlines. The **United States Tour Operators Association**'s website (www.ustoa.com) has a search engine that allows you to look for operators that offer packages to a specific destination. Travel packages are also listed in the travel section of your local Sunday newspaper. **Liberty Travel** (© **888/271-1584;** www.libertytravel.com), one of the biggest packagers in the Northeast, often runs full-page ads in Sunday

papers. Or check ads in the national travel magazines such as *Arthur Frommer's Budget Travel Magazine, Travel & Leisure, National Geographic Traveler,* and *Condé Nast Traveler.*

THE PROS & CONS OF PACKAGE TOURS

Packages can save you money because they are sold in bulk to tour operators, who sell them to the public. They offer group prices but allow for independent travel. The disadvantages are that you're usually required to make a large payment up front; you may end up on a charter flight; and you have to deal with your own luggage and with transfers between your hotel and the airport, if transfers are not included in the package price. Packages often don't allow for complete flexibility or a wide range of choices. For instance, you may prefer a quiet inn but have to settle for a popular chain hotel instead. Your choice of travel days may be limited as well.

QUESTIONS TO ASK IF YOU BOOK A PACKAGE TOUR

- What are the **accommodations choices** available and are there price differences? Once you find out, look them up in a Frommer's guide.
- What **type of room** will you be staying in? Don't take whatever is thrown your way. Request a non-smoking room, a quiet room, a room with a view, or whatever you fancy.
- Look for hidden expenses. Ask whether airport departure fees and taxes are included in the total cost.

9 Planning Your Trip Online

Researching and booking your trip online can save time and money. Then again, it may not. It is simply not true

that you always get the best deal online. Most booking engines do not include schedules and prices for budget airlines, and from time to time you'll get a better last-minute price by calling the airline directly, so it's best to call the airline to see if you can do better before booking online.

On the plus side, Internet users today can tap into the same travel-planning databases that were once accessible only to travel agents—and do it at the same speed. Sites such as **Frommers.com, Travelocity.com, Expedia.com,** and **Orbitz.com** allow consumers to comparison shop for airfares, access special bargains, book flights, and reserve hotel rooms and rental cars.

But don't fire your travel agent just yet. Although online booking sites offer tips and hard data to help you bargain shop, they cannot endow you with the hard-earned experience that makes a seasoned, reliable travel agent an invaluable resource, even in the Internet age. And for consumers with a complex itinerary, a trusty travel agent is still the best way to arrange the most direct flights to and from the best airports.

Still, there's no denying the Internet's emergence as a powerful tool in researching and plotting travel time.

The benefits of researching your trip online can be well worth the effort.

Last-minute specials, such as weekend deals or Internet-only fares, are offered by airlines to fill empty seats. Most of these are announced on Tuesday or Wednesday and must be purchased online. They are only valid for travel that weekend, but some can be booked weeks or months in advance. Sign up for weekly e-mail alerts at airline websites or check mega-sites that compile comprehensive lists of last-minute specials, such as **Smarter Living** (smarterliving.com) or **WebFlyer** (www.webflyer.com).

Some sites, such as Expedia.com, will send you **e-mail notification** when a cheap fare becomes available to your favorite destination. Some will also tell you when fares to a particular destination are lowest.

TRAVEL PLANNING & BOOKING SITES

Keep in mind that because several airlines are no longer willing to pay commissions on tickets sold by online travel agencies, these agencies may either add a $10 surcharge to your bill if you book on that carrier—or neglect to offer those carriers' schedules.

 Frommers.com: The Complete Travel Resource

For an excellent travel-planning resource, we highly recommend **Frommers.com** (www.frommers.com). We're a little biased, of course, but we guarantee that you'll find the travel tips, reviews, monthly vacation giveaways, and online-booking capabilities thoroughly indispensable. Among the special features are our popular **Message Boards,** where Frommer's readers post queries and share advice (sometimes even our authors show up to answer questions); **Frommers.com Newsletter,** for the latest travel bargains and inside travel secrets; and Frommer's **Destinations Section,** where you'll get expert travel tips, hotel and dining recommendations, and advice on the sights to see for more than 2,500 destinations around the globe. When your research is done, the **Online Reservation System** (www.frommers.com/booktravelnow) takes you to Frommer's favorite sites for booking your vacation at affordable prices.

Tips Air Canada CyberDeals

One site that's particularly worth checking out is **Air Canada** (www.air canada.ca). On Wednesday, it offers deeply discounted flights to Canada for that weekend. You need to reserve on Wednesday or Thursday to fly on Friday (after 7pm only) or Saturday (all day) and return on Monday or Tuesday (all day). Once you register with Air Canada's Web Specials page, you'll receive an e-mail every Wednesday about available discounts.

The list of sites below is selective, not comprehensive. Some sites will have evolved or disappeared by the time you read this.

- **Travelocity** (www.travelocity.com or www.frommers.travelocity.com) and **Expedia** (www.expedia.com) are among the most popular sites, each offering an excellent range of options. Travelers search by destination, dates and cost.
- **Orbitz** (www.orbitz.com) is a popular site launched by United, Delta, Northwest, American, and Continental airlines. With this site, you're granted access to the largest data bank of rates on airline tickets (including available fares from more than 450 airlines), rental cars, hotels, vacation packages, and other travel products.
- **Qixo** (www.qixo.com) is another powerful search engine that allows you to search for flights and accommodations from some 20 airline and travel-planning sites (such as Travelocity) at once. Qixo sorts results by price.
- **Priceline** (www.priceline.com) lets you "name your price" for airline tickets, hotel rooms, and rental cars. For airline tickets, you can't say what time you want to fly—you have to accept any flight between 6am and 10pm on the dates you've selected, and you may have to make one or more stopovers. Tickets are nonrefundable, and no frequent-flier miles are awarded.

SMART E-SHOPPING

The savvy traveler is armed with insider information. Here are a few tips to help you navigate the Internet successfully and safely.

- **Know when sales start.** Last-minute deals may vanish in minutes. If you have a favorite booking site or airline, find out when last-minute deals are released to the public. (For example, Southwest's specials are posted every Tues at 12:01am central time.)
- **Shop around.** If you're looking for bargains, compare prices on different sites and airlines—and against a travel agent's best fare. Try a range of times and alternative airports before you make a purchase.
- **Stay secure.** Book only through secure sites (some airline sites are not secure). Look for a key icon (Netscape) or a padlock (Internet Explorer) at the bottom of your Web browser before you enter credit card information or other personal data.
- **Avoid online auctions.** Sites that auction airline tickets and frequent-flier miles are the number-one perpetrators of Internet fraud, according to the National Consumers League.
- **Maintain a paper trail.** If you book an E-ticket, print out a confirmation, or write down your confirmation number, and keep it safe and accessible—or your trip could be a virtual one!

Easy Internet Access Away from Home

There are a number of ways to get your e-mail on the Web, using any computer.

- Your **Internet Service Provider (ISP)** may have a Web-based interface that lets you access your e-mail on computers other than your own. Just find out how it works before you leave home. The major ISPs maintain local access numbers around the world so that you can go online by placing a local call. Check your ISP's website or call its toll-free number and ask how you can use your current account away from home, and how much it will cost. Also ask about the cost of the service before you leave home.

- You can open an account on a free, web-based **e-mail provider** before you leave home, such as Microsoft's **Hotmail** (www. hotmail.com) or **Yahoo! Mail** (http://mail.yahoo.com). Your home ISP may be able to forward your home e-mail to the Web-based account automatically.

- Check out **www.mail2web.com**. This amazing free service allows you to type in your regular e-mail address and password and retrieve your e-mail from any Web browser, anywhere, so long as your home ISP hasn't blocked it with a firewall.

- Call your hotel in advance to see whether Internet connection is possible from your room.

- For recommended cybercafes in Toronto, see "Fast Facts: Toronto," in chapter 3. Another option: rent online time from Kinko's, which has various locations around the city. The charge is about C$15 per hour, but time is billed by the minute.

ONLINE TRAVELER'S TOOLBOX

Veteran travelers usually carry some essential items to make their trips easier. Following is a selection of online tools to bookmark and use.

- **Visa ATM Locator** (www.visa. com), for locations of PLUS ATMs worldwide, or **MasterCard ATM Locator** (www.mastercard. com), for locations of Cirrus ATMs worldwide.

- **Intellicast** (www.intellicast.com) and **Weather.com** (www.weather. com). Gives weather forecasts for Toronto and cities around the world.

- **Mapquest** (www.mapquest.com). This best of the mapping sites lets

you choose a specific address or destination, and in seconds, it will return a map and detailed directions.

- **Cybercafes.com** (www.cybercafes. com) or **Net Café Guide** (www. netcafeguide.com/mapindex. htm). Locate Internet cafes at hundreds of locations around the globe. Catch up on your e-mail and log onto the Web for a few dollars per hour.

- **Universal Currency Converter** (www.xe.net/currency). See what your dollar or pound is worth in more than 100 other countries.

- **U.S. State Department Travel Warnings** (www.travel.state.gov/ travel_warnings.html). Reports on places where health concerns or unrest might threaten U.S. travelers. It also lists the locations of U.S. embassies around the world.

10 Tips on Accommodations

Toronto has a wealth of great places to stay. Major chains such as Hyatt, Fairmont, Four Seasons, Marriott, Sheraton, Westin, Holiday Inn, and Ramada are all represented, and there are several smaller boutique hotels as well (see chapter 4 for reviews). The only difficulty is in getting a deal, particularly in the downtown core. Here are some ways to ensure that you get the best price possible.

TIPS FOR SAVING ON YOUR HOTEL ROOM

The **rack rate** is the maximum rate that a hotel charges for a room. It's the rate you'd get if you walked in off the street and asked for a room for the night. Hardly anybody pays these prices, however, and there are many ways around them.

- **Don't be afraid to bargain.** Most rack rates include commissions of 10% to 25% for travel agents, which some hotels may be willing to reduce if you make your own reservations and haggle a bit. Always ask whether a room less expensive than the first one quoted is available, or whether any special rates apply to you. You may qualify for corporate, student, military, senior, or other discounts. Be sure to mention membership in AAA, AARP, frequent-flier programs, or trade unions, which may entitle you to special deals as well. Find out the hotel policy on children—do kids stay free in the room or is there a special rate?
- **Rely on a qualified professional.** Certain hotels give travel agents discounts in exchange for steering business their way, so if you're shy about bargaining, an agent may be better equipped to negotiate discounts for you.
- **Dial direct.** When booking a room in a chain hotel, compare the rates offered by the hotel's local line with that of the toll-free number. Also check with an agent and online. A hotel makes nothing on a room that stays empty, so the local hotel reservation desk may be willing to offer a special rate unavailable elsewhere.
- **Remember the law of supply and demand.** Resort hotels are most crowded and therefore most expensive on weekends, so discounts are usually available for midweek stays. Business hotels in downtown locations are busiest during the week, so you can expect big discounts over the weekend. Avoid high-season stays whenever you can: Planning your vacation just a week before or after official peak season can mean big savings.
- **Look into group or long-stay discounts.** If you come as part of a large group, you should be able to negotiate a bargain rate, since the hotel can then guarantee occupancy in a number of rooms. Likewise, if you're planning a long stay (at least 5 days), you might qualify for a discount. As a general rule, expect one night free after a seven-night stay.
- **Avoid excess charges.** When you book a room, ask whether the hotel charges for parking. Many hotels charge a fee just for dialing out on the phone in your room. Find out whether your hotel imposes a surcharge on local and long-distance calls. A pay phone, however inconvenient, may save

you money, although many calling cards charge a fee when you use them on pay phones. Finally, ask about local taxes and service charges, which could increase the cost of a room by 25% or more.

- **Watch for coupons and advertised discounts.** Scan ads in your local Sunday newspaper travel section, an excellent source for up-to-the-minute hotel deals.
- **Consider a suite.** If you are traveling with your family or another couple, you can pack more people into a suite (which usually comes with a sofa bed), and thereby reduce your per-person rate. Remember that some places charge for extra guests.
- **Book an efficiency.** A room with a kitchenette allows you to shop for groceries and cook your own meals. This is a big money saver, especially for families on long stays.
- Join hotel **frequent-visitor clubs,** even if you don't use them much. You'll be more likely to get upgrades and other perks.
- Many hotels offer **frequent-flier points.** Don't forget to ask for yours when you check in.
- **Investigate reservations services.** These outfits usually work as consolidators, buying up or reserving rooms in bulk, and then dealing them out to customers at a profit. You can get 10 to 50 percent off; but remember, these discounts apply to inflated rack rates that savvy travelers rarely end up paying. You may get a decent rate, but always call the hotel as well to see if you can do better.

Among the more reputable reservations services, offering both telephone and online bookings, are: **Accommodations Express** (© **800/950-4685;** www.accommodationsexpress.com); **Hotel Reservations Network** (© **800/715-7666;** www.hoteldiscounts.com or www.180096HOTEL.com); **Quikbook** (© **800/789-9887,** includes fax-on-demand service; www.quikbook.com). Online, try booking your hotel through **Frommers.com** (www.frommers.com). **Microsoft Expedia** (www.expedia.com) features a "Travel Agent" that will also direct you to affordable lodgings.

LANDING THE BEST ROOM

Somebody has to get the best room in the house. It might as well be you.

Always ask about a corner room. They're often larger and quieter, with more windows and light, and they often cost the same as standard rooms.

When you make your reservation, ask if the hotel is renovating; if it is, request a room away from the construction. Ask about nonsmoking rooms, rooms with views, rooms with twin, queen- or king-size beds. If you're a light sleeper, request a quiet room away from vending machines, elevators, restaurants, bars, and discos. Ask for one of the rooms that have been most recently renovated or redecorated. If you aren't happy with your room when you arrive, talk to the front desk. If they have another room, they may be willing to accommodate you. Join the hotel's frequent visitor club; you may qualify for upgrades.

11 Recommended Reading

Though it hasn't always played itself in the movies (doubling often as other major cities instead), Toronto does have quite a literary legacy to call its own. It's the hometown of authors Margaret Atwood, Michael Ondaatje, and media theorist and writer Marshall McLuhan.

Atwood's *The Robber Bride* pays homage to her hometown with a story that covers three decades of life in the city. *In the Skin of a Lion* by Michael Ondaatje, the celebrated author of *The English Patient*, is a moving love story that brings the city's landmarks to life. Another notable novel is *Cabbagetown* by Hugh Gardner, the story of the fight to survive in a Toronto slum in the 1930s (Cabbagetown was famous as the largest Anglo-Saxon slum in North America).

If you're interested in architecture, an especially good read is *Emerald City: Toronto Revisited*, by John Bentley Mays. *Emerald City* explores all of Toronto's special places, from the majesty of Casa Loma to the colorful bedlam of Kensington Market.

3

Getting to Know Toronto

Toronto is a wonderful city in which to get lost. Start anywhere in the downtown core and walk in any direction for no more than 15 minutes. You'll see eclectic modern buildings side by side with neo-Gothic and Art Deco architecture, catch a fair glimpse of the city's ethnic spectrum, and walk right into a pleasing patch of greenery.

This is a happy coincidence because the layout and organization of the city mean you *will* get lost at least once during your stay. Streets have names, not numbers, and they have a crazy-making habit of changing their monikers as they go along. In Midtown, the must-see Avenue Road, for example, turns into Queen's Park Crescent and then into University Avenue as you head south, and into Oriole Parkway if you go north. My best advice: Relax and enjoy the ride. In this chapter, you'll find information on the highways, byways, and services that make Toronto tick.

1 Orientation

ARRIVING

BY PLANE

Most flights arrive at **Pearson International Airport,** in the northwest corner of Metro Toronto, approximately 30 minutes from downtown. The trip takes 10 to 15 minutes longer during the weekday morning rush (7–9am). A few (mostly commuter) flights land at the **Toronto Island Airport,** a short ferry ride from downtown.

Pearson serves more than 50 airlines. The most impressive of its three (at the moment) terminals is the **Trillium Terminal 3** (© **905/612-5100**). This airy, modern facility has moving walkways, a huge food court, and many retail stores. An equally grand terminal, currently under construction, will replace the existing **Terminals 1 and 2.** (Terminal 1 has the distinction of being the gloomiest, ugliest airport terminal this travel writer has ever seen.) Its opening has been delayed, but with any luck it will open for business in 2003.

To get from the airport to downtown, take Highway 427 south to the Gardiner Expressway East. A **taxi** costs about C$36 (US$25). A slightly sleeker way to go is by flat-rate **limousine,** which costs around C$40 (US$27). Two limo services are **Aaroport** (© **416/745-1555**) and **AirLine** (© **905/676-3210**). You don't need a reservation. Most first-class hotels run their own **hotel limousine** services; check when you make your reservation.

The convenient **Airport Express bus** (© **905/564-6333**) travels between the airport, the bus terminal, and major downtown hotels—the Westin Harbour Castle, Fairmont Royal York, The Sheraton Centre Toronto, and the Delta Chelsea—every 20 minutes, from 4:55am to 12:55am, with one extra run around 2:30am. The adult fare is C$12.50 (US$9) one-way, C$21.50 (US$15) round-trip; children under 11 accompanied by an adult ride free.

The cheapest way to go is by **bus and subway,** which takes about an hour. From Terminal 2, take the #58 bus to Lawrence West station, the #192 "Airport Rocket" bus to Kipling station, or the #307 bus to Eglinton West station. Only the #192 bus serves Terminal 3; there are no public buses from Terminal 1 (though there is a shuttle that will drop you off at Terminal 2 or 3). The fare of C$2.25 (US$1.50) includes free transfer to the subway. It doesn't matter which bus you use; they all take roughly the same amount of time. (The Airport Rocket reaches the subway fastest, but the subway ride to downtown is more than twice as long as from the other stations.) For more information, call the Toronto Transit Commission, or TTC (© **416/393-4636**).

BY TRAIN

Trains arrive at Union Station on Front Street, 1 block west of Yonge Street, opposite the Fairmont Royal York hotel. The station has direct access to the subway, so you can easily reach any Toronto destination.

VISITOR INFORMATION

For hotel, dining, and other tourist information, head to (or write to) **Tourism Toronto,** 207 Queens Quay W., Suite 590, Toronto, ON M5J 1A7 (© **800/ 363-1990** or 416/203-2600; www.torontotourism.com). It's in the Queens Quay Terminal at Harbourfront, and is open Monday to Friday from 9am to 5pm. Take the LRT (light rapid transit system) from Union Station to the York Street stop. The website has up-to-the-minute city calendar and events information.

More convenient is the drop-in **Ontario Visitor Information Centre,** in the Eaton Centre, on Yonge Street at Dundas Street. It's on Level 1 (one floor below street level) and is open Monday to Friday from 10am to 9pm, Saturday from 9:30am to 6pm, and Sunday from noon to 5pm.

The **Community Information Centre,** 425 Adelaide St. W. (© **416/392-0505**), specializes in social, government, and health-service information for residents or potential residents. Staff members will try to answer questions, and if they can't, they will direct you to someone who can.

To pick up brochures and a map at **Pearson International Airport,** stop by the **Transport Canada Information Centre** (© **905/676-3506** or 416/247-7678). There's one in each terminal. A staff fluent in a dozen languages can answer questions about attractions, ground transportation, and more.

PUBLICATIONS & WEBSITES

Toronto has four daily newspapers: the *Globe and Mail,* the *National Post,* the *Toronto Star,* and the *Toronto Sun.* All have some local listings, but the best are in the *Star,* which lists events, concerts, theater performances, first-run films, and the like.

Even better bets are the free weeklies *Now* and *Eye,* both published on Thursday and available in news boxes and at cafes and shops around town. *Xtra!* is another weekly freebie; it lists events, seminars, and performances, particularly those of interest to the gay and lesbian community. A free annual directory called *The Pink Pages* targets Torontonians, but out-of-towners will find the information about gay- and lesbian-friendly restaurants, bars, and other businesses quite useful. It's available at shops, restaurants, and bars along Church Street.

Underground Toronto

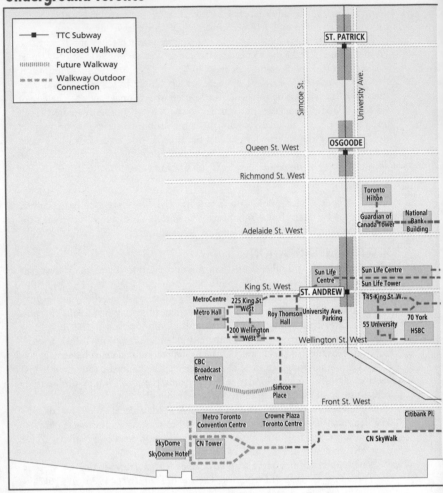

- ■— TTC Subway
- Enclosed Walkway
- Future Walkway
- Walkway Outdoor Connection

ST. PATRICK

Simcoe St.

University Ave.

Queen St. West — OSGOODE

Richmond St. West

Toronto Hilton

Guardian of Canada Tower

National Bank Building

Adelaide St. West

Sun Life Centre

Sun Life Centre

Sun Life Tower

King St. West — ST. ANDREW

MetroCentre

225 King St. West

145 King St. W.

Metro Hall

Roy Thomson Hall

University Ave. Parking

70 York

55 University

200 Wellington West

HSBC

Wellington St. West

CBC Broadcast Centre

Simcoe Place

Front St. West

Metro Toronto Convention Centre

Crowne Plaza Toronto Centre

Citibank Pl.

SkyDome
SkyDome Hotel

CN Tower

CN SkyWalk

Where Toronto is a glossy monthly magazine that lists events, attractions, restaurants, and shops; it's available free at most hotels in the city and at some restaurants in the Theater District. *Toronto Life* is an award-winning lifestyle magazine that has excellent listings of kids' events, theater, speeches, and art exhibitions; the April issue contains a dining guide. *Toronto Life Fashion* magazine will be of interest to serious shoppers.

Toronto.com (www.toronto.com), operated by the *Toronto Star,* offers extensive restaurant reviews, events listings, and feature articles. *Toronto Life*'s website (www.torontolife.com) is another popular choice, particularly for its restaurant reviews and contests. It includes events, shopping, and services listings.

CITY LAYOUT

Toronto is laid out in a grid . . . with a few interesting exceptions. **Yonge Street** (pronounced *Young*) is the main north-south street, stretching from Lake Ontario

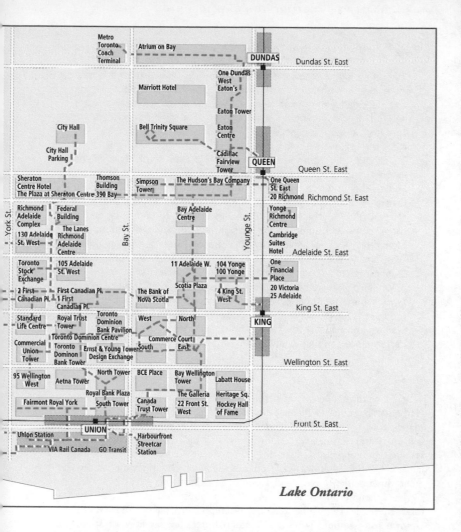

Metro Toronto Coach Terminal

Atrium on Bay

DUNDAS

Dundas St. East

One Dundas West
Eaton's

Marriott Hotel

Eaton Tower

City Hall

Bell Trinity Square

Eaton Centre

City Hall Parking

Cadillac Fairview Tower

QUEEN

Queen St. East

Sheraton Centre Hotel
The Plaza at Sheraton Centre

Thomson Building
390 Bay

Simpson Tower

The Hudson's Bay Company

One Queen St. East
20 Richmond

Richmond St. East

York St.

Richmond Adelaide Complex

Federal Building

The Lanes
Richmond Adelaide Centre

Bay St.

Bay Adelaide Centre

Yonge Richmond Centre

Cambridge Suites Hotel

Adelaide St. East

130 Adelaide St. West

Toronto Stock Exchange

105 Adelaide St. West

11 Adelaide W.

104 Yonge
100 Yonge

One Financial Place

Yonge St.

2 First Canadian Pl.

First Canadian Pl.
1 First Canadian Pl.

The Bank of Nova Scotia

Scotia Plaza

4 King St. West

20 Victoria
25 Adelaide

King St. East

Standard Life Centre

Royal Trust Tower

Toronto Dominion Bank Pavilion

West

North

KING

Commercial Union Tower

Toronto Dominion Centre
Toronto Dominion Bank Tower

Ernst & Young Tower
Design Exchange

Commerce Court South

East

Wellington St. East

95 Wellington West

Aetna Tower

North Tower

Royal Bank Plaza

BCE Place

Bay Wellington Tower

Labatt House

Fairmont Royal York

South Tower

Canada Trust Tower

The Galleria
22 Front St. West

Heritage Sq.

Hockey Hall of Fame

Front St. East

UNION

Union Station

VIA Rail Canada

GO Transit

Harbourfront Streetcar Station

Lake Ontario

in the south well beyond Highway 401 in the north. Yonge Street divides western cross streets from eastern cross streets. The main east-west artery is **Bloor Street,** which cuts through the heart of downtown.

"Downtown" usually refers to the area from Eglinton Avenue south to the lake, between Spadina Avenue in the west and Jarvis Street in the east. Because this is such a large area, I have divided it into five sections. **Downtown West** runs from the lake north to College Street; the eastern boundary is Yonge Street. **Downtown East** goes from the lake north to Carlton Street (once College St. reaches Yonge, it becomes Carlton St.); the western boundary is Yonge Street. **Midtown West** extends from College Street north to Davenport Road; the eastern boundary is Yonge Street. **Midtown East/The East End** runs from Carlton Street north to Davenport and farther east along Danforth Avenue; the western boundary is Yonge Street. **Uptown** is the aea north of Davenport Road.

Underground Toronto

It is not enough to know the streets of Toronto; you also need to navigate the labyrinth of walkways beneath the pavement. If the weather's bad, you can eat, sleep, dance, shop, and go to the theater without even donning a coat. Consult our map, "Underground Toronto," on p. 44, or look for the large, clear underground PATH maps throughout the concourse.

You can walk from the Dundas subway station south through the Eaton Centre until you hit Queen Street, turn west to the Sheraton Centre, then head south. You'll pass through the Richmond-Adelaide Centre, First Canadian Place, and Toronto Dominion Centre, and go all the way (through the dramatic Royal Bank Plaza) to Union Station. En route, branches lead off to the stock exchange, Sun Life Centre, and Metro Hall. Additional walkways link Simcoe Plaza to 200 Wellington West and to the CBC Broadcast Centre. Other walkways run around Bloor Street and Yonge Street and elsewhere in the city.

While its wide-ranging network makes this an excellent way to get around the downtown core when the weather is grim, the underground city has its own attractions, too. First Canadian Place in particular is known for free lunch-hour lectures, opera and dance performances, and art exhibits.

In Downtown West, you'll find many of the lakeshore attractions—Harbourfront, Ontario Place, Fort York, Exhibition Place, and the Toronto Islands. It also boasts the CN Tower, City Hall, SkyDome, Chinatown, the Art Gallery, and the Eaton Centre. Downtown East includes the St. Lawrence Market, the Hummingbird Centre, the St. Lawrence Centre for the Arts, and St. James Cathedral. Midtown West contains the Royal Ontario Museum, the Gardiner Museum, the University of Toronto, Markham Village, and chic Yorkville, a prime area for browsing and dining alfresco. Midtown East/The East End features Riverdale Farm, the historic Necropolis cemetery, and Greektown. Uptown has traditionally been a residential area, but it's now a fast-growing entertainment area, too. Its attractions include the Sunnybrook park system and the Ontario Science Centre.

North Toronto is another burgeoning area, with theaters, such as the Toronto Centre for the Arts, galleries, and some excellent dining. It's not yet a prime tourist destination, but it gets a few mentions throughout this guide.

Toronto sprawls so widely that quite a few of its primary attractions lie outside the downtown core. They include the Toronto Zoo, Paramount Canada's Wonderland, and the McMichael Canadian Art Collection. Be prepared to journey somewhat.

FINDING AN ADDRESS   This isn't as easy as it should be. Your best bet is to call ahead and ask for directions, including landmarks and subway stations. Even the locals need to do this.

NEIGHBORHOODS IN BRIEF

DOWNTOWN WEST

The Toronto Islands These three islands in Lake Ontario—Ward's, Algonquin, and Centre—are home to a handful of residents and no cars. They're a spring and summer haven where Torontonians go to in-line skate, bicycle, boat, and picnic. Centre Island, the most visited, holds the children's theme park Centreville. Catch the ferry at the foot of Bay Street by the Westin Harbour Castle hotel.

Harbourfront/Lakefront The landfill where the railroad yards and dock facilities once stood is now a glorious playground opening onto the lake. This is home to Queen's Quay, a major antiques market, and the Harbourfront Centre, one of the most important literary, artistic, and cultural venues in Canada.

Financial District Toronto's major banks and insurance companies have their headquarters here, from Front Street north to Queen Street, between Yonge and York streets. Toronto's first skyscrapers rose here; fortunately, some of the older structures have been preserved. Ultramodern BCE Place incorporated the facade of a historic bank building into its design.

Theater District An area of dense cultural development, this neighborhood stretches from Front Street north to Queen Street, and from Bay Street west to Bathurst Street. King Street West is home to most of the important sights, including the Royal Alexandra Theatre, the Princess of Wales Theatre, Roy Thomson Hall, and Metro Hall. Farther south are the Convention Centre and the CN Tower.

Chinatown Dundas Street West from University Avenue to Spadina Avenue, and north to College Street are the boundaries of Chinatown. As the Chinese community has grown, it has extended along Dundas Street and north along Spadina Avenue. Here you'll see a fascinating mixture of old and new. Hole-in-the-wall restaurants share the sidewalks with glitzy shopping centers built with Hong Kong money.

Queen Street West This stretch from University Avenue to Bathurst Street is youngish, hip, and home to many of the city's up-and-coming fashion designers. It offers an eclectic mix—antiques stores, secondhand bookshops, fashion boutiques, and vintage clothing emporiums. It's also home to Toronto's gourmet ghetto, with bistro after trattoria after cafe lining the street. There's excellent food along this strip, but it's too frequently served with heaps of attitude. Despite the intrusion of mega-retailers, many independently owned boutiques flourish.

Little Italy This thriving, lively area, filled with open-air cafes, trattorias, and shops, serves the Italian community along College Street between Euclid and Shaw. The trendies can't seem to stay away, which has driven up prices in this once-inexpensive neighborhood.

DOWNTOWN EAST

Old Town/St. Lawrence Market During the 19th century, this area, east of Yonge Street between the Esplanade and Adelaide Street, was the focal point of the community. Today the market's still going strong, and attractions like the glorious St. James Cathedral draw visitors.

The Beaches Communal, youthful, safe, and comfortable—these adjectives best describe the Beaches, just 15 minutes from downtown at the end of the Queen Street East streetcar line. It was a summer resort in the mid-1800s, and its boardwalk and beach continue to make it a casual, family-oriented neighborhood.

MIDTOWN WEST

Queen's Park and the University Home to the Ontario Legislature and many of the colleges and buildings that make up the University of Toronto, this neighborhood extends from College Street to Bloor Street between Spadina Avenue and Bay Street.

Yorkville Originally a village outside the city, this area north and west of Bloor and Yonge streets became Toronto's Haight-Ashbury in the 1960s. Now, it's a *haute, haute, haute* district filled with designer boutiques, galleries, cafes, and restaurants.

The Annex This area fell into neglect for many years, but since the early 1980s much of it has been lovingly restored. It stretches from Bedford Road to Bathurst Street, and from Harbord Street to Dupont Avenue. Many of the tremendous turn-of-the-century homes are still single-family dwellings, though as you walk west it segues into the U of T student ghetto. Revered urban-planning guru Jane Jacobs has long called this area home.

Koreatown The bustling blocks along Bloor Street West between Bathurst and Christie streets are filled with Korean restaurants, alternative-medicine practitioners such as herbalists and acupuncturists, and shops filled with made-in-Korea merchandise. One of the first Korean settlements in Toronto, it is now primarily a business district.

MIDTOWN EAST/THE EAST END

Rosedale Meandering tree-lined streets with elegant homes and manicured lawns are the hallmarks of this residential community, from Yonge and Bloor streets northeast to Castle Frank and the Moore Park Ravine. Named after Sheriff Jarvis's residence, its name is synonymous with Toronto's wealthy elite.

Church Street Between Gerrard Street and Bloor Street East along Church Street lies the heart of Toronto's gay and lesbian community. Restaurants, cafes, and bars fill this relaxed, casual neighborhood. Church Street is where 19th-century Toronto's grandest cathedrals stood.

Cabbagetown Once described by writer Hugh Garner as the largest Anglo-Saxon slum in North America, this gentrified neighborhood of Victorian and Edwardian homes stretches east of Parliament Street to the Don Valley between Gerrard Street and Bloor Street. The sought-after residential district got its name because the front lawns of the homes, occupied by Irish immigrants (who settled here in the late 1800s), were, it is said, covered with row upon row of cabbages. Riverdale, Toronto's only inner-city farm, is at the southeastern end of this district.

Greektown Across the Don Valley Viaduct, Bloor Street becomes the Danforth, which marks the beginning of **Greektown.** It's lined with old-style Greek tavernas and hip Mediterranean bars and restaurants that are crowded from early evening until early morning. The densest wining-and-dining area starts at Broadview Avenue and runs 6 blocks east.

UPTOWN

Forest Hill Second to Rosedale as the city's prime residential area, Forest Hill is home to Upper Canada College and Bishop Strachan School for girls. It stretches west of Avenue Road between St. Clair Avenue and Eglinton Avenue.

Eglinton Avenue The neighborhood surrounding the intersection of Yonge Street and Eglinton Avenue is jokingly known as "Young and Eligible." It's a bustling area filled with restaurants—including some of the town's top-rated—and nightclubs. To the east, it intersects with the 243-hectare (600-acre) Sunnybrook park system and with the Ontario Science Centre.

2 Getting Around

BY PUBLIC TRANSPORTATION

The **Toronto Transit Commission,** or TTC (✆ **416/393-4636** for 24-hr. information; recordings available in 18 languages; www.city.toronto.on. ca/ttc), operates the subway, bus, streetcar, and light rapid transit (LRT) system.

Fares, including transfers to buses or streetcars, are C$2.25 (US$1.50) or 10 tickets for C$18 (US$12) for adults. Students under 20 and seniors pay C$1.50 (US$1) or 10 tickets for C$12 (US$8), and children under 12 pay C50¢ (US35¢) or 10 tickets for C$4 (US$2.70). You can buy a special day pass for C$7.50 (US$5) that's good for unlimited travel for one person after 9:30am on weekdays, and good for up to six people (a maximum of two adults) anytime on Sunday and holidays. There's no Saturday pass, and no multiple-day deals.

For surface transportation, you need a ticket, a token, or exact change. You can buy tickets and tokens at subway entrances and at authorized stores that display the sign TTC TICKETS MAY BE PURCHASED HERE. Bus drivers do not sell tickets, nor will they make change. Always obtain a free transfer *where you board the train or bus,* in case you need it. In the subways, use the push-button machine just inside the entrance. On streetcars and buses, ask the driver for a transfer.

THE SUBWAY   It's fast (especially when you compare it to snarled surface traffic), clean, and very simple to use. There are two major lines—Bloor-Danforth and Yonge-University-Spadina—and one smaller line, Sheppard, which is supposed to be up and running in 2003 (the project has been slow going, so don't be surprised if there's another delay). The Bloor Street east-west line runs from Kipling Avenue in the west to Kennedy Road in the east (where it connects with Scarborough Rapid Transit to Scarborough Centre and McCowan Rd.). The Yonge Street north-south line runs from Finch Avenue in the north to Union Station (Front St.) in the south. From there, it loops north along University Avenue and connects with the Bloor line at the St. George station. A Spadina extension runs north from St. George to Downsview station at Sheppard Avenue. The new Sheppard line connects only with the Yonge line at Sheppard Station, and runs east through north Toronto for just 6km (10 miles).

The light rapid transit (LRT) system connects downtown to Harbourfront. The fare is one ticket or token. It runs from Union Station along Queen's Quay to Spadina, with stops at Queen's Quay ferry docks, York Street, Simcoe Street, and Rees Street, then continues up Spadina to the Spadina subway station. The transfer from the subway to the LRT (and vice versa) at Union Station is free.

The subway operates Monday to Saturday from 6am to 1:30am, and Sunday from 9am to 1:30am. From 1am to 5:30am, the Blue Night Network operates on basic surface routes. It runs about every 30 minutes. For route information, pick up a "Ride Guide" at subway entrances or call ✆ **416/393-4636.**

Multilingual information is available. You can also use the automated information service at ℂ **416/393-8663.**

Smart commuters park their cars at subway terminal stations at Kipling, Islington, Finch, Wilson, Warden, Kennedy, York Mills, Victoria Park, and Keele. Certain conditions apply. Call ℂ **416/393-8663** for details. You'll have to get there very early.

BUSES & STREETCARS   Where the subway leaves off, buses and streetcars take over. They run east-west and north-south along the city's arteries. When you pay your fare (on bus, streetcar, or subway), always pick up a transfer so that you won't have to pay again if you want to transfer to another mode of transportation. For complete TTC information, call ℂ **416/393-4636.**

BY TAXI

As usual, this is an expensive mode of transportation. It's C$2.50 (US$1.70) the minute you step in, and C25¢ (US20¢) for each additional 0.2km (about ¼ mile). Fares can quickly mount up, especially during rush hours. You can hail a cab on the street, find one in line in front of a big hotel, or call one of the major companies—**Diamond** (ℂ **416/366-6868**), **Royal** (ℂ **416/777-9222**), or **Metro** (ℂ **416/504-8294**). If you experience problems with cab service, call the Metro Licensing Commission (ℂ **416/392-3082**).

BY CAR

Toronto is a rambling city, but that doesn't mean that a car is the best way to get around. Toronto has the dubious distinction of being recognized as the worst city in Canada in which to drive. It has gotten so bad that the government has started monitoring certain intersections with cameras. Driving can be a frustrating experience because of the high volume of traffic, drivers' disregard for red lights, and meager but pricey parking options. This is particularly true downtown, where traffic inches along and parking lots are scarce. I strongly recommend that you avoid driving in the city.

RENTAL CARS   If you decide to rent a car, try to make arrangements in advance. Companies with outlets at Pearson International Airport include **Thrifty** (ℂ 800/367-2277), **Budget** (ℂ 800/527-0700), **Avis** (ℂ 800/331-1084), **Hertz** (ℂ 800/654-3001), **National** (ℂ 800/227-7368), and **Enterprise** (ℂ 800/736-8222). Keep in mind that there's usually a steep fee when you rent a vehicle in one city and drop it off in another. The rental fee depends on the type of car you want, but the starting point is around C$45 (US$31) a day—not including the 15% in sales taxes. This also does not include insurance; if you pay with a particular credit card, you might get automatic coverage (check with your credit-card issuer before you go). Be sure to read the fine print of the rental agreement—some companies add conditions that will boost your bill if you don't fulfill certain obligations, like filling the gas tank before returning the car. See "Health & Insurance," in chapter 2, for more information.

Note: If you're under 25, check with the company—many will rent on a cash-only basis, some only with a credit card, and others will not rent to you at all.

PARKING   Parking lots downtown run about C$4 to $6 (US$2.70–$4.10) per half hour, with a C$16 to $20 (US$11–$14) maximum between 7am and 6pm. After 6pm and on Sunday, rates drop to around C$8 (US$5). Generally, the city-owned lots, marked with a big green "P," are slightly cheaper than private facilities. Observe the parking restrictions—otherwise the city will tow your car away, and it'll cost more than C$100 (US$68) to get it back.

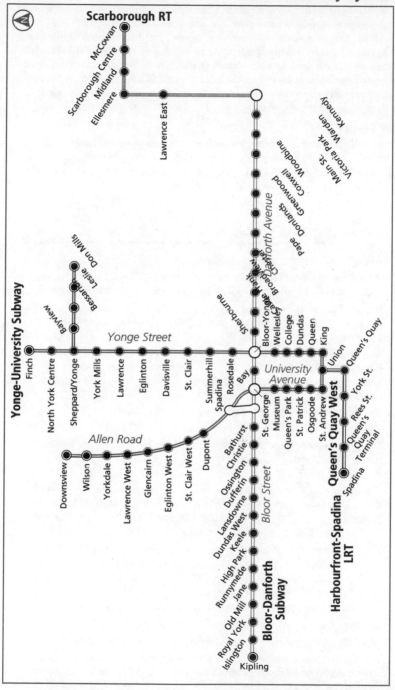

DRIVING RULES A right turn at a red light is permitted after coming to a full stop, unless posted otherwise. The driver and front-seat passengers must wear seat belts; if you're caught not wearing one, you'll incur a substantial fine. The speed limit in the city is 50kmph (30 mph). You must stop at pedestrian crosswalks. If you are following a streetcar and it stops, you must stop well back from the rear doors so passengers can exit easily and safely. (Where there are concrete safety islands in the middle of the street for streetcar stops, this rule does not apply, but exercise care nonetheless.) Radar detectors are illegal.

BY FERRY

Toronto Parks and Recreation operates ferries that travel to the Toronto Islands. Call ℂ **416/392-8193** for schedules and information. Round-trip fares are C$5 (US$3.40) for adults, C$3 (US$2) for seniors and students 15 to 19 (with valid ID), and C$2 (US$1.30) for children 15 and under.

 FAST FACTS: **Toronto**

Airport See "Getting There," in chapter 2.

Area Code Toronto's area codes are **416** and **647**; outside the city, the code is **905** or **289**. You must dial all 10 digits for all local phone numbers.

Babysitting Hotel concierges can suggest reliable sitters if there aren't child-care facilities on site. In a pinch, call **Care-on-Call** (ℂ **416/975-1313**), a 24-hour service.

Business Hours Banks are generally open Monday to Thursday 10am to 3pm, Friday 10am to 6pm. Most stores are open Monday to Wednesday 10am to 6pm and Saturday and Sunday 10am to 5pm, with extended hours (until 8–9:30pm) on Thursday and usually Friday.

Car Rentals See "Getting Around," earlier in this chapter.

Climate See "When to Go," in chapter 2.

Currency Exchange Generally, the best place to exchange your currency is at an ATM or bank. You can also change money at the airport, but at a less favorable rate.

Dentist For emergency services from 8am till midnight, call the **Dental Emergency Service** (ℂ **416/485-7121**). After midnight, your best bet is the **Toronto Hospital**, 200 Elizabeth St. (ℂ **416/340-3948**). Otherwise, ask the front-desk staff or concierge at your hotel.

Doctor The staff or concierge at your hotel should be able to help you locate a doctor. You can also call the **College of Physicians and Surgeons,** 80 College St. (ℂ **416/967-2600,** ext. 626), for a referral between 9am to 5pm. See also "Emergencies," below.

Documents See "Entry Requirements & Customs," in chapter 2.

Driving Rules See "Getting Around," earlier in this chapter.

Electricity It's the same as in the United States—110 volts, 50 cycles, AC.

Embassies/Consulates All embassies are in Ottawa, the national capital. They include the **Australian High Commission,** 50 O'Connor St., Suite 710, Ottawa, ON K1P 6L2 (ℂ **613/236-0841**); the **British High Commission,** 80 Elgin St., Ottawa, ON K1P 5K7 (ℂ **613/237-1530**); the **Irish Embassy,** 130

Albert St., Ottawa, ON K1P 5G4 (© **613/233-6281**); the **New Zealand High Commission,** 727–99 Bank St., Ottawa, ON K1P 6G3 (© **613/238-5991**); the **South African High Commission,** 15 Sussex Dr., Ottawa, ON K1M 1M8 (© **613/744-0330**); and the **U.S. Embassy,** 100 Wellington St., Ottawa, ON K1P 5T1 (© **613/238-4470**). Consulates in Toronto include **Australian Consulate-General,** 175 Bloor St. E., Suite 314, at Church Street (© **416/323-1155**); **British Consulate-General,** 777 Bay St., Suite 2800, at College (© **416/593-1290**); and the **U.S. Consulate,** 360 University Ave. (© **416/595-1700**).

Emergencies Call © **911** for fire, police, or ambulance. The **Toronto General Hospital,** 200 Elizabeth St., provides 24-hour emergency service (© **416/340-3946** for emergency or 416/340-4611 for information). Also see "Hospitals," below.

Hospitals In the downtown core, go to **Toronto General,** 200 Elizabeth St. (© **416/340-4611,** or 416/340-3946 for emergency); **St. Michael's,** 30 Bond St. (© **416/360-4000,** or 416/864-5094 for emergency); or **Mount Sinai,** 600 University Ave. (© **416/596-4200,** or 416/586-5054 for emergency). Also downtown is the **Hospital for Sick Children,** 555 University Ave. (© **416/813-1500**). Uptown, there's **Sunnybrook Hospital,** 2075 Bayview Ave., north of Eglinton (© **416/480-6100,** or 416/480-4207 for emergency). In the eastern part of the city, go to **Toronto East General Hospital,** 825 Coxwell Ave. (© **416/461-8272,** or 416/469-6435 for emergency).

Hot Lines **Poison Information Centre** (© 416/813-5900); **Distress Centre** suicide prevention line (© 416/598-1121); **Rape Crisis Line** (© 416/597-8808); **Assaulted Women's Help Line** (© 416/863-0511); **AIDS & Sexual Health InfoLine** (© 800/668-2437); **Toronto Prayer Line** (© 416/929-1500). For kids or teens in distress, there's **Kids Help Phone** (© 800/668-6868).

Internet Access As in most other North American cities, the Web is a social magnet in Toronto. **Insomnia,** 563 Bloor St. W. (© **416/588-3907**), is more social than your average Net cafe—maybe it's the sign over the door that reads, "The Internet is a strange place. Don't surf alone." There are several curtained computer terminals (C$10/US$6 per hr.), as well as comfortable couches and a big-screen TV. The pizza and panini are usually pretty good. Open daily from noon to 1am. Subway: Bathurst.

In the heart of Toronto's gay and lesbian community, **Ciber Village,** 449 Church St. at Alexander St. (© **416/928-6060**), is a good deal. Open from 10am to 10pm, it offers Web surfing for a mere C$6 (US$4.10) an hour, or C10¢ (US7¢) per minute, with no minimum. Subway: College.

Laundry/Dry Cleaning **Bloor Laundromat,** 598 Bloor St. W., at Bathurst Street (© **416/588-6600**), is conveniently located. At the **Laundry Lounge,** 531 Yonge St., at Wellesley Street (© **416/975-4747**), you can do your wash while sipping a cappuccino and watching TV in the lounge. It's open daily from 7am to 11pm. **Careful Hand Laundry & Dry Cleaners Ltd.** has outlets at 195 Davenport Rd. (© **416/923-1200**), 1415 Bathurst St. (© **416/530-1116**), and 1844 Avenue Rd. (© **416/787-6006**); for pickup and delivery, call © **416/787-6006.**

Liquor Laws The minimum drinking age is 19. Drinking hours are daily from 11am to 2am. The government is the only retail vendor. **Liquor**

Control Board of Ontario (LCBO) stores sell liquor, wine, and some beers. They're open Monday to Saturday. Most are open from 10am to 6pm; some stay open evenings, and a few are open Sunday from noon to 5pm.

Wine lovers will want to check out **Vintages** stores (also operated by the LCBO), which carry a more extensive, specialized selection of wines. The most convenient downtown locations are in the lower-level concourse of Hazelton Lanes (© **416/924-9463**) and at Queen's Quay (© **416/864-6777**). The **Wine Rack,** 560 Queen St. W. (© **416/504-3647**), and 77 Wellesley St. E., at Church (© **416/923-9393**), sells only Ontario wines.

Most branches of the **Beer Store** (also part of the LCBO) are open Monday to Friday from 10am to 10pm, and Saturday from 10am to 8pm. There's a downtown location at 614 Queen St. W. (© **416/504-4665**).

Lost Property If you leave something on a bus, a streetcar, or the subway, call the **TTC Lost Articles Office** (© **416/393-4100**) at the Bay Street subway station. It's open Monday to Friday from 8am to 5pm.

Luggage Storage/Lockers Lockers are available at Union Station and at the Eaton Centre.

Mail Postage for letters and postcards to the United States costs C55¢ (US40¢); overseas, C90¢ (US65¢). Mailing letters and postcards within Canada costs C45¢ (US30¢).

Postal services are available at convenience and drug stores. Almost all sell stamps, and many have a separate counter where you can ship packages from 8:30am to 5pm. Look for the sign in the window indicating such services. There are also post-office windows in **Atrium on Bay** (© **416/506-0911**), in **Commerce Court** (© **416/956-7452**), and at the **TD Centre** (© **416/360-7105**).

Maps Free maps of Toronto are available in every terminal at **Pearson International Airport** (look for the Transport Canada Information Centre signs), the Metropolitan Toronto Convention & Visitors Association at **Harbourfront,** and the Visitor Information Centre in the **Eaton Centre,** on Yonge Street at Dundas Street. Convenience stores and bookstores sell a greater variety of maps. Or try **Canada Map Company,** 63 Adelaide E., between Yonge and Church streets (© **416/362-9297**), or **Open Air Books and Maps,** 25 Toronto St., near Yonge and Adelaide streets (© **416/363-0719**).

Newspapers & Magazines The four daily newspapers are the *Globe and Mail,* the *National Post,* the *Toronto Star,* and the *Toronto Sun. Eye* and *Now* are free arts-and-entertainment weeklies. *Xtra!* is a free weekly targeted at the gay and lesbian community. In addition, many English-language ethnic newspapers serve Toronto's Portuguese, Hungarian, Italian, East Indian, Korean, Chinese, and Caribbean communities. *Toronto Life* is the major monthly city magazine; its sister publication is *Toronto Life Fashion. Where Toronto* is usually free at hotels and some Theater District restaurants.

Pharmacies One big chain is **Pharma Plus,** which has a store at 68 Wellesley St., at Church Street (© **416/924-7760**). It's open daily from 8am to midnight. Other Pharma Plus branches are in College Park, Manulife

Centre, Commerce Court, and First Canadian Place. The only 24-hour drugstore near downtown is **Shopper's Drug Mart**, 700 Bay St., at Gerrard Street West (② **416/979-2424**).

Police   In a life-threatening emergency, call ② **911**. For all other matters, contact the Metro police, 40 College St. (② **416/808-2222**).

Post Office   See "Mail," above.

Radio   The Canadian Broadcasting Corporation offers a great mix of intelligent discussion and commentary as well as drama and music. In Toronto, the **CBC** broadcasts on 740AM and 94.1FM. **CHIN** (1540AM and 100.7FM) will get you in touch with the ethnic and multicultural scene in the city; it broadcasts in more than 30 languages.

Restrooms   Finding a public restroom is usually not difficult. Most tourist attractions have them, as do hotels, department stores, and public buildings. There are restrooms at major subway stations such as Yonge/Bloor, but they are best avoided.

Safety   As large cities go, Toronto is generally safe, but be alert and use common sense, particularly at night. The Yonge/Bloor, Dundas, and Union subway stations are favorites with pickpockets. In the downtown area, Moss Park is considered one of the toughest areas to police. Avoid Allan Gardens and other parks at night.

Taxes   The provincial retail sales tax is 8%; on accommodations it's 5%. There is an additional 7% national goods-and-services tax (GST).

In general, nonresidents may apply for a tax refund. They can recover the accommodations tax, the sales tax, and the GST for nondisposable merchandise that will be exported for use, provided it is removed from Canada within 60 days of purchase. The following do not qualify for rebate: meals and restaurant charges, alcohol, tobacco, gas, car rentals, and such services as dry cleaning and shoe repair.

The quickest and easiest way to secure the refund is to stop at a duty-free shop at the border. You must have proper receipts with GST registration numbers. Or you can apply through the mail, but it will take about 4 weeks to receive your refund. For an application form and information, you can contact **Visitor Rebate Program, Canada Customs and Revenue Agency,** Ottawa, ON K1A 0L8 (fax 613/954-3577; www.ccra-adrc.gc.ca); forms are also available at tourism kiosks around town. You can also contact **Ontario Travel,** Queen's Park, Toronto, ON M7A 2R9 (② **800/668-2746** or 416/314-0944).

Taxis   See "Getting Around," earlier in this chapter.

Telephone   A local call from a telephone booth costs C25¢ (US20¢). Watch out for hotel surcharges on local and long-distance calls; often a local call will cost at least C$1 (US70¢) from a hotel room. The United States and Canada are on the same long-distance system. To make a long-distance call between the United States and Canada, use the area codes as you would at home. Canada's international prefix is **1**.

Time   Toronto is on eastern time. Daylight saving time is in effect from April to October.

Tipping Basically it's the same as in major U.S. cities: 15% in restaurants (up to 20% in the finer spots), 10% to 15% for taxis, C$1 (US70¢) per bag for porters, C$2 (US$1.40) per day for hotel housekeepers.

Transit Information For information on the subway, bus, streetcar, and light rapid transit (LRT) system, call the TTC at ☎ **416/393-4636** (www.city.toronto.on.ca/ttc).

Weather Call the **talking yellow pages** (☎ **416/292-1010**) for a current weather report and lots of other information. Or check the *Toronto Star*'s website, www.thestar.com.

4

Where to Stay

Toronto has no shortage of hotels. Whether you're seeking Old World elegance in a historic building or looking for all the conveniences of the office in your home away from home, you'll find it here. But there is one catch: Bargains are hard to come by, particularly in the downtown core.

The city has become increasingly popular with both business and leisure travelers, and demand has driven prices skyward. In exchange for proximity to top attractions like the Harbourfront Centre, SkyDome, and the Eaton Centre, even budget hotels charge more than C$100 (US$68) a night in the high season, which runs from April through October. Factor in the 5% accommodations tax and the 7% GST (which are refundable to nonresidents), and you're looking at spending a sizable sum of money (although you can apply for a tax refund; see "Fast Facts" in chapter 3, for details).

There are some ways around the problem. First, always ask for a discount when you book your accommodations. Even the most expensive luxury hotel will reduce its rates during the low season and on weekends, and sometimes simply because the hotel isn't full. This discount can be anywhere from 20% to 50%—after all, having a guest pay a reduced rate is preferable to having an empty room that generates no revenue.

Do not be shy—always ask for a deal. If you belong to a group (such as the military, seniors, students, or an auto club), so much the better. You'll qualify for an instant discount as long as you have appropriate ID. Members of frequent flyer clubs may qualify for discounts, room upgrades, or other perks—if they ask for them. A hotel may offer special packages, which might include theater tickets, meals, or museum passes with the cost of your accommodations. At the risk of sounding like a broken record, I will say it again: Always ask for a deal.

When you make your reservations, it's important to keep in mind what you're planning to see and do. Toronto is a vast metropolis, with attractions, dining districts, and ethnic communities scattered throughout. If you're spending money and time to reach the areas that interest you, even a great deal is no bargain.

I have grouped accommodations by price and location. Most are in the neighborhoods defined in chapter 3 as Downtown West, Downtown East, Midtown West, the East End, and Uptown. I've also included a few hotels to the east of the city and close to Pearson International Airport.

TWO IMPORTANT NOTES ON PRICES The prices quoted in this chapter are rack rates; discounts can knock the price down as much as 50%. The 5% accommodations tax and the 7% GST are refunded to nonresidents upon application (see "Taxes" under "Fast Facts: Toronto," in chapter 3).

A NOTE TO NONSMOKERS Hotels that reserve floors for nonsmokers are now commonplace, so we don't single them out in this guide. However, people who want a smoke-free room should make that clear when making a reservation. Rooms for smokers are concentrated on particular floors, and the rooms and even the hallways in those areas tend to smell strongly of smoke, even in the cleanest hotels. Never assume that you'll get a smoke-free room if you don't specifically request one.

BED & BREAKFASTS   A B&B can be an excellent—and relatively inexpensive—alternative to standard hotel accommodations. **Toronto Bed & Breakfast,** 253 College St., P.O. Box 269, Toronto, ON M5T 1R5 (© 877/922-6522 or 416/588-8800; www.torontobandb.com), has a lengthy list of accommodations in the city. Doubles cost roughly C$75 to $125 (US$51–$85). The organization will make your reservation and send you a confirmation. The **Downtown Association of Bed-and-Breakfast Guesthouses,** P.O. Box 190, Station B, Toronto, ON M5T 2W1 (© **416/ 368-1420;** www.bnbinfo.com), lists only nonsmoking B&Bs. Doubles range from C$70 to $130 (US$48–$88). **Bed and Breakfast Homes of Toronto,** P.O. Box 46093, College Park Post Office, 44 Yonge St., Toronto, ON M5B 2L8 (© **416/ 363-6362;** www.bbcanada.com), is a cooperative of about 20 independent B&B operators. Doubles run from about C$65 to $100 (US$44–$68).

ACCOMMODATIONS SERVICES If you're having trouble finding a hotel, call **Tourism Toronto** (© **800/ 363-1990** or 416/203-2600), for advice and special deals.

FOR TRAVELERS IN NEED   If you run into trouble in Toronto, call the **Travellers Aid Society of Toronto** (© **416/366-7788**); the organization provides shelter for people in crisis situations.

1 Downtown West

EXPENSIVE

Fairmont Royal York 😾😾   Looming across from Union Station, Toronto's hub for rail travel, is the Fairmont Royal York, a historic hotel built by the Canadian-Pacific Railroad in 1929. Fairmont hotels across the country tend to the mono-lithic, and this one is no exception, with 1,365 guest rooms and suites, and 35 meeting and banquet rooms. The old-fashioned lobby is magnificent, and just sitting on a plush couch and watching the crowd is an event. Still, you have to decide whether you want to stay under the same roof with more than 1,000 others—business travelers, shoppers, tour groups, and particularly conventioneers. Service is remarkably efficient but necessarily impersonal; the downtown location, just steps from the Theater District and the Hummingbird Centre, is excellent.

Guest rooms, though furnished with charming antique reproductions, are a mixed bag. Some are reasonably airy, but there's generally not much spare space. If you're willing to spring for a Fairmont Gold room, you'll stay on a private floor with superior, spacious rooms, separate check-in and concierge, a private lounge, and complimentary breakfast (the extra cost is well worth it, in my opinion).

If you're interested in pampering yourself, ask about special spa packages—the Elizabeth Milan Day Spa, in the shopping arcade, is one of the best in the city. Among the multitude of dining and drinking spots in the hotel, the don't-miss ones are Epic (see review on p. 86), and the Library Bar, which serves the best martinis in the city.

In July 2002, the Fairmont launched its VIP (Very Important Pets) program: for an extra C$30 (US$20) per night, guests and their furry friends can stay in a special "dog friendly" room that comes with toys, treats, and other amenities. (Part of the extra fee is donated to the Toronto Humane Society.)

Downtown West Accommodations

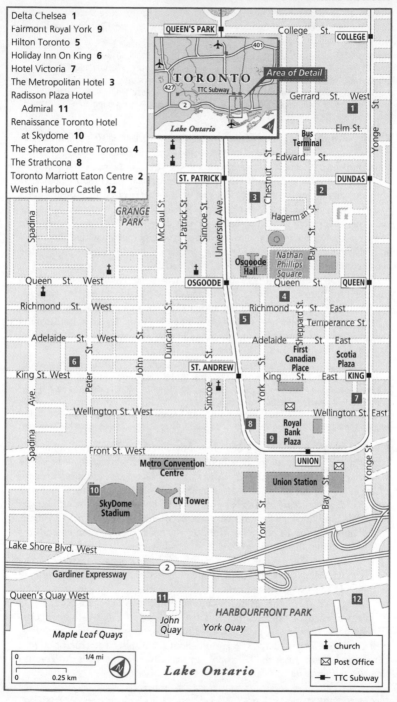

Delta Chelsea **1**
Fairmont Royal York **9**
Hilton Toronto **5**
Holiday Inn On King **6**
Hotel Victoria **7**
The Metropolitan Hotel **3**
Radisson Plaza Hotel
  Admiral **11**
Renaissance Toronto Hotel
  at Skydome **10**
The Sheraton Centre Toronto **4**
The Strathcona **8**
Toronto Marriott Eaton Centre **2**
Westin Harbour Castle **12**

QUEEN'S PARK   College   St.   COLLEGE

Area of Detail

TORONTO
427
TTC Subway
2
Lake Ontario

Gerrard   St.   West
1

Bus
Terminal   Elm   St.

Edward   St.

ST. PATRICK   **2**   DUNDAS

3   Chestnut   St.

Hagerman   St.

GRANGE
PARK

Nathan
Phillips
Square

Osgoode
Hall   Queen   St.   QUEEN

Queen   St.   West   OSGOODE   **4**

Richmond   St.   West   Richmond   St.   East
5   Temperance St.

Adelaide   St.   West   Adelaide   St.   East

6   First
Canadian
Place   Scotia
Plaza

King St. West   ST. ANDREW   King   St.   East   KING
7

Wellington St. West   Wellington St. East

8   Royal
Bank
9   Plaza

Front St. West   UNION

Metro Convention
Centre   Union Station

10
SkyDome
Stadium   CN Tower

Lake Shore Blvd. West

Gardiner Expressway   2

Queen's Quay West   **11**   **12**

HARBOURFRONT PARK
John
Quay   York Quay

Maple Leaf Quays

0   1/4 mi
0   0.25 km   Lake Ontario

✝ Church
✉ Post Office
TTC Subway

59

Also of note, the hotel also pays particular attention to accessibility, with adaptations specially designed for wheelchair users, the hearing impaired, and the visually impaired.

100 Front St. W., Toronto, ON M5J 1E3. ✆ 800/441-1414. Fax 416/368-9040. www.fairmont.com. 1,365 units. C$175–$370 (US$119–$252) double. Packages available. AE, DC, DISC, MC, V. Parking C$26 (US$18). Subway: Union. Pets accepted. **Amenities:** 5 restaurants; 4 bars/lounges; skylit indoor pool; fitness center; spa (with special packages for guests); Jacuzzi; sauna; concierge; car-rental desk; business center; shopping arcade; salon; 24-hr. room service; babysitting; same-day dry cleaning/laundry. *In room:* A/C, TV, dataport, minibar, coffeemaker, hair dryer, iron.

Hilton Toronto ★★

The Hilton Toronto isn't what it used to be: With a gorgeous C$25 million (US$17 million) renovation completed in the spring of 2000, it became one of the most attractive hotels in the city. On the western edge of the Financial District, the 32-story Hilton boasts generously sized rooms decorated with streamlined luxury in mind. Because of the hotel's excellent location overlooking the wide boulevard of University Avenue, many rooms (and the glass elevators) have superb vistas. Because of its proximity to the Financial District, the Hilton is a favorite among business travelers. Executive rooms include perks such as an ultraplush terry bathrobe, a trouser press, and access to a private lounge that serves complimentary breakfast and evening snacks.

The Hilton is more cutting-edge than you'd expect from a business hotel, making it a sophisticated choice. The design of the grand foyer is dramatic, with an illuminated canopy, floor lights and backlights, and copious use of glass. There are photographic art exhibits on the public floors. Last but not least, as part of its renovation, the Hilton unveiled the magnificent Tundra, which serves top-notch Canadian cuisine (see review on p. 85).

145 Richmond St. W., Toronto, ON M5H 2L2. ✆ 800/445-8667 or 416/869-3456. Fax 416/869-1478. www.hilton.com. 601 units. C$269–$449 (US$183–$305) double. Extra person C$22 (US$15). Children 18 and under stay free in parents' room. Weekend packages available. AE, DC, MC, V. Parking C$22 (US$15). Subway: Osgoode. **Amenities:** 3 restaurants; bar; indoor and outdoor lap pools; fitness center with exercise room, Jacuzzi, and sauna; children's programs; concierge; business center; 24-hr. room service; massage; babysitting; same-day dry cleaning/laundry. *In room:* A/C, TV, dataport, minibar, coffeemaker, hair dryer, iron.

The Metropolitan Hotel ★★★

One of the few major hotels in Toronto that isn't part of a large chain, the Metropolitan prides itself on offering a boutique atmosphere. The hotel caters to a business-oriented clientele, and it offers many of the same features and amenities as its competitors at a comparatively lower cost (which is not to say it's inexpensive, just very competitive). Just off Dundas Street West, the hotel is a 5-minute stroll north of the business district and about two minutes west of the Eaton Centre. But why walk when you can take advantage of the complimentary limo service to any downtown core address?

That perk is just one of the ways in which the Metropolitan attempts to compete with its pricier competitors. Rooms are well sized and furnished with comfort in mind. The luxury and executive suites boast Jacuzzis, Dolby Surround Sound televisions, and CD players. Many rooms also feature two-line cordless phones.

The two restaurants are huge draws. Lai Wah Heen (p. 87), which serves classic Cantonese cuisine, is a top choice for business entertaining with natives as well as visitors. The modern-style ground-floor Hemispheres restaurant offers a continental menu. Also, the Metropolitan has a partnership with the Toronto Symphony Orchestra, which offers guests special packages.

108 Chestnut St., Toronto, ON M5G 1R3. ✆ 416/977-5000. Fax 416/977-9513. www.metropolitan.com. 425 units. C$280–$310 (US$190–$211) double. Children under 18 stay free in parents' room. AE, DC, DISC, MC, V. Valet parking C$24 (US$16), self C$19 (US$13). Subway: St. Patrick. **Amenities:** 2 restaurants; bar; indoor

pool; fitness center with sauna, Jacuzzi, and massage treatments; concierge; courtesy limo; 24-hr. business center (with PCs and Macs); room service from 6am to 11pm; babysitting; same-day dry cleaning/laundry. *In room:* A/C, TV, dataport, minibar, coffeemaker, hair dryer, iron, safe.

Radisson Plaza Hotel Admiral ⓕ   While not exactly small, the Radisson has an intimate, clubby feel. It overlooks Lake Ontario and is steps from the Harbourfront Centre. Its location can be seen as a big plus or a big minus. On the one hand, guests have beautiful lakefront vistas, as well as close access to one of Canada's premier arts centers and to the Toronto Islands. But this area of town can feel completely desolate at night. Toronto's waterfront, south of the hideous Gardiner Expressway, is woefully underdeveloped, making it a must to travel northward to seek good food, shopping, and entertainment. If your primary concern is location, this probably isn't the hotel for you.

What the Radisson does well is exploit its location for those who want to feel that they're getting away from the city without actually leaving it. This works especially well in summer. Its nautical-theme decor includes lacquered wood and gleaming brass in the lobby, with oil paintings of marine scenes littering the walls. The rooms are generally not large, but they are nicely appointed and boast floor-to-ceiling windows. Lakefront rooms offer superb views, and all guests can enjoy the sights (and a dip in the outdoor pool) on the roof deck.

249 Queen's Quay W., Toronto, ON M5J 2N5. ⓒ 800/333-3333 or 416/203-3333. Fax 416/203-3100. www. radisson.com/torontoca_admiral. 157 units. C$189–$299 (US$129–$203) double. Extra person C$20 (US$14). Weekend packages available. AE, DC, DISC, MC, V. Parking C$18 (US$12). Subway: Union, then LRT to Rees St. **Amenities:** Restaurant; bar; outdoor pool; exercise room; Jacuzzi; concierge; business center; 24-hr. room service; laundry service. *In room:* A/C, TV, dataport, coffeemaker, hair dryer, iron.

Renaissance Toronto Hotel at SkyDome ⓕ   A while ago, I was traveling and met a woman who had just visited Toronto. I asked where she'd stayed, and she told me that it was at "that hotel where they filmed people having sex and put it on a big screen." This is that hotel. It's a dream come true for diehard baseball fans—70 rooms overlook the diamond's verdant Astroturf. Unfortunately, those who enjoy the view should remember that it goes both ways: Just after it opened, the hotel became notorious when the amorous antics of a pair of guests ended up on the JumboTron (the giant screen that's supposed to be showing the on-field action). The incident is now a minor local legend. The lesson: All rooms have shades—remember to use them.

The hotel finished a C$10 million (US$6.3 million) renovation and refurbishment in 2001. The guest rooms are pretty much all a good size, but there's a definite pecking order: Rooms that face the city are the least expensive, with uninspiring views. Still, this is a strong contender as a tourist hotel—it's in a great location for theater, dining, and sights.

1 Blue Jays Way, Toronto, ON M5V 1J4. ⓒ 800/237-1512 or 416/341-7100. Fax 416/341-5091. www. renaissancehotels.com/yyzbr. 348 units. City view from C$189 (US$129) double; field side from C$305 (US$207) double. AE, DC, DISC, MC, V. Parking C$18 (US$12). Subway: Union. **Amenities:** Restaurant; bar; indoor pool; squash courts; fitness center with sauna; concierge; business center; 24-hr. room service; sameday dry cleaning/laundry. *In room:* A/C, TV, dataport, coffeemaker, hair dryer, iron.

The Sheraton Centre Toronto ⓕⓕ (Kids)   A convention favorite, the Sheraton is across the street from New City Hall, a block from the Eaton Centre, and a short stroll from the trendy restaurant and boutique area of Queen Street West. It's entirely possible to stay here and never venture outside—the Sheraton complex includes restaurants, bars, and a cinema, and the building connects to Toronto's fabled underground city. If you long for a patch of green, the hotel provides that,

too: The south side of the lobby contains a manicured garden with a waterfall. Am I making the place sound like a monolith? Well, it is. But it's an excellent home base for families because of its location and extensive list of child-friendly features, including a children's center and huge pool.

Most of the guest rooms in this skyscraper-heavy neighborhood lack a serious view, though as you near the top of the 46-story complex, the sights are inspiring indeed. Designed for business travelers, Club Level rooms were renovated in 2001; they contain mini business centers with a fax/printer/copier and two-line speakerphone.

123 Queen St. W., Toronto, ON M5H 2M9. ℂ **800/325-3535** or 416/361-1000. Fax 416/947-4854. www. sheratoncentretoronto.com. 1,377 units. C$260–$295 (US$177–$201) double. Extra person C$20 (US$14). 2 children under 18 stay free in parents' room. Packages available. AE, DC, MC, V. Parking C$28 (US$19). Subway: Osgoode. **Amenities:** 2 restaurants; bar; gigantic heated indoor/outdoor pool; fitness center with sauna and Jacuzzi; spa; children's center; concierge; activities desk; business center; shopping arcade; 24-hr. room service; babysitting; dry cleaning/laundry. *In room:* A/C, TV, dataport, coffeemaker, hair dryer, iron.

Toronto Marriott Eaton Centre 𝒜

Attention, shoppers: Those who want proximity to Toronto's central shrine to commerce should seriously consider checking in here. Connected to the Eaton Centre, the Marriott is just a few minutes' walk from the Financial and Theater districts, Chinatown, and Sky-Dome. This hotel caters to the tourist crowd: While a good concierge at any hotel can point you in the direction of, say, a hot restaurant, the Marriott has desks set up to facilitate day-trip planning and other activities. Because of its unmatched location, this is an excellent choice for determined sightseers. One caveat is that the area immediately surrounding the Eaton Centre veers toward the grungy and depressing; it isn't dangerous, but it is pickpocket heaven.

Most of the Marriott's guest rooms are well sized—all the better to store your loot. The views from many of the rooms aren't the best, because you'll find office towers in all directions. A pleasant surprise is the view of the beautiful 19th-century Holy Trinity Church from the Parkside restaurant.

525 Bay St. (at Dundas St.), Toronto, ON M5G 2L2. ℂ **800/905-0667** or 416/597-9200. Fax 416/597-9211. www.marriotteatoncentre.com. 459 units. C$189–$239 (US$129–$163) double. AE, DC, DISC, MC, V. Parking C$16 (US$11). Subway: Dundas. **Amenities:** 2 restaurants; 2 bars; indoor rooftop swimming pool; fitness center with Jacuzzi, sauna, and massage rooms; concierge; activities desk; car-rental desk; business center; 24-hr. room service, same-day dry cleaning. *In room:* A/C, TV, dataport, coffeemaker, hair dryer, iron.

Westin Harbour Castle 𝒜

A popular spot for conventions, the Westin is on the lakefront, just across from the Toronto Islands ferry docks and down the road from the Harbourfront Centre and Queen's Quay. Not surprisingly, the views are among the best in the city. The trade-off is that, like the nearby Radisson Plaza Hotel Admiral, this hotel is somewhat out of the way. It's a 5-minute walk to Union Station, but to get there you have to cross under the Gardiner Expressway, one of the ugliest and most desolate patches of the city. The hotel tries to get around this difficulty with shuttle bus service; there's also a public-transit stop and a queue of cabs at the hotel. But it's unlikely you'll want to go for an evening stroll around here.

Perhaps recognizing the lack of things to do in the vicinity, management has populated the hotel with attractions. The dining options are extremely fine: The excellent new restaurant, Toula, is attracting Toronto residents as well as visitors in droves. There are also terrific sports facilities, giving this monolithic hotel the feel of a resort. Who needs to go outside anyway?

1 Harbour Sq., Toronto, ON M5J 1A6. ℂ **800/WESTIN-1** or 416/869-1600. Fax 416/361-7448. www.westin. com/harbourcastle. 977 units. C$180–$360 (US$122–$245) double; from C$335 (US$228) suite. Extra person

C$30 (US$20). Children stay free in parents' room. Weekend packages available. AE, DC, MC, V. Parking C$25 (US$17). Subway: Union, then LRT to Queen's Quay. **Amenities:** 2 restaurants; bar; indoor pool; 2 outdoor tennis courts; excellent health club with Jacuzzi, sauna, and steam room; 2 squash courts; spa; children's center; concierge; business center; salon; 24-hr. room service; dry cleaning/laundry. *In room:* A/C, TV, dataport, minibar, coffeemaker, hair dryer, iron.

MODERATE

Delta Chelsea *Kids* *Value*   While not a budget hotel, the Delta Chelsea offers bang for the buck. Its downtown location draws heaps of tour groups and a smattering of business travelers, its family-friendly facilities lure those with tykes, and its weekend packages capture the cost-conscious. It's impossible for a hotel to be all things to all people, but the Delta Chelsea comes pretty close. Luxury seekers should look elsewhere, and backpackers won't be able to afford it, but the Delta Chelsea is talented at meeting the needs of everyone in between.

The Delta Chelsea celebrated its 25th anniversary in 2000, when it opened Bb33 Bistro and Brasserie, a two-in-one restaurant with a formal dining room and a fuss-free buffet room. The guest rooms, many of which were renovated in 2001, are as bright and cheery as ever; a few have kitchenettes. On the Signature Club floor for business travelers, rooms have cordless speakerphones, faxes, well-stocked desks, and ergonomic chairs.

One special feature of the Delta Chelsea is its entertainment department. The hotel has partnerships with CanStage, Soupepper Theatre, the CN Tower, and the Canadian National Exhibition, to mention a few. Guests enjoy access to tickets for everything from blockbuster shows to special events.

33 Gerrard St. W., Toronto, ON M5G 1Z4. ℂ 800/243-5732 or 416/595-1975. Fax 416/585-4362. www.delta hotels.com. 1,590 units. C$129–$340 (US$88–$231) double; C$149–$360 (US$101–$245) deluxe double; C$195–$380 (US$133–$258) Signature Club double (business floor); from C$475 (US$323) suite. Extra person C$20 (US$14). Children under 18 stay free in parents' room. Weekend packages available. AE, DC, DISC, MC, V. Valet parking C$26 (US$18); self-parking C$21 (US$14); parking available only to 575 cars). Subway: College. **Amenities:** 3 restaurants; 3 bars; 2 pools (1 for adults only); fitness center with Jacuzzi and sauna; children's center; billiards room; concierge; activities desk; business center; salon; babysitting; dry cleaning/laundry. *In room:* A/C, TV, coffeemaker, hair dryer, iron.

Holiday Inn on King   The blinding-white facade of this building suggests that some architect mistook Toronto for the tropics. No matter—its location is hot, with the Theater District, gourmet ghetto, Chinatown, and SkyDome nearby (in fact, its location is better than that of any other hotel in this price category except the Delta Chelsea). It's also close to the Financial District, which explains the mix of business travelers and vacationers. Half the floors are office space; guest rooms start at the 9th floor and go up to the 20th. The good-sized, pastel-colored rooms are vintage Holiday Inn.

370 King St. W. (at Peter St.), Toronto, ON M5V 1J9. ℂ 800/263-6364 or 416/599-4000. Fax 416/599-7394. www.hiok.com. 431 units. C$179–$319 (US$122–$217) double. Extra person C$15 (US$10). AE, DISC, MC, V. Parking C$18 (US$12). Pets accepted. Subway: St. Andrew. **Amenities:** Restaurant; bar; small outdoor pool; fitness center with exercise room, Jacuzzi, and sauna; massage. *In room:* A/C, TV, coffeemaker, hair dryer.

INEXPENSIVE

The Strathcona *Value*   The Strathcona has a unique status: it's pretty much the only budget hotel in the Financial District, and for years it has been one of the best buys in the city. It sits in the shadow of the Royal York, making this hotel a short walk from all major downtown attractions. If you want to be in this neighborhood but don't want to pay a bundle, this is your best option. The trade-offs aren't as extensive as you might think. The Strathcona's rooms may be on the small side, but they are designed with efficiency in mind.

The hotel doesn't have a health club, but guests have access to the nearby Wellington Club for a C$10 (US$6.80) fee.

60 York St., Toronto, ON M5J 1S8. ✆ **800/268-8304** or 416/363-3321. Fax 416/363-4679. www.thestrathcona hotel.com. 193 units. May–Oct C$129–$179 (US$88–$122) double; Nov–Apr C$109–$139 (US$74–$95) double. AE, DC, MC, V. Parking nearby C$20 (US$14). Subway: Union. **Amenities:** Cafe; bar; access to nearby health club; bike rental; children's center; concierge; tour desk; car-rental desk; babysitting; limited room service; dry cleaning/laundry. *In room:* A/C, TV, hair dryer, iron.

Hotel Victoria   In a landmark downtown building near the Hummingbird Centre and the Hockey Hall of Fame, the Victoria boasts the glamorous touches of an earlier age, such as crown moldings and marble columns in the lobby. It's Toronto's second-oldest hotel (built in 1909), but all of the guest rooms underwent a complete renovation in 2000, and the facilities are upgraded yearly. Because of its small size, the 56-room hotel offers an unusually high level of personal service and attention, which you normally wouldn't expect in a budget accommodation; the staff is fluent in several languages. Standard rooms are very small; select rooms are larger.

56 Yonge St. (at Wellington St.), Toronto, ON M5E 1G5. ✆ **800/363-8228** or 416/363-1666. Fax 416/363-7327. www.hotelvictoria-toronto.com. 56 units (38 with tub/shower combination, 18 with shower only). C$129–$169 (US$88–$115) double. Extra person C$15 (US$10). AE, DC, MC, V. Parking C$20 (US$14). Subway: King. **Amenities:** Restaurant; access to nearby health club; babysitting; dry cleaning/laundry. *In room:* A/C, TV, dataport, coffeemaker, hair dryer, iron.

2 Downtown East

VERY EXPENSIVE

Cambridge Suites Hotel 🏵🏵   This hotel has three main selling points: location, location, and location. Sitting on the edge of the Financial District, it caters to a corporate crowd that never wants to be more than a few steps from the office. Of course there are other drawing cards, such as the fact that all units are suites. The emphasis is on luxury, and the Cambridge succeeds in making its point.

The suites start at a generous 550 square feet and move up to deluxe duplexes. (In fact, the Jacuzzi-outfitted penthouse suites have come to the attention of celebrities tired of Toronto's tried-and-true star-catering hotels; the views are breathtaking.) The amenities for business travelers are solid. If you can drag yourself away from the comfy desk area, which has two two-line telephones and a fax, you can enjoy some of the comforts of home: refrigerator, microwave, and dining ware, plus coffee, tea, and snacks. And if you hand over your shopping list, the staff will stock the fridge, too.

15 Richmond St. E. (near Yonge St.), Toronto, ON M5C 1N2. ✆ **800/463-1990** or 416/368-1990. Fax 416/601-3751. www.cambridgesuiteshotel.com. 231 units. From C$219 (US$149). Rates include continental breakfast. AE, DC, DISC, MC, V. Parking C$20 (US$14). Subway: Queen. **Amenities:** Restaurant; bar; small health club with Jacuzzi and sauna; access to much larger health club nearby; spa; concierge; business center; limited room service; babysitting; dry cleaning/laundry. *In room:* A/C, TV, fax, dataport, minibar, fridge, microwave, coffeemaker, hair dryer, iron.

Le Royal Meridien King Edward 🏵🏵   At one time, the King Eddy was the only place in Toronto that Hollywood royalty like Liz Taylor and Richard Burton would consider staying. In the 1980s, after many years of neglect, a group of local investors spent C$40 million (US$27 million) to rescue it. The result recalls its former glory, with rosy marble columns and a glass-domed rotunda dominating the lobby. The sense of grandeur carries into the accommodations. Not every room is spacious, but they are all charmingly appointed; unlike those at many

Downtown East Accommodations

Bond Place Hotel **3**
Cambridge Suites Hotel **4**
Days Inn **1**
Le Royal Meridien King Edward **6**
Neill-Wycik College Hotel **2**
Quality Hotel **5**

† Church
⊠ Post Office
━■ TTC Subway

(Kids) Family-Friendly Hotels

Delta Chelsea (p. 63)   This is a perennial family favorite—with good cause. To ease the burden on frazzled parents, a children's creative center and babysitting services are available between 9:30am and 10pm. Kids will enjoy the in-room family movies, Super Nintendo, cookie jar (replenished daily), and nightly turndown gift. Further reducing the strain on the family purse, kids have a half-price menu at the Delta Chelsea's restaurants.

Four Seasons Hotel Toronto (p. 67)   A hop and a skip from the Children's Own Museum and the Royal Ontario Museum, this hotel has its own attractions. There are free bicycles and video games for borrowing, and an indoor-outdoor pool. Upon arrival, room service brings the kids complimentary cookies and milk. The concierge and housekeeping staff work magic, including conjuring up excellent babysitting services.

The Sheraton Centre (p. 61)   The endless attractions of this complex—including restaurants with special menus for tykes, and a cinema—mean there's a lot to keep the kiddies entertained. There's a supervised play center as well as on-call babysitting services. Kids also enjoy in-room video games and a welcome gift. There are a limited number of Family Guest Rooms, which boast a toy chest, some kiddie-size furniture, a fridge and a microwave.

uptown competitors, the rooms feel personally designed. The bathrooms are particularly nice, with generously proportioned marble tubs. Ongoing renovations through spring 2003 will introduce 165 "Art & Tech" rooms, which blend streamlined (but luxe!) decor with tech goodies (like the wall-mounted 42-inch plasma-screen TV and high-speed Internet access).

The formal dining room, Café Victoria, wins solid reviews for its seafood starters. But with goldfish swimming in bowls on many tables, you might wish to stick to the decadent desserts. Just off the lobby is a mirrored lounge that serves traditional English afternoon tea; it's a favorite haunt of would-be literary types. The wood-paneled Consort Bar is wonderfully clubby, and its 2.5m (8-ft.) -high windows afford fun people-watching.

37 King St. E., Toronto, ON M5C 2E9. (© **800/543-4300** or 416/863-3131. Fax 416/367-5515. www.lemeridien-kingedward.com. 294 units. C$375–$450 (US$255–$306) double; from C$800 (US$544) suite. Children 12 and under stay free in parents' room. AE, DC, MC, V. Parking C$26 (US$18). Subway: King. Pets accepted. **Amenities:** 2 restaurants; bar; fitness center with Jacuzzi and sauna; concierge; 24-hr. room service, babysitting; dry cleaning/laundry. *In room:* A/C, TV, fax, dataport, minibar, hair dryer, iron.

MODERATE

Bond Place Hotel   The location is right—a block from the Eaton Centre, around the corner from the Pantages and Elgin theaters—and so is the price. Perhaps that's why this hotel tends to be popular with tour groups. (The fact that the staff speaks several European and Asian languages doesn't hurt, either.) The rooms are on the small side, but all were freshened up in a 2002 renovation and refurbishment

65 Dundas St. E., Toronto, ON M5B 2G8. (© **800/268-9390** or 416/362-6061. Fax 416/360-6406. www.bond placehoteltoronto.com. 287 units. High season C$140 (US$95) single or double; low season C$79 (US$54)

single or double. Extra person C$15 (US$10). Weekend packages available. AE, DC, DISC, MC, V. Parking C$12 (US$8.15). Subway: Dundas. **Amenities:** Restaurant; bar; concierge; tour desk; car-rental desk; limited room service; dry cleaning/laundry. *In room:* A/C, TV, hair dryer, iron.

Days Inn & Conference Centre Toronto Downtown   Now that Maple Leaf Gardens is semi-retired (hockey has moved to the Air Canada Centre), the Days Inn's location isn't what it used to be. Still, this hotel isn't far from the downtown core, and its reasonable rates continue to draw business, particularly with those traveling for leisure (and on a budget). Also, extensive renovations in 2000 and ongoing improvements through 2002 have really spruced up both the public areas and the guest rooms.

30 Carlton St., Toronto, ON M5B 2E9. ℂ **800/329-7466** or 416/977-6655. Fax 416/977-0502. www.days inn.com. 536 units. C$99–$169 (US$67–$115) double. Extra person C$15 (US$10). Children under 18 stay free in parents' room. Summer discounts available. AE, DISC, MC, V. Parking C$15 (US$10). Subway: College. **Amenities:** Restaurant; bar; indoor pool; sauna; concierge; tour desk; car-rental desk; dry cleaning/laundry. *In room:* A/C, TV, dataport, coffeemaker; fridge, hair dryer, iron.

INEXPENSIVE

Neill-Wycik College Hotel   During the school year, this is a residence for nearby Ryerson Polytechnic University. Some students work here in the summer, when the Neill-Wycik morphs into a guesthouse. Travelers on tight budgets won't mind the minimalist approach—rooms have beds, chairs, desks, and phones, but no air-conditioning or TVs. Groups of five bedrooms share two bathrooms and one kitchen with a refrigerator and stove. It's less than a 5-minute walk to the Eaton Center. The neighborhood is not as appealing as that around Victoria University at the University of Toronto, which offers a similar arrangement (p. 72).

96 Gerrard St. E. (between Church and Jarvis sts.), Toronto, ON M5B 1G7. ℂ **800/268-4358** or 416/977-2320. Fax 416/977-2809. www.neill-wycik.com. 300 units (none with private bathroom). C$61 (US$41) double; C$70 (US$48) family (2 adults plus children). MC, V. Closed Sept to early May. Limited parking nearby C$10 (US$6.80). Subway: College. **Amenities:** Cafe; 2 roof decks (on the 5th and 23rd floors); TV lounge; sauna; 24-hr. laundry room.

Quality Hotel   Close to the Financial District and the Eaton Centre, this hotel always seems to be running a special promotion, so be sure to ask for a deal. Rooms tend to be small, though they do have all the standard amenities. This is basically a no-frills hotel whose main selling point is its location. Rates include a Continental breakfast buffet.

111 Lombard St. (between Adelaide and Richmond sts.), Toronto, ON M5C 2T9. ℂ **800/4-CHOICE** or 416/367-5555. Fax 416/367-3470. www.choicehotels.ca/cn311. 196 units. C$109–$209 (US$74–$142) double. Children 18 and under stay free in parents' room. AE, DC, DISC, MC, V. Parking C$16 (US$11). Subway: King or Queen. **Amenities:** Exercise room; dry cleaning/laundry. *In room:* A/C, TV, coffeemaker, hair dryer, iron.

3 Midtown West

VERY EXPENSIVE

Four Seasons Hotel Toronto ★★ *Kids*   The Four Seasons is famous as the favored haunt of many visiting celebrities. The Rolling Stones call it home in Toronto, and during the Toronto International Film Festival every September you can't get in here for love or money. The hotel, in the ritzy Yorkville district, has earned a reputation for offering fine service and complete comfort. While not even close to being the largest hotel in the city, the building—with its myriad ballrooms, meeting rooms, and restaurants—is monolithic. It's easy to get lost inside (I've done it myself).

Midtown Toronto Accommodations

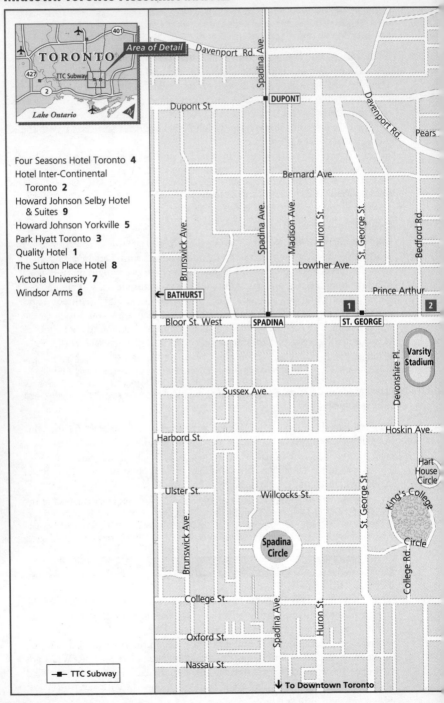

Four Seasons Hotel Toronto **4**
Hotel Inter-Continental
  Toronto **2**
Howard Johnson Selby Hotel
  & Suites **9**
Howard Johnson Yorkville **5**
Park Hyatt Toronto **3**
Quality Hotel **1**
The Sutton Place Hotel **8**
Victoria University **7**
Windsor Arms **6**

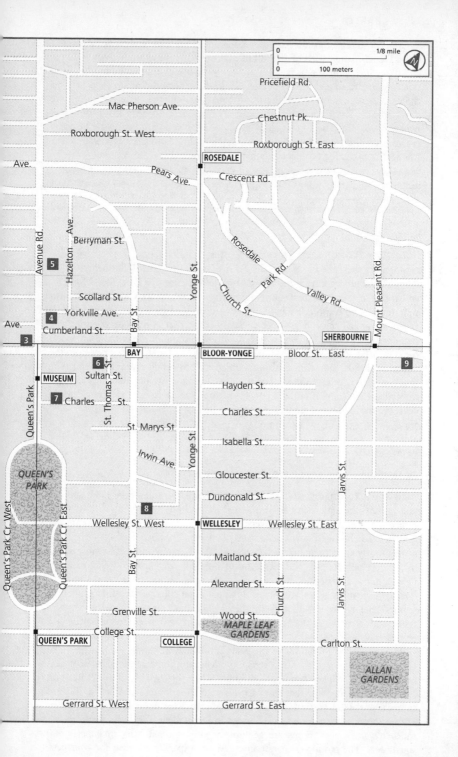

Even if you do get lost, it's an interesting place. The public areas are decorated like a French parlor, with marble floors and dramatic floral arrangements. Once you make it to your room, you'll find that while it may tend to be on the small side (a standard model is only about 325 sq. ft.), it's well designed and easy on the eye. Corner rooms have charming balconies—all the better to appreciate street scenes. The formal dining room, Truffles, is a Toronto institution (see review on p. 97). The second-floor Studio Cafe is a favorite with the business crowd; its menu features many health-conscious, low-fat dishes. The Avenue bar is a perfect perch for people-watching—it overlooks Yorkville Avenue.

21 Avenue Rd., Toronto, ON M5R 2G1. © 800/268-6282 or 416/964-0411. Fax 416/964-2301. www.four seasons.com. 380 units. C$305–$440 (US$207–$299) double; from C$485 (US$330) suite. Weekend discounts and packages available. AE, DC, DISC, MC, V. Parking C$25 (US$17). Subway: Bay. **Amenities:** 2 restaurants; 2 bars/lounges; indoor/outdoor pool; health club with Jacuzzi; bike rental; concierge; weekday courtesy limo to downtown; business center; 24-hr. room service, in-room massage; babysitting; same-day dry cleaning/ laundry. *In room:* A/C, TV, dataport, minibar, hair dryer, iron, safe.

Hotel Inter-Continental Toronto 🎔
Just a little west of its higher-profile competitors the Park Hyatt and the Four Seasons, the Inter-Continental is less than a 5-minute walk from the Royal Ontario Museum, the Bata Shoe Museum, and Yorkville, one of the best shopping districts in the city. It's a favorite with business travelers, who appreciate its attentive, personalized service. The atmosphere is exclusive but low-key. It doesn't get the starry crowd that its rivals draw, either, and that can be a blessing (anyone who has witnessed some of the weird behavior of the stars will know exactly what I mean). The building looks nondescript from the street, but inside, abundant European and Art Deco details give it character. The spacious guest rooms contain stylish love seats and roomy desks. The focus throughout the hotel is on business, from room design to the extensive business center to the Signatures restaurant, which is perfect for entertaining.

220 Bloor St. W., Toronto, ON M5S 1T8. © 800/267-0010 or 416/960-5200. Fax 416/960-8269. www.toronto. intercontinental.com. 210 units. C$275–$400 (US$178–$258) double. AE, DC, MC, V. Parking C$27 (US$18). Subway: St. George. **Amenities:** Restaurant; bar; indoor pool; fitness center with sauna; concierge; tour desk; business center; 24-hr. room service; in-room massage; babysitting; same-day dry cleaning/laundry. *In room:* A/C, TV/VCR, fax, dataport, minibar, fridge, coffeemaker, hair dryer, iron, safe.

Park Hyatt Toronto 🎔🎔🎔
With its ongoing C$60 million (US$41 million) renovations, the Park Hyatt has cemented its reputation for being the last word in luxe. It is, in my opinion, the very best hotel in Toronto at the moment, and it's where I'd choose to stay if price were no object. Chicago-based Hyatt has renovated nearly every corner of the 70-year-old Art Deco building. The most recent major development was the unveiling of the Stillwater Spa in 2001, which is unique in both its design and some of its treatments (one signature therapy is a "watsu"-style massage, in which you float in a water-filled room while a therapist applies shiatsu moves—it's very soothing). The next plan is to redecorate and refurbish the rooms in the South Tower; this work will be complete by the end of January 2003.

The location is prime: It's in the posh Yorkville district, steps from the Royal Ontario Museum and the Children's Own Museum. Its neighbor, the Four Seasons, has for years been luring the glitterati, while the Park Hyatt prides itself on luring the literati. Now that the Park Hyatt is the official hotel of the Toronto International Film Festival, it's the venue of choice for many stars, too.

A glamorous lobby dotted with Eastern-inspired objets d'art links the north and south towers. Guest rooms are generously proportioned—the smallest is 500 square feet. The ground-floor restaurant Annona (p. 97) is a treat for gourmets.

The 18th-floor Roof Lounge is a favorite meeting spot for journalists, who congregate on couches in front of the fireplace; but in summer, the lounge's open-air balcony is the place to be for a perfect view of the city (and an impressive daiquiri).

4 Avenue Rd., Toronto, ON M5R 2E8. ℭ **800/233-1234** or 416/925-1234. Fax 416/924-6693. www.park toronto.hyatt.com. 346 units. C$225–$499 (US$153–$339) double; from C$299 (US$203) suite. Weekend packages available. AE, DC, DISC, MC, V. Parking C$25 (US$17). Subway: Museum or Bay. Pets accepted. **Amenities:** Restaurant; 2 bars; fitness center with sauna and Jacuzzi; spa; concierge; business center; 24-hr. room service; babysitting; dry cleaning/laundry. *In room:* A/C, TV, fax, dataport, minibar, coffeemaker, hair dryer, iron, safe.

Windsor Arms ⭐ Take one exquisite neo-Gothic building, tear it down, and replace it with an identical structure that incorporates some of the original's elements. That's the recipe the new owner of the Windsor Arms followed in re-creating the hotel, which was built in 1927 and closed in 1991. The result is a stunning mix of new and old, with state-of-the-art technology behind leaded-glass windows. Only 4 of the 15 stories contain hotel rooms; the rest consists of million-dollar condominiums.

The guest rooms and suites are exquisite confections of ivory, celadon, and silver. All feature a "butler's cupboard," with a door from the hallway and another in the room (in case you want room service but don't feel like answering the door). The generously proportioned bathrooms have Jacuzzi jets in the tubs.

118 St. Thomas St., Toronto, ON M5S 3E7. ℭ **416/971-9666.** Fax 416/971-3303. www.windsorarms hotel.com. 28 units. From C$375 (US$255) double. Weekend discounts available. AE, DC, DISC, MC, V. Parking C$26 (US$18). Subway: Bay. **Amenities:** Restaurant; bar; lap pool; sauna; concierge; 24-hr. room service; spa with massage, aromatherapy, and aquatherapy treatments; dry cleaning/laundry; walk-in humidor. *In room:* A/C, TV, dataport, minibar, hair dryer.

EXPENSIVE

The Sutton Place Hotel ⭐⭐ Although it towers over the intersection of Bay and Wellesley, The Sutton Place boasts the advantages of a small hotel—particularly detail-oriented, personalized service. In addition to hosting a galaxy of stars and celebrities, the hotel draws sophisticated business and leisure travelers in search of serious pampering. The emphasis is on sophistication—famous guests expect to be left alone, and management protects their privacy. In other words, no autograph seekers.

The hotel aims for European panache, littering the public spaces with antiques and tapestries. The spacious guest rooms are decorated in a similar, though scaled-down, style, and all were refurbished in 2001. A few suites have full kitchens. Not that you'd want to cook while you're here—the lovely ground-floor Accents restaurant serves continental fare, and across the street the star-studded Bistro 990 produces perfect French cuisine. One downside is that The Sutton Place stands alone in its neighborhood. It's about a 10- to 15-minute walk to attractions such as the Royal Ontario Museum and the Yorkville shopping district.

955 Bay St., Toronto, ON M5S 2A2. ℭ **800/268-3790** or 416/924-9221. Fax 416/924-1778. www.sutton place.com. 294 units. C$235–$325 (US$160–$221) double; from C$400 (US$272) suite. Extra person C$20 (US$14). Children under 18 stay free in parents' room. Weekend discounts available. AE, DC, MC, V. Valet parking C$28 (US$19); self-parking C$20 (US$14). Subway: Wellesley. Pets accepted. **Amenities:** Restaurant; bar; indoor pool; fitness center with sauna; concierge; business center; salon; 24-hr. room service; massage; babysitting; dry cleaning/laundry. *In room:* A/C, TV, dataport, minibar, coffeemaker, hair dryer, iron, safe.

MODERATE

Howard Johnson Yorkville Formerly the Venture Inn, this hotel is a bargain in a very expensive neighborhood. It's a little more expensive than it used to be, but it also has a few more amenities now. The Yorkville location is excellent, which is the trade-off for small rooms. As with many value-priced hotels, you're not going to want to spend much time in your room.

89 Avenue Rd., Toronto, ON M5R 2G3. *C* 800/446-4656 or 416/964-1220. Fax 416/964-8692. 71 units. C$89–$229 (US$61–$156) double. Rates include continental breakfast. AE, DC, MC, V. Parking C$10 (US$6.80). Subway: Bay or Museum. Pets accepted. **Amenities:** Concierge; dry cleaning/laundry. *In room:* A/C, TV, dataport, hair dryer, iron.

Quality Hotel *(Value)* Considering this hotel's tony location—steps from Yorkville and several museums, including the Royal Ontario Museum—the price is hard to beat. The rooms are small but comfortable, and outfitted with well-lit worktables. Choice Club members have access to in-house secretarial services; executive rooms have fax-modem hookups. However, there aren't many other amenities or services. This is a good home base for a leisure traveler who prizes location over other considerations. If you're not planning on hanging out a lot in your hotel room, it's a small tradeoff to make for the price.

280 Bloor St. W. (at St. George St.), Toronto, ON M5S 1V8. *C* 416/968-0010. www.choicehotels.ca. 210 units. C$139–$209 (US$95–$142) double. Weekend and other packages available. AE, DC, DISC, MC, V. Parking C$12 (US$8.15). Subway: St. George. **Amenities:** Restaurant; coffee shop; access to nearby health club; limited room service; dry cleaning/laundry. *In room:* A/C, TV, coffeemaker, hair dryer, iron.

INEXPENSIVE

Howard Johnson Selby Hotel & Suites *(Finds)* This hotel is one of Toronto's better-kept secrets. Ornate chandeliers, stucco moldings, and high ceilings make the 1890s Victorian building an absolute stunner. In a predominantly gay neighborhood, the Selby attracts gay and straight couples, as well as seniors (the latter group gets special discounts). All of the rooms now have private bathrooms, but only a few have an old-fashioned claw-footed tub. The staff is very friendly, and while there's no concierge, there's no shortage of advice and recommendations for what to see and do.

592 Sherbourne St., Toronto, ON M4X 1L4. *C* 800/387-4788 or 416/921-3142. Fax 416/923-3177. 82 units. C$79–$119 (US$54–$81) double; C$125–$165 (US$85–$112) suite. Rates include continental breakfast. Senior discounts available. AE, DISC, MC, V. Parking C$10 (US$6.80). Subway: Sherbourne. **Amenities:** Access to nearby fitness center; laundry room. *In room:* A/C, TV, coffeemaker.

Victoria University *(Value)* This is a summer steal: You could not find a better deal in this part of town. From early May to late August, Victoria University (which is federated with the University of Toronto) makes its student accommodations available to travelers. Furnishings are simple—a bed, desk, and chair are standard—but the surroundings are splendid. Many of the rooms are in Burwash Hall, a 19th-century building that overlooks a peaceful, leafy quad. All rooms are down the street from the Royal Ontario Museum, and up the street from Queen's Park. Guests are provided with linens, towels, and soap.

140 Charles St. W., Toronto, ON M5S 1K9. *C* 416/585-4524. Fax 416/585-4530. Accom.victoria@ utoronto.ca. 700 units (none with private bathroom). C$66 (US$45) double. Rates include breakfast. Senior and student discounts available. MC, V. Closed Sept–April. Nearby parking C$12 (US$8.15). Subway: Museum. **Amenities:** Tennis courts; access to fitness center with Olympic-size pool; laundry room. *In room:* No phone.

4 Uptown

MODERATE

Best Western Roehampton Hotel & Suites The Roehampton is removed from downtown attractions, but still well located—for some people. It is a short walk from one of the best dining districts in the city, and a short bus ride from the Ontario Science Centre and 243 hectares (600 acres) of parkland (including hiking and cross-country skiing trails, and the Sunnybrook stables). The large, nicely furnished rooms boast big windows and peaceful views. With the wealth of hotels downtown, there's no reason to come this far north unless you need to—but if you do, this is a nice, relatively inexpensive place to stay.

808 Mount Pleasant Rd., Toronto, ON M4P 2L2. (✆ 800/387-8899 or 416/487-5101. Fax 416/487-5390. www. bestwestern.com. 112 units. C$145–$175 (US$99–$119) double. Packages available. Children 17 and under stay free in parents' room. AE, DC, DISC, MC, V. Valet parking C$8 (US$5.45). Subway: Eglinton. **Amenities:** Restaurant; outdoor rooftop pool; exercise room; concierge; limited room service; babysitting; dry cleaning/ laundry. *In room:* A/C, TV, dataport, minibar, coffeemaker, hair dryer, iron.

5 The East End

Although it's not close to the downtown attractions, this area has many sights that are worth noting. They include the Ontario Science Centre, the Toronto Zoo, the Scarborough Bluffs (which homesick English settlers compared to the white cliffs of Dover), and the Scarborough Town Centre, a vast shopping complex.

There are a number of moderately priced chain hotels in this area. They include **Embassy Suites,** 8500 Warden Ave., Markham, ON L6G 1A5 (✆ 905/ 470-8500); **Howard Johnson,** 940 Progress Ave., Scarborough, ON M1G 3T5 (✆ 800/446-4656); **Radisson,** 1250 Eglinton Ave. E., Don Mills, ON M3C 1J3 (✆ 416/449-4111); **Ramada,** 185 Yorkland Blvd., Don Mills, ON M2J 4R2 (✆ 800/2-RAMADA); and **Sheraton,** 2035 Kennedy Rd., Scarborough, ON M1T 3G2 (✆ 416/299-1500).

EXPENSIVE

Westin Prince Hotel ✿   This hotel is less than half an hour from downtown, but its location and 6 hectares (15 acres) of parkland make it feel like a secluded resort. The generously proportioned rooms are designed for comfort. Many have a bay window or balcony, and the view makes Toronto look like one big forest. Standard features include a refrigerator, two phones, and a marble bathroom.

900 York Mills Rd., Don Mills, ON M3B 3H2. (✆ 800/WESTIN-1 or 416/444-2511. Fax 416/444-9597. www. westin.com. 384 units. C$150–$320 (US$102–$218) double. Extra person C$20 (US$14). Children 17 and under stay free in parents' room. Weekend packages available. AE, DC, MC, V. Free parking. Subway: York Mills. **Amenities:** 3 restaurants; bar; outdoor heated pool; tennis court; fitness center with sauna; 9-hole putting green; children's center; concierge; business center; 24-hr. room service; dry cleaning/laundry. *In room:* A/C, TV, coffeemaker, hair dryer, iron.

INEXPENSIVE

University of Toronto at Scarborough   Like the downtown U of T campus, this student residence opens to travelers from mid-May to late August. The greenery-surrounded student village consists of townhouses that sleep a maximum of six. Each has a complete kitchen, but none has air-conditioning, a telephone, or a TV.

Student Village. Scarborough Campus, University of Toronto, 1265 Military Trail, Scarborough, ON M1C 1A4. (✆ 416/287-7356. Fax 416/287-7323. C$180 (US$122) double for 2-night minimum; each additional night C$90 (US$61). Family rates available. MC. V. Closed Sept to mid-May. Free parking. Subway: Kennedy, then Scarborough Rapid Transit to Ellesmere, then bus no. 95 or 95B to college entrance. By car: take exit 387 north from Hwy. 401. **Amenities:** Cafeteria; pub; access to fitness center with squash and tennis courts. *In room:* No phone.

6 At the Airport

Don't be fooled by anyone who tells you that the airport isn't far from the city. It's at least a 30-minute drive to downtown, depending on traffic. A taxi downtown costs roughly C$36 (US$25); the cheap public-transit options from the airport take an hour. Many of the hotels along the airport strip cater to business travelers. Others may wish to stay in this area if they're planning to divide their time between Toronto and its outlying areas, such as the Niagara region. Serious golfers come here for the area's many golf courses, including the 18-hole championship layout at the Royal Woodbine Golf Club.

EXPENSIVE

Hilton Toronto Airport 🛋   I'm not enthusiastic about staying out by Pearson International Airport, but one of the luxuries of doing so is that you can expect a spacious room. The Hilton certainly makes good on this opportunity. In fact, one of its main attractions is its 152 minisuites—all of which have a king-size bed in the bedroom, a sofa bed in the living room, a color TV in both rooms, and three phones. Another lure is the chain's well-regarded array of business-oriented amenities. The building underwent a C$9 million (US$6 million) face-lift in 1999, and a smaller renovation in the fall of 2001.

5875 Airport Rd., Mississauga, ON L4V 1N1. ☎ 800/567-9999 or 905/677-9900. Fax 905/677-7782. www.hilton.com. 413 units. From C$219 (US$149) double; from C$244 (US$166) minisuite. Extra person C$25 (US$17). Children stay free in parents' room. Weekend packages available. AE, DC, DISC, MC, V. Parking C$12 (US$8.15). Take the Gardiner Expressway. west to Hwy. 427 north, to Airport Expressway. (Dixon Rd. exit). **Amenities:** Restaurant; bar; indoor pool; nearby golf course; health club with sauna; spa; children's center; concierge; car-rental desk; business center; 24-hr. room service; same-day dry cleaning/laundry. *In room:* A/C, TV, fax, dataport, minibar, coffeemaker, hair dryer, iron.

Sheraton Gateway Hotel in Toronto International Airport 🛋   Talk about convenience: You don't even need to go outdoors to get here—just take the skywalk from Terminal 3 (or a free shuttle from the other terminals). If you're planning a very short trip that requires flying out of the city almost as soon as you fly in, this hotel makes an awful lot of sense. Rooms are comfortable, spacious, and, more to the point, fully soundproofed (remember, you're still at the airport!). Club rooms have extra inducements, such as ergonomic chairs, a fax/printer/copier, and access to a private lounge that serves complimentary breakfast and snacks.

Toronto AMF, Box 3000, Toronto, ON L5P 1C4. ☎ 800/325-3535 or 905/672-7000. Fax 905/672-7100. www.sheraton.com. 474 units. C$190–$280 (US$129–$190) double. AE, DC, DISC, MC, V. Parking C$19 (US$13). Pets accepted. **Amenities:** Restaurant; bar; indoor pool; fitness center with Jacuzzi and sauna; concierge; business center; 24-hr. room service; in-room massage; babysitting; dry cleaning/laundry. *In room:* A/C, TV, dataport, minibar, coffeemaker, hair dryer, iron, safe.

Wyndham Bristol Place 🛋🛋   For a hotel by the airport, the Wyndham has a lot to offer. I'd never recommend staying near the airport unless you absolutely have to, but if you do, the Wyndham is an excellent choice. This is undoubtedly the most glamorous hotel for miles around—and the only one with a waterfall in its lobby. The decor throughout the building is sophisticated, but the hotel's real claim to fame is its personalized service. (You'll need to register for the Wyndham by Request program, which you can do online at www.wyndham.com; it's free, and filling out the questionnaires about everything from your dining to bedding preferences will improve your stay immeasurably.)

Guest rooms are well lit and spacious. Because it's a 30-minute journey to downtown Toronto, the good news is that the Wyndham boasts lots of amenities to keep you in the vicinity. The main dining room, Zachary's, aims high, with a seasonal menu and glamorously appointed dining room.

950 Dixon Rd., Toronto, ON M9W 5N4. ☎ 800/WYNDHAM or 416/675-9444. Fax 416/675-4426. www.wyndham.com. 287 units. C$175–$295 (US$119–$201) double; from C$400 (US$272) suite. Extra person

C$20 (US$14). Children under 18 stay free in parents' room. Packages available. AE, DC, DISC, MC, V. Parking C$12 (US$8.15). **Amenities:** 2 restaurants; bar; large skylit indoor pool; health club with sauna; concierge; business center; 24-hr. room service; babysitting; dry cleaning/laundry. *In room:* A/C, TV, dataport, minibar, coffeemaker, hair dryer, iron.

MODERATE

Regal Constellation Hotel 🏕   This hotel has steadily grown into one of the best bets in the airport region. Its excellent meeting space makes it a favorite for trade shows and conventions. Because the hotel was constructed piece by piece, the rooms vary greatly from floor to floor. Every unit is a minisuite with a king or two double beds, a sturdy desk, and an L-shaped sofa. Not surprisingly, given the location, the hotel is a self-contained entertainment complex. There are two restaurants: the Royal Chinese, for formal dining, and the more casual Atrium. The Banyan Bar offers live entertainment on Friday and Saturday evenings.

900 Dixon Rd., Toronto, ON M9W 1J7. ☎ **800/222-8888** or 416/675-1500. Fax 416/675-4611. www.royal constellation.com. 710 units. C$115–$195 (US$78–$133). Extra person C$15 (US$10). Children 17 and under stay free in parents' room. Weekend and honeymoon packages available. AE, DC, MC, V. Parking C$8 (US$5.45). **Amenities:** 2 restaurants; bar; indoor/outdoor pool; exercise room and sauna; concierge; car-rental desk; business center; salon; 24-hr. room service, dry cleaning/laundry. *In room:* A/C, TV, dataport, coffeemaker, hair dryer, iron.

Toronto Airport Marriott Hotel   One of the newest airport hotels, the Marriott is popular with business travelers. Of course, everything out here is really for business travelers. However, the Marriott is trying to attract leisure travelers, too, so expect a weekend discount of up to 50%. Rooms are comfortable and spacious. The amenities are in keeping with the Marriott name—no surprises here. There are two restaurants off the lobby: Take note of the Mikado, a Japanese restaurant where your meal can be cooked right at your table (think food as performance art).

901 Dixon Rd, Toronto, ON M9W 1J5. ☎ **800/905-2811** or 416/674-9400. Fax 416/674-8292. www.marriott. com. 424 units. C$120–$245 (US$82–$167) double. Extra person C$15 (US$10). Weekend packages available. AE, DC, DISC, MC, V. Parking C$8 (US$5.45). **Amenities:** 2 restaurants; bar; skylit indoor pool; nearby golf course; health club with Jacuzzi and sauna; concierge; car-rental desk; business center; 24-hr. room service; babysitting; same-day dry cleaning/laundry. *In room:* A/C, TV, dataport, minibar, coffeemaker, hair dryer, iron.

INEXPENSIVE

Belaire Hotel Toronto Airport   Formerly a Comfort Inn, this hotel offers simple rooms at reasonable rates. Rooms are decorated in pine, and just big enough to hold a queen-size bed, dresser, desk and chair, and plush armchair or loveseat.

240 Belfield Rd., Rexdale, ON M9W 1H3. ☎ **416/241-8513.** Fax 416/249-4203. 114 units. C$90–$140 (US$61–$95) double. Extra person C$10 (US$6.80). Children under 18 stay free in parents' room. Rates include continental breakfast. AE, DC, DISC, MC, V. Free parking. Take Hwy. 27 north to Belfield Rd. **Amenities:** Restaurant; lounge; limited room service; dry cleaning/laundry. *In room:* A/C, TV, hair dryer.

Days Hotel—Toronto Airport   For the price, this is a very good bet on the airport strip; the facilities are similar to those at pricier hotels. The guest rooms are bright and cheery, and 20 of them were recently renovated to become Corporate Plus rooms geared towards business travelers. Upgraded units have bathrobes (unusual at a hotel in this price range), irons and ironing boards, and fax-modem hookups. The Garden Café Restaurant is open all day.

6257 Airport Rd., Mississauga, ON L4V 1N1. ☎ **800/387-6891** or 905/678-1400. Fax 905/678-9130. www.daysinn.com. 201 units. C$90–$169 (US$61–$115) double. Extra person C$10 (US$6.80). Children under 17 stay free in parents' room. Weekend packages available. AE, DC, DISC, MC, V. Parking C$6 (US$4.10) per day, C$18 (US$12) per week. **Amenities:** Restaurant; outdoor pool; exercise room; sauna; limited room service; small laundry room. *In room:* A/C, TV, coffeemaker, hair dryer.

Delta Meadowvale Resort & Conference Centre Set on 9 hectares (23 acres) of greenery, the Delta has all the attributes of a restful resort. There are hiking and biking trails, tennis and squash courts, and indoor and outdoor swimming pools. The cozy rooms have modern wooden furniture, and each boasts a small balcony, a refrigerator, and two phones. The Regatta Bar & Grille serves a variety of dishes throughout the day; there are also two lounges for evening drinks (one only in summer, as it's out of doors).

6750 Mississauga Rd. (at Hwy. 401), Mississauga, ON L5N 2L3. © **800/422-8238** or 905/821-1981. Fax 905/542-4036. www.deltahotels.com. 374 units. C$110–$240 (US$75–$163) double. Weekend discounts available. AE, DC, DISC, MC, V. Free parking. Downtown shuttle C$11 (US$7.50) one-way. **Amenities:** 2 restaurants; 2 bars; children's center; business center; salon; 24-hr. room service; babysitting; dry cleaning/laundry. *In room:* A/C, TV, coffeemaker, hair dryer.

Four Points Sheraton Toronto Airport Talk about getting away from it all: on a 2.5-hectare (6-acre) woodland site, the Four Points Sheraton offers a relaxing—dare I say pastoral?—setting. Guest rooms were last renovated in 2002, with bathrooms, carpets, and draperies singled out for attention. The lobby, business center and meeting rooms were also renovated in 2002.

5444 Dixie Rd. (at Hwy. 401), Mississauga, ON L4W 2L2. © **800/737-3211** or 905/624-1144. Fax 416/ 624-9477. www.fourpoints.com/torontoairport. 296 units. C$119–$265 (US$81–$180) double. Extra person C$15 (US$10). Weekend discounts available. AE, DC, DISC, MC, V. Free parking. **Amenities:** Restaurant; indoor pool; fitness center with Jacuzzi and sauna; children's center; business center; 24-hr. room service; babysitting; same-day dry cleaning/laundry. *In room:* A/C, TV, dataport, fridge, coffeemaker, hair dryer, iron.

5

Where to Dine

Dining out is nothing short of a passion in Toronto. It's not that we're too lazy to cook, but we are spoiled by the embarrassment of edible riches in all parts of the city. Many restaurants are just as busy on a Wednesday as they are on a weekend, because dining out is a hallmark of the local culture.

The city is a restaurant-goer's nirvana for a wealth of reasons. For starters, there are more than 5,000 eateries. They represent cooking styles from any country or nationality you can name, making Toronto's culinary scene both eclectic and palate teasing. Eating out is also remarkably affordable: While the most expensive restaurants have some entrees priced above C$40 (US$27), many more boast top-notch cooking for bargain-basement prices—it's a very competitive market. (Keep in mind, too, that for American visitors, even the most expensive Toronto restaurants aren't so pricey given the weak Canadian dollar.)

Mediterranean and Asian cuisines dominate the scene—and often appear on the same plate. Fusion cooking caught on big here and has never lost its steam. Many restaurants that started out as, say, Italian, have incorporated ingredients and cooking styles from Southeast Asia and North Africa, among other *haute* spots. Each wave of immigration has carried new ideas and flavors.

While restaurants of all descriptions are found across the city, certain neighborhoods are renowned for their specialties: Little Italy for its trattorias,

Chinatown for its Chinese and Vietnamese eateries, and the Danforth for its Greek tavernas.

DINING NOTES Dining out does not have to be an expensive venture, but the tax level is high. Meals are subject to the 8% provincial sales tax and to the 7% GST. In other words, tax and tip together can add 30% to your bill. Restaurants normally leave tipping to the diners' discretion, unless there are six or more people at the table. The usual amount for good service is 15%, jumping to 20% at the pricier establishments. The price of a bottle of wine is generally quite high because of the tax on imports; get around it by ordering an Ontario vintage—local wines enjoy a rising international reputation. Remember that there is a 10% tax on alcohol, whatever you're sipping.

NOTES ON THE REVIEWS Restaurants are grouped by neighborhood and listed alphabetically under the following main-course price ranges (not counting tax and tip): Very Expensive, C$30 (US$20) and up; Expensive, C$20 to $29 (US$14–$20); and Moderate, C$10 to $19 (US$6.80–$13). At Inexpensive restaurants, it's possible to eat an entire meal for C$15 (US$10) or less. Many restaurants' offerings veer into higher and lower categories, so the ranges are general guidelines. Keep in mind that many restaurants change their menus and policies at a moment's notice. If a listing says a restaurant doesn't accept reservations, but you have your heart set on eating there, it doesn't hurt to call and ask if a reservation (or an exception) could be made.

⌒Tips A Note on Smoking

Almost all Toronto restaurants are nonsmoking, the result of an anti-smoking bylaw that went into effect on June 1, 2001. Exceptions are made for patios and separately ventilated dining rooms. Some restaurants chose to designate themselves as bars to get around the restriction, but this led to another problem, since they had to ban people under the age of 19 from the premises. Restaurateurs vowed to fight the regulation, which subjects both patrons and establishments to fines of C$200 to C$5,000 (US$136–$3,400) for infractions, but they've been unsuccessful to date. When making a reservation, ask about the restaurant's smoking policy.

1 Restaurants by Cuisine

AMERICAN

Far Niente ☆☆ (Downtown West, $$$, p. 87)

Jump Café and Bar ☆☆ (Downtown West, $$$, p. 87)

ASIAN

Kubo (Downtown East, $, p. 95)

Monsoon ☆ (Downtown West, $$$$, p. 84)

Queen Mother Café (Downtown West, $, p. 92)

Rain ☆ (Downtown West, $$$, p. 88)

SpringRolls (Midtown West, $, p. 105)

BELGIAN

Café Brussel ☆ (Midtown East/East End, $$$, p. 106)

BISTRO

Biff's ☆ (Downtown East, $$$, p. 93)

Cities (Downtown West, $$, p. 88)

Lakes ☆ (Uptown, $$$, p. 111)

La Palette ☆ (Downtown West, $$, p. 89)

Le Select Bistro (Downtown West, $$, p. 89)

Pony (Downtown West, $$, p. 90)

Roxborough's ☆ (Uptown, $$$, p. 112)

Stork on the Roof ☆ (Uptown, $$, p. 113)

Torch Bistro ☆ (Downtown East, $$$, p. 94)

CAJUN

Southern Accent (Midtown West, $$, p. 103)

CANADIAN

Canoe Restaurant & Bar ☆ (Downtown West, $$$$, p. 84)

Jamie Kennedy at the Museum ☆☆ (Midtown West, $$$, p. 100)

Patriot ☆☆ (Midtown West, $$$, p. 101)

Splendido Bar and Grill ☆ (Midtown West, $$$, p. 101)

Tundra ☆☆ (Downtown West, $$$$, p. 85)

CHINESE

Grand Yatt ☆ (North of the City, $$, p. 116)

Happy Seven (Downtown West, $, p. 91)

Lai Wah Heen ☆☆☆ (Downtown West, $$$, p. 87)

Lee Garden (Downtown West, $, p. 92)

Sang Ho ☆ (Downtown West, $$, p. 90)

CONTINENTAL

Café Societa ☆ (Downtown West, $$$, p. 86)

Key to Abbreviations: $$$$ = Very Expensive $$$ = Expensive $$ = Moderate $ = Inexpensive

Centro ★★ (Uptown, $$$$,
  p. 110)
Opus ★ (Midtown West, $$$$,
  p. 97)
Oro ★ (Downtown West, $$$,
  p. 88)
360 Revolving Restaurant ★
  (Downtown West, $$$$, p. 85)
Truffles ★ (Midtown West, $$$$,
  p. 97)

DELI

Lox, Stock & Bagel (Midtown
  West, $, p. 105)
Shopsy's (Downtown East, $,
  p. 96)

ECLECTIC

Avalon ★★ (Downtown West,
  $$$$, p. 81)
Citron (Downtown West, $$,
  p. 88)
The Fifth ★★ (Downtown West,
  $$$$, p. 84)
Goldfish ★★ (Midtown West, $$,
  p. 101)
Messis ★ (Midtown West, $$,
  p. 103)
Mildred Pierce ★★ (Downtown
  West, $$, p. 90)
Octavia (Midtown East/East End,
  $$, p. 108)
Rouge ★★ (Midtown West, $$,
  p. 103)
Swan (Downtown West, $$, p. 90)
Taro Grill ★ (Downtown West,
  $$, p. 91)

ETHIOPIAN

Lalibela (Midtown West, $, p. 105)

FRENCH

Auberge du Pommier ★ (Uptown,
  $$$$, p. 110)
Bistro 990 ★★★ (Midtown West,
  $$$$, p. 96)
Jacques Bistro du Parc (Midtown
  West, $$, p. 102)
La Bodega (Downtown West, $$,
  p. 89)

Matignon (Midtown West, $$,
  p. 102)
Quartier ★ (Uptown, $$$, p. 112)

FUSION

Boba ★ (Midtown West, $$$,
  p. 97)
Pangaea ★ (Midtown West, $$$,
  p. 100)
The Rivoli ★★ (Downtown West,
  $, p. 92)
Susur ★★★ (Downtown West,
  $$$$, p. 84)
Veni Vidi Vici ★★ (Downtown
  West, $$, p. 91)

GREEK

Astoria (Midtown East/East End,
  $, p. 108)
Avli ★ (Midtown East/East End,
  $, p. 108)
Christina's (Midtown East/
  East End, $$, p. 106)
Gus ★★ (Midtown West, $$,
  p. 102)
Mezes (Midtown East/East End, $,
  p. 109)
Myth ★★ (Midtown East/
  East End, $$, p. 108)
Octavia (Midtown East/East End,
  $$, p. 108)
Ouzeri (Midtown East/East End,
  $, p. 109)
Pan on the Danforth ★ (Midtown
  East/East End, $$, p. 108)
Penelope (Downtown West, $,
  p. 92)

INDIAN

Indian Rice Factory ★ (Midtown
  West, $, p. 104)
Nataraj (Midtown West, $, p. 105)

INTERNATIONAL

Annona ★ (Midtown West, $$$,
  p. 97)
Courthouse Market Grille ★
  (Downtown East, $$$, p. 93)
Epic ★★ (Downtown West, $$$,
  p. 86)
North 44 ★★★ (Uptown, $$$$,
  p. 110)

Rosewater Supper Club 🍴 (Downtown East, $$$, p. 93)

Scaramouche 🍴 (Uptown, $$$$, p. 111)

Senses 🍴🍴 (Midtown West, $$$, p. 101)

Terra 🍴🍴 (North of the City, $$$, p. 114)

YYZ 🍴🍴 (Downtown West, $$$$, p. 85)

Zoom Caffe & Bar 🍴 (Downtown East, $$$, p. 94)

ITALIAN

Amore Trattoria 🍴🍴 (Uptown, $$, p. 112)

Café Nervosa (Midtown West, $$, p. 101)

Dante's 🍴🍴 (North of the City, $, p. 116)

Ecco La (Downtown West, $$, p. 88)

Florentine Court (Downtown East, $$, p. 95)

Gio's (Uptown, $$, p. 112)

Grano 🍴 (Uptown, $$, p. 113)

Il Posto Nuovo 🍴 (Midtown West, $$$, p. 100)

La Bruschetta 🍴 (Uptown, $$$, p. 111)

Mistura 🍴 (Midtown West, $$$, p. 100)

Serra (Midtown West, $, p. 105)

Sotto Sotto 🍴🍴 (Midtown West, $$, p. 103)

Terroni (Uptown, $$, p. 113)

Veni Vidi Vici 🍴🍴 (Downtown West, $$, p. 91)

JAPANESE

Hiro Sushi 🍴 (Downtown East, $$$, p. 93)

Japan Deli (Midtown West, $, p. 104)

LAOTIAN

Vanipha Lanna 🍴🍴 (Uptown, $$, p. 114)

LIGHT FARE

Bloor Street Diner (Midtown West, $, p. 104)

Hello Toast (Downtown East, $, p. 95)

Hannah's Kitchen (Uptown, $, p. 114)

Kalendar 🍴🍴 (Downtown West, $, p. 91)

Peter Pan (Downtown West, $$, p. 90)

Rebel House (Uptown, $, p. 114)

Sottovoce (Downtown West, $, p. 92)

Terroni (Uptown, $$, p. 113)

MEDITERRANEAN

Agora 🍴 (Downtown West, $$$, p. 85)

Kensington Kitchen 🍴🍴 (Midtown West, $, p. 104)

Lolita's Lust 🍴 (Midtown East/East End, $$, p. 107)

Millie's Bistro 🍴🍴 (Uptown, $$$, p. 111)

Myth 🍴🍴 (Midtown East/East End, $$, p. 108)

Octavia (Midtown East/East End, $$, p. 108)

MIDDLE EASTERN

Cedar's (Midtown West, $, p. 104)

Mezzetta (Uptown, $$, p. 113)

PORTUGUESE

Chiado 🍴 (Downtown West, $$$, p. 86)

QUEBECOIS

Le Papillon (Downtown East, $, p. 96)

Montreal Bistro and Jazz Club (Downtown East, $$, p. 95)

SEAFOOD

Joso's (Midtown West, $$, p. 102)

Rodney's Oyster House (Downtown East, $$, p. 95)

STEAK

Barberian's 🍴 (Downtown West, $$$$, p. 81)

TEX-MEX

Tortilla Flats (Downtown West, $, p. 92)

THAI

Thai Magic ⋆ (Uptown, $$$,
p. 112)

Vanipha Lanna ⋆⋆ (Uptown, $$,
p. 114)

Young Thailand ⋆⋆ (Downtown
East, $, p. 96)

VEGETARIAN

Annapurna Vegetarian Restaurant
(Midtown West, $, p. 115)

Fressen (Downtown West, $$,
p. 115)

Juice for Life (Downtown West, $,
p. 115)

VIETNAMESE

Pho Hung (Midtown West, $,
p. 105)

---

2 Downtown West

This is where you will find Toronto's greatest concentration of great restaurants.
Little Italy, which runs along **College Street,** and **Chinatown,** which radiates
from **Spadina Avenue,** has more restaurants than any other parts of the city.

You'll see a lot of high-price, low-quality eateries in the area, too. There also
tends to be more attitude from wait staffs, particularly along the gourmet ghetto
of **Queen Street West.** I'm a firm believer that even the best food can't make up
for shoddy service, so the restaurants I've selected generally get high marks in
both categories. Because service is so important to me, you won't find reviews of
restaurants where it's totally substandard. A case in point is Little Italy's **Trattoria
Giancarlo,** which has gained renown for its very good cooking and its celeb
sightings. Unfortunately, you pretty much have to be a star to even a glass of
water brought to your table. Personally, no matter how charming a meal is, I find
that lousy service leaves a bad taste in my mouth.

VERY EXPENSIVE

Avalon ⋆⋆ ECLECTIC   Follow the slim marble staircase into the elegant,
compact dining room. Careful attention to detail is clear, whether in the spray
of fresh flowers on each table or the daily chef's menu. (The regular menu
changes with the seasons.) Avalon has one of the most inventive kitchens in the
city, and it demonstrates its creativity through pairings of flavors rather than a
showy multiplicity of ingredients. Main courses favor fish and fowl, such as
steamed Boston fluke and Alaskan king crab with a sweet-pea sauce, or lightly
smoked Moulard duck breast with pommes Anna and a blackcurrant coulis.
Desserts include treats like pear-and-elderflower sorbet and a wide selection of
cheeses. The globe-trotting wine list represents New World and Old.

270 Adelaide St. W. (at John St.). ℭ 416/979-9918. Reservations required. Main courses C$29–$40
(US$20–$27). AE, DC, MC, V. Thurs noon–2pm; Mon–Sat 5:30–10pm. Subway: St. Andrew.

Barberian's ⋆ STEAK   Not getting enough protein? Get thee to Harry Bar-
berian's upscale steakhouse, which has been going strong since 1959 (his son,
Arron, has since taken over). The room is cozy in a clubby way, with dark woods,
framed newspapers, and pre-Confederation doodads. The menu rarely changes,
but you won't hear any grousing—the crowd is too busy slurping martinis. The
highlights are the 8 steaks, from 9-ounce sirloin to 23-ounce porterhouse, all
served with rice and spuds. The less traditional can partake of dishes like cheese
or beef fondue for two, which is on the late-night menu (10pm–midnight). For
all intents and purposes, there is only one dessert: Grand Marnier soufflé for
two. The wine list is about 1,000 strong, so bring your reading specs. Celebrity
sightings aren't uncommon, but autograph seeking is frowned upon.

Downtown Toronto Dining

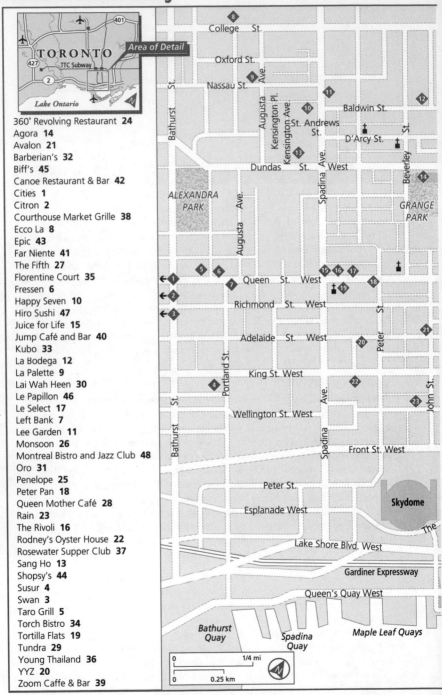

360° Revolving Restaurant **24**
Agora **14**
Avalon **21**
Barberian's **32**
Biff's **45**
Canoe Restaurant & Bar **42**
Cities **1**
Citron **2**
Courthouse Market Grille **38**
Ecco La **8**
Epic **43**
Far Niente **41**
The Fifth **27**
Florentine Court **35**
Fressen **6**
Happy Seven **10**
Hiro Sushi **47**
Juice for Life **15**
Jump Café and Bar **40**
Kubo **33**
La Bodega **12**
La Palette **9**
Lai Wah Heen **30**
Le Papillon **46**
Le Select **17**
Left Bank **7**
Lee Garden **11**
Monsoon **26**
Montreal Bistro and Jazz Club **48**
Oro **31**
Penelope **25**
Peter Pan **18**
Queen Mother Café **28**
Rain **23**
The Rivoli **16**
Rodney's Oyster House **22**
Rosewater Supper Club **37**
Sang Ho **13**
Shopsy's **44**
Susur **4**
Swan **3**
Taro Grill **5**
Torch Bistro **34**
Tortilla Flats **19**
Tundra **29**
Young Thailand **36**
YYZ **20**
Zoom Caffe & Bar **39**

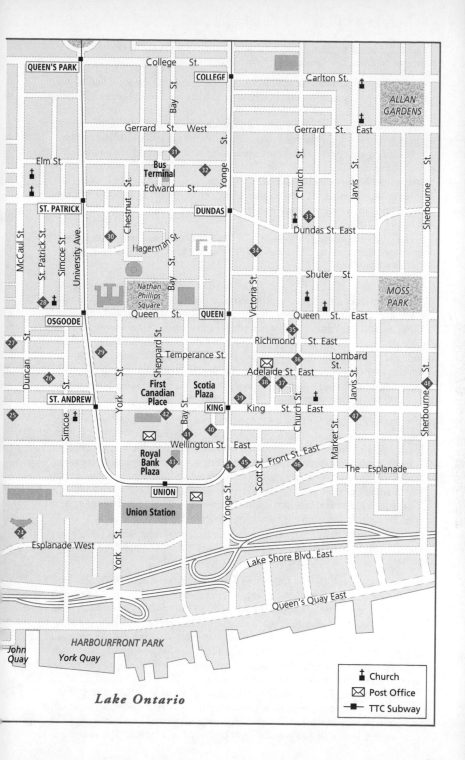

7 Elm St. ⓒ **416/597-0335.** Reservations required. Main courses C$22–$37 (US$15–$25). AE, DC, MC, V. Mon–Fri noon–2:30pm; daily 5pm–midnight. Subway: Dundas.

Canoe Restaurant & Bar 𝕽 CANADIAN   The inspiring view makes this the place to see Toronto lit up at night. The interior isn't so shabby, either, with polished wooden floors and furnishings. Corporate types predominate, not only because Canoe is in the Financial District, but also because the prices best suit expense accounts. The meat-heavy menu showcases modern Canadian cuisine. Grilled veal tenderloin served with acorn squash and warm sage-infused goat cheese vies for attention with Maritime sea scallops served with a tartlet of caramelized potatoes and double-smokes bacon. A few "spa inspired" dishes are lower in fat. The wine list only scratches the surface—roughly two-thirds of the bottles in stock aren't included—so if you're craving a certain vintage, be sure to ask.

54th floor, Toronto Dominion Tower, 66 Wellington St. W. ⓒ **416/364-0054.** www.oliverbonacini.com. Reservations required. Main courses C$24–$40 (US$16–$27). AE, DC, MC, V. Mon–Fri 11:45am–2:30pm and 5–10:30pm. Subway: King.

The Fifth 𝕽𝕽 ECLECTIC   *Je pense que Le Cinquième n'est pas comme des autres.* Ah, *pardon,* was I just speaking French? I must have been confused by the menu at The Fifth, which insists on listing all its plates *en français* and *en anglais.* *Crème Arlequin* is translated as—get ready for this—crème Arlequin (no, I'm not joking). *Ça va?* In fairness, though, the kitchen does serve stellar fare, like fluke stuffed with scallop mousse. The delectable food and first-rate service attract an upscale, chic crowd. Now if they could just fire the translator . . .

225 Richmond St. W. ⓒ **416/979-3005.** www.easyandthefifth.com. Reservations required. 3-course prix-fixe menu C$80 (US$54). Thurs–Sat 6pm–midnight. Subway: Osgoode.

Monsoon 𝕽 ASIAN   Monsoon is more famous for its award-winning interior design than for its food. That's a pity, because, while the brown-on-black Zen-like setting and the fabulously flattering lighting are easy on the eye, the cooking is subtly sensual. Sophisticated palates are familiar with Thai, Chinese, Japanese, and Indian flavors, but it's unusual to find them so seductively intertwined with North American staples—take for example the exquisite beef tenderloin in a Cabernet-teriyaki reduction that is teamed up with wasabi mashed potatoes. The wine list runs the gamut from French Bordeaux to Australian shiraz.

100 Simcoe St. ⓒ **416/979-7172.** www.monsoonrestaurant.ca. Reservations required. Main courses C$21–$37 (US$14–$25). AE, DC, MC, V. Mon–Fri noon–2:30pm; Mon–Sat 5:30pm–midnight. Subway: St. Andrew.

Susur 𝕽𝕽𝕽 FUSION   If you visited Toronto a few years ago, you might have had the good fortune to dine at an exquisite restaurant called Lotus. The eatery's chef and owner, Susur Lee, broke the hearts of the city's foodies when he decided to close it and travel abroad. After some stints in foreign kitchens—he got as far away as Singapore—Lee is back and better than ever. Susur is a delight. For such a high-end establishment, its decor is refreshingly low-key, with stark white walls and oyster-pale upholstery warmed with colored lights. There is no pretension here, in either the ambience or the fine service.

But the biggest draw is what's on the plate. Lee serves stellar cuisine in the true fusion spirit, blending Asian and Western ingredients, cooking methods, and presentation. The menu changes frequently, with bold, savory offerings like rare venison loin with Gorgonzola–haw berry–red wine sauce. The cooking is complex, and the wine list, while pricey, has been put together with extreme care. When in doubt, ask the well-informed serving staff for recommendations.

601 King St. W. © 416/603-2205. Reservations required. Main courses C$29–$43 (US$20–$29). AE, MC, V. Mon–Sat 6–10pm. Subway: St. Andrew. Take streetcar west to Bathurst Ave. and walk one block west to Portland St.

360 Revolving Restaurant 🌾 *Overrated* CONTINENTAL   Let's be frank: Most people do not come here for the food. The view's the thing, a breathtaking, awe-inspiring panorama that will make you see the city in a new light. Unfortunately, the kitchen doesn't keep pace—it offers uninspiring fare like cold crab and shrimp salad on Bibb lettuce. The highlight of the dessert list is a chocolate rendition of the CN Tower. The wine list makes for interesting viewing, with its collection of three-figure vintages, though there are a few choices by the glass.

CN Tower, 301 Front St. W. © 416/362-5411. Reservations required. Main courses C$25–$40 (US$17–$27). AE, DC, MC, V. May–Sept daily 10:30am–2:30pm; year-round daily 4:30–10:30pm. Subway: Union.

Tundra 🌾🌾 CANADIAN   A key element of the Hilton's recent C$25 million (US$15.8 million) renovation was the creation of this luxurious restaurant just off its foyer. Sophisticated and opulent, the restaurant is designed to evoke elements of the Canadian landscape. How does one suggest the majesty of, say, a giant redwood? With columns wrapped in semi-transparent fabric and lit from within, of course! (The stunning result is like a gargantuan Naguchi lamp.) Every detail, from the one-armed wing chairs to the Frette linens, is beautifully executed.

The sense of theater doesn't stop with the design—the cuisine is just as artful. Arctic char (a fish that's often called a hybrid of salmon and trout) is paired with Malapeque oysters and fried leeks; Nova Scotia lobster mates with tomato-avocado-bean salad and Yukon Gold potatoes. The results are elegantly complex. While the wine list is exhaustive, don't hesitate to ask for recommendations—service is well informed and helpful.

Hilton Toronto, 145 Richmond St. W. © 416/860-6800. Reservations strongly recommended. Main courses C$28–$40 (US$19–$27). AE, DC, MC, V. Daily 6:30–10:30am; Mon–Fri 11:30am–2pm; daily 5:30–11pm. Subway: Osgoode.

YYZ 🌾🌾 INTERNATIONAL   If you visited Toronto in 2001 or earlier, you might have had the good fortune to dine at the Mercer Street Grill. While that restaurant is no more, its owner, Simon Bower, has created a striking new spot in YYZ. Named after the call letters of Toronto's airport, the setting brings to mind a futuristic lounge—all chrome, steel, and glass. While the palette veers to the cool (unlike the city's other modernist spaces, there's not so much as a hint of greenery to temper its android appeal), this is now home to some of the hottest cooking in town. For starters, rare duck breast is paired with both spicy ginger and sweet pineapple. The substantial mains, like the rack of lamb with a celery-root-and-potato mash and mint puree, are artfully done. Do try to save space for dessert: the warm pumpkin tart is a great way to finish.

345 Adelaide St. W. © 416/599-3399. Reservations required. Main courses C$26–$34 (US$18–$23). AE, MC, V. Mon–Sat 5–10:30pm. Subway: Osgoode.

EXPENSIVE

Agora 🌾 MEDITERRANEAN   I'm biased—restaurants attached to larger institutions usually scare me off. Agora and Jamie Kennedy at the Museum (see p. 100) are exceptions. Located in the beautiful Tannenbaum sculpture gallery of the AGO, and open only for lunch and brunch, Agora serves food that's inventive without being artsy. It's worth a trip even if you're not visiting the gallery. The menu does have its precious moments, like "Still life with aubergine," but the food is uniformly delightful. Some dishes play it straight with a continental flair, like grilled niçoise-style tuna with French green beans. The weekend brunch glams up scrambled eggs with fresh truffle shavings and chives; the cinnamon crepes with an almond-ricotta filling and apricot coulis are a treat.

At the Art Gallery of Ontario, 317 Dundas St. W. ℂ 416/977-0414. Reservations recommended for lunch. Main courses C$12–$20 (US$8.15–$14). AE, DC, MC, V. Tues–Fri noon–2:30pm, Sat–Sun 11am–3pm. Subway: St. Patrick.

Café Societa ⭐ CONTINENTAL   The Lilliputian dining room is cramped, the menu is the shortest in the city, and yet the crowds can't stay away. Why? Simply because the food is seductive. The trick is in the unusual marriages of fruits and vegetables flavoring many of the dishes. Rosti and rhubarb compote enliven a veal chop, and it turns out that grilled calamari tastes better with citrus fruit. Who knew? The highlight of the triad of desserts is chocolate mousse with heavy cream and paper-thin pear shavings.

796 College St. ℂ 416/588-7490. Reservations recommended. Main courses C$12–$21 (US$8.15–$14). MC, V. Sat–Sun 11am–3pm; daily 6–11pm. Subway: Queen's Park, then any streetcar west to Ossington Ave.

Chiado ⭐ PORTUGUESE   Alone in this Mediterranean-obsessed part of town, Chiado serves modern Portuguese cuisine. Designed to evoke opulence, with marble floors, oil paintings, and fresh orchids, it draws a sophisticated crowd. Servers are models of Euro professionalism, attentive without hovering. The menu favors seafood, from starters—such as grilled squid with roasted peppers—to entrees, such as poached or grilled salted cod. Fresh fish is flown in daily. The fowl and game dishes include a choice of braised rabbit or capon. Don't skimp on the lovingly prepared sweets. The wine list is a treat. It includes many unfamiliar but rich and complex wines, most priced in the bargain range.

484 College St. (at Concorde Ave.). ℂ 416/538-1910. Reservations required. Main courses C$17–$30 (US$12–$20). AE, DC, MC, V. Mon–Sat noon–3pm; Mon–Thurs 5–10pm, Fri–Sat 5pm–midnight. Subway: Queen's Park, then any streetcar west to Bathurst St.

Epic ⭐⭐ INTERNATIONAL   Not that I would ever counsel a visitor to stay within the confines of his or her hotel, but this stunning restaurant at the Fairmont Royal York is definitely worth a visit. The scene here is one of unabashed luxury, with velvety banquettes and Murano glass chandeliers. The attentive service is in keeping with the elegant atmosphere—don't come here if you don't want to be pampered.

The menu holds up its end of the deal, with luxurious ingredients that are cleverly matched up. The starters set the tone—think Dungeness crab salad with Segruva caviar, or a seafood tower that is built with the freshest lobster, scallops, and oysters. Mains are equally well turned out, varying from truffle-polenta-stuffed pheasant with asparagus and shallots, to the morel-crusted venison loin with seared Quebec foie gras. One of my favorite dishes—the tempura-fried halibut and hand-cut fries (an upscale version of fish 'n' chips)—is available only at lunch.

Fairmont Royal York, 100 Front St. W. ℂ 416/860-6949. Reservations recommended. Main courses C$22–$34 (US$15–$23). AE, DC, MC, V. Mon–Thurs 7–10am, noon–2pm, 5:30–10pm; Fri 7–10am, noon–2pm, 5:30–11pm; Sat 7–11am, 5:30–11pm; Sun 7am–2pm, 5:30–10pm.

Far Niente ☆☆ AMERICAN   A hangout favored by the suited set, this restaurant offers fine cuisine in a casual setting. The room recalls California, with an earthy palette, mounds of greenery, wine racks, and simple wooden tables and chairs. The kitchen uses garden-fresh ingredients and a light touch. The menu designates many staples—including tuna steak, grilled salmon, and even a Caesar salad—as "living well" dishes, which have reduced fat, cholesterol, and calories. You might try Sonoma spinach salad with cherry tomatoes, button mushrooms, and bean sprouts; the pumpkin ravioli with cranberries and pecans in apple cider butter sauce; or the skillet-seared sea bass in a saffron-vanilla sauce with ginger-scented veggies and mashed Yukon Gold potatoes. Steaks are a specialty, with filet mignon and New York strip loin available in 6- to 14-ounce cuts.

Downstairs is **Soul of the Vine,** a wine bar that has its own menu, mainly appetizers and pasta. The room can get loud and smoky, so serious eaters should stay upstairs.

187 Bay St. (at Wellington St.). ℂ **416/214-9922.** Reservations recommended. Main courses C$18–$36 (US$12–$25). AE, DC, MC, V. Mon–Fri 11:30am–11pm, Sat–Sun 5–11pm. Subway: King.

Jump Café and Bar ☆☆ AMERICAN   Jump is, appropriately enough, always hopping. A sprawling space in Commerce Court, it can be tricky to find. Just follow the buzz—as the decibel level rises (above romantic, but not uncomfortable), you'll know you're on the right track. Power brokers drop by for lunch or after-work drinks. The dinner scene is a mix of celebratory couples and suits in deal-making mode. The restaurant is such a see-and-be-seen spot that you might suspect it's all show and no substance. Actually, the food is anything but an afterthought. To start, consider steamed mussels in ginger-and-coconut-milk broth, or grilled tiger shrimps on Thai mango-peanut salad. The menu features "suit-able" dishes like grilled 10-ounce New York black Angus steak with Yukon Gold fries, salsa, and mushroom gravy. The more adventurous have other choices, such as roasted sea bass with fragrant coconut basmati rice and green curry, or *osso buco* with spinach-and-lemon risotto. The wine list favors the New World, and there are a fair number of selections by the glass. Luxe desserts will set your diet back by about a month. Service is smooth, and the only complaint I could possibly make is that Jump never seems to settle down.

1 Wellington St. W. ℂ **416/363-3400.** Reservations required. Main courses C$19–$32 (US$13–$22). AE, DC, MC, V. Mon–Fri 11:30am–11pm, Sat 4:30–11pm. Subway: King.

Lai Wah Heen ☆☆☆ CHINESE   This is one hotel dining room where you'll find more locals than visitors. The interior is vintage Art Deco; spare pictograms dominate the walls of the two-level space. A suited-up crowd dominates at lunch; at dinner, a few dolled-up couples manage to sneak in. The massive menu is mainly Cantonese, with some Sichuan specialties. It offers more than a dozen shark's fin soups, from thick broth with bamboo fungi to Alaska king crab bisque. Abalone gets similar attention, shredded and stir-fried with bean sprouts or braised with fresh vegetables and oyster sauce. Those with tamer tastes (or restricted budgets) can choose from meat or noodle dishes; the dim sum list alone goes on for several pages. There are several lunch and dinner prix-fixe specials, which offer five or six dishes for C$38 (US$26) and up.

In the Metropolitan Hotel, 110 Chestnut St. ℂ **416/977-9899.** Reservations recommended. Main courses C$16–$30 (US$11–$20). AE, DC, MC, V. Daily 11:30am–3pm; Sun–Thurs 5:30–10:30pm, Fri–Sat 5:30–11pm. Subway: St. Patrick.

Oro *✿* CONTINENTAL   The trappings of modern luxury set the scene, with blond wood, a tile floor, and a substantial fireplace that warms that room (figuratively if not always literally). In its Eaton Centre neighborhood, Oro is uniquely sophisticated. Softly lit tables sit far apart—this is the perfect spot for a romantic rendezvous. The menu ventures further and further from its Italianate roots, with showstoppers like West-meets-East hoisin-tamarind glazed pork tenderloin accompanied by cumin-scented red onion puree. Desserts like the white chocolate cheesecake bombe are equally delightful. The lengthy wine list leans toward Italy and America, with only a select few by the glass. The oft-praised service is relaxed but attentive.

45 Elm St. *©* **416/597-0155.** www.ororestaurant.com. Reservations recommended. Main courses C$18–$40 (US$12–$27). AE, DC, MC, V. Mon–Fri noon–2:30pm, Mon–Sat 5:30–10:30pm. Subway: Dundas.

Rain *✿* ASIAN   One of Toronto's newest hot spots, Rain has gained a certain notoriety for employing a bouncer at the door; word has it that the bouncer determines who's chic enough to make it into this den of cool, reservations be damned. The *Toronto Star*'s restaurant critic was turned away, despite having a reservation; most famously, pop star Nelly Furtado was refused entry to her own private party (the restaurant's owners refuse to discuss the incident). You either love it or you hate it—Rain evokes strong emotions. Everyone agrees that the decor is a seductive hit, with its waterfall walls, backlit frosted-glass bars and screens, and sophisticated low black banquettes. The menu is equally sleek, albeit a tad confusing: Instead of dividing appetizers from entrees, it jumbles dishes together, with only their price tags indicating their relative size. The cooking is lovely, with some standouts like five-spice Peking duck roll, and miso black cod atop tatsoi greens. While the service is adequate, it's a little clunky for such a swank place.

19 Mercer St. *©* **416/599-7246.** Reservations required. Dishes C$10–$30 (US$6.80–$20). AE, MC, V. Tues–Sat 5:30–11pm. Subway: St. Andrew.

MODERATE

Cities BISTRO   This charming bistro, where a rococo Elvis presides over the bar, personifies the pleasures and problems of metropolitan life. It's overcrowded—19 tables for two cram the narrow room, forcing neighbors to rub elbows. The food, however, makes it all worthwhile. The menu is deliberately short, allowing the kitchen to focus hothouse-flower care on its featured selections: rack of lamb, Atlantic salmon, veal tenderloin. Starters, like three-mushroom salad, get equal attention.

859 Queen St. W. *©* **416/599-7720.** Main courses C$12–$20 (US$8.15–$14). AE, MC, V. Daily noon–2:30pm and 5–10:30pm. Subway: Osgoode, then any streetcar west to Bathurst St.

Citron ECLECTIC   At once chic and attitude-free, Citron draws casual but hip 20-somethings. The menu borrows heavily from every corner of the globe, favoring seafood and vegetarian offerings. North African couscous stew, Tex-Mex lasagna, and Thai-spiced salmon compete for attention. For dessert, my sweet-tooth side recommends the divine white chocolate cheesecake.

813 Queen St. W. *©* **416/504-2647.** Reservations not accepted. Main courses C$12–$20 (US$8.15–$14). AE, MC, V. Mon–Thurs 5–10:30pm, Fri–Sat 5–11pm. Subway: Osgoode, then any streetcar west to Bathurst St.

Ecco La ITALIAN   Tiny trattorias litter Little Italy, but Ecco La stands out. The rustic dining room is all red brick and ochre walls, with a wood-burning pizza oven as the centerpiece. Arugula and smoked salmon make a good match for robust tomatoes and Parmesan. There's also pasta (rigatoni goes nicely with wild mushrooms, sage cream, and truffle essence), and tender, meaty main dishes, which include capon and salmon. The menu always offers a vegetarian risotto, too. Desserts are strictly for chocolate lovers.

356 College St. © 416/926-9899. Reservations recommended. Main courses C$10–$21 (US$6.80–$14). AE, MC, V. Mon–Fri 11am–1am, Sat–Sun 4pm–1am. Subway: Queen's Park, then any streetcar west to Brunswick Ave.

La Bodega FRENCH This is a quiet spot infused with Gallic charm. In a turn-of-the-century town house, La Bodega is a short walk from the Art Gallery of Ontario. The two dining rooms have fireplaces, and tapestries and gilt-framed mirrors line the walls. The menu is traditional French, with a focus on meats. Grilled beef tenderloin soaks up cognac sauce, and duck breast mixes well with wild blueberries. The wine list boasts some Bordeaux *grandes dames,* and there's a nice mix of Ontario vintages, too.

30 Baldwin St. © 416/977-1287. Reservations recommended. Main courses C$15–$27 (US$10–$18). AE, DC, MC, V. Mon–Fri 11:30am–2:30pm; Mon–Sat 5–11pm. Subway: St. Patrick.

La Palette ⚜ BISTRO This is a terrific, offbeat addition to the Kensington Market neighborhood. It's so good, in fact, that you almost wonder why no one else ever thought of locating a classic French bistro on the edge of Chinatown. A quartet of Gallic flags announces its presence; inside, the 30-seat dining room is cozy and informal, with considerate, low-key service. The menu is classic, from ballantine of chicken stuffed with peppers and rice to lamb chops with a crusty coating of mustard and rosemary. If you're as much as a dessert fiend as I am, save room for irresistible citron tart and dark chocolate cake.

256 Augusta Ave. © 416/929-4900. Reservations recommended. Main courses C$10–$18 (US$6.80–$12). AE, MC, V. Sun–Thurs 5:30–11pm, Fri–Sat noon–midnight. Subway: St. Patrick, then streetcar west to Augusta Ave.

Le Select Bistro BISTRO What says Paris bistro to you? Le Select sets the tone with posters, decorative objects straight from *grand-mère*'s attic, and sultry jazz in the background. Breadbaskets hang from the ceiling above each table, and require gentle coaxing to reach the diners. The menu emphasizes traditional

---

⌒Kids **Family-Friendly Restaurants**

Grano (p. 113) Don't worry that a noisy babe-in-arms might disrupt diners—this lively, slightly chaotic eatery welcomes families. The owners have four kids, and they love to fuss over the *bambini.*

Kensington Kitchen (p. 104) Whimsically decorated, with colorful toys and model airplanes. It seems to be easier to get kids to eat their greens when veggies are tucked into pita sandwiches, like the ones here.

Millie's Bistro (p. 111) This is a perennially popular spot with families. There's a special menu for tykes, and most of the Mediterranean food can be eaten without cutlery.

Shopsy's (p. 96) When the kids are sick of eating out and craving comfort food, this is where to take them. Home-style chili and macaroni and cheese hit the spot, and ice cream dominates a whole section of the menu.

rib-sticking fare such as steak frites and cassoulet, all nicely done. The service can be a trifle slow, but the casually dressed professionals don't seem to mind.

328 Queen St. W. ⓒ **416/596-6405.** www.leselect.com. Reservations recommended. Main courses C$13–$33 (US$8.85–$22). AE, DC, MC, V. Daily 11:30am–11:30pm. Subway: Osgoode.

Mildred Pierce ⭐⭐ ECLECTIC   Named after a Joan Crawford film, this restaurant is appropriately theatrical. Murals of a Roman feast cover the walls (a local in-joke, they depict characters including the restaurant's owner). The menu fits right in, rich in inspiration and dramatic flourishes borrowed from different countries. Grilled salmon accompanies saffron risotto and a ragout of fennel, baby beets, and bok choy, while a Thai hot pot boasts tiger shrimp, scallops, mussels, and clams brewing in a coconut-lime-cilantro sauce. The short wine list includes options from Italy, Spain, South Africa, and California. Lush desserts include maple crème brûlée, and a rustic cranberry and walnut tart.

99 Sudbury St. ⓒ **416/588-5695.** Reservations recommended for lunch and dinner; not accepted for Sun brunch. Main courses C$17–$26 (US$12–$18). AE, DC, MC, V. Mon–Fri noon–2pm, Sun 10am–3pm; Sun–Thurs 5:30–10pm, Fri–Sat 5:30–11pm. Subway: Osgoode, then any streetcar west to Dovercourt; walk south on Dovercourt and turn right at Sudbury.

Peter Pan LIGHT FARE   When I was in high school, Peter Pan was the classy restaurant you went to for pre-prom dinner or a big date. The crowd at this fun, relaxed place is forever young, easily impressed by the old-fashioned bar, ever-changing art exhibits, and friendly service. The menu is awash in Eurasian food-speak; simpler dishes are best. The Peter Pan burger is always a top choice. Desserts are strictly for sweet tooths.

373 Queen St. W. ⓒ **416/593-0917.** Reservations recommended. Main courses C$10–$18 (US$6.80–$12). AE, MC, V. Mon–Wed noon–midnight, Thurs–Sat noon–1am, Sun noon–11pm. Subway: Osgoode.

Pony BISTRO   On the periphery of hyper-trendy Little Italy, Pony is nevertheless the kind of place where you can relax. The candlelit dining room is charming, the upholstered chairs are comfy, and the service is smooth. The menu sticks mainly to bistro classics, such as roasted chicken stuffed with prosciutto, smoked mozzarella, and apple slices. The Caesar salad has the creamiest dressing in town—even a devoted calorie-counter won't be able to resist.

488 College St. ⓒ **416/923-7665.** Reservations recommended. Main courses C$16–$25 (US$11–$17). AE, MC, V. Mon–Sat 5–11pm. Subway: Queen's Park, then any streetcar west to Bathurst.

Sang Ho ⭐ CHINESE   There's no end of eateries in the eastern end of Chinatown, but Sang Ho will be the one with the longest queue out front. The restaurant boasts not only a top-notch kitchen, but also a lovely dining room filled with several teeming aquariums. The regular menu of 100-plus dishes never changes; wall-mounted boards list many specials of the day. Seafood—shrimp, clams, or red snapper—is the obvious choice. Service is speedy and responsive. Try to go on a weeknight, when there's no more than a short wait for a table.

536 Dundas St. W. ⓒ **416/596-1685.** Reservations not accepted. Main courses C$8–$18 (US$5.45–$12). MC, V. Sun–Thurs noon–10pm, Fri–Sat noon–11pm. Subway: St. Patrick.

Swan ECLECTIC   The room brings to mind a retro soda fountain, with a counter and swirly stools on one side, and booths with Formica tables on the other. Just don't expect to find a strawberry-banana float on the menu. The youngish hipsters who congregate here slurp up martinis and oysters. Happily, the menu avoids the trendy trap, managing both roasted capon with bourbon gravy and corn fritters, and braised beef short ribs marinated in beer and marmalade.

There's a nice selection of wines, almost all available by the glass. The popular weekend brunch features the usual eggy plates as well as some surprises: spicy Moroccan olives or smoked arctic char salad, anyone?

892 Queen St. W. ✆ 416/532-0452. Reservations recommended. Main courses C$15–$20 (US$10–$14). AE, DC, MC, V. Mon–Fri noon–4:30pm; Sun–Fri 5–10:30pm, Sat 5–11pm; Sat–Sun 11:30am–2:30pm. Subway: Osgoode, then any streetcar west to Euclid Ave.

Taro Grill ✿ ECLECTIC   Pass through the curtain hanging at the door, and enter a hip new world. Actually, it's not that new, but the Taro Grill has something that most hot spots of the moment can't claim—staying power. Its secret? A mix of clever cooking, helpful service, and a glamorous high-ceilinged space. The menu refuses to be easily characterized. Just when you think you've pegged the Cal-Ital pizza-pasta-salad triad, out of the blue comes tempura veggies or Asian-influenced New Zealand lamb. Affordable bottles, mainly from Australia and South Africa, fill the wine list.

492 Queen St. W. ✆ 416/504-1320. Reservations recommended. Main courses C$13–$20 (US$8.85–$14). AE, MC, V. Daily noon–4pm and 6–10pm. Subway: Osgoode, then any streetcar west to Bathurst St.

Veni Vidi Vici ✿✿ ITALIAN/FUSION   This is Little Italy's brightest new addition, a little gem that serves delicious food in a swanky setting—but, unlike many of its neighborhood cousins, it does so without attitude. I like it even better than established neighborhood favorite Ecco La. There's no sign outside, just a gilt-covered fresco of a mustachioed deity looming over the doorway. Inside, the staff is quick to usher diners to high-backed velvet banquettes.

The menu can be divided into two parts. On the Italian side, there are pasta dishes such as linguine with mixed seafood, or risotto with portobello, cremini, and porcini mushrooms. But the Asian-inspired fusion plates are the showstoppers: think cashew-studded sea bass with fennel, or phyllo-wrapped salmon with basmati rice. Desserts return to the classics, like crème brûlée with fresh berries. The wine list is particularly strong in Italian reds.

650 College St. (at Grace St.). ✆ 416/536-8550. Reservations recommended. Main courses C$13–$25 (US$8.85–$17). AE, MC, V. Tues–Sun 11am–3pm and 5pm–midnight. Subway: Queen's Park, then streetcar west to Grace St.

INEXPENSIVE

Happy Seven CHINESE   This eatery boasts kitschy touches like plastic Buddhas and a tank full of fish and crawly critters. They may not be everybody's cup of (green) tea, but the kitchen is widely acknowledged as one of the best in Chinatown. The menu is classic Cantonese, with a few Sichuan choices. Seafood dishes are a favorite, though there are many plates for vegetarians; portions are extremely generous.

358 Spadina Ave. ✆ 416/971-9820. Reservations not accepted. Main courses C$7–$15 (US$4.75–$10). MC, V. Daily 4pm–5am. Subway: Spadina, then LRT south to Baldwin St.

Kalendar ✿✿ LIGHT FARE   I can't go to this restaurant without snickering at the menu, but the food inspires satisfied sighs. There are sandwiches stuffed with portobello mushrooms, havarti, and roasted red peppers, and five "scrolls"—phyllo pastries filled with delights like artichoke hearts, eggplant, and hummus. The "nannettes" (pizzas) are baked nan breads topped with ingredients like smoked salmon, capers, and red onions. The ambiance recalls a French bistro. In summer the sidewalk patio is just the place to sit and watch the world.

546 College St. (just west of Bathurst St.). ✆ 416/923-4138. Main courses C$10–$13 (US$6.80–$8.85). MC, V. Mon–Fri 11am–4pm. Subway: Queen's Park, then any streetcar west to Bathurst St.

Lee Garden CHINESE   If lines are a measure of the success of a restaurant, then Lee Garden is, deservedly, the hands-down Toronto champ. The draw is a Cantonese menu weighted heavily toward seafood. Although there's no shark fin, there's no shortage of shrimp, lobster, and cod. The signature dish is fork-tender grandfather smoked chicken with honey and sesame seeds. The kitchen works wonders with tofu, too.

331 Spadina Ave. © **416/593-9524.** Reservations not accepted. Main courses C$10–$22 (US$6.80–$15). AE, MC, V. Daily 4pm–midnight. Subway: Spadina, then LRT south to Baldwin St.

Penelope GREEK   If you're in a rush to see a show at the Royal Alex or Roy Thomson Hall, this is one of your best bets. Give the friendly staff an hour or less, and they will stuff you with spanakopita, moussaka, or souvlaki. This is the home of hearty food in a hurry.

225 King St. W. © **416/351-9393.** Reservations recommended for pre-theater dinner. Main courses C$13–$22 (US$8.85–$15). AE, DC, MC, V. Mon–Wed 11:30am–10pm, Thurs–Fri 11:30am–11:30pm, Sat 4:30–11:30pm. Subway: St. Andrew.

Queen Mother Café ASIAN   Fussy dowager this is not. Beloved by vegetarians, trend-hoppers, and reformed hippies, the Queen Mum is a Queen Street West institution with old-fashioned wooden furnishings and an underlit interior. The menu's lengthy descriptions are required reading. "Ping Gai" turns out to be chicken breast marinated in garlic, coriander, and peppercorns, served with lime sauce atop steamed rice. "Salmon Sottha" is served with hotter-than-hot Cambodian chili sauce and black rice. The menu is anything but pricey, so the wine list is a surprise, with few bargains in sight.

208 Queen St. W. © **416/598-4719.** Reservations accepted only for groups of 6 or more. Main courses C$11–$18 (US$7.50–$12). AE, MC, V. Daily noon–1am. Subway: Osgoode.

The Rivoli ⚔⚔ FUSION   The Riv is better known as a club than as a restaurant—the 125-seat back room plays host to live music, stand-up comics, and poetry readings. What most people don't know is that the kitchen is just as creative. Chicken marinated in jerk spices comes with sautéed spinach and plantain chips; mussels are steamed in green curry jazzed up with coconut and lime. The less adventurous can partake of the spinach-and-pear salad or the house burger (beef on a challah bun with caramelized onions). The low prices draw a mixed crowd of starving artists, budget-conscious boomers, and Gen-Xers. *One caveat:* If you're planning to talk over dinner, get there before the back room starts filling up.

332 Queen St. W. © **416/597-0794.** www.rivoli.ca. Reservations accepted only for groups of 6 or more. Main courses C$9–$19 (US$6.10–$13). AE, MC, V. Daily noon–2am. Subway: Osgoode.

Sottovoce LIGHT FARE   The name of this tiny eatery is more than a little misleading. *Sotto* (soft) it isn't. Forget trying to have a conversation and instead try to score one of the window seats, which afford a full view of College Street. The youngish crowd that mills in after 7pm enjoys the pumped-up music that refuses to stay in the background. In the middle of this frenetic scene you will find the most lovingly prepared, and least expensive, salads and focaccia sandwiches in town. There are daily pasta specials, and many wines by the glass.

595 College St. © **416/536-4564.** Reservations not accepted. Main courses C$6–$12 (US$4.10–$8.15). AE, MC, V. Mon–Sat 5:30–11pm. Subway: Queen's Park, then any streetcar west to Clinton St.

Tortilla Flats TEX-MEX   Park your fear of sour cream and oil at the door, because it will spoil the fun. The dining room is all riotous color and southwestern knickknacks; think Georgia O'Keeffe meets Salvador Dalí. The crowd is mainly 20- to 30-something, and a number of boomers come for the weekend brunch and the best frozen margaritas in town. The menu never changes, though there are some daily specials. Potato skins piled high with bacon and sharp cheddar are at the top of my list; the enchilada and chimichurri platters, which include rice, salad, and refried beans, are pretty satisfying, too.

429 Queen St. W. ℂ 416/593-9870. Reservations accepted only for groups of 5 or more. Main courses C$8–$20 (US$5.45–$14). MC, V. Sun–Wed noon–10pm, Thurs–Sat noon–11pm. Subway: Osgoode, then any streetcar west to Spadina Ave.

3 Downtown East

EXPENSIVE

Biff's ✿ BISTRO   The same team that created a trio of excellent eateries with Jump, Canoe, and Auberge du Pommier have been hard at work again. The intent this time was to create a classic bistro, with dishes priced somewhat lower than at the other establishments (in keeping with true bistro tradition, *naturellement*). The setting hits all the right notes, with wood paneling and potted palms among the cozy-but-chic touches. The menu is equally fine, with pan-fried halibut covered with a second skin of thinly sliced potatoes, and traditional roast leg of lamb. The prime downtown location is a boon for Financial District types at lunch and theatergoers in the evening (the St. Lawrence and the Hummingbird centers are a stone's throw away).

4 Front St. E. (at Yonge St.). ℂ 416/860-0086. Reservations strongly recommended. Main courses C$18–$28 (US$12–$19). AE, DC, MC, V. Mon–Fri 11:30am–2:30pm; Mon–Sat 5:30–11pm. Subway: Union or King.

Courthouse Market Grille ✿ INTERNATIONAL   This hangout for the suited set boasts gargantuan fluted columns, sky-high ceilings, swinging chandeliers, and miles of marble. Pretty good for an 1850 building that used to be a jail. Financial District types lap it up, along with generous martinis. The menu features grilled and rotisserie meats of excellent quality, though timid seasoning will not please daring palates. Appetizers are uniformly fine, with simple but well-executed numbers like steamed Prince Edward Island mussels in creamy white wine sauce. The wine list includes some impressive vintages—and prices.

57 Adelaide St. E. ℂ 416/214-9379. Reservations required. Main courses C$15–$32 (US$10–$22). AE, DC, MC, V. Mon–Wed 11:30am–10pm, Thurs–Fri 11:30am–midnight, Sat 5:30pm–midnight. Subway: King.

Hiro Sushi ✿ JAPANESE   Widely regarded as the best sushi chef in the city, Hiro Yoshida draws a horde of Financial District types at lunch and mainly couples at dinner. The monochromatic setting is comfortably minimalist, and diners are encouraged to relax and leave their meal in Hiro's capable hands. The sushi varieties range from the expected to the inventive; you can also choose sashimi, tempura, and bento box combinations. Service can be rather slow. Forget the few wines listed in favor of sake or beer.

171 King St. E. ℂ 416/304-0550. Reservations recommended. Main courses C$20–$30 (US$14–$20). AE, DC, MC, V. Mon–Fri noon–2:30pm; Mon–Sat 6–10:30pm. Subway: King.

Rosewater Supper Club ✿ INTERNATIONAL   This triple-decked pleasure dome is packed almost every night with dressed-up diners who pass the time checking each other out. Personally, I'm still caught on the scenery: Marble, moldings, and a waterfall make quite the impression. So does the menu, which casually tours the globe. First up are delectables like carpaccio of seared caribou with a citrus-gin relish. Main courses include roast sirloin of lamb with parsnip gratin and hazelnut sauce, and coq au vin with butternut squash. The can't-miss desserts include rhubarb apple crisp with a vanilla-plum sorbet. The serious wine list focuses mainly on France and California, with some excellent Ontario vintages.

19 Toronto St. (at Adelaide). © **416/214-5888.** Reservations required. Main courses C$20–$32 (US$14–$22). AE, DC, MC, V. Mon–Fri 11:30am–2:30pm and 5:30–10:30pm, Sat 5:30–11:30pm. Subway: King.

Torch Bistro ⭐ BISTRO   The Senator Restaurant brought back the days when red meat, rich food, and cigar smoking weren't considered a threat to one's health. It closed in 2000 to make way for the Torch Bistro, a paean to the classic French bistro. The decor is much the same, with etched-glass doors and heavy wood paneling, but the menu is entirely new: think smoked duck breast with shiitake mushroom risotto, or grilled provimi calves liver with braised red cabbage and crispy pancetta. Upstairs, things haven't changed at all: there's jazz at the glamorous Top O' the Senator (see chapter 9), and the Victory Lounge for cigar aficionados.

253 Victoria St. © **416/364-7517.** Reservations required for dinner. Main courses C$16–$36 (US$11–$25). AE, DC, MC, V. Tues–Thurs 5–11pm, Fri–Sat 5pm–midnight, Sun 5–10pm. Subway: Dundas.

Zoom Caffe & Bar ⭐ INTERNATIONAL   Perhaps because its design is so striking, Zoom has had some trouble being taken seriously as a restaurant. Located in the space of a long-gone bank, it has a vaulted ceiling, velvet lounges, and halogen lighting—a lovely setting for the Beautiful People. Its oft-overlooked menu is short but to the point. It features creations like taro root–encrusted foie gras as a

---

Tips **Savory Surfing**

Trying to decide between two equally tantalizing restaurants? Why not sneak a peek at their menus online? The websites listed here will give you different perspectives on the city's eateries.

Toronto Life Online (www.torontolife.com)   Look to this magazine's "Best of T.O." section to learn where to find the city's best bets for gelato, falafel, or panini. The site also offers a section filled with reviews of just about every restaurant around town. There's a $25 Gourmet Guide for those who want to dine well without breaking the bank.

Toronto.com (www.toronto.com)   This site boasts a lot of features, but its restaurant reviews are the biggest draw for me. A photo or two usually accompanies the reviews, to give you a sense of what that space is like.

Send Me Food (www.sendmefood.com)   If you're tired from a day of sightseeing and want dinner to come to you, a visit to this site is essential. Simply select your favorite food and your Toronto neighborhood or suburb, and the guide will cook up a list of names and numbers.

TorDine (www.tordine.com)   This award-winning site purports to be the best Toronto dining guide. You'll find restaurant reviews penned by average food-loving folks, as well as coupons and special deals. You can search the directory by name, food type, or price, and you can make reservations online. Each entry gives descriptive details, from dress codes to wheelchair access.

starter, and a main course of "wonder spiced" lamb loin with smoked corn polenta and plantains. Desserts are less esoteric, though no less satisfying (I can't resist the chocolate mud pie). On the wine list, bargains are in short supply. And this is *the* spot for private parties, so be sure to call ahead.

18 King St. E. ✆ 416/861-9872. www.zoomrestaurant.com. Reservations recommended. Main courses C$18–$36 (US$12–$25). AE, DC, MC, V. Mon–Fri noon–3pm; Mon–Tues 5–11pm, Wed–Sat 5pm–midnight. Subway: King.

MODERATE

Florentine Court ITALIAN   The granddaddy of Toronto's many Italian restaurants, the Florentine Court has been going strong since 1968. The kitchen hasn't changed much over the years, because its saucy Northern Italian specialties have never gone out of vogue. Veal scaloppine appears in various guises, served straight up with white-wine sauce or lightly breaded and paired with herbed tomato sauce. Homemade pastas come with creamy sauces, and there's a selection of surf 'n' turf dishes, too. The list of Italian vintages—all personally selected by the restaurant's owner—is a delight.

97 Church St. ✆ 416/364-3687. Reservations recommended. Main courses C$13–$40 (US$8.85–$27). AE, DC, MC, V. Tues–Fri noon–2pm; Tues–Sat 5:30–10:30pm. Subway: Queen.

Montreal Bistro and Jazz Club QUEBECOIS   Ontario and Quebec share a border, but it's no mean feat to find top-notch *tourtière* (traditional beef, veal, and pork pie) in Toronto. Anyone who craves Quebecois staples like pea soup and smoked-meat sandwiches can return their train ticket and stop at this bistro. Besides being a restaurant, this is one of the city's premier jazz clubs, so you can *écouter* while you *manger.*

65 Sherbourne St. (at Adelaide). ✆ 416/363-0179. www.montrealbistro.com. Reservations recommended. Main courses C$10–$22 (US$6.80–$15). AE, DC, MC, V. Mon–Fri 11:30am–3pm; Mon–Thurs 6–11pm, Fri–Sat 6pm–midnight. Subway: King, then any streetcar east to Sherbourne St.

Rodney's Oyster House SEAFOOD   You could pass this restaurant a half-dozen times and not see it from the street. The tiny sign points, Alice-in-Wonderland style, to a flight of stairs down to the basement. Follow them into a series of aquarium-cluttered rooms with fishing nets around the walls. A favorite with the Financial District set, Rodney's is rowdy at all times of day. The main draw is oysters, and the lobster and salmon dishes are worth more than a look. The drink list is a mile long, though there are only about a dozen wines.

469 King St. W. ✆ 416/363-8105. Reservations recommended. Main courses C$16–$40 (US$11–$27). AE, DC, MC, V. Mon–Sat 11:30am–midnight. Subway: St. Andrew.

INEXPENSIVE

Hello Toast LIGHT FARE   Humorist Fran Lebowitz once asked why there were places called Bonjour Croissant but not Hello Toast. Well, now there is. Gleaming toasters and retro furniture bedeck the kitschy dining room. The menu is a mix of pizza and pasta specials, with a few salads, soups, and rich desserts mixed in. If you're springing for toast, choose the inspired challah.

993 Queen St. E. ✆ 416/778-7299. Main courses C$7–$15 (US$4.75–$10). MC, V. Tues–Sun noon–10pm. Subway: Queen, then any streetcar east to Pape Ave.

Kubo ASIAN   From its perch just east of the Eaton Centre, Kubo beckons. The scene is all swanky minimalism, with loft-like ceilings and manicured plants. Pretty cool for an old Sears warehouse. The short menu bestows goofy names on its Asian-inspired offerings ("To Fumanchu With Love" is a tofu stir-fry with broccoli, shiitake mushrooms, and oyster sauce). The real attraction for the so-hip-it-hurts 20-something crowd? Divine drinks, like the sake martini.

155 Dalhousie St. (at Dundas St. W.). ✆ 416/366-5826. Main courses C$10–$14 (US$6.80–$9.50). AE, MC, V. Mon–Sat 6–10:30pm, Sun 11am–3pm. Subway: Dundas.

Le Papillon QUEBECOIS   If you thought crepes were simply for breakfast, stop by Le Papillon for re-education. While there are many fruit-filled numbers, the best are savory crepes, which combine, for example, bacon, apples, and ched-dar. Created from a mixture of white and buckwheat flour, the crepes make a satisfying lunch. For dinner, add some onion soup and a green salad, or go for *tourtière,* a traditional Quebecois pie that includes beef, veal, *and* pork.

16 Church St. (between Front St. E. and Esplanade). ✆ 416/363-0838. www.lepapillon.ca. Reservations recommended. Crepes C$6–$10 (US$4.10–$6.80). AE, DC, MC, V. Tues–Fri noon–2:30pm; Tues–Wed 5–10pm, Thurs 5–11pm, Fri 5pm–midnight; Sat 11:30am–midnight; Sun noon–10pm. Subway: Union.

Shopsy's (Kids DELI   This Toronto institution has been in business for more than three-quarters of a century. Its large patio, festooned with giant yellow umbrellas, draws crowds for breakfast, lunch, and dinner and in between. This is where you go for heaping corned beef or smoked-meat sandwiches served on fresh rye. There's also a slew of comfort foods, like macaroni and cheese and chicken potpie. Shopsy's also boasts one of the largest walk-in humidors in the city (which is not subject to the new smoking crackdown).

33 Yonge St. ✆ 416/365-3333. Reservations accepted only for groups of 6 or more. Sandwiches and main courses C$7–$14 (US$4.75–$9.50). AE, MC, V. Mon–Wed 6:30am–11pm, Thurs–Fri 6:30am–midnight, Sat 8am–midnight, Sun 8am–10pm. Subway: Union or King.

Young Thailand ✰✰ THAI   Wandee Young was one of the first chefs to awake Toronto's taste buds to the joys of Thai cuisine. That was more than two decades ago, and Young Thailand is still going strong, with several locations around the city. The large dining room contains a few Southeast Asian decorative elements, but it's the low-priced, high-quality cuisine that attracts the hip-but-broke and boomers alike. The bargain buffet at lunch is always a mob scene. The dinner menu is a la carte, with popular picks like spiced chicken and bamboo shoots in coconut milk, satays with fiery peanut sauce, and the ever-present pad Thai. Soups tend to be sinus-clearing, and mango salads offer a sweet antidote.

81 Church St. (south of Lombard St.). ✆ 416/368-1368. Reservations recommended. Lunch buffet C$9.95 (US$6.75); main courses C$8–$16 (US$5.45–$11). AE, DC, MC, V. Mon–Fri 11:30am–2pm; daily 4:30–11pm. Subway: Queen or King.

4 Midtown West

VERY EXPENSIVE

Bistro 990 ✰✰✰ FRENCH   Because Hollywood types frequent Toronto, it's no surprise to see the stars out for a night on the town. Bistro 990 is just across the street from the tony Sutton Place Hotel, so it drags in more than its fair share of big names. (One friend has had a couple of Whoopi Goldberg sightings here. Why do these things never happen when I'm around?) In any case, the Gallic dining room is charming, and the service is all-around attentive. The menu offers updated hors d'oeuvres, such as octopus and veggies in citrus marinade. Main dishes stick to grand-mère's recipes, like the satisfying roasted half chicken with garlicky mashed potatoes, and calf's liver in white-wine sauce. Sweets, such as the pineapple tarte tatin with kiwi coulis and blueberry ice cream, are made daily. The three-course prix fixe menus are an excellent value, at C$19.90 (US$13.50) for lunch and C$24.90 (US$16.90) for dinner.

990 Bay St. (at St. Joseph). © 416/921-9990. Reservations required. Main courses C$19–$40 (US$13–$27). AE, DC, MC, V. Mon–Fri noon–3pm; Mon–Sat 5–11pm. Subway: Wellesley.

Opus ⚘ CONTINENTAL   Popular with the price-is-no-object set, Opus is nonetheless low-key. Smooth, personable servers make you feel at home in the elegant renovated town house, which contains several small dining areas. The look is casually chic, and there's no shortage of suits. The menu changes every other month, and always features classic French as well as lightened-up dishes. Tuna tartare meets its match with black sesame seeds and lotus chips, and beef tenderloin with dauphinoise potatoes and rosemary-shallot *jus* is memorable. Desserts are easy on the eye and the palate. The wine list runs to volumes, with highlights of New and Old worlds; the knowledgeable staff can set you straight.

37 Prince Arthur Ave. © 416/921-3105. Reservations recommended. Main courses C$25–$39 (US$17–$27). AE, DC, MC, V. Daily 5:30–11:30pm; bar until 2am. Subway: St. George.

Truffles ⚘ CONTINENTAL   On the second floor of the Four Seasons Hotel, this formal dining room is a study in elegance. Every last detail has been attended to, from the exotic sculptures to the stunning marquetry floor. The clientele is a mix of hotel guests and local businesspeople—it's a bit of an older crowd. Appetizers boast exquisite ingredients, with results such as pan-seared foie gras atop pineapple and mango chutney. Main courses, such as bacon-wrapped veal tenderloin served side-by-side with morel mushroom ravioli, are more down-to-earth. Desserts like peach Napoleon and lemon soufflé are uniformly delightful. The mile-long wine list frequently veers into the stratosphere.

In the Four Seasons Hotel, 21 Avenue Rd. © 416/928-7331. Reservations required. Main courses C$34–$46 (US$23–$31). AE, DC, MC, V. Mon–Fri 6–11pm, Sat 5:30–10:30pm. Subway: Bay.

EXPENSIVE

Annona ⚘ INTERNATIONAL   Why are so many of the city's fascinating restaurants in hotels? Annona, at the Park Hyatt, is the latest case in point. This street-level dining room is an exercise in elegance, with dusky blue draperies and banquettes, gold accents, and floor-to-ceiling windows (all the better to people-watch, my dears). It draws a business crowd, Yorkville shoppers, and hotel guests, serving scrambled eggs with smoked salmon and capers for breakfast, seafood risotto with morel mushrooms and asparagus at lunch, and pan-seared Black Angus medallions in red wine sauce for dinner. The desserts are to die for, especially the caramelized pineapple tart with rum ice cream.

Park Hyatt Toronto, 4 Avenue Rd. © 416/924-5471. Reservations recommended for dinner. Main courses C$16–$30 (US$11–$20). AE, DC, MC, V. Mon–Fri 6:30am–11pm, Sat–Sun 7am–11pm. Subway: Museum or Bay.

Boba ⚘ FUSION   There is no shortage of stunning turn-of-the-century houses in this part of town, and Boba happens to be in one of the most charming. Set back from the street, it has a front patio for summer dining. Inside, the pastel-hued walls and tasseled lampshades exude warmth, Provençal style. Boba is a scene every night, with a mix of dressed-up and dressed-down professionals table-hopping with abandon. What draws them is the inventive cuisine, which has turned co-chefs Barbara Gordon and Bob Bermann into local celebrities. One highlight is Gordon's wonderful Muscovy duck two ways, with the breast cooked rare and the leg braised. Grilled salmon is also just so, nicely mated with curried vegetable risotto. Desserts are overwhelming, particularly the Valrhona chocolate triangle with crème fraîche ice cream, raspberries, and berry coulis.

Midtown & Uptown Toronto Dining

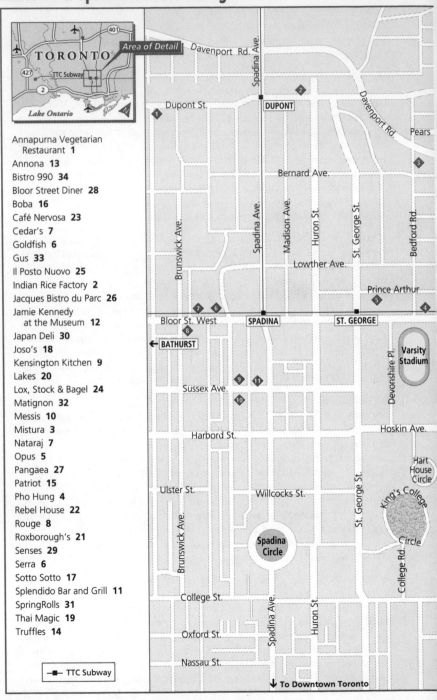

Annapurna Vegetarian Restaurant **1**
Annona **13**
Bistro 990 **34**
Bloor Street Diner **28**
Boba **16**
Café Nervosa **23**
Cedar's **7**
Goldfish **6**
Gus **33**
Il Posto Nuovo **25**
Indian Rice Factory **2**
Jacques Bistro du Parc **26**
Jamie Kennedy at the Museum **12**
Japan Deli **30**
Joso's **18**
Kensington Kitchen **9**
Lakes **20**
Lox, Stock & Bagel **24**
Matignon **32**
Messis **10**
Mistura **3**
Nataraj **7**
Opus **5**
Pangaea **27**
Patriot **15**
Pho Hung **4**
Rebel House **22**
Rouge **8**
Roxborough's **21**
Senses **29**
Serra **6**
Sotto Sotto **17**
Splendido Bar and Grill **11**
SpringRolls **31**
Thai Magic **19**
Truffles **14**

TTC Subway

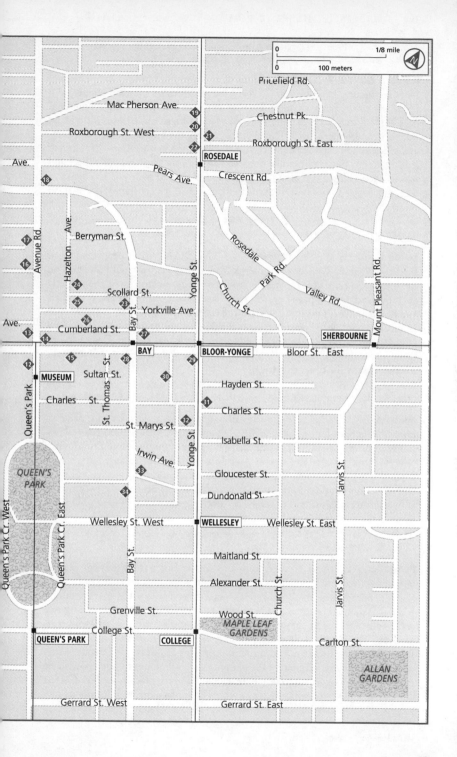

90 Avenue Rd. ⓒ **416/961-2622.** Reservations recommended. Main courses C$20–$34 (US$14–$23). AE, DC, MC, V. Mon–Sat 5:45–10pm. Subway: Bay.

Il Posto Nuovo ⓐ ITALIAN   All of those ladies who lunch can't be wrong. Now celebrating its 20th year, Il Posto Nuovo (formerly known simply as Il Posto) has new management and a new direction—and business is booming. Still, some things don't change: white-linened tables sit cheek-by-jowl, making this an eavesdropper's Eden. The service is among the best in the city, considerate, efficient, and well versed in the intricacies of the menu. And what a menu it is, rich with classic dishes like bresaola salad (thinly sliced air-cured beef and Asiago cheese atop a bed of arugula), and ravioli stuffed with veal and spinach. The wine cellar favors Italy, France, and California; it's constantly updated, so do ask for recommendations.

148 Yorkville Ave. (at Avenue Rd.). ⓒ **416/968-0469.** Reservations required. Main courses C$14–$25 (US$9.50–$17). AE, DC, MC, V. Mon–Sat noon–2:30pm and 6–11pm. Subway: Bay or Museum.

Jamie Kennedy at the Museum ⓐⓐ CANADIAN   Most people who visit the Royal Ontario Museum never suspect that there's a top-rated restaurant on the fifth floor. Accessible by one elevator, the serene, secluded spot is open only for lunch and draws a power crowd. Jamie Kennedy is one of the city's top chefs and an aficionado of organic produce. The menu staple is steak frites served with lemon mayo; other delightful choices include herbed goat cheese and tomato tart, and terrine of foie gras with walnuts and marinated veggies. Desserts work wonders with phyllo and cream. Most dishes come with wine suggestions, making the lengthy list easier to navigate.

Royal Ontario Museum, 100 Queen's Park Crescent. ⓒ **416/586-5578.** www.rom.on.ca. Reservations recommended. Main courses C$13–$20 (US$8.85–$14). AE, MC, V. Daily 11:30am–3pm. Subway: Museum.

Mistura ⓐ ITALIAN   While the curvy bar up front is a favorite place to meet, the modern Italian menu is the real draw for the well-dressed 20- and 30-somethings who dine at Mistura. The food is satisfying without being overly heavy—think spinach and ricotta gnocchi with light but creamy Gorgonzola sauce and toasted walnuts. The meaty entrees might include a tender veal chop with rosemary roasted potatoes and portobello mushrooms, or sweetbreads with chickpea polenta and caramelized root veggies. The well-organized wine list is heavy with Italian and California vintages.

265 Davenport Rd. ⓒ **416/515-0009.** Reservations recommended. Main courses C$20–$28 (US$14–$19). AE, DC, MC, V. Mon–Sat 5–11pm. Subway: Bay.

Pangaea ⓐ FUSION   I used to think this location was cursed. For years, I watched restaurants open with a bang and fold with a whimper. Well, Pangaea seems to have broken that losing streak—and deservedly so. The massive dining room is as dramatic as ever, complete with an undulating aluminum ceiling and coral walls. Perhaps to compete with the surroundings, the chic crowd likes to dress up. The menu changes every month. Appetizers such as white asparagus soup with roasted shallots and morel mushrooms are classically French. Main dishes strike boldly in different directions: glazed salmon with bok choy, water chestnuts, and ginger, for example, or rack of lamb roasted in sunflower seeds and honey and served with whiskey sauce. The professional staff knows its way around the wide-ranging wine list, which favors the Western Hemisphere.

1221 Bay St. ⓒ **416/920-2323.** Reservations recommended. Main courses C$22–$28 (US$15–$19). AE, DC, MC, V. Mon–Sat 11:30am–11:30pm. Subway: Bay.

Patriot ★★ CANADIAN   Canadians are often accused of lacking patriotism; perhaps this elegant eatery was designed to arouse some national pride? Most of the menu staples, from veal to lobster to cheeses to mushrooms, are proudly sourced in Canada. But what really counts is what the kitchen makes of its bounty. The results are compelling, like the pairing of artichoke and oka cheese atop rich carrot soup, or slightly seared lamb carpaccio served with beet juice, basil oil, and balsamic vinegar. Because Canadians hail from all parts of the globe, it's only fair to throw in a few foreign elements, as the excellent pineapple tarte Tatin demonstrates. Canadian vintages dominate the wine list.

131 Bloor St. W. ℂ 416/922-0025. Reservations recommended. Main courses C$17–$27 (US$12–$18). AE, MC, V. Mon–Sat 11am–11pm. Subway: Museum or Bay.

Senses ★★ INTERNATIONAL   Harry Wu, who already has two excellent restaurants—Lai Wah Heen (p. 87) and Hemispheres—at the Metropolitan Hotel, is the man behind this venture. Senses is a combination bakery, gourmet food emporium (see chapter 8), and restaurant, all in one sophisticated, romance-minded space. Dining here is an experience for—what else?—all the senses. The serene sandy tones are serious eye candy, the background music soothes, and velvety banquettes rub you the right way. Smell and taste get revved up for starters like the Spanish goat cheese empanada with olives and beet-root salad. The main-dish squab breasts with prawn sausage and wild rice pancake is beautifully executed. Service is extremely well informed and professional.

15 Bloor St. W. ℂ 416/935-0400. www.senses.ca. Reservations required. Main C$19–$46 (US$13–$31). AE, DC, MC, V. Mon–Fri 11:30am–2:30pm, Sat 11:30am–3pm; Mon–Sat 5–10pm. Subway: Yonge/Bloor.

Splendido Bar and Grill ★ CANADIAN   This longstanding favorite is under new ownership, and the resulting renovation has made it look even more like a private club than before: the dining room pairs brown with beige (much more attractive than it sounds), dark wood and leather chairs. The menu has also taken a new direction, with the Northern Italian standards taking a backseat to modern innovations that highlight Canadian produce. Mains run the gamut from a seared B.C. halibut filet in a leek-and-champagne vinaigrette to an Ontario butternut squash ravioli. For dessert, the lemon pudding cake with caramelized mango is hard to beat. The international wine list is pricey, but some nice vintages are available by the glass.

88 Harbord St. ℂ 416/929-7788. Reservations required. Main courses C$20–$30 (US$14–$20). AE, DC, MC, V. Mon–Sat 5–11pm. Subway: Spadina, then LRT south to Harbord St.

MODERATE

Café Nervosa ITALIAN   There are reed-thin models playing with their food at the next table, leopard skin decking the room, and limos parked out front. Where are you? One possible answer is Café Nervosa, a casually hip Yorkville hangout. The name is borrowed from the coffee shop on TV's "Frasier," with a wacky ambiance all its own. The menu boasts nicely constructed panini, pizzas, and salads, and the portions tend to be generous (curious, given the you-can-never-be-too-rich-or-too-thin crowd).

75 Yorkville Ave. ℂ 416/961-4642. www.cafenervosa.ca. Reservations only for groups of 6 or more. Main courses C$10–$25 (US$6.80–$17). AE, DC, MC, V. Mon–Sat 11am–11pm, Sun 10:30am–3pm. Subway: Bay.

Goldfish ★★ (Value) ECLECTIC   Behind the floor-to-ceiling front window, dining at this new hot spot is rather like being in a fishbowl. The cool, crisp lines of Scandinavian design mix with miniature Japanese plants for an upscale Zen ambiance. While the look may be trendier-than-thou, the staff's attitude is consistently considerate. The menu is far less austere than the surroundings. Main dishes run the gamut from ostrich tenderloin with lobster orzo and cranberry coulis to orange-poppy-seed-crusted salmon in an apple cider reduction. Even the simplest green salad benefits from dollops of pumpkin seeds and a light dressing that contains a hint of lavender emulsion. The short dessert list includes some inventive pairings, such as delicious apple tart with rosemary ice cream. The wine list is short but contains 10 selections by the glass.

372 Bloor St. W. ℂ 416/513-0077. www.goldfishrestaurant.net. Reservations strongly recommended. Main courses C$13–$27 (US$8.85–$18). AE, DISC, MC, V. Wed–Fri 11:30am–3:30pm, Sat–Sun 10am–3pm, Daily 5:30–10:30pm. Subway: Spadina.

Gus ⭐⭐ GREEK   This restaurant is out of its element so far as locale is concerned—Toronto's Greek restaurants tend to congregate along the Danforth (see "Midtown East/The East End" on p. 106). But this midtown newcomer is a welcome addition to the neighborhood. Created by the husband-and-wife team responsible for Lolita's Lust (see review on p. 107), Gus injects some creative cookery—and a pleasantly relaxed vibe—into an area that could benefit from cutting loose a little. Main courses run the gamut from rack of lamb in a sour-cherry reduction to seared tuna steak with a classic avgolemono sauce. Side plates, including the delicious feta-scalloped potatoes, are ordered separately. Portions are on the generous side, but do try to save space for the light but luscious Pavlova. The wine list has some well-chosen bottles, but the cocktail list is more of a draw: the lychee martini is a house specialty.

1033 Bay St. ℂ 416/923-8159. Reservations recommended. Main courses C$16–$25 (US$11–$17). AE, MC, V. Mon–Fri 5pm–midnight, Sat 6pm–2am.

Jacques Bistro du Parc FRENCH   There are about three ladies who lunch for every lad who happens by Jacques Bistro du Parc around noontime. In the evening, the ratio evens out. The menu is that of a genuine French brasserie, with omelets, quiches, and niçoise salads galore. There are meatier main courses, too, like green peppercorn steak and Dijon-coated rack of lamb. Many wines are available by the glass, and bottles tend to be reasonably priced. Service can be considered relaxed or slow, depending on your mood.

126A Cumberland St. ℂ 416/961-1893. Reservations recommended on weekends. Main courses C$12–$30 (US$8.15–$20). AE, MC, V. Mon–Sat 11:30am–3pm and 5–10:30pm. Subway: Bay.

Joso's SEAFOOD   This Annex mainstay keeps packing 'em in, drawing a crowd of regulars and a sprinkling of celebrities. The Spralja family has a show-biz history (chef Joso was half of the folk-singing duo of Malka and Joso, who appeared on *The Tonight Show*), which may explain the theatricality of the surroundings. The two-story house is crammed with art depicting the female form in all its naked glory. Tables are inches apart, foiling intimate conversation but letting you get to know your neighbors. Fresh seafood is carted to your table for inspection, then returned to the kitchen for cooking. There is also a selection of pastas, such as delightful spaghettini al Leonardo, which combines shrimp, octopus, and capers. Desserts range from jam-filled crepes to sorbets.

202 Davenport Rd. (just east of Avenue Rd.). ℂ 416/925-1903. Reservations recommended. Main courses C$14–$44 (US$9.50–$30); pasta dishes C$10–$16 (US$6.80–$11). AE, MC, V. Mon–Fri 11:30am–2:30pm; Mon–Sat 5:30–11pm. Subway: Bay.

Matignon *Finds* FRENCH   A bit off the beaten track, this small restaurant offers the thrill of discovery. Spread over two floors, the intimate rooms are festooned with all things French. The crowd includes many regulars, and the ambiance is that of a low-key bistro. The short menu is filled with classics from the old country, including Angus steak rolled in crushed pepper and flambéed with cognac, and rack of lamb with mustard and herbs of Provence. Desserts, like vanilla ice cream under hot chocolate sauce, stay on the same track.

51 St. Nicholas St. ℭ **416/921-9226.** Reservations recommended. Main courses C$14–$18 (US$9.50–$12). AE, MC, V. Mon–Fri 11:30am–2:30pm; Mon–Thurs 5–10pm, Fri–Sat 5–11pm. Subway: Wellesley.

Messis *(Value* ECLECTIC   This is one of Toronto's prime training grounds for up-and-coming young chefs. The food is for gourmets, though the prices are comparatively low. That explains the presence of earnest artsy types and casual boomers in the small, saffron-walled dining room. The menu changes frequently, keeping as its mainstays Italian pastas and Mediterranean meat dishes, and ranging into Asia, too. For a starter, the herbed goat cheese and cumin phyllo pastry is a delicious choice. Main courses include oven-roasted Atlantic salmon with jasmine rice and sun-dried fruit. Service is well-intentioned though occasionally clunky. The California-dominated wine list is as reasonably priced as the food.

97 Harbord St. ℭ **416/920-2186.** Main courses C$11–$21 (US$7.50–$14). AE, MC, V. Sun–Thurs 5:30–10pm; Fri–Sat 5:30–11pm. Subway: Spadina, then LRT south to Harbord St.

Rouge *ECLECTIC   Oh, make me blush—not another minimalist, modernist eatery along Bloor Street West. Alright, that's exactly what it is -but it has nothing to be ashamed of. This skinny little room with its crimson walls and Japanese-inspired flower boxes is serving up some stellar fare. Appetizers go from sweet—tomato salad with roasted baby onions in a balsamic vinaigrette—to sophisticated, like the seared foie gras with brioche and roasted pears. There are several impressive pastas, such as the gnocchi with double-smoked bacon and savory, as well as strong mains (the duo of Quebec leg of lamb and Australian lamb rack with gratin dauphinois offers a fascinating taste test for gourmets).

467 Bloor St. W. ℭ **416/413-0713.** Reservations recommended. Main courses C$12–$24 (US$8.15–$16). AE, MC, V. Daily 6–11pm. Subway: Spadina.

Sotto Sotto *NORTHERN ITALIAN   Imagine the Bat Cave decorated by a Florentine, with aged frescoes, wall-mounted stonework, and wax-dripping candelabra. A few steps down from street level, this restaurant transports diners a world away. Tables are cheek-by-jowl, but the jovial suits and couples don't seem to mind. Efficient service lacks warmth, though the kitchen makes up for it. The menu leans to the lightweight, with a few irresistible creamy-sauced pastas. Main courses of meat or fish, like Cornish hen and swordfish, are nicely grilled. The risotto is fine—though, annoyingly, at least two people at the table must order it. There's a nice wine list, with many selections available by the glass.

116A Avenue Rd. (north of Bloor St.). ℭ **416/962-0011.** Reservations required. Main courses C$14–$24 (US$9.50–$16). AE, DC, MC, V. Daily 5:30–midnight. Subway: Bay or Museum.

Southern Accent CAJUN   Cajun food isn't Toronto's claim to fame, so this down-home Annex eatery is a find. Background blues and zydeco set the tone, and the menu attracts casual neighborhood boomers. Anyone who has admired the work of New Orleans celebrity chef Paul Prudhomme will cotton to the blackened entrees—chicken, steak, lamb, and fish all get the treatment. Gumbo and crawfish make occasional appearances, too. *Warning:* The corn bread is a mite addictive.

595 Markham St. ℭ **416/536-3211.** Reservations recommended on weekends. Main courses C$13–$26 (US$8.85–$18). AE, DC, DISC, MC, V. Tues–Sun 5:30pm–1am. Subway: Bathurst.

INEXPENSIVE

Bloor Street Diner LIGHT FARE   If you've shopped until you've dropped along Bloor Street West, this is just the place to grab a bite to eat and let your feet and your credit card recover. It's two restaurants in one: Le Café/Terrasse is an informal bistro that serves decent soups, salads, and sandwiches all day; La Rotisserie is a slightly more upscale dining room with heartier Provençal-style fare. The basics are what they do best. Try to snag a seat on the umbrella-covered patio overlooking Bay Street (all the better for people-watching).

In the Manulife Centre, 55 Bloor St. W. ℂ 416/928-3105. Main courses C$10–$18 (US$6.80–$12). AE, DC, MC, V. Daily 7am–1am. Subway: Bay or Yonge/Bloor.

Cedar's MIDDLE EASTERN   As the evening goes on, the decibel level rises, and throngs of diners and Middle Eastern music vie for attention. The menu is mainly Lebanese, with plates of nibbles such as grilled zucchini and *moujarar-dara* (rice and lentils with onions). Main courses include a variety of meaty shish kebabs. Servers are pleasant but prone to vanishing.

394 Bloor St. W. ℂ 416/923-3277. Reservations not accepted. Main courses C$11–$14 (US$7.50–$9.50). MC, V. Mon–Thurs noon–10pm, Fri–Sat noon–11pm. Subway: Spadina or Bathurst.

Indian Rice Factory ⋐ INDIAN   A Toronto institution since it opened in the late 1970s, the Indian Rice Factory is in a league of its own. The corduroy banquettes and macramé wall hangings still draw boomers who started coming here 20 years ago. The Punjabi-influenced menu features heaping helpings of beef *dhansak* (braised with lentil-eggplant-tomato curry) and chicken *khashabad*, stuffed with almonds, cashews, and raisins in coconut-milk cream. There are many beers from local microbreweries, and a small but well-chosen wine list.

414 Dupont St. ℂ 416/961-3472. Reservations recommended. Main courses C$8–$16 (US$5.45–$11). AE, DC, MC, V. Mon–Sat noon–11pm, Sun 5–10pm. Subway: Dupont.

Japan Deli JAPANESE   Tucked into a cubbyhole on a side street just off Bloor Street West, Japan Deli succeeds at bringing tempura and teriyaki to the masses. Fine Japanese cuisine takes hours to prepare, but this is more like what time-pressed Tokyo residents are used to—a friend who used to live in Japan swears that this is as close as you can get to the experience without boarding a plane. Complete dinners include miso soup, salad, a meat dish, side vegetables, and fresh fruit for dessert—all nicely prepared, and all for under C$10 (US$6.80).

11 Balmuto St. ℂ 416/920-2051. Reservations not accepted. Complete dinners C$7–$9 (US$4.75–$6.10). MC, V. Mon–Sat noon–10pm. Subway: Yonge/Bloor.

Kensington Kitchen ⋐⋐ (Kids) MEDITERRANEAN   Drawing a crowd of regulars—students and profs—from the nearby University of Toronto, Kensington Kitchen is a perennial gem. The decor hasn't changed in years, with Oriental carpets covering the walls, a painted wood floor, and decorative objects scattered about. The tradition of big portions at small cost stays constant, too. The menu ventures between the ports of the Mediterranean. There's angel-hair pasta with heaps of shrimp, scallops, and mussels in tomato-coriander sauce; saffron paella with chicken and sausage; and Turkish-style braised lamb stuffed with raisins, eggplant, apricots, and figs. In clement weather, head to the rooftop patio, in the shade of a mighty Manitoba maple.

124 Harbord St. ℂ 416/961-3404. Reservations recommended. Main courses C$10–$14 (US$6.80–$9.50). AE, DC, MC, V. Mon–Sat 11:30am–11pm, Sun 11:30am–10pm. Subway: Spadina, then LRT south to Harbord St.

Lalibela ETHIOPIAN   Perhaps it's the fact that you don't need cutlery to dine in Ethiopian style that makes it so much fun. A flatbread called *injera* takes the place of flatware as you scoop up spicy hot meats and thick lentil stews. Lalibela has numerous choices for vegetarians and meat-lovers, and the helpful staff will arrange mixed plates with three different dishes for tasting.

869 Bloor St. W. © 416/535-6615. Main courses C$5–$9 (US$3.40–$6.10). MC, V. Mon–Thurs 6–10pm, Fri–Sat 6–11pm. Subway: Christie.

Lox, Stock & Bagel DELI   If you're tuckered out while shopping in Yorkville—and not feeling up to facing the chic scene at the neighborhood's many bistros—head to the sanctuary of Lox, Stock & Bagel. Located in a courtyard of the Hazelton Lanes shopping complex, this deli serves snacks, salads, and sandwiches. The menu isn't sophisticated, but it's hard to resist comfort foods like cheese blintzes, matzo ball soup, and a classic Reuben sandwich. There are a few hot dishes too, such as vegetarian lasagna. Of course, you could always just grab a bagel, too.

Hazelton Lanes, 55 Avenue Rd. © 416/968-8850. Reservations only for groups. Main courses C$8–$12 (US$5.45–$8.15). AE, DC, MC, V. Daily 7:30am–9pm. Subway: Bay or Museum.

Nataraj INDIAN   There's usually a bit of a wait for a table—Nataraj's upscale cuisine is popular with Annex residents, and its downscale prices are affordable to U of T students. But the service is swift, so tables do open up rather quickly. The cooking is from the northern part of the subcontinent, so there are lots of fish and seafood dishes. A number of plates will appeal to vegetarians. The tandoor-baked breads are simply sublime.

394 Bloor St. W. © 416/928-2925. Reservations not accepted. Main courses C$7–$12 (US$4.80–$8.15). MC, V. Mon–Sat 5:30–10:30pm. Subway: Spadina.

Pho Hung VIETNAMESE   Pho usually translates as "soup," but that's a bit of a misnomer—it's more like a meal in a bowl. There are 15 good choices here, and the lemongrass- or coriander-scented broths are chock-full of meat, noodles, and vegetables. There's also a range of chicken, pork, and seafood dishes, and a tangy beef fondue. The clientele includes both suits and students, and the wine list is longer and better than you might expect.

200 Bloor St. W. © 416/963-5080. Reservations recommended for groups of 4 or more. Main courses C$7–$15 (US$4.75–$10). V. Mon–Sat 11am–10pm. Subway: St. George or Museum.

Serra ★★ ITALIAN   This diminutive eatery would fit in nicely in Little Italy. The diners are casually chic, and the look is sleek, with a wood-paneled bar in one corner and mahogany tables for two. The trattoria-worthy fare includes thin-crust pizza topped with olives, prosciutto, and goat cheese; light-sauced pasta dishes teeming with shrimp; and grilled focaccia sandwiches.

378 Bloor St. W. © 416/922-6999. www.serrarestaurant.com. Main courses C$10–$18 (US$6.80–$12). AE, DC, MC, V. Daily noon–10:30pm. Subway: Spadina.

SpringRolls ASIAN   What to have for dinner tonight: Chinese, Vietnamese, Thai, Singaporean? If you can't decide, your best bet is SpringRolls. The name may make you think its offerings are meager, but the multi-page menu will set you straight. Tenderly executed barbecued pork and fried shrimp dishes abound. Vegetarians don't have as many choices as you might expect, though there are a few top-notch vermicelli-and-veggie plates.

693 Yonge St. © 416/972-7655. Reservations recommended. Main courses C$6–$15 (US$4.10–$10). MC, V. Sun–Thurs 11am–11pm, Fri–Sat 11am–midnight. Subway: Yonge/Bloor.

Great Greasy Spoons

While I'm enchanted by Toronto's top-notch dining spots, I just can't resist the lure of the greasy spoon. You know the kind of place I mean: fluorescent lighting, a bottle of ketchup on every Formica tabletop, vinyl-upholstered booths, and aromas of strong coffee and frying bacon. Some suggestions:

Perhaps Toronto's best-known greasy spoon, **Mars,** 432 College St. at Bathurst St. (© **416/921-6332**), sports a neon sign that claims the diner is "Just out of this world." In addition to the all-day breakfast menu, it boasts cheese blintzes, grilled burgers, and a great turkey club. There's another location at 2363 Yonge St., just north of Eglinton Ave. (© 416/322-7111), but its kitschy mock-diner decor doesn't hold a candle to the real McCoy.

Avenue Coffee Shop, 222 Davenport Rd. at Avenue Rd. (© **416/924-5191**), is just up the street from the Park Hyatt and the Four Seasons hotels, which explains the frequent celebrity sightings (signed and framed photos stand as a permanent record of stars' visits). In business since 1946, the Avenue serves a steady supply of omelets, French toast, and hamburgers.

The Goof, 2379 Queen St. E. (© **416/694-3605**), is officially named the Garden Gate Restaurant. But certain letters burned out of the neon "Good Food" sign, giving this Beaches neighborhood mainstay its name. In addition to the usual diner grub, this spot has star power, as evidenced by recent Jennifer Lopez sightings.

5 Midtown East/The East End

Just about everything *will* be Greek to you in the East End along Danforth Avenue. Known appropriately enough as Greektown, this is where to come for low-cost, delicious dining, or for a midnight meal—the tavernas generally stay open until the wee hours, even on weeknights.

EXPENSIVE

Café Brussel ⭐ BELGIAN   Perhaps this was to be a challenge to the supremacy of Greek food in this neighborhood. The Café Brussel is defiantly . . . Belgian? The only such eatery in the city, it draws a neighborhood crowd. The menu could pass for French in most regards, with staples like onion soup and duck confit. This is food you could get drunk on—try beef simmered in dark ale (*carbonnades flamandes*), or seafood with shots of hard stuff (*moules au bourbon*). There's also a great selection of European lagers and wines.

124 Danforth Ave. © **416/465-7363.** Reservations recommended. Main courses C$15–$28 (US$10–$19). AE, MC, V. Mon–Sat 5:30–11pm, Sun 11:30am–11pm. Subway: Broadview.

MODERATE

Christina's GREEK   This restaurant takes itself a little more seriously than its nearby cousins. The walls are plastered with photographs of celebrities caught in the act of dining here. (There's one infamous old snapshot of "Friends" star Matt LeBlanc dining with Alanis Morissette.) The menu offers reliable souvlaki and

Dining: Chinatown to Bloor Street

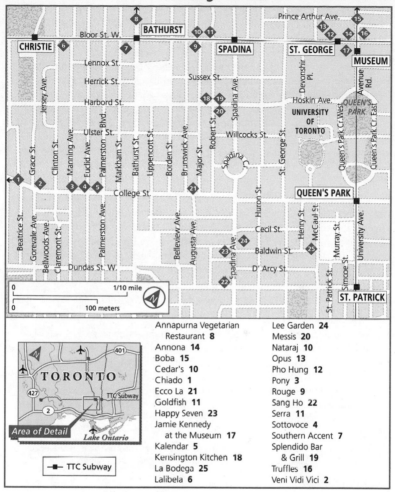

Annapurna Vegetarian
   Restaurant **8**
Annona **14**
Boba **15**
Cedar's **10**
Chiado **1**
Ecco La **21**
Goldfish **11**
Happy Seven **23**
Jamie Kennedy
   at the Museum **17**
Kalendar **5**
Kensington Kitchen **18**
La Bodega **25**
Lalibela **6**

Lee Garden **24**
Messis **20**
Nataraj **10**
Opus **13**
Pho Hung **12**
Pony **3**
Rouge **9**
Sang Ho **22**
Serra **11**
Sottovoce **4**
Southern Accent **7**
Splendido Bar
   & Grill **19**
Truffles **16**
Veni Vidi Vici **2**

eggplant pies, but it veers into pasta and burger territory, too. The hearty all-day breakfast of feta-spiked omelets and herbed taters is a popular choice.

492 Danforth Ave. ✆ **416/463-4418.** Reservations recommended. Main courses C$10–$24 (US$6.80–$16). AE, DC, MC, V. Daily 11am–4am. Subway: Chester.

Lolita's Lust ⚘ MEDITERRANEAN   Lolita's is a bit of a tease. The front window is painted acid green, leaving the smallest hint of glass peering through. Perhaps the hush-hush air is a draw, because the restaurant has been packed since it first opened; it's a favorite port of call for casually dressed boomers. The menu travels around the Mediterranean, from Greece to Morocco to Italy. Pan-seared tuna goes well with green lentil sauce, though there are more than a few odd-couple pairings, like roasted beets with Gorgonzola. The wait staff occasionally suffers memory lapses.

513 Danforth Ave. ✆ **416/465-1751.** Main courses C$10–$25 (US$6.80–$17). AE, MC, V. Sun–Thurs 6–11pm, Fri–Sat 6pm–midnight. Subway: Pape.

Myth 👭👭 GREEK/MEDITERRANEAN Part trendy bar, part restaurant, this generous space is large enough to encompass both. The ambience is classical Greece meets MTV. Ornate oversized shields share space with a series of TVs running an endless loop of mythic movies. Who can pay attention to what's on the plate with so much going on? Fortunately, the food calls attention to itself. Starters, ranging from traditional spanakopita (spinach pie) to tuna tartar with beet and taro-root chips, are impossible to ignore. Main courses, such as rabbit braised in port and cinnamon, or pizza topped with spiced lamb, zucchini and onion puree, are just as demanding. As the night goes on, the crowd gathers at the bar, where a DJ starts spinning music at 11pm.

417 Danforth Ave. (between Logan and Chester). ✆ **416/461-8383.** Reservations recommended. Main courses C$14–$26 (US$9.50–$18). AE, MC, V. Mon–Wed 5pm–11pm, Thurs–Sun noon–11pm ; bar open till 2am nightly. Subway: Chester.

Octavia ECLECTIC/GREEK/MEDITERRANEAN Who brought Thai satays onto the Danforth? The name of this swanky new addition to the Greektown strip fits right in, but its sensibility is decidedly different. The look is polished, with velvety banquettes against one wall and French doors that open to the sidewalk. Most of the main courses, such as grilled seafood and squid-ink pastas, come from the Mediterranean, but there's room on the menu for California salads and satays.

414 Danforth Ave. ✆ **416/461-3562.** Reservations not accepted. Main courses C$14–$22 (US$9.50–$15). AE, MC, V. Sun–Thurs 5pm–midnight, Fri–Sat 5pm–2am. Subway: Chester.

Pan on the Danforth 👭 GREEK To the best of my knowledge, Pan was a god of music, not of food. I must have mixed it up, because if he is the inspiration for this restaurant, he certainly knows his way around a kitchen. This long-established eatery updates classic Greek dishes with panache. Salmon is stuffed with mushrooms and spinach and wrapped in phyllo pastry, and a smoked baked pork chop comes with feta scalloped potatoes and zucchini relish. The well-chosen wine list favors the New World. The crowd is fairly sophisticated, which may explain the cryptic message over the bar: "You've done it already."

516 Danforth Ave. ✆ **416/466-8158.** Reservations accepted only for parties of 3 or more. Main courses C$13–$19 (US$8.85–$13). AE, DC, MC, V. Sun–Thurs 5–11pm, Fri–Sat 5pm–midnight. Subway: Chester or Pape.

INEXPENSIVE

Astoria GREEK The restaurant subtitles itself a shish-kebab house, but its offerings are much broader. And it's more upscale than the name would suggest, with a patio fountain and colorful decor. Whatever the protein, it seems to respond well to broiling—beef, lamb, chicken, and seafood all get similar treatment. There are several choices for vegetarians, including souvlaki and moussaka. Expect a wait if you arrive after 8:30 or so on weekends.

390 Danforth Ave. ✆ **416/463-2838.** Reservations recommended; accepted on weekdays only. Main courses C$9–$15 (US$6.10–$10). AE, MC, V. Mon–Wed and Fri–Sat 11am–1am, Thurs and Sun 11am–midnight. Subway: Chester.

Avli 👭 GREEK A white stucco archway contributes to the cave-like feel of the narrow street-level room, though the recent expansion to the second floor has created an airier place to dine. Always noisy, occasionally raucous, this taverna serves up some of the best food on the Danforth—non-greasy, thoughtfully prepared, and carefully seasoned. Meze starters are standard: *kopanisti* (spicy feta with peppers) and hummus for those who want cold food, grilled octopus and

Sleepless in Toronto: What to Do When the Midnight Munchies Attack

There are cities that never sleep. Well, Toronto isn't one of them. The city starts to doze off around 11:30pm, even on weekends. Sure, there are 24-hour doughnut shops, but if you're looking for something more substantial, try one of the following late-night options:

- **Caribbean Roti Corner,** 607 Queen St. W. (C 416/504-9558), provides takeout dishes of jerk chicken, rice and peas, and meaty stews until 4am on weekends. Subway: Osgoode, then streetcar west to Spadina Ave.
- **Happy Seven** (p. 91) serves reliable Chinese food in a kitschy setting until 5am.
- **7 West Café,** 7 Charles St. W. (C 416/928-9041), is open 24 hours a day. Delish sandwiches and pasta platters hit the spot. Those with severe sugar cravings can indulge in cakes and pies from several of the city's best bakers. Subway: Yonge/Bloor.
- If you're on the Danforth, you're in luck: Many of the terrific Greek tavernas and restaurants there, like **Myth** (p. 108), **Octavia** (p. 108), and **Christina's** (p. 106), stay open until the wee hours even on weeknights.

steamed mussels for those who like it hot. Main courses are standouts. The half chicken stuffed with cashews, dates, apples, and rice is exquisite, and the meat moussaka is the best around.

401 Danforth Ave. C 416/461-9577. www.avlirestaurant.com. Reservations recommended. Main courses C$9–$19 (US$6.10–$13). AE, DC, MC, V. Daily noon–midnight. Subway: Chester.

Mezes GREEK   This sophisticated space doles out exactly what it promises. *Mezes* are the Greek equivalent of tapas—light snacks meant to keep you going until you have a real dinner in front of you. Still, it's worth spoiling your appetite to indulge in these appetizers. Choices range from grilled calamari and octopus to spicy eggplant dip and leek pie. Do try to save room for the honey-sweet baklava.

456 Danforth Ave. C 416/778-5150. Reservations not accepted. Appetizers C$4–$10 (US$2.70–$6.80). AE, MC, V. Mon–Thurs 11am–midnight, Fri–Sat 11am–1am, Sun noon–midnight. Subway: Chester.

Ouzeri GREEK   One of the longtime stars of the neighborhood, Ouzeri has been packing in the crowds for years and shows no sign of slowing down. Just inside the foyer, TV sets make it look like a sports bar. Farther inside, colorful ceramic tiles and wrought iron surround terrazzo tables and wicker chairs. Charming as the interior is, if you're lucky you'll be outside on the small patio. Portions of main dishes, such as lamb pies and pork kebabs, tend to be quite generous. As the evening goes on, the convivial atmosphere evolves into festival-like celebration; on Tuesday nights, there's live Greek music.

500A Danforth Ave. C 416/778-0500. Reservations recommended. Main courses C$8–$18 (US$5.45–$12). AE, DISC, MC, V. Sun–Mon and Wed–Thurs 11am–midnight, Tues and Fri–Sat 11am–2am. Subway: Chester.

6 Uptown

This area is too large to be considered a neighborhood, stretching as it does from north of Davenport Road to Steeles Avenue. While it doesn't have the concentration of restaurants that the downtown area enjoys, a number of stellar options make the trip north worthwhile.

VERY EXPENSIVE

Auberge du Pommier ⭐ FRENCH   Don't have time to drop by your French country house this weekend? To the rescue comes Auberge du Pommier, a cozy chateau that exudes Provençal-style charm. Diners outfitted in business casual relax in the care of expert servers. The menu doesn't offer many surprises, but what it does, it does well. Appetizers set a high standard, with dishes like creamy lobster and white-bean soup, and baked artichokes stuffed with French goat cheese. Entrees, like pan-seared scallops with braised oxtail in a Cabernet *jus,* keep up the pace.

4150 Yonge St. 🕿 416/222-2220. Reservations recommended. Main courses C$33–$38 (US$22–$26). AE, DC, DISC, MC, V. Mon–Fri 11:30am–2:30pm; Mon–Sat 5–10pm. Subway: York Mills.

Centro ⭐⭐ CONTINENTAL   The palace-grand main room, with its oxblood walls, is always bustling. The dressed-up all-ages crowd often starts out schmoozing at the wine bar downstairs, moves up to the main floor for dinner, then migrates back downstairs for R&B music and a nightcap (the wine bar stays open until 2am). The seasonal menu pays tribute to the restaurant's Northern Italian origins, with pasta dishes like homemade egg tagliolini with smoked chicken in a truffle emulsion. Many choices lean to contemporary Canadiana, like the grain-fed Quebec capon paired with a foie gras mousse and sun-dried cherries, or French modern, like the rack of lamb in a Provençal honey mustard crust. Delicious desserts run the gamut from traditional tiramisu to warm banana bread pudding. The stellar wine list is sure to thrill oenophiles.

2472 Yonge St. 🕿 416/483-2211. www.centro.ca. Reservations required. Main courses C$28–$42 (US$19–$29). AE, DC, MC, V. Mon–Sat 5–11:30pm. Subway: Eglinton.

North 44 ⭐⭐⭐ INTERNATIONAL   This is the one restaurant that even people who've never set foot in Toronto have heard about. It's profiled extensively in food and travel magazines, but can it possibly live up to its reputation? In a word, yes. The spare Art Deco decor recently got a face-lift, and the results are stunning. The soft lighting and strategically situated mirrors wrap the dining room—and its occupants—in a gorgeous glow. The menu, which changes with the seasons, borrows from Mediterranean, American, and Asian sources. The results are inspiring to the palate and the eye. On the list of main courses you might find grilled veal tenderloin with orange peppercorns, toasted barley, and root veggies, or roasted Muscovy duck breast with orange-soy marinade and foie gras. There are always a few pasta and pizza choices, such as caramelized squash ravioli with black truffle essence. It's impossible to come here without being seduced into a three-course meal. The desserts, like lemon meringue mille-feuille, are among the best in the city, and there's a wide selection of accompanying ice wines. The wine list is comprehensive, though most of the prices veer off into the stratosphere. What really sets North 44 apart is its seamless service. Those who don't like to be pampered should stay away.

2537 Yonge St. 🕿 416/487-4897. Reservations required. Main courses C$27–$45 (US$18–$31). AE, DC, MC, V. Mon–Sat 5–11pm. Subway: Eglinton.

Scaramouche ☆ INTERNATIONAL   This is a contender for those who don't mind spending top dollar on splendid food. Tucked into an upscale apartment building, it isn't easy to find. That enhances its snob appeal—and the crowd here is more old money than the patrons at either of its uptown competitors, Centro and North 44. Scaramouche is blessed with one of the most romantic settings in the city. Floor-to-ceiling windows afford a panoramic view of the downtown skyline. (Securing a window seat is no mean feat, but fortunately most tables have decent sightlines.) The unobtrusive servers pay attention to the details. The menu is laden with caviar, foie gras, truffles, and oysters; main dishes include the likes of venison loin wrapped in smoke bacon in a red wine glaze. The wine list has a broad reach, and there's a nice selection of cognacs.

1 Benvenuto Place (off Avenue Rd.). ⓒ **416/961-8011.** Reservations required. Main courses C$25–$40 (US$17–$27); pasta dishes C$16–$25 (US$11–$17). AE, DC, MC, V. Dining room: Mon–Sat 5:30–10pm; pasta bar: Mon–Fri 5:30–10:30pm, Sat 5:30–11pm. Subway: St. Clair, then streetcar west to Avenue Rd., and walk four blocks south to Edmund Ave.; Benvenuto is the first street on the left.

EXPENSIVE

La Bruschetta ☆ ITALIAN   Star sightings are common in Toronto, but at La Bruschetta they're almost an everyday event. The entryway is covered from floor to ceiling with plates decorated by celebs such as Kelsey Grammer and Bette Midler. It's a surprise, then, to find the homey, kitchen-like dining room. Owner Benito Piantoni, who charms patrons with tales of Italy and Hollywood gossip, provides local color. The menu lists a dozen pastas, with cream sauces ranging from brandy to Gorgonzola. Mouth-watering main courses include veal medallions simply presented in white-wine sauce with garlic and mushrooms. After a rich meal, you'll welcome the delicate lemon ice for dessert.

1317 St. Clair Ave. W. ⓒ **416/656-8622.** Reservations recommended. Main courses C$14–$26 (US$9.50–$18). AE, DC, MC, V. Mon–Fri 5–10:30pm. Subway: St. Clair West, then any streetcar west to Dufferin St.

Lakes ☆ BISTRO   Plush banquettes and close-set tables heighten the sense of intimacy in the narrow dining room. A casually well-dressed crowd drops by during the week; on Saturday, couples spend candlelit quality time. The menu changes every few months, with jazzed-up bistro classics such as duck confit with cranberry-shallot glaze and garlic mashed potatoes, grilled provimi veal liver, and Gruyère-and-Emmenthal fondue for two making frequent appearances. The banana crème brûlée is a perennial favorite dessert.

1112 Yonge St. ⓒ **416/966-0185.** Reservations strongly recommended. Main courses C$14–$26 (US$9.50–$18). AE, DC, MC, V. Mon–Fri noon–3pm and 5:30–11pm, Sat 6–11pm. Subway: Rosedale.

Millie's Bistro ☆☆ *(Kids)* MEDITERRANEAN   Subtle as its signage is, Millie's is hard to miss. The sole gastronomic draw in this neighborhood, it lures even jaded downtown dwellers. It attracts an unusual mix of young-to-middle-age courting couples, families with tiny tykes, and groups gearing up for a night on the town. The sprawling menu includes dishes from Spain, southern France, Italy, Turkey, and Morocco. There is a kids' menu, too. Start with tapas—perhaps Catalan-style goat cheese with basil and olive oil; Turkish flatbread with a topping of lamb, yogurt, and mint; or a *b'stilla* (aromatic chicken wrapped in herbed semolina). Better still, sample them all—the cheery staff will arrange them on ceramic platters for sharing. Main dishes include paella with saffron, shrimp, clams, quail and chorizo sausage. Sweets are seductive, though generous portions make saving room for dessert almost impossible. On the wide-ranging wine list, Spanish selections are a particularly good value.

1980 Avenue Rd. (south of York Mills). © **416/481-1247.** Reservations recommended. Main courses C$10–$27 (US$6.80–$18). AE, DC, MC, V. Daily 11:30am–11pm. Subway: York Mills, then walk west or take a taxi (about C$5/US$3.40).

Quartier ☆ FRENCH   The Old World elegance is palpable as you step into this refined bistro. Is it the languid sound of Edith Piaf's voice? Perhaps the baroque mirrors and look-again prints on the walls? No matter. The French-born proprietor, Marcel Rethore, has created a romance-tinged atmosphere for a casually chic crowd. The menu boasts classic dishes such as duck confit with sautéed potatoes and garlic-dressed endive, and Breton bouillabaisse. Desserts, for those who have room, include a tender lemon-cream mille-feuille and a delicate crème brûlée. The short wine list is particularly well chosen—it's hard to go wrong.

2112 Yonge St. © **416/545-0505.** Reservations recommended. Main courses C$17–$27 (US$12–$18). AE, MC, V. Mon–Fri 11:30am–2:30pm; Mon–Sat 5:30–10:30pm. Subway: Eglinton.

Roxborough's ☆ BISTRO   This glamorous bistro boasts soft lighting, strategically placed privacy screens, and smooth service—the perfect setting for a grown-up night on the town. The crowd is a mix of locals and visitors drawn from far-flung areas who made a special trip for dinner. And Roxborough's makes it all worthwhile, with a stylish seasonal menu that features main courses like red snapper served atop cumin- and mint-scented couscous, or Atlantic salmon in a sauce of tomato, lemon, and olive with leeks and baby potatoes. The desserts, particularly the caramel-drenched bread pudding, are classics.

1055 Yonge St. (at Roxborough Ave.). © **416/323-0000.** Reservations strongly recommended. Main courses C$20–$26 (US$14–$18). AE, DC, MC, V. Mon–Sat 5:30–10:30pm. Subway: Rosedale.

Thai Magic ☆ THAI   Arrangements of orchids, cascading vines, and Thai statuary grace the enchanting entry. The serene staff handles frenetic crowds with ease; this spot is filled with locals, especially on Thursday and Friday nights. The meal is served Western-style, rather than in the Thai fashion of bringing all courses to the table at once. Delicate appetizers like chicken-filled golden baskets vie for attention with not-too-spicy soups. Entrees range from chicken with cashews and whole dried chilies to a coriander-infused lobster in the shell.

1118 Yonge St. © **416/968-7366.** Reservations recommended. Main courses C$12–$20 (US$8.15–$14). AE, MC, V. Mon–Sat 5–11pm. Subway: Summerhill.

MODERATE

Amore Trattoria ☆☆ ITALIAN   This double-decker restaurant is a neighborhood favorite with groups and families alike. Pandemonium reigns on the first floor; upstairs, the cognoscenti can gaze over a balcony at the tumult below. The cheerful staff takes it all in stride. Reading the menu takes much too long: With 22 pastas, 21 pizzas, 6 meat dishes, and daily specials, it can be an intimidating experience for the indecisive. Fortunately, the kitchen consistently produces top-notch dishes, from simple salads of mesclun and goat cheese to spaghetti in brandy-tomato sauce with sweet Bermuda onion. Wine is served in tumblers in classic rustic-Italian style.

2425 Yonge St. © **416/322-6184.** Reservations recommended; accepted only for groups of 6 or more. Main courses C$10–$18 (US$6.80–$12). AE, MC, V. Daily noon–3pm and 5:30–10:30pm. Subway: Eglinton.

Gio's ITALIAN   Ask any local where you might find this tiny trattoria, and you'll be told to look for the nose—in lieu of a sign, a schnozz of Durante-like proportions looms over Yonge Street. The sense of fun keeps up inside, where ceramic crockery, grappa bottles, and pastoral paintings cover the 8-foot-wide dining room. Waiters rush about, occasionally breaking into song. Prices look inexpensive, but portions aren't large, so ordering three or four courses is the norm. In true Italian style, pasta is not a main course but an appetizer; the list of entrees is mainly for meat-eaters, and you'll have to order veggies separately. This isn't the place for intimate conversation, but it's great fun with a group.

2070 Yonge St. ℂ **416/932-2306.** Reservations not accepted. Main courses C$8–$14 (US$5.45–$9.50). AE, MC, V. Mon–Thurs 5:30–10:30pm, Fri–Sat 5:30–11pm. Subway: Eglinton.

Grano ⋇ *Kids* ITALIAN   While Toronto has no shortage of Italian eateries, few spots have as much ambiance as Grano. The old-fashioned trattoria contains several dining areas, with wooden furnishings, distressed stucco, and piles of greenery. The small courtyard at the back is heaven on sunny days. This is a high-energy spot that attracts celebratory groups (one clever friend of mine had her wedding rehearsal dinner here); it's also welcoming to families accompanied by *bambini*. The cooking is hearty, from tender *osso buco* to ricotta gnocchi paired with shrimp in white-wine sauce. The desserts are a serious draw—I insist that everyone try the divine white chocolate and raspberry tart at least once.

2035 Yonge St. ℂ **416/440-1986.** Reservations recommended. Main courses C$11–$20 (US$7.50–$14). AE, DC, MC, V. Mon–Fri 9:30am–11pm, Sat 9am–11pm. Subway: Davisville or Eglinton.

Mezzetta MIDDLE EASTERN   Tapas bars are a dime a dozen in Madrid, but in Toronto they're few and far between. Mezzetta is one such gem. Everything on the menu is served in appetizer-sized portions, from cold salads of feta, olives, and tomatoes to steamy kofta, an Egyptian dish of beef, lamb, and potato in a spicy sauce. There are also pita sandwiches and barbecued items. Much of the menu will appeal to vegetarians. The wine list is short but priced for value, and there's a lengthy list of brews, too.

681 St. Clair Ave. W. ℂ **416/658-5687.** Reservations recommended on weekends. Appetizers C$3 (US$2.05). MC, V. Tues–Fri noon–2:30pm, Tues–Sun 5–10:30pm. Subway: St. Clair.

Stork on the Roof ⋇ BISTRO   The stork in question is a Dutch sign of good fortune. And luck it is to discover this charming bistro. The menu abounds with pan-European classics warmed by exotic elements, such as grilled pork tenderloin with lemon curry sauce. Asian inspirations are in evidence, particularly in seafood dishes, like sautéed squid served with satay-worthy peanut sauce and pickled vegetables. For dessert, Dutch spiced apple pie is the standout.

2009 Yonge St. ℂ **416/483-3747.** Reservations required. Main courses C$15–$17 (US$10–$12). AE, MC, V. Wed–Fri noon–2pm; Tues–Sat 6–10pm. Subway: Davisville.

Terroni ITALIAN/LIGHT FARE   From its humble beginnings on Queen Street West, Terroni has grown into a local mini-chain with three locations. The newest one, at Yonge and St. Clair, is the most ambitious undertaking yet. The setting is informal, with kitchen-style tables and chairs and a wall-mounted chalkboard that heralds the daily specials. The antipasti, salads, and pizzas, essentially the same at all three locations, are uniformly delightful. They range from the simplest margherita pizza (tomato, mozzarella, basil) to a gourmet salad of cooked oyster mushrooms drizzled with balsamic vinegar and served atop a bed of arugula. With its larger kitchen, the uptown Terroni offers a number of other options, including pastas and meat dishes. Beef carpaccio with truffles is a standout.

1 Balmoral Ave. ℂ **416/925-4020** (other locations at 720 Queen St. W. and 106 Victoria St.). Main courses C$10–$18 (US$6.80–$12). MC, V. Sun–Wed 9am–10pm, Thurs–Sat 9am–11pm. Subway: St. Clair.

Vanipha Lanna ⭐⭐ LAOTIAN/THAI   There's no shortage of Thai eateries in Toronto, but only a few specialize in the cooking of Thailand's northwestern Lanna region. Many Laos natives have relocated to Lanna, and strong, spicy Laotian influences permeate the cooking. One of the house specialties is grilled chicken and garlic served with lime-chili sauce. The busy dining room attracts casually dressed diners of all ages, all of whom the thoughtful staff treats with care.

471 Eglinton Ave. W. ⓒ **416/484-0895.** www.vanipha.ca. Reservations recommended. Main courses C$8–$15 (US$5.45–$10). AE, MC, V. Mon–Thurs 5–10:30pm; Fri–Sat 5–11:30pm. Subway: Eglinton.

INEXPENSIVE

Hannah's Kitchen LIGHT FARE   National magazines and newspapers have published several of its recipes, but this cubbyhole-like eatery remains defiantly low-key. Diners seat themselves at wooden banquettes or tiny tables. The menu includes many pasta dishes, both cold (pesto radiatore salad with chicken and pine nuts is the top pick) and hot (penne arrabiata has the spiciest sauce in town), with three or four daily specials. Occasional forays into the exotic include a few Indonesian rice dishes and the ever-popular pad Thai. Desserts are a must, so check out the selection behind the counter on your way in.

2221 Yonge St. ⓒ **416/481-0185.** Reservations not accepted. Main courses C$7–$12 (US$4.75–$8.15). MC, V. Mon–Fri 10am–10pm. Subway: Eglinton.

Rebel House LIGHT FARE   This casual spot is beloved by locals. Is the draw the warm welcome, the better-than-average pub grub, or the impressive selection of microbrews? The crowd is mainly 20- to 30-somethings decked out in designer casualwear, more intent on socializing than eating. The specialty of the house is hearty, simple fare; grilled Atlantic salmon and seared Angus strip loin are top picks. Pastas and salads are worth a taste, too.

1068 Yonge St. ⓒ **416/927-0704.** Reservations not accepted. Main courses C$8–$18 (US$5.45–$12). AE, MC, V. Mon–Sat 11:30am–11pm, Sun 11:30am–10pm (bar open till 1am Mon–Sat and 11pm Sun). Subway: Rosedale.

7 North of the City

Toronto is a sprawling city, and as it has expanded, new and inspiring restaurants have cropped up in formerly out-of-the-way regions. The area north of Steeles Avenue is experiencing a remarkable boom. These restaurants are beyond the reach of the Toronto subway system. If you've rented a car to go to the McMichael Canadian Art Collection in Kleinburg or to the Canada's Wonderland theme park, you might want to stop on the way back downtown. (For driving directions, see chapter 6.)

EXPENSIVE

Terra ⭐⭐ INTERNATIONAL   This restaurant feels as if it was airlifted out of the downtown core. Sleek and sophisticated, it is the sibling of uptown's North 44, and the cooking at Terra is appropriately splendid. The kitchen favors seafood, from appetizers like butter-poached lobster with shallots and honey mushrooms to entrees like pan-fried sea bream with baby bok choy, candied beets and fava beans. There are several steak plates, with everything from a 10-ounce filet of beef to a 16-ounce porterhouse. Believe it or not, there are also numerous vegetarian offerings. Desserts include classic crème brûlée and a more unusual pecan and blueberry cheesecake. The lengthy wine list hits all the international high notes, though most bottles are quite pricey.

Vegetarian Delights

It used to be that vegetarian dining in Toronto was often more of an exercise in virtue than in good taste. Crunchy granola might be healthful for the body, but it's hell on the palate. But now a new wave of vegetarian eateries are making meat-free meals a gourmet's delight. Several of the city's finest restaurants are also offering special vegetarian tasting menus. Here are some of the best bets:

- **Annapurna Vegetarian Restaurant,** 1085 Bathurst St. (© 416/537-8513; subway: Bathurst). Annapurna has been around for more than 20 years, and it's still serving Indian vegetable dishes, hearty tofu burgers, and a variety of fruit and vegetable juices to a crowd of students and boomers. In keeping with the aura of health, Annapurna hosts free meditation classes every week. Main courses C$8–$12 (US$5–$8); MC, V; Mon–Tues, Thurs–Sat 11:30am–9pm, Wed 11:30am–6:30pm.

- **Fressen,** 478 Queen St. W. (© 416/504-5127; subway: Osgoode). This is a vegetarian oasis for sophisticates. From the freshly baked beet-infused buns to tender tofu with both hot tomato and sweet teriyaki sauces, this new hot spot makes every mouthful a gourmet delight. It's a hit with vegetarians *and* their carnivorous friends. Main courses C$12–$14 (US$8–$9); MC, V; Mon–Thurs 5:30–10pm, Fri 5:30–11pm, Sat 10:30am–3:30pm and 5:30–11pm, Sun 10:30am–3:30pm and 5:30–10pm.

- **Juice for Life,** 336 Queen St. W. (© 416/599-4442; subway: Osgoode). If there's such a thing as an elixir of life, one of the bartenders at this Annex favorite is sure to find it one day. They've already developed a Bionic Brain Tonic (peach, strawberry, and orange juices with gotu kola and ginseng) and about 40 other blends intended to boost your immune system, sex drive, or mood. The noodle and rice dishes have equally esoteric names (Buddha, Green Goddess), though their contents are down-to-earth. The high-protein almond grain burgers and hemp-seed bread get top marks. Main courses C$8–$12 (US$5–$8); Mon–Fri 8:30am–6:30pm, Sat 9am–6:30pm, Sun 10am–6pm.

- **Kalendar** (p. 91) may be a small bistro, but its list of vegetarian offerings is substantial.

- **Mezzetta** (p. 113) offers a collection of Middle Eastern appetizers, few of which contain meat; ordering a selection of three of four makes for a substantial meal.

- **Millie's Bistro** (p. 111) has a vegetarian lasagna with portobello mushrooms, sweet roasted peppers, and leeks that will make you wonder why anyone would want to add beef. The Mediterranean menu has many meat-free plates.

- **Senses** (p. 101) offers a vegetarian tasting menu that changes frequently, but might include curried-squash ravioli or a salad of Jerusalem artichoke, olives, and beets. Yum!

- **Truffles** (p. 97) is another top-notch restaurant with a vegetarian tasting menu. Called the Menu Terroir, it might feature the likes of white bean and truffle soup, or a salad of frisee with Roquefort, walnuts, and apples; C$65 (US$44) for five courses.

8199 Yonge St. (just south of Hwy. 407). (© **905/731-6161.** www.terrarestaurant.ca. Reservations recommended. Main courses C$17–$49 (US$12–$33). AE, DC, MC, V. Tues–Sun 6–11pm.

MODERATE

Grand Yatt 🛪 CHINESE   There's a Grand Yatt restaurant at the Westin Harbour Castle hotel; this is the original. The large space is quite plain in comparison with its downtown offspring, but the cooking here is widely considered better. This is Cantonese cuisine at its finest. The seafood—black cod, geoduck (a large clam), or jumbo shrimp—is fresh as a daisy, and needs only light seasoning to bring out the intense natural flavors. Shark's fin soup is a perennial favorite. The swift servers are extremely helpful.

19019 Bayview Ave. (© **905/882-9388.** Main courses C$12–$18 (US$8.15–$12). AE, MC, V. Daily 9am–3pm and 6–10pm.

INEXPENSIVE

Dante's 🛪🛪 ITALIAN   Predating the current boom in the area, Dante's has been the favorite local spot for down-home cooking since 1976. It's not hard to figure out why. The menu has something for everyone, the food is consistently good, and the prices are reasonable. Don't expect to find exotic risottos—stick to heaping plates of pasta like rigatoni with black and green olives, or homemade cannelloni. One serving of chicken parmigiano can feed two adults.

267 Baythorn Dr. (just off Yonge St.). (© **905/881-1070.** Main courses C$7–$14 (US$4.75–$9.50). AE, MC, V. Mon–Thurs noon–10pm, Fri–Sat noon–midnight.

6

What to See & Do in Toronto

First the good news: Toronto has amazing sights to see and places to be that appeal to travelers of all stripes. The bad news? No matter how long your stay, you won't be able to fit everything in. Toronto is a sprawling city, and while downtown and midtown boast a sizable collection of attractions, some wonderful sights are in less accessible areas.

Another difficulty is that many attractions could take up a whole day. Ontario Place, Harbourfront, the Ontario Science Centre, and Paramount Canada's Wonderland all come to mind. That's not even mentioning the parks, the arts scene, or the shopping possibilities. My best advice is to relax and bring a good pair of walking shoes. There's no better way to appreciate Toronto than on foot.

SUGGESTED ITINERARIES
If You Have 1 Day
Start out early in the morning in **Kensington Market,** and pick up breakfast from one of the Middle Eastern, Asian, or North African cafes. Kensington adjoins Toronto's main **Chinatown;** stroll down Spadina Avenue and head east along Dundas Street to enjoy it. Along Dundas you'll find the **Art Gallery of Ontario;** spend at least a couple of hours there, and be sure to take in the collection of sculptures by British artist Henry Moore. For lunch, head to the gallery's marvelous restaurant, Agora, or to nearby Baldwin Street for Chinese food. It's a short walk from here to **Queen's Park,** where the Ontario Legislature meets; the surrounding greenery affords a respite from the asphalt jungle. If you're a museum lover, the **Royal Ontario Museum** is just up the street, but I wouldn't recommend exploring two major institutions (like the AGO and the ROM) in 1 day. Instead, head up to

trendy **Yorkville,** with its small galleries, boutiques, and cafes. If you have kids in tow, you might want to check out the **Children's Own Museum.** Before dinner, try to buy same-day tickets to a show in the adjoining **Theater District.** Then check out one of the fine restaurants in **Yorkville,** or head back downtown to **Queen Street West** (see chapter 5 for suggestions). If you didn't get theater tickets, Queen Street West offers varied nightlife options.

If You Have 2 Days
On the first day, follow the itinerary for 1 day. On day 2, start by wandering the grounds of **Exhibition Place,** and arrive at the gates of **Ontario Place** at 10am sharp; allow about half a day for Ontario Place. If it's a clear sunny day, go from there to the top of the **CN Tower** and drink in the matchless view. Glance over at **SkyDome** as you pass by. Head up to the architectural wonder that is **City Hall at Nathan**

Phillips Square, then continue east to the **Eaton Centre.** After you've shopped until you drop, ride a streetcar to **Little Italy,** along College Street. There's no end of dining options; try to score a patio seat if the weather's fine. This is another prime neighborhood for nightlife, so unless you've scored tickets to a game at the **Air Canada Centre,** you can hang out here.

If You Have 3 Days

This is when I'd recommend going a little farther afield. (You could also just allot more time to the previously mentioned sights.) Start your day at the highly interactive **Ontario Science Centre.** If the weather's good, you could spend the rest of the day reveling in the 600 acres of **Sunnybrook Park,** which has hiking trails and a horseback riding center. If the weather isn't so clement, this could be your afternoon to explore the **Royal Ontario Museum** or the **Hockey Hall of Fame.** If another museum isn't your thing, head to the **Harbourfront Centre,** which offers restaurants, a daily antiques market, activities for kids, and varied events. At night, go to **Greektown** along the Danforth, where the many tavernas stay open as late as 4am even on weeknights.

If You Have 4 Days or More

Now you can really start to explore Toronto. If you've followed the itinerary for the first 3 days, you might want to return to some sights. Otherwise, you could head north of Toronto to see the **McMichael Canadian Art Collection** in Kleinburg or, if the kids outvote you, to spend the day at **Paramount Canada's Wonderland.** There's no better way to spend a day than picnicking on the lush **Toronto Islands,** where you can rent bicycles, take the kids to **Centreville** amusement park, and get a whole new view of the city. A less traveled site is scenic **Cabbagetown,** with its Edwardian and Queen Anne–style architecture, **Riverdale Farm,** and Gothic **Necropolis.** With 4 days or more, you should also be able to sample the city's lively arts scene, taking in a **theater** or **dance performance.** Try to hit a **comedy club** while you're at it, and check out one of Toronto's **sports** teams, too.

1 The Top Attractions

ON THE LAKEFRONT

Harbourfront Centre ★★ Kids   In 1972, the federal government took over a 38-hectare (96-acre) strip of prime waterfront land to preserve the vista. Since then, Torontonians have rediscovered their lakeshore. Abandoned warehouses, shabby depots, and crumbling factories have been refurbished, and a tremendous urban park now stretches on and around the old piers. Today it's one of the most popular hangouts for locals and visitors—a great place to spend a day sunbathing, picnicking, biking, shopping, and sailing.

Queen's Quay, at the foot of York Street, is the closest quay to town, and it's the first one you'll encounter as you approach from the Westin Harbour Castle. From here, boats depart for harbor tours, and ferries leave for the Toronto Islands. In this renovated warehouse you'll find the Premiere Dance Theatre (which was designed for dance performances), and two floors of shops, restaurants, and waterfront cafes.

After exploring Queen's Quay, walk west along the glorious waterfront promenade to **York Quay.** You'll pass the **Power Plant,** a contemporary art gallery, and behind it, the **Du Maurier Theatre Centre.** At York Quay Centre, you can

Booked seat 6A, open return.

Rented red 4-wheel drive.

Reserved cabin, no running water.

Discovered space.

With over 700 airlines, 50,000 hotels, 50 rental car companies and 8,000 cruise and vacation packages, you can create the perfect getaway for you. Choose the car, the room, even the ground you walk on.

Travelocity.com
A Sabre Company
Go Virtually Anywhere.

Book your air, hotel, and transportation all in one place.

Hotel or hostel? Cruise or canoe? Car? Plane? Camel? Wherever you're going, visit Yahoo! Travel and get total control over your arrangements. Even choose your seat assignment. So. One hump or two? travel.yahoo.com

powered by
COMPAQ

YAHOO!
Travel

pick up information on Harbourfront programming. Galleries here include the **Craft Studio,** where you can watch artisans blow glass, throw pots, and make silk-screen prints. On the other side of the center, you can attend a free outdoor concert, held all summer long at Molson Place. Also on the quay is the Water's Edge Cafe, overlooking a small pond for electric model boats (there's skating here in the winter) and a children's play area.

Take the footbridge to John Quay, crossing over the sailboats moored below, to the stores and restaurants on **Pier 4**—Wallymagoo's Marine Bar and the Pier 4 Storehouse. Beyond, on Maple Leaf Quay, lies the Nautical Centre. At the **Harbourside Boating Centre** (part of the Nautical Centre), 283 Queen's Quay W. (② **416/203-3000**), you can rent sailboats and powerboats or sign up for sailing lessons (see "Boating/Canoeing," later in this chapter).

The **Harbourfront Antiques Market,** 390 Queen's Quay W., at the foot of Spadina Avenue (② **416/260-2626**), will keep antique-lovers busy browsing for hours. More than 100 dealers spread out their wares—jewelry, china, furniture, toys, and books. Indoor parking is adjacent to the market, and a cafeteria serves fresh salads, sandwiches, and desserts. It's open Tuesday through Sunday from 10am to 6pm.

At the west end of the park stands **Bathurst Pier,** with a large sports field plus two adventure playgrounds, one for older kids and the other (supervised) for 3- to 7-year-olds.

More than 4,000 events take place annually at Harbourfront, including the **Harbourfront Reading Series** in June and the **International Festival of Authors** in October. Other happenings include films, dance, theater, music, children's events, multicultural festivals, and marine events.

235 Queen's Quay W. ② **416/973-3000** for information on special events, or 416/973-4000 (box office). www.harbourfront.on.ca. Subway: Union, then LRT to York Quay.

Ontario Place ❀ *(Kids*   When this 38-hectare (96-acre) recreation complex on Lake Ontario opened in 1971, it seemed futuristic. Thirty-two years later, it still does. (The 1989 face-lift no doubt helped.) From a distance, you'll see five steel-and-glass pods suspended on columns 32m (105 ft.) above the lake, three artificial islands, and a huge geodesic dome. The five pods contain a multimedia theater, a children's theater, a high-technology exhibit, and displays that tell the story of Ontario in vivid kaleidoscopic detail. The dome houses Cinesphere, where a 18-by-24m (60-by-80-ft.) screen shows specially made IMAX movies year-round.

Under an enormous orange canopy, the Children's Village is the most creative playground you'll find anywhere. In a well-supervised area, children under 13 can scramble over rope bridges, bounce on an enormous trampoline, explore the foam forest, or slide down a twisting chute. The most popular activity allows them to squirt water pistols and garden hoses, swim, and generally drench one another in the water-play section. Afterward, parents can pop wet clothes into the convenient dryers before moving on to other amusements.

A stroll around the complex reveals two marinas full of yachts and other craft, the HMCS *Haida* (a destroyer, open for tours, that served in World War II and the Korean War), an 18-hole miniature golf course, and plenty of grassland for picnicking and romping. The restaurants and snack bars serve everything from Chinese, Irish, and German food to hot dogs and hamburgers. And don't miss the wildest rides in town—the Hydrofuge, a tube slide that allows you to reach speeds over 30 mph; the Rush River Raft Ride, which carries you along a lengthy flume; the pink twister and purple pipeline (water slides); plus bumper boats

Downtown Toronto Attractions

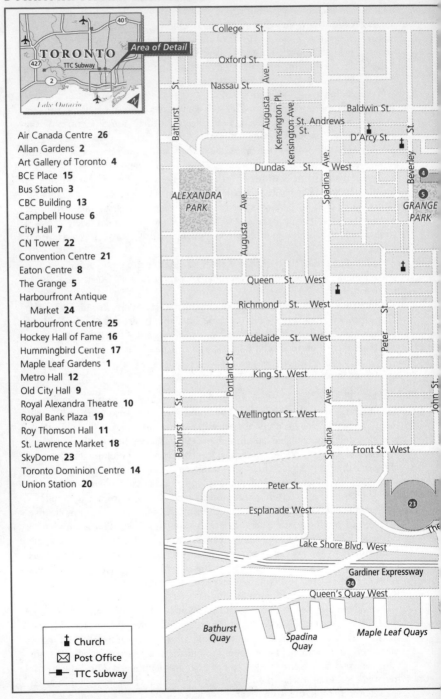

Air Canada Centre **26**
Allan Gardens **2**
Art Gallery of Toronto **4**
BCE Place **15**
Bus Station **3**
CBC Building **13**
Campbell House **6**
City Hall **7**
CN Tower **22**
Convention Centre **21**
Eaton Centre **8**
The Grange **5**
Harbourfront Antique
   Market **24**
Harbourfront Centre **25**
Hockey Hall of Fame **16**
Hummingbird Centre **17**
Maple Leaf Gardens **1**
Metro Hall **12**
Old City Hall **9**
Royal Alexandra Theatre **10**
Royal Bank Plaza **19**
Roy Thomson Hall **11**
St. Lawrence Market **18**
SkyDome **23**
Toronto Dominion Centre **14**
Union Station **20**

✝ Church
⊠ Post Office
-■- TTC Subway

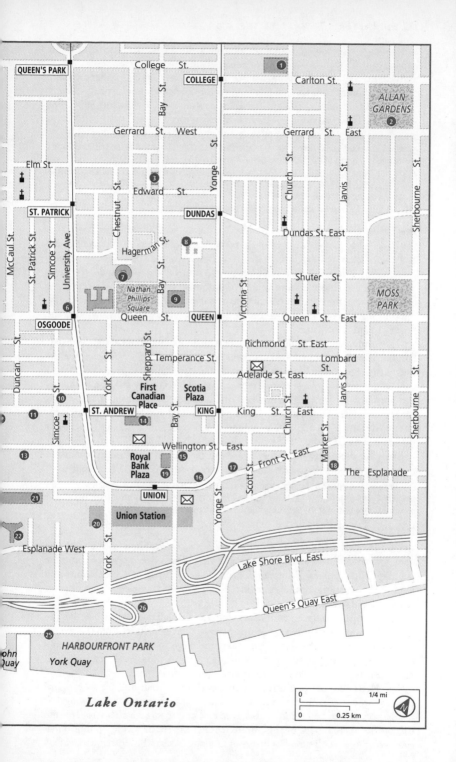

and go-karts. For something more peaceful, you can navigate pedal boats or remote-control boats between the artificial islands.

At night, the **Molson Amphitheatre** accommodates 16,000 under a copper canopy and outside on the grass. It features top-line entertainers such as Kenny G, James Taylor, and the Who. For information, call © **416/260-5600.** For tickets, call **Ticketmaster** (© **416/870-8000**).

955 Lakeshore Blvd. W. © **416/314-9811,** or 416/314-9900 for recorded info. www.ontarioplace.com. Admission to grounds and Children's Village only is C$10 (US$6.80) (all ages); separate fees for rides and events. Play All Day pass C$25 (US$17) adults and children 5 and over, C$12 (US$8.15) children aged 4, free for children 3 and under. IMAX movies after Labour Day (otherwise included in Play All Day pass) C$8 (US$5.45) adults, C$6 (US$4.10) seniors and children under 14. Mid-May to Labour Day, daily 10am–dusk; evening events end and dining spots close later. Closed (except Cinesphere) early Sept to early May. Parking C$10 (US$6.80). Subway: Bathurst or Dufferin, then Bathurst streetcar south.

The Toronto Islands 🎯 *Kids*   In only 7 minutes, an 800-passenger ferry takes you to 245 hectares (612 acres) of island parkland crisscrossed by shaded paths and quiet waterways—a glorious spot to walk, play tennis, bike, feed the ducks, putter around in boats, picnic, or lap up the sun. Of the 14 islands, the three major ones are **Centre, Ward's,** and **Algonquin.** The first is the busiest; the other two are home to about 600 people who live in modest cottages. Originally, the land was a peninsula, but in the mid-1800s a series of storms shattered the finger of land into islands.

On Centre Island, families enjoy **Centreville** (© **416/203-0405**), an old-fashioned amusement park that's been in business since 1966. You won't see the usual neon signs, shrill hawkers, and greasy hot-dog stands. Instead you'll find a turn-of-the-century village complete with a Main Street, tiny shops, a firehouse, and even a small working farm where the kids can pet lambs and chicks and enjoy pony rides. They'll also love trying out the antique cars, fire engines, old-fashioned train, authentic 1890s carousel, flume ride, and aerial cars. An all-day ride pass costs C$15.50 (US$11) for those less than 124cm (49 in.) tall, C$22 (US$15) for those over 1.25m (4 ft.). Centreville is open 10:30am to 6pm, daily from mid-May to Labour Day, and weekends in early May and September.

Lake Ontario. © **416/392-8193** for ferry schedules. Round-trip fare C$5 (US$3.40) adults, C$3 (US$2.05) seniors and youths 14–19, C$2 (US$1.35) children 13 and under; free for children 2 and under. Ferries leave from docks at the bottom of Bay St. Subway: Union Station, then LRT to Queen's Quay.

DOWNTOWN

Art Gallery of Ontario 🎯 *Kids*   The exterior gives no hint of the light and openness inside this beautifully designed gallery. The space is dramatic, and the paintings imaginatively displayed. Throughout, audiovisual presentations and interactive computer exhibits provide information on particular paintings or schools of painters.

The European collections are fine, but the Canadian galleries are the real treat. The paintings by the Group of Seven—which includes Tom Thomson, F. H. Varley, and Lawren Harris—are extraordinary. In addition, other galleries show the genesis of Canadian art from earlier to more modern artists. And don't miss the extensive collection of Inuit art.

The **Henry Moore Sculpture Centre,** with more than 800 pieces (original plasters, bronzes, maquettes, woodcuts, lithographs, etchings, and drawings), is the largest public collection of his works. The artist gave them to Toronto because he was so moved by the citizens' enthusiasm for his work—public dona-tions bought his sculpture *The Archer* to decorate Nathan Phillips Square at City

Hall after politicians refused to free up money for it. In one room, under a glass ceiling, 20 or so of his large works stand like silent prehistoric rock formations. Along the walls flanking a ramp are color photographs showing Moore's major sculptures in their natural locations, which reveal their magnificent dimensions.

The European collection ranges from the 14th century to the French impressionists and beyond. Works by Pissarro, Monet, Boudin, Sisley, and Renoir fill an octagonal room. De Kooning's *Two Women on a Wharf* and Karel Appel's *Black Landscape* are just two of the modern pieces. There are several works of particular interest to admirers of the pre-Raphaelite painters, including one by Waterhouse. Among the sculptures, you'll find two beauties—Picasso's *Poupée* and Brancusi's *First Cry.*

Behind the gallery, connected by an arcade, stands the Grange (1817), Toronto's oldest surviving brick house, which was the gallery's first permanent space. Originally the home of the Boulton family, it was a gathering place for many of the city's social and political leaders and for such eminent guests as Matthew Arnold, Prince Kropotkin, and Winston Churchill. Meticulously restored and furnished to reflect the 1830s, it is a living museum of mid-19th-century Toronto life. Entrance is free with admission to the art gallery.

The gallery has an attractive restaurant, Agora (see chapter 5 for a review), which is open for lunch, as well as a cafeteria and a gallery shop. There's also a full program of films, concerts, and lectures.

317 Dundas St. W. (between McCaul and Beverley sts.). (©) 416/977-0414. www.ago.net. Admission C$12 (US$8.15) adults, C$9 (US$6.10) seniors and students, C$6 (US$4) youths 6–16, free for children 5 and under. Free admission Wed 6–8:30pm. Tues and Thurs–Fri 11am–6pm, Wed 11am–8:30pm, Sat–Sun 10am–5:30pm. Grange House Tues–Sun noon–4pm, Wed noon–9pm. Closed Jan 1, Dec 25. Subway: St. Patrick.

CN Tower *Kids*   As you approach the city, whether by plane, train, or automobile, the first thing you notice is this slender structure. Glass-walled elevators glide up the 553m (1,815-ft.) tower, the tallest freestanding structure in the world. The elevators stop first at the 346m-high (1,136-ft.) LookOut level. (It takes just 58 seconds, so prepare for popping ears.) You can walk down one level to experience the Glass Floor, my favorite spot at the tower: through it you can see all the way down to street level (even as your heart drops into your shoes). As a bonus, if you wait long enough, you'll undoubtedly see some alpha males daring each other to jump on the glass (they do, and no, it doesn't break—the glass can withstand the weight of 14 adult hippos).

The tower attractions are often revamped. Some perennial draws are the IMAX theater and two airplane simulators (one gentle and calm, the other a rugged ride through caves and over mountains). A series of interactive displays showcases the CN Tower along with such forerunners as the Eiffel Tower and the Empire State Building. The LookOut also contains broadcasting facilities, a nightclub, and the underwhelming **360 Revolving Restaurant** (© **416/362-5411;** see chapter 5 for a review).

Fun Fact **Tough Enough**

The CN Tower is built of sturdy stuff to resist the elements—contoured reinforced concrete covered with thick glass-reinforced plastic—and designed to keep ice accumulation to a minimum. The structure can withstand high winds, snow, ice, lightning, and earth tremors.

Above the LookOut is the world's highest public observation gallery, the Sky Pod, 447m (1,465 ft.) above the ground (C$7/US$4.75 additional charge). From here, on a clear day you can't quite see forever, but the sweeping vista stretches to Niagara Falls, 161km (100 miles) south, and to Lake Simcoe, 193km (120 miles) north. Unless you're really taken with the tower, I wouldn't recommend it—the view from the Glass Floor is majestic enough for me. Atop the tower sits a 102m (335-ft.) antenna mast erected over 31 weeks with the aid of a giant Sikorsky helicopter. It took 55 lifts (and no hippos) to complete the operation.

301 Front St. W. ⓒ 416/868-6937. www.cntower.ca. Basic admission C$16 (US$11) adults, C$14 (US$9.50) seniors, C$11 (US$7.50) children 4–12; Total Tower Experience (includes Skypod, film, and 2 rides) C$30 (US$19) all ages. Motion simulator rides C$7.50 (US$5). Combination tickets from C$23 (US$16). Daily May–Sept 8am–11pm, Oct–Apr 9am–10pm. Subway: Union, then walk west on Front St.

MIDTOWN

George R. Gardiner Museum of Ceramic Art   Across the street from the ROM, North America's only specialized ceramics museum houses a great collection of 15th- to 18th-century European pieces in four galleries. The pre-Columbian gallery contains fantastic Olmec and Maya figures, and objects from Ecuador, Colombia, and Peru. The majolica gallery displays spectacular 16th- and 17th-century salvers and other pieces from Florence, Faenza, and Venice, and a Delftware collection that includes fine 17th-century chargers.

Upstairs, the galleries contain 18th-century continental and English porcelain—Meissen, Sèvres, Worcester, Chelsea, Derby, and other great names. All are spectacular. Among the highlights are objects from the Swan Service—a 2,200-piece set that took 4 years (1737–41) to make—and an extraordinary collection of commedia dell'arte figures.

111 Queen's Park. ⓒ 416/586-8080. www.gardinermuseum.on.ca. Admission C$10 (US$6.80) adults, C$6 (US$4.10) seniors and students. Free admission on the first Tuesday of every month. Mon, Wed, Fri 10am–6pm; Tues, Thurs 10am–8pm; Sat–Sun 10am–5pm. Closed Jan 1, Dec 25. Subway: Museum.

Royal Ontario Museum 🏛🏛🏛 *Kids*   This is one of my favorite museums anywhere. The ROM (rhymes with "tom"), as it's affectionately called, is Canada's largest museum, with more than 6 million objects in its collections. Among the many highlights are the world-renowned **T. T. Tsui Galleries of Chinese Art,** which contain priceless Ming and Qing porcelains, embroidered silk robes, and objects made of jade and ivory. One of the collection's treasures is the procession of 100 earthenware figures, including ox-drawn carts, soldiers, musicians, officials, and attendants, dating from the early 6th to the late 7th century. Another is the collection of 14 monumental Buddhist sculptures from the 12th to the 16th century. Visitors can also see outstanding examples of early weapons and tools, oracle bones, bronzes, ceramic vessels, human and animal figures, and jewelry.

⌒ *Finds* **Serenity Now**

While the ROM's permanent collections and special exhibitions are impressive, the best room in the entire gallery is barely known—and usually empty. It's the **Bishop White Gallery,** and it houses a group of serene Southeast Asian Buddhas. They stand in the center of the room, facing out; murals from the region cover the walls. Some of the Buddhas are in better shape than others (you'll see wounds and scars where jewels were plucked out), but all of them radiate peace. This is one place I go to recharge.

The **Sigmund Samuel Canadiana galleries** display a premier collection of early Canadian decorative arts and historical paintings. More than 1,200 objects in elaborate period room settings reveal the French and English contributions to Canadian culture.

Other highlights include the **Ancient Egypt Gallery,** which features several mummies, the **Roman Gallery** (the most extensive collection in Canada), the excellent textile collection, and nine life-science galleries (devoted to evolution, mammals, reptiles, and botany). The **Gallery of Indigenous Peoples** features changing exhibitions that explore the past and present cultures of Canada's indigenous peoples. A recent addition is the **Gallery of Korean Art,** the largest exhibit of its kind in North America. It holds more than 200 works from the Bronze Age through modern times.

A favorite with kids is the **Bat Cave Gallery,** a miniature replica of the St. Clair bat cave in Jamaica. It's complete with more than 3,000 lifelike bats roosting and flying through the air amid realistic spiders, crabs, a wildcat, and snakes. Kids also enjoy the spectacular **Dinosaur Gallery,** with 13 realistically displayed skeletons, and the **Discovery Gallery,** a mini-museum where youngsters (and adults) can touch authentic artifacts from Egyptian scarabs to English military helmets.

The ROM's light, airy dining lounge, **Jamie Kennedy at the Museum** (© **416/586-5578;** see chapter 5 for a review), has a small terrace with outdoor seating. Under the expert supervision of Jamie Kennedy, one of Canada's top chefs, it's well worth a stop for lunch.

100 Queen's Park. © 416/586-8000. www.rom.on.ca. Admission C$16.50 (US$11) adults, C$12 (US$8.15) seniors and students with valid ID, C$10 (US$6.80) children 5–14, free for children 4 and under. Pay what you can Fri 4:30–9:30pm. Mon–Thurs 10am–6pm; Fri 10am–9:30pm; Sat 10am–6pm; Sun 11am–6pm. Closed Jan 1, Dec 25. Subway: Museum.

ON THE OUTSKIRTS

The McMichael Canadian Art Collection   In Kleinburg, 40km (25 miles) north of the city, the McMichael is worth a visit for the setting as well as the art. The collection occupies a log-and-stone gallery that sits amid quiet stands of trees on 40 hectares (100 acres) of conservation land. Specially designed for the landscape paintings it houses, the gallery is a work of art. The lobby has a pitched roof that soars 8m (27 ft.) on massive rafters of Douglas fir; throughout the gallery, panoramic windows look south over white pine, cedar, ash, and birch.

The collection includes the work of Canada's famous circle of landscape painters, the Group of Seven, as well as David Milne, Emily Carr, and their contemporaries. An impressive collection of Inuit and contemporary Native Canadian art and sculpture is also on display. In addition, four galleries contain changing exhibitions of works by contemporary artists.

Founded by Robert and Signe McMichael, the gallery began in 1965 when they donated their property, home, and collection to the province of Ontario. The collection has expanded to include more than 6,000 works. The museum has a good book and gift store, filled with reproductions as well as one-of-a-kind crafts, carvings and wall hangings by Canadian artisans.

10365 Islington Ave., Kleinburg. © 888/213-1121 or 905/893-1121. www.mcmichael.com. Admission C$12 (US$8.15) adults, C$9 (US$6.10) seniors and students, free for children 5 and under. Daily 10am–4pm. Closed Dec 25. Parking C$5 (US$3.40). By car: From downtown, take Gardiner Expressway to Hwy. 427 north, follow it to Hwy. 7, and turn east. Turn left (north) at first light onto Hwy. 27. Turn right (east) at Major Mackenzie Dr. and left (north) at first set of lights to Islington Ave. and the village of Kleinburg. Or take Hwy. 401 to Hwy. 400 north. At Major Mackenzie Dr., go west to Islington Ave. and turn right. By bus: From Islington station, take the #37 bus to Steeles Ave., then take the York Region #13 bus to the museum driveway (it's about a 10-min. walk up the driveway from the bus stop); note: separate fares are required for the 2 buses.

Midtown Toronto Attractions

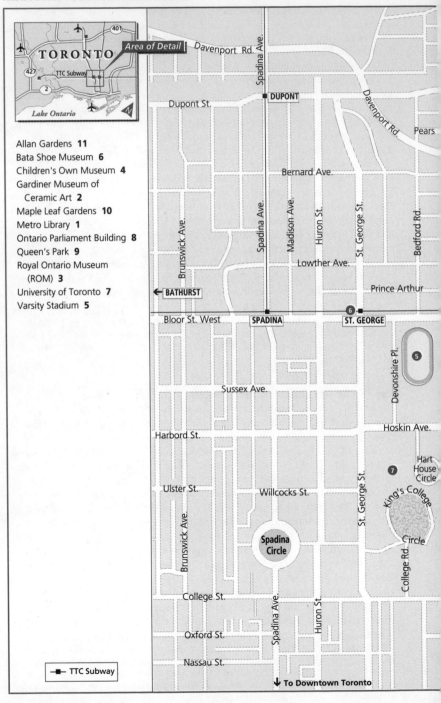

Allan Gardens **11**
Bata Shoe Museum **6**
Children's Own Museum **4**
Gardiner Museum of
  Ceramic Art **2**
Maple Leaf Gardens **10**
Metro Library **1**
Ontario Parliament Building **8**
Queen's Park **9**
Royal Ontario Museum
  (ROM) **3**
University of Toronto **7**
Varsity Stadium **5**

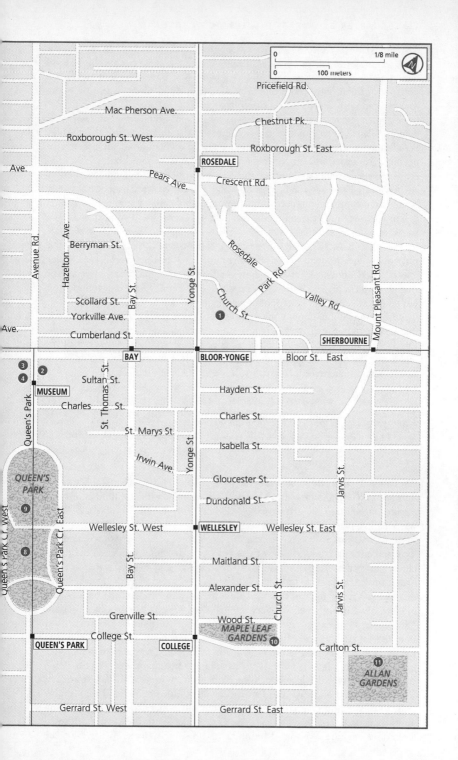

Ontario Science Centre *(Kids)* Described as everything from the world's most technical fun fair to a hands-on museum for the 21st century, the Science Centre holds a series of wonders for children—800 interactive exhibits in 10 cavernous exhibit halls. More than a million people visit every year, so it's best to arrive promptly at 10am to see everything.

Wherever you look, there are things to touch, push, pull, or crank. Test your reflexes, balance, heart rate, and grip strength; surf the Internet; watch frozen-solid liquid nitrogen shatter into thousands of icy shards; study slides of butterfly wings, bedbugs, fish scales, or feathers under a microscope; tease your brain with a variety of optical illusions; land a spaceship on the moon; watch bees making honey; see how many lights you can light or how high you can elevate a balloon with your own pedal power. The fun goes on and on through the 10 exhibit halls.

Throughout, small theaters show film and slide shows, and you can see regular 20-minute demonstrations of lasers, metal casting, and high-voltage electricity (which will literally make your hair stand on end). Another draw is the Omnimax Theatre, with a 24m (79-ft.) domed screen that creates spectacular effects. There are two eateries on-site: Galileo's Bistro, a buffet-style restaurant that serves alcohol, and Valley Marketplace, a cafeteria. The Mastermind shop has a vast collection of educational toys and games.

While most of the Ontario Science Centre's offerings are fun for the small fry, one area that adults will appreciate is the re-creation of a rain-forest environment. On the bottom level of the building, it's large enough that you can wander a bit and forget the noise and blinking lights of the science arcade just beyond. One caveat: Roam in here for long and you'll feel as if you've hit a sauna.

770 Don Mills Rd. (at Eglinton Ave. E.). © 416/696-3127, or 416/696-1000 for Omnimax tickets. www. ontariosciencecentre.ca. Admission C$13 (US$8.85) adults, C$9 (US$6.10) seniors and youths 13–17, C$7 (US$4.75) children 5–12, free for children 4 and under. Omnimax admission C$10 (US$6.80) adults, C$7 (US$4.75) seniors and youths 13–17, C$6 (US$4.10) children 5–12. Combination discounts available. July 1–Sept 4 Daily 10am–6pm, Sept 5–June 30 Daily 10am–5pm. Closed Dec 25. Parking C$7 (US$4.80). Subway: Yonge St. line to Eglinton, then no. 34 Eglinton bus east to Don Mills Rd. By car: From downtown, take Don Valley Pkwy. to Don Mills Rd. exit and follow signs.

Paramount Canada's Wonderland *(Kids)* Thirty minutes north of Toronto lies Canada's answer to Disney World. The 120-hectare (300-acre) park features more than 140 attractions, including 60 rides, an 8-hectare (20-acre) water park, a play area for tiny tots (KidZville), and live shows.

Adults and kids alike come for the thriller rides. Because the park relies on the local audience, it introduces new rides every year. In 2002, it opened both Psyclone, a gravity-defying pendulum, and Riptide Racer, an 8-track water raceway. Other top attractions include: the Fly, a roller coaster designed to make every seat feel as if it's in the front car (the faint of heart can't hide at the back of this one!); Drop Zone, in which riders free-fall 70m (230 ft.) in an open cockpit; Cliffhanger, a "super swing" that executes 360-degree turns and makes riders feel immune to gravity; and the Xtreme Skyflyer, a hang-gliding and skydiving hybrid that plunges riders 46m (150 ft.) in a free fall. The roller coasters range from the looping, inverted Top Gun, to the track-free suspended Vortex.

The Splash Works water park offers a huge wave pool and 16 water rides, from speed slides and tube rides to special scaled-down slides and a kids' play area. You'll also find Hanna-Barbera characters, including Scooby-Doo, strolling around the park (and ready to get their picture taken with the kids). Additional attractions include Wonder Mountain and its high divers (they take the

---

(*Finds* **Retro Thrills**

With the fanfare given to the new rides Paramount Canada's Wonderland introduces each summer, many park-goers overlook the older attractions. The Wilde Beaste is one of the original roller coasters, and it's still one of the best. The first few times you hurtle along the track you'll be convinced that the whole rickety structure is about to fall down at any moment. Guess what—it was designed to feel that way! (Wonderland's safety standards are top-notch, so have no worries on that front.) Other tried-and-true favorites include the Minebuster and the Dragon Fire. A bonus: shorter queues!

20m/66-ft. plunge down Victoria Falls to the mountain's base), restaurants, and shops. The Kingswood Theatre books top-name entertainers.

You'll definitely want to take a full day to see everything. If you picnic on the grounds and forgo souvenirs, a family of four can "do" the park for about C$200 (US$136), depending on the age of the kids. Watch out, though, for the extra attractions not included in the admission pass.

9580 Jane St., Vaughan. (*C*) **905/832-7000** or 905/832-8131. www.canadas-wonderland.com. Pay-One-Price Passport (includes unlimited rides and shows but not parking, special attractions, or Kingswood Music Theater) C$47 (US$32) adults and children 7 and up, C$23.50 (US$16) seniors and children 3–6, free for children 2 and under. Admission only (no rides) C$25 (US$17). June 1–25 Mon–Fri 10am–8pm, Fri–Sat 10am–10pm; June 26–Labour Day daily 10am–10pm; late May and early Sept to early Oct Sat–Sun 10am–8pm. Closed mid-Oct to mid-May. Parking C$7 (US$4.75). Subway: Yorkdale or York Mills, then GO Express Bus to Wonderland. By car: From downtown, take Yonge St. north to Hwy. 401 and go west to Hwy. 400. Go north on Hwy. 400 to Rutherford Rd. exit and follow signs. By car from the north, exit at Major Mackenzie.

The Toronto Zoo (*Kids*)   Covering 284 hectares (710 acres) of parkland, this unique zoological garden contains some 5,000 animals, plus an extensive botanical collection. Pavilions—including Africa, Indo-Malaya, Australasia, and the Americas—and outdoor paddocks house the plants and animals.

One popular zoo attraction is at the **African Savannah** project. It re-creates a market bazaar and safari through Kesho (Swahili for "tomorrow") National Park, past such special features as a bush camp, rhino midden, elephant highway, and several watering holes. In the summer of 2002, the zoo opened Splash Island, a kids-only water park that includes a replica of a Canadian Coast Guard ship.

Ten kilometers (6 miles) of walkways offer access to all areas of the zoo. During the warmer months, the Zoomobile takes visitors around the major walkways to view the animals in the outdoor paddocks. The zoo has restaurants, a gift shop, first aid, and a family center. Visitors can rent strollers and wagons, and borrow wheelchairs. The African pavilion has an elevator for strollers and wheelchairs. There's ample parking and plenty of picnic areas with tables.

Meadowvale Rd. (north of Hwy. 401 and Sheppard Ave.), Scarborough. (*C*) **416/392-5900.** www.toronto zoo.com. Admission C$17 (US$12) adults, C$11 (US$7.50) seniors, C$9 (US$6.10) children 4–12, free for children 3 and under. Summer daily 9am–7:30pm; spring and fall 9am–6pm; winter 9:30am–4:30pm. Last admission 1 hour before closing. Closed Dec 25. Parking C$6 (US$4.10). Subway: Bloor–Danforth line to Kennedy, then bus no. 86A north. By car: From downtown, take Don Valley Pkwy. to Hwy. 401 east, exit on Meadowvale Rd., and follow signs.

2 More Museums

The Bata Shoe Museum (*R*)   Imelda Marcos—or anyone else obsessed with shoes—will love this museum, which houses the Bata family's 10,000-item

---

Finds **Pssst . . . Want in on a Secret?**

Toronto has a unique museum that is one of the city's best-kept secrets. It's the **History of Contraception Museum**, at the Janssen-Ortho building, 19 Green Belt Drive (© **416/449-9444**). The collection occupies an airy atrium and contains more than 600 items, some of which will make your jaw drop. (Ever wonder what mule earwax, weasel testicles, and crocodile dung have in common? This is your chance to find out.) The museum is extremely well curated, and many of the prophylactics have fascinating stories behind them.

The only downside to the museum is that it's far off the beaten track—though the Ontario Science Centre is just a 5-minute drive away. If you've already made it that far, hop on a southbound Don Mills Road bus; there's a stop at Green Belt Drive, and the Janssen-Ortho building is a 2-minute walk up the street. It's open Monday through Friday from 9am to 5pm, and admission is free.

---

collection. The building, designed by Raymond Moriyama, is spectacular. The main gallery, "All About Shoes," traces the history of footwear. It begins with a plaster cast of some of the earliest known human footprints (discovered in Africa by anthropologist Mary Leakey), which date to 4 million B.C.

You'll come across such specialty shoes as spiked clogs used to crush chestnuts in 17th-century France, Elton John's 12-inch-plus platforms, and Prime Minister Pierre Trudeau's well-worn sandals. One display focuses on Canadian footwear fashioned by the Inuit, while another highlights 19th-century ladies' footwear. The second-story galleries house changing exhibits.

327 Bloor St. W. (at St. George St.). © 416/979-7799. www.batashoemuseum.ca. Admission C$6 (US$4.10) adults, C$4 (US$2.70) seniors and students, C$2 (US$1.35) children 5–14; C$12 (US$8.15) family (2 adults, 2 children). Free to all first Tues of the month. Tues–Wed and Fri–Sat 10am–5pm, Thurs 10am–8pm, Sun noon–5pm. Subway: St. George.

Black Creek Pioneer Village (Kids Life here moves at the gentle pace of rural Ontario as it was 100 years ago. You can watch the authentically dressed villagers going about their chores, spinning, sewing, rail splitting, sheep shearing, and threshing. Enjoy the villagers' cooking, wander through the cozily furnished homesteads, visit the working mill, shop at the general store, or rumble past the farm animals in a horse-drawn wagon. The beautifully landscaped village has more than 30 restored buildings to explore. Special events take place throughout the year, from a great Easter egg hunt to Christmas by lamplight.

The dining room (open May–Thanksgiving and Dec) serves lunch and afternoon tea.

1000 Murray Ross Pkwy. (at Steeles Ave. and Jane St.), Downsview. © 416/736-1733. www.blackcreek.ca. Admission C$10 (US$6.80) adults, C$9 (US$6.10) seniors, C$6 (US$4.10) children 5–14, free for children 4 and under. May–June Mon–Fri 9:30am–4:30pm, Sat–Sun and holidays 10am–5pm; July–Sept daily 10am–5pm; Oct–Dec Mon–Fri 9:30am–4pm, Sat–Sun and holidays 10am–4:30pm. Closed Jan–Apr, Dec 25. Parking C$6 (US$4.10). Subway: Finch, then bus no. 60 west to Murray Ross Parkway.

Design Exchange In the old Stock Exchange Building, this has become Toronto's design center. It showcases professionals' work, but its main purpose is to nurture designers of all types—graphic, industrial, interior, landscape, and urban. It also serves as a clearinghouse and resource center for the design community. Small free exhibitions on the first floor are open daily, while those in the upstairs Exhibition Hall are generally on view for 3 to 6 months and require admission. There's also a good bookstore and Cafe Deco, a relaxed eatery open Monday through Friday from 7:30am to 5pm.

234 Bay St. ⓒ 416/363-6121. www.dx.org. Admission C$5 (US$3.40) adults, C$3.50 (US$2.40) students and seniors, free for children under 14. Mon–Fri 10am–6pm, Sat–Sun noon–5pm. Subway: King.

Museum of Contemporary Canadian Art   This 8-year-old gallery's original mission was to collect and exhibit the best Canadian art created since 1985; however, it is now showing some works by international artists, too. Currently, the Canadian collection includes works by Stephen Andrews, Genevieve Cadieux, Ivan Eyre, Betty Goodwin, Micah Lexier, Arnaud Maggs, and Roland Poulin.

Toronto Centre for the Arts, 5040 Yonge St., Toronto. ⓒ 416/395-0067. www.mocca.toronto.on.ca. Free admission. Tues–Sun noon–5pm. Subway: North York Centre.

Textile Museum of Canada ⓡ   This fascinating museum is internationally recognized for its collection of more than 8,000 historic and ethnographic textiles and related artifacts. You'll find fine Oriental rugs, and cloth and tapestries from all over the world. One gallery presents the work of contemporary artists. The museum is small, so only a tiny portion of the collection is on display, but you'll always find a vibrant, interesting show.

55 Centre Ave. ⓒ 416/599-5321. www.museumfortextiles.on.ca. Admission C$8 (US$5.45) adults, C$6 (US$4.10) students seniors, and kids 5 and up. Pay what you can on Wednesday from 5–8pm. Tues and Thurs–Fri 11am–5pm, Wed 11am–8pm, Sat–Sun noon–5pm. Subway: St. Patrick.

3 Exploring the Neighborhoods

Toronto is a patchwork of neighborhoods, and the best way to discover its soul and flavor is to meander along its streets. On foot you can best appreciate the sights, sounds, and smells—those elements that lend a particular area its unique character. These are some of the most interesting neighborhoods.

DOWNTOWN WEST

CHINATOWN ⓡ   Stretching along Dundas Street west from Bay Street to Spadina Avenue and north and south along Spadina Avenue, Chinatown is home to some of Toronto's 350,000 Chinese-Canadian residents. Packed with fascinating shops and restaurants, it even has bilingual street signs.

In **Dragon City,** a large shopping mall at Spadina and Dundas, you'll find all kinds of stores. Some sell Chinese preserves (like cuttlefish, lemon ginger, whole mango, ginseng, and antler), and others specialize in Asian books, tapes, records, fashion, and food. Downstairs, a fast-food court features Korean, Indonesian, Chinese, and Japanese cuisine.

As you stroll through Chinatown, stop at the **Kim Moon Bakery,** 438 Dundas St. W. (ⓒ 416/977-1933) for Chinese pastries and a pork bun, or go to one of the tea stores. A walk through Chinatown at night is especially exciting—the sidewalks fill with people, and neon lights shimmer everywhere. You'll pass windows where ducks hang, gleaming noodle houses, record stores selling the Top 10 in Chinese, and trading companies filled with Asian produce. Another stop might be the **New Asia Supermarket,** 299 Spadina Ave. (ⓒ 416/591-9314), around the corner from Dundas Street.

To get to Chinatown, take the subway to St. Patrick and walk west. For more details, see "Walking Tour: Chinatown & Kensington Market," in chapter 7.

LITTLE ITALY   Along College Street between Euclid and Shaw, Little Italy vies with Queen Street for the hottest spot in the city. The area hums at night, as people crowd the coffee bars, pool lounges, nightclubs, and trattorias. To get there, ride any College Street streetcar west to Euclid Avenue.

QUEEN STREET WEST   This street has over the years been known as the heart of Toronto's avant-garde scene. It's home to several clubs—the **BamBoo** and the **Rivoli,** in particular—where major Canadian artists and singers have launched their careers (see chapter 9). An eclectic mix of stores and businesses lines the street. Although recent trends have brought mainstream stores to the street, it retains a certain edginess.

Here in the heart of the gourmet ghetto, there's a broad selection of bistros and restaurants, a number of fine antiquarian bookstores, and a lot of funky fashion stores. You'll also see outright junk shops, nostalgic record emporiums, kitchen supply stores, and discount fabric houses. East of Bathurst, the street is being slowly gentrified, but beyond Bathurst it retains its rough-and-ready energy.

To start exploring, take the subway to Osgoode and walk west along Queen Street West.

DOWNTOWN EAST
THE BEACHES   This is one of the neighborhoods that makes Toronto a unique city. Here, near the terminus of the Queen Street East streetcar line, you can stroll or cycle along the lakefront boardwalk. Because of its natural assets, it has become a popular residential neighborhood for young boomers and their families, and there are plenty of browseable stores along Queen Street. Just beyond Waverley Road, you can turn down through Kew Gardens to the board-walk and walk all the way past the Olympic Pool to Ashbridge's Bay Park. To get to the Beaches, take any Queen Street East streetcar to Woodbine Avenue.

MIDTOWN WEST
YORKVILLE   This area stretches north of Bloor Street, between Avenue Road and Bay Street. Since its founding in 1853 as a village outside the city proper, Yorkville has experienced many transformations. In the 1960s, it was Toronto's Haight-Ashbury, the countercultural mecca for young suburban runaways other-wise known as hippies. In the 1980s, it became the shopping ground of the chic, who dropped their money liberally at such boutiques as Hermès, Courrèges, Gianni Versace, Cartier, and Turnbull & Asser, and at the neighborhood's many fine art galleries. In the early 1990s, the recession left its mark—a fact that became glaringly obvious when Creeds, a Toronto institution, shut its doors. The restored town houses began to look a little forlorn, but today the energy is back. Bloor Street and Hazelton Lanes continue to attract high-style stores, including a branch of Tiffany's.

Stroll around and browse—or sit out in the sun at one of the many cafes on Yorkville Avenue or Cumberland Avenue, and watch the parade go by.

Make sure you wander through the labyrinths of Hazelton Lanes, between Avenue Road and Hazelton Avenue. You'll find a maze of shops and offices clustered around an outdoor court in the center of a building that is topped with apartments—one of the most sought-after addresses in the city. The court-yard plays host to outdoor dining in summer and skating in winter.

While you're in the neighborhood (especially if you're an architecture buff), take a look at the red-brick building on Bloor Street at the end of Yorkville Avenue that houses the **Toronto Reference Library.** Step inside and you'll find one of Toronto's most serene spots. To reach Yorkville, take the subway to Bay.

MIRVISH VILLAGE   One of the city's most illustrious characters is Honest Ed Mirvish, who started his career in the 1950s with a no-frills department store at the corner of Markham and Bloor streets (1 block west of Bathurst). Even from blocks away, neon signs race and advertisements touting bargains hit you from every direction. Among his other accomplishments, Mirvish saved the Royal Alexandra Theatre on King Street from demolition, established a row of adjacent restaurants for theater patrons, and developed this block-long area with art galleries, restaurants, and bookstores. He was responsible for saving and renovating London's Old Vic, too.

Stop by and browse, and don't forget to step into **Honest Ed's** (see "The Best Bargains," in chapter 8). To start your visit, take the subway to Bathurst.

THE EAST END
THE DANFORTH   This eclectic area along Danforth Street east of the Don River is hot, hot, hot. It swings until the early hours, when the restaurants and bars are still crowded and frenetic. During the day, visitors can browse the traditional Greek stores—like **Akropol**, a Greek bakery at no. 458 (© **416/465-1232**) that displays stunning multi-tiered wedding cakes in the window. Along with the Greek food vendors and travel agents, you'll find stores like **Blue Moon**, no. 375 (© **416/778-6991**), which sells beautiful crafts from the developing world (the store supports only producers that provide healthy working conditions and fair pay); **El Pipil**, no. 267 (© **416/465-9625**), which has colorful clothing, knapsacks, and jewelry; and some New Age and alternative stores. To get to the Danforth, ride the subway to Broadview and walk east.

4 Architectural Highlights

Casa Loma ⏏ *Kids*   Every city has its folly, and Toronto has an unusually charming one. It's complete with Elizabethan-style chimneys, Rhineland turrets, secret passageways, an underground tunnel, and a mellifluous name: Casa Loma.

Sir Henry Pellatt, who built it between 1911 and 1914, had a lifelong fascination with castles. He studied medieval palaces and gathered materials and furnishings from around the world, bringing marble, glass, and paneling from Europe, teak from Asia, and oak and walnut from North America. He imported Scottish stonemasons to build the massive walls that surround the 2.5-hectare (6-acre) site.

It's a fascinating place to explore. Wander through the majestic Great Hall, with its 18m-high (60-ft.) hammer-beam ceiling; the Oak Room, where three artisans took 3 years to fashion the paneling; and the Conservatory, with its elegant bronze doors, stained-glass dome, and pink-and-green marble. The castle encompasses battlements and a tower; Peacock Alley, designed after Windsor Castle; and a 1,700-bottle wine cellar. A 244m (800-ft.) tunnel runs to the stables, where the luxury of Spanish tile and mahogany surrounded the horses.

⸨Finds⸩ Walk This Way

Several doors on the first story of Casa Loma open to a grand terrace that overlooks the gardens; most visitors step out, look at the gorgeous fountain and flowers below, and then proceed with the castle tour. Their mistake. From the terrace, it's almost impossible to see the entrances to several winding paths that lead around the extensive grounds and command amazing views. Follow the grand staircase down and enjoy a leisurely ramble.

I find it amusing to compare the Pellatts' private suites. Lady Mary's is overwhelmingly extravagant—you could house a family of four in her bathroom, never mind the bedroom, sitting area, sunroom, and so on. Sir Henry's suite is surprisingly modest: it's relatively tiny, with the greatest extravagance being the 18-inch-diameter shower head in the bathroom. It does make you wonder which of them was the *real* driving force behind the building of the castle.

The tour is self-guided; pick up an audiocassette, available in eight languages, upon arrival. From May to October, the gardens are open, too. There are special events every March, July, and December.

1 Austin Terrace. (©) 416/923-1171. www.casaloma.org. Admission C$10 (US$6.80) adults, C$6.50 (US$4.40) seniors and youths 14–17, C$6 (US$4.10) children 4–13, free for children 3 and under. Daily 9:30am–5pm (last entry at 4pm). Parking C$2.30 (US$1.60) per hour. Closed Jan 1 and Dec 25. Subway: Dupont, then walk 2 blocks north.

City Hall ⊛   An architectural spectacle, City Hall houses the mayor's office and the city's administrative offices. Daringly designed in the late 1950s by Finnish architect Viljo Revell, it consists of a low podium topped by the flying-saucer-shaped Council Chamber, enfolded between two curved towers. Its interior is as dramatic as its exterior.

In front stretches **Nathan Phillips Square** (named after the mayor who initiated the project). In summer you can sit and contemplate the flower gardens, fountains, and reflecting pool (which doubles as a skating rink in winter), as well as listen to concerts. Here you'll find Henry Moore's *The Archer* (formally, *Three-Way Piece No. 2*), purchased through a public subscription fund, and the Peace Garden, which commemorates Toronto's sesquicentennial in 1984. In contrast, to the east stands the **Old City Hall,** a green-copper-roofed Victorian Romanesque-style building.

100 Queen St. W. (©) 416/338-0338. www.city.toronto.on.ca. Free admission. Self-guided tours Mon–Fri 8:30am–4:30pm. Subway: Queen, then walk west to Bay.

Eaton Centre   Buttressed at both ends by 30-story skyscrapers, this high-tech center, which cost over C$250 million (US$170 million) to build, stretches from Dundas Street south along Yonge Street to Queen Street, an area that encompasses 6 million square feet. **Eatons** department store takes up 1 million square feet, and more than 285 stores and restaurants and two garages fill the rest. Some 20 million people shop here annually.

Inside, the structure opens into the impressive **Galleria,** a 264m-long (866-ft.) glass-domed arcade dotted with benches, orchids, palm trees, and fountains; it's further adorned by Michael Snow's 60 soaring Canada geese, titled *Step Flight.* The birds are made from black-and-white photos mounted on cast fiber-glass frames. Three tiers rise above, reached by escalator and glass elevators,

---

(Finds A Place in the Sun

While it's easy to get carried away in the shops of Eaton Centre, don't overlook Trinity Square, on the west side of the building near Eatons department store. The complex surrounds two of Toronto's oldest landmarks: **Trinity Church,** dating to 1847, and **Scadding House** ((©) 416/598-4521), home of Trinity's rector. Concerned citizens demanded that the developers not block sunlight from reaching the buildings. They got their way—the sun continues to shine on the church's twin towers.

which afford glorious views over this Crystal Palace and Milan–style masterpiece designed by Eb Zeidler (who also designed Ontario Place). Don't be surprised by the twittering of sparrows, some of which have decided that this environment is as pleasant as the outdoors.

Dundas and Yonge sts. ℂ **416/598-8700.** www.torontoeatoncentre.com. Mon–Fri 10am–9pm, Sat 9:30am–7pm, Sun noon–6pm. Subway: Dundas or Queen.

Ontario Legislature 𝕉   At the northern end of University Avenue, with University of Toronto buildings to the east and west, lies Queen's Park. Embedded in its center is the rose-tinted sandstone-and-granite Ontario Legislature, with stately domes, arches, and porte cocheres. At any time of year other than summer, drop in around 2pm—when the legislature is in session—for some pithy comments during the question period, or take one of the regular tours. It's best to call ahead to check times.

111 Wellesley St. W. (at University Ave.). ℂ **416/325-7500.** www.ontla.on.ca. Free admission. Mon–Fri year-round; Sat–Sun Victoria Day–Labour Day. Weekend tours every ½ hour 9–11:30am and 1–4pm; call ahead at other times. Subway: Queen's Park.

Royal Bank Plaza   Shimmering in the sun, Royal Bank Plaza looks like a pillar of gold, and with good reason. During its construction, 2,500 ounces of gold went into the building's 14,000 windows as a coloring agent. More important, the structure is a masterpiece of architectural design. Two triangular towers of bronze mirror glass flank a 40m-high (130-ft.) glass-walled banking hall. The external walls of the towers are built in a serrated configuration so that they reflect a phenomenal mosaic of color from the skies and surrounding buildings.

In the banking hall, hundreds of aluminum cylinders hang from the ceiling, the work of Venezuelan sculptor Jesús Raphael Soto. Two levels below, there's a waterfall and pine-tree setting that's naturally illuminated from the hall above.

Front and Bay sts. Free admission. Subway: Union.

Toronto Reference Library   Step inside—a pool and a waterfall gently screen out the street noise, and the space opens dramatically to the sky. Light and air flood every corner. This structure is another masterwork by Toronto architect Raymond Moriyama, who also designed the Bata Shoe Museum.

789 Yonge St. ℂ **416/393-7000.** Free admission. Year-round Mon–Thurs 10am–8pm, Fri–Sat 10am–5pm; Thanksgiving–Apr Sun 1:30–5pm. Subway: Bloor.

5 Historic Buildings

Campbell House   Just across from Osgoode Hall (see below) sits the 1822 mansion of Sir William Campbell, a Loyalist and sixth chief justice of Upper Canada. In 1829, he retired to this mansion, where he lived until his death in 1834. It was moved several blocks from its original location in 1972. The beautifully restored building features a collection of period furniture. Guided tours take about half an hour and provide insight into Toronto's early history.

160 Queen St. W. (at University Ave.). ℂ **416/597-0227.** Admission C$4.50 (US$3.05) adults; C$3 (US$2.05) students, C$2.50 (US$1.70) seniors, C$2 (US$1.35) children; C$10 (US$6.80) family (2 adults, 2 children). Year-round Mon–Fri 9:30am–4:30pm, May–October also Sat–Sun noon–4:30pm. Subway: Osgoode.

Colborne Lodge   This charming, English-style Regency cottage with a three-sided verandah was built in 1836–37 to take advantage of the view of Lake Ontario and the Humber River. At the time, it was considered way out in the country, and a bother to travel to during the harsh winters. In 1873, the owner, a Toronto surveyor and architect named John Howard, donated the house and surrounding land to the city in return for an annual salary. That created High Park (see "Parks & Gardens," below), a great recreational area.

High Park. ℂ 416/392-6916. Admission C$3.50 (US$2.40) adults, C$2.75 (US$1.90) seniors and youths 13–18, C$2.50 (US$1.70) children 12 and under. Tues–Sun 10am–4pm. Call ahead; hours vary. Subway: High Park.

Fort York *(Kids* Established by Lieutenant Governor Simcoe in 1793 to defend "little muddy York," as Toronto was then known, Americans sacked Fort York in 1813. You can tour the soldiers' and officers' quarters, clamber over the ramparts, and view demonstrations. The fort really comes to life in summer, with daily demonstrations of drill, music, and cooking. The fort is a few blocks west of the CN Tower and 2 blocks east of Exhibition Place.

100 Garrison Rd., off Fleet St., between Bathurst St. and Strachan Ave. ℂ 416/392-6907. Admission C$5 (US$3.40) adults, C$3.25 (US$2.20) seniors and youths 13–18, C$3 (US$2.05) children 6–12, free for children under 6. Free parking. Mid-May–Labor Day Daily 10am–5pm; September to mid-May Mon–Fri 10am–4pm, Sat–Sun 10am–5pm. Subway: Bathurst, then streetcar no. 911 south.

Mackenzie House This typical mid-19th-century brick row house, 2 blocks east of Yonge and south of Dundas, gives some idea of what Toronto must have looked like when the streets were lined with similar buildings. Concerned friends and fund-raisers bought it for William Lyon Mackenzie, leader of the 1837 rebellion, and he lived here from 1859 to 1861. It's furnished in 1850s style, and in the back there's a print shop designed after Mackenzie's own.

82 Bond St. ℂ 416/392-6915. Admission C$3.50 (US$2.40) adults, C$2.75 (US$1.90) seniors and youths 13–18, C$2.50 (US$1.70) children 5–12. May–Sept 1 Tues–Sun noon–5pm, Sept 2–Dec Tues–Sun noon–4pm; Jan–Apr Sat–Sun noon–5pm. Subway: Dundas.

Osgoode Hall West of City Hall, an impressive, elegant wrought-iron fence extends in front of an equally gracious public building, Osgoode Hall. Folklore has it that the fence was built to keep cows from trampling the flowerbeds. Tours of the interior reveal the splendor of the grand staircase, the rotunda, the Great Library, and the fine portrait and sculpture collection. Construction began in 1829, and troops were billeted here after the Rebellion of 1837. It's currently the home of the Law Society of Upper Canada, the headquarters of Ontario's legal profession. The Court of Appeal for Ontario has several magnificent courtrooms here. The courts are open to the public.

130 Queen St. W. ℂ 416/947-3300. www.lsuc.on.ca. Free admission. Mon–Fri 9am–6pm. Free tours July–Aug Mon–Fri 1:15pm. Subway: Osgoode.

Spadina House ⚘ Here's a trick locals play on unsuspecting visitors: get them to pronounce "Spadina." In the case of the avenue, it's "spa-DYE-na"; for this lovely landmark, it's "spa-DEE-na." Why? Who knows! But if you want to see how the leading lights of the city lived in days gone by, visit the historic home of financier James Austin. The exterior is beautiful, the interior even more impressive. Spadina House contains a remarkable collection of art, furniture, and decorative objects. The Austin family occupied the house from 1866 to 1980, and successive generations modified and added to the house and its decor.

Tours (the only way to see the house) start on the quarter hour. Be warned that while the guides are excellent, the video that they force you to watch before the tour is laughable (the narrator is the "spirit of the house," and his rambling comments—paired with a stagy Irish brogue—will make you wonder if the video is a joke). In summer, you can also tour the gorgeous gardens.

Finds **Park Yourself Here**

Spadina House is the next-door neighbor of Casa Loma (see "Architectural Highlights," above). Between the two is a small but lovely park that is almost hidden by the trees that shade it. Many visitors don't notice it, but locals love it. Grab a bench here if you want to take a breather.

---

285 Spadina Rd. (*C*) **416/392-6910.** Guided tour C$5 (US$3.40) adults, C$3.50 (US$2.40) seniors and youths, C$3 (US$2.05) children under 13. Tues–Fri noon–4pm, Sat–Sun noon–5pm. Subway: Dupont.

6 For Sports Fans

Air Canada Centre   Toronto's newest sports and entertainment complex is home to the Maple Leafs (hockey) and the Raptors (basketball). Longtime fans were crushed when the Leafs moved here in 1999 from Maple Leaf Gardens—the arena that had housed the team since 1931—but the Air Canada Centre has quickly become a fan favorite. Seating 18,700 for hockey, 19,500 for basketball, and 20,000 for concerts, the center was designed with comfort in mind. Seating is on a steeper-than-usual grade so that even the "nosebleed" sections have decent sightlines, and the seats are wider . . . and upholstered.

40 Bay St. (at Lakeshore Blvd.). (*C*) **416/815-5500.** www.theaircanadacentre.com. Tours C$10 (US$6.80) adults, C$8 (US$5.45) students and seniors, C$7 (US$4.75) children 12 and under. Tours on the hour daily 11am–3pm. Call ahead; no tours during events. Subway: Union, then LRT to Queen's Quay.

Canada's Sports Hall of Fame   In the center of Exhibition Place, this three-floor space celebrates the country's greatest male and female athletes in all major sports. Complementing the displays are touch-screen computers that tell you everything you could want to know about particular sports personalities and Canada's athletic heritage.

Exhibition Place. (*C*) **416/260-6789.** Free admission. Mon–Fri 10am–4:30pm. Subway: Bathurst, then streetcar no. 511 south to end of line.

Hockey Hall of Fame *★ (Kids)*   Ice hockey fans will be thrilled by the artifacts collected here. They include the original Stanley Cup (donated in 1893 by Lord Stanley of Preston), a replica of the Montreal Canadiens' locker room, Terry Sawchuck's goalie gear, Newsy Lalonde's skates, and the stick Max Bentley used. You'll also see photographs of the personalities and great moments in hockey history. Most fun are the shooting and goalkeeping interactive displays, where you can take a whack at targets with a puck or don goalie gear and face down flying video pucks or sponge pucks.

In BCE Place, 30 Yonge St. (at Front St.). (*C*) **416/360-7765.** www.hhof.com. Admission C$12 (US$8.15) adults, C$8 (US$5.45) seniors and children 4–18, free for children 3 and under. Late June through Labour Day Mon–Sat 9:30am–6pm, Sun 10am–6pm; Sept through mid-June Mon–Fri 10am–5pm, Sat 9:30am–6pm, Sun 10:30am–5pm. Closed Jan 1, Dec 25. Subway: Union.

SkyDome   In 1989, the opening of 53,000-seat SkyDome, home to the Toronto Blue Jays baseball team and the Toronto Argonauts football team, was a gala event. In 1992, SkyDome became the first Canadian stadium to play host to the World Series, and the Blue Jays won the championship for the first of two consecutive years. The stadium represents an engineering feat, featuring the world's first fully retractable roof, which spans more than 3 hectares (8 acres),

---

Finds Say Cheese

One Kensington Market spot I can't resist is the **Global Cheese Shoppe,** 76 Kensington Ave. (© **416/593-9251**). It stocks excellent offerings from around the world, and the staff is happy to let you try anything. One irresistible choice is the made-in-Ontario goat cheese. Mmm . . .

---

and a gigantic video scoreboard. It is so large that a 31-story building would fit inside the complex when the roof is closed.

1 Blue Jays Way. © **416/341-2770.** www.skydome.com. Tours C$12.50 (US$8.50) adults, C$8 (US$5.45) students 12–17 and seniors, C$7 (US$4.75) children 4–11, free for children 3 and under. Tours on the hour daily 11am–3pm.Call ahead; no tours during events. Parking C$6.50 (US$4.40). Subway: Union.

7 Markets

Kensington Market 🏵 This colorful, lively area should not be missed. If you can struggle out of bed to get here around 5am, you'll see squawking chickens being carried from trucks to the stalls. You'll hear Caribbean, Portuguese, Italian, and other accents as merchants spread out their wares—squid and crabs in pails, chickens, pigeons, bread, cheese, apples, pears, peppers, ginger, and mangoes from the West Indies, salted fish from Portuguese dories, lace, fabrics, and other colorful remnants. There's no market on Sunday.

Bounded by Dundas St., Spadina Ave., Baldwin St., and Augusta Ave. No central phone. Most stores open Mon–Sat. Subway: St. Patrick, then Dundas St. streetcar west to Kensington.

St. Lawrence Market This handsome food market is in a vast building constructed around the façade of the second city hall, built in 1850. Vendors sell fresh meat, fish, fruit, vegetables, and dairy products as well as other foodstuffs. The best time to visit is early Saturday morning, shortly after the farmers arrive.

92 Front St. E. © **416/392-7219.** Tues–Thurs 8am–6pm, Fri 8am–7pm, Sat 5am–5pm. Subway: Union.

8 Parks & Gardens

Allan Gardens George William Allan gave the city these gardens. He was born in 1822 to wealthy merchant and banker William Allan, who gave him a vast estate (it stretched from Carlton St. to Bloor St. between Jarvis and Sherbourne). George married into the ruling Family Compact when he wed John Beverley Robinson's daughter. A lawyer by training, he became a city councilor, mayor, senator, and philanthropist. Today the park is rather seedy and should be avoided at night, but stroll by during the day to take in the glass-domed Victorian glory of the Palm House conservatory.

Between Jarvis, Sherbourne, Dundas, and Gerrard sts. © **416/392-1111.** Free admission. Daily dawn–dusk. Subway: Dundas.

Edwards Gardens 🏵 This quiet, formal 14-hectare (35-acre) garden is part of a series of parks that stretch over 240 hectares (600 acres) along the Don Valley. Gracious bridges arch over a creek, rock gardens abound, and roses and other seasonal flowers add color and scent. The garden is famous for its rhododendrons. The Civic Garden Centre operates a gift shop and offers free walking tours on Tuesday and Thursday at 11am and 2pm. The Centre also boasts a fine horticultural library.

777 Lawrence Ave. E. (at Leslie St.). ℂ **416/397-8186.** Free admission. Daily dawn–dusk. Subway: Eglinton, then no. 51 (Leslie) or no. 54 (Lawrence) bus.

High Park This 160-hectare (400-acre) park was surveyor and architect John G. Howard's gift to the city. He lived in Colborne Lodge, which still stands in the park. The grounds contain a large lake called Grenadier Pond (great for ice-skating), a small zoo, a swimming pool, tennis courts, sports fields, bowling greens, and vast expanses of green for baseball, jogging, picnicking, bicycling, and more.

1873 Bloor St. W., stretching south to the Gardiner Expressway. No phone. Free admission. Daily dawn–dusk. Subway: High Park.

9 Cemeteries

Mount Pleasant Cemetery 🏵 Home to one of the finest tree collections in North America, this cemetery is also the final resting place of many fascinating people. Of particular note are Glenn Gould, the celebrated classical pianist; Dr. Frederick Banting and Dr. Charles Best, the University of Toronto researchers who discovered insulin in 1922; golfer George Knudson; the Massey and Eaton families, whose mausoleums are impressive architectural monuments; Prime Minister William Lyon Mackenzie King; Canada's greatest war hero, Lieutenant Colonel William Barker; and writer and editor Jim Cormier.

375 Mount Pleasant Rd., north of St. Clair Ave. ℂ **416/485-9129.** www.mountpleasantgroupof cemeteries.ca. Free admission. Daily 8am–dusk. Subway: St. Clair.

Necropolis This is one of the city's oldest cemeteries, dating to 1850. Many of the remains were originally buried in Potters Field, where Yorkville stands today.

Before strolling through the cemetery, pick up a History Tour at the office. You'll find the graves of William Lyon Mackenzie, leader of the 1837 rebellion, as well as those of his followers Samuel Lount and Peter Matthews, who were hanged for their part in the rebellion. Anderson Abbot, the first Canadian-born black surgeon; Joseph Tyrrell, who discovered dinosaurs in Alberta; world-champion oarsman Ned Hanlan; and many more notable Torontonians lie in the 15-acre cemetery. Henry Langley, who is also buried here, designed the porte cochere and Gothic Revival chapel.

200 Winchester St. (at Sumach St.). ℂ **416/923-7911.** www.mountpleasantgroupofcemeteries.ca. Free admission. Daily 8am–dusk. Subway: Castle Frank, then #65 bus south on Parliament St to Wellesley and walk 3 blocks east to Sumach.

10 Especially for Kids

The city puts on a fabulous array of special events for children at **Harbourfront.** In March, the **Children's Film Festival** screens 40 entries from 15 countries. In April, **Spring Fever** celebrates the season with egg decorating, puppet shows, and more; on Saturday mornings in April, the 5-to-12 set enjoys **cushion concerts.** In May, the **Milk International Children's Festival** brings 100 international performers to the city for a week of great entertainment. For additional information, call ℂ **416/973-3000.**

For 30 years, the **Young Peoples Theatre,** 165 Front St. E., at Sherbourne Street (ℂ **416/862-2222** for box office or 416/363-5131 for administration), has been entertaining youngsters. Its season runs from August to May.

Help! We've Got Kids is an all-in-one directory for attractions, events, shops and services appropriate for kids under 13 in the Greater Toronto area. It doesn't provide a lot of detail about most of the entries, but the listings make a great starting point. A print copy costs C$11.95 (US$8); info is free at **www.helpweve gotkids.com.**

Look in the sections above for the following Toronto-area attractions that have major appeal for kids of all ages. The first five on the list are tied for best venue, at least from a kid's point of view. The others suit more specialized interests.

- **Ontario Science Centre** (p. 128)   Kids race to be the first at this paradise of hands-on games, experiments, and push-button demonstrations—800 of them.
- **Paramount Canada's Wonderland** (p. 128)   The kids can't wait to get on the theme park's roller coasters and daredevil rides. And don't forget to budget for video games.
- **Harbourfront** (p. 118)   Kaleidoscope is an ongoing program of creative crafts, active games, and special events on weekends and holidays. There's also a pond, winter ice-skating, and a crafts studio.
- **Ontario Place** (p.119)   The Children's Village, water slides, huge Cinesphere, futuristic pod, and other entertainment are the big hits at this recreational and cultural park. In the Children's Village, kids under 13 can scramble over rope bridges, bounce on an enormous trampoline, or drench one another in the water-play section.
- **Toronto Zoo** (p. 129)   One of the best in the world, modeled after San Diego's—the animals in this 284-hectare (710-acre) park really do live in a natural environment.
- **Toronto Islands—Centreville** (p. 122)   Riding a ferry to this turn-of-the-century amusement park is part of the fun.
- **CN Tower** (p. 123)   Especially for the interactive simulator games and the terror of the glass floor.
- **Royal Ontario Museum** (p. 124)   The top hits are the dinosaurs and the spooky bat cave.
- **Fort York** (p. 136)   For its reenactments of battle drills, musket and cannon firing, and musical marches with fife and drum.
- **Hockey Hall of Fame** (p. 137)   Who wouldn't want the chance to tend goal against Mark Messier and Wayne Gretzky (with a sponge puck), and to practice with the fun and challenging video pucks?
- **Black Creek Pioneer Village** (p. 130)   For craft and other demonstrations.
- **Casa Loma** (p. 133)   The stables, secret passageway, and fantasy rooms capture children's imaginations.
- **Art Gallery of Ontario** (p. 122)   For its hands-on kids' exhibit.

Children's Own Museum   The ROM's next-door neighbor is another favorite with tykes. At the Children's Own Museum, everything is designed with kids ages 1 to 8 in mind. This interactive learn-while-you-play center includes a sensory tunnel, construction site, garden, animal clinic, mini putting courses (for kids 4–8), and theater. Well-trained staff members are on hand to answer the inevitable endless questions.

In the McLaughlin Planetarium Building, 90 Queen's Park. © **416/542-1492.** www.childrensownmuseum.org. Admission C$5.75 (US$3.90). Pay what you can Tues 1–5pm. Tues–Sat 10am–5pm, Sun noon–5pm Subway: Museum.

Chudleigh's   A day here introduces kids to life on a farm. They'll enjoy hayrides, pony rides, and, in season, apple picking. There's a playground, a straw maze, and more. The store sells pies, cider, and other produce.

9528 Hwy. 25 (3km/1.8 miles north of Hwy. 401), Milton. ℂ 905/826-1252. www.chudleighs.com. Orchard admission C$5 (US$3.40); free for children 3 and under. Family admission C$12 (US$8.15; 2 adults, 2 children). July–Oct daily 10am–5pm. By car: From downtown, take Highway 401 west to Highway 25 (exit 320); follow Hwy. 25 north for about 3km (1.8 miles).

Cullen Gardens & Miniature Village

The half-scale village has great appeal. The 11 hectares (27 acres) of gardens, the playground (with two splash ponds), the shopping, and the live entertainment only add to the fun. There are special events year-round, including various flower festivals in summer, Halloween pumpkin carving in October, and fireworks at midnight on New Year's Eve.

Taunton Rd., Whitby. ℂ 905/686-1600. www.cullengardens.com. Admission C$12 (US$8.15) adults, C$9 (US$6.10) seniors, C$5 (US$3.40) children 3–12. Free parking. Daily summer 9am–8pm, spring and fall 10am–6pm. Closed early Jan to mid-Apr. By car: From downtown, take Highway 401 east to Highway 12 (exit 410); drive north on Highway 12 to Taunton Rd.; turn left (west) at Taunton Rd. and drive 1 km (.5 miles).

Playdium

The Playdium is an interactive pleasure palace, with its 33,000-square-foot space filled with more than 200 games and simulators. It also has rock-climbing walls, a 1.2km (three-quarter-mile) Go-Kart track, an IMAX theater, batting cages, mini golf, and a lounge and restaurant. Beyond the sliding steel door activated by an infrared sensor, you'll discover a surreal scene of huge TV screens, circuit boards, and neon and strobe-lit "alien squid mushrooms."

99 Rathburn Rd. W. ℂ 905/273-4810. www.playdium.com. C$2–$23 (US$1.40–$16) per game or attraction. Sun–Thurs 11am–11pm, Fri–Sat 10am–2am. By car: Take Hwy 401 to Hwy 10 (Hurontario St.), and go south to Rathburn Rd. W.

Riverdale Farm

Idyllically situated on the edge of the Don Valley Ravine, this working farm right in the city is a favorite with small tots. They enjoy watching the cows and pigs, and petting the other animals. There are farming demonstrations daily at 10:30am and 1:30pm.

201 Winchester St. (at Sumach St.). ℂ 416/392-6794. Free admission. Daily 9am–5pm. Subway: Castle Frank, then #65 bus south on Parliament St to Wellesley and walk 3 blocks east to Sumach.

Wild Water Kingdom

A huge water theme park, Wild Water Kingdom encompasses a 20,000-square-foot wave pool, tube slides, speed slides, giant hot tubs, and thrilling water rides (try the Midnight Express, which spirals through some very dark tunnels). There are bumper boats, pedal boats, canoes, batting cages, and mini golf, too. Note that the park may not be open in inclement weather, so call ahead if in doubt.

Finch Ave., 1.6km (1 mile) west of Hwy. 427, Brampton. ℂ 416/369-0123 or 905/794-0565; www.wildwater kingdom.com. Admission C$23.50 (US$16) adults and children 10 and up, C$17.50 (US$12) seniors and children 4–9, free for children 3 and under; flat rate of C$13.50 (US$9.20) per person after 4pm. June daily 10am–6pm; July–mid-August daily 10am–8pm; late August–Sept 2 10am–6pm. By car: Take Hwy. 401 to Hwy. 427 north; exit at Finch Ave. and drive 1.6km (1 mile) west. Or from downtown, take Queen Elizabeth Way (QEW) to Hwy. 427 north; exit at Finch Ave. and drive 1.6km (1 mile) west.

11 Guided Tours

INDUSTRIAL TOURS

Canadian Broadcasting Centre

The headquarters for the CBC's English Networks, this building was designed by Bregman and Hamann and Scott, with John Burgee and Philip Johnson as consultants. It's one of the most modern broadcasting facilities in North America. From the minute visitors enter, they know they're in a studio facility—there's even a lobby viewing studio. When you come for your tour, check out the **CBC Museum,** a series of interactive exhibits and film clips showcasing the CBC's broadcast history (open weekdays 9am–5pm).

250 Front St. W. ✆ 416/205-8605. www.cbc.ca. Tour C$7 (US$4.75) adults, C$5 (US$3.40) seniors, students, and children; tours by appointment only. Subway: Union.

ChumCity   This innovative television station contrasts dramatically with the CBC's formality. It's a television factory where cameras are not hard-wired to studios or control rooms, but can be plugged into any one of 35 hydrants that allow them to go on-air in minutes. Instead of formal shows confined to studios, programs can flow minute by minute from any working area in the building, including the hallways and rooftop. From this location, the cutting-edge company operates three channels. **Citytv** is a popular local TV station. **MuchMusic,** which is similar to MTV, and **Bravo,** a 24-hour arts channel, are available on many American cable systems. The staff is young and cutting-edge, with an impressive, fast-response news team. ChumCity has 100 permanently fixed remote-control cameras, 25 mobile news cruisers, plus remote terminals at key locations such as City Hall, Metro Hall, the TTC, and police headquarters. The results air on "CityPulse" at noon, 6, and 11pm.

This futuristic, interactive TV station even invites casual visitors to air their opinions and grievances. Simply enter **Speakers Corner,** a video booth at the corner of John and Queen streets, and bare your soul before the camera. If you're compelling or bizarre enough, you'll get your 15 seconds of fame on a weekly half-hour show, or in short blurbs on Citytv and MuchMusic.

299 Queen St. W. (at John St.). ✆ 416/591-7400, ext 2770. www.citytv.com. Free tours; by appointment only. Subway: Osgoode.

Stock Market Place at the Toronto Stock Exchange   With C$1 billion (US$680 million) of stock being traded every business day, this is the second-largest stock exchange in North America. **Barter to Bytes** traces the history of commerce from the days of bartering, and several interactive exhibits give kids the chance to be pint-size CEOs.

Exchange Tower, 130 King St. W. (at York St.). ✆ 416/947-4670. Free admission. Call ahead to ensure site is open that day. Mon–Fri 10am–5pm. Subway: St. Andrew.

ORGANIZED TOURS

For summer weekends, it's always a good idea to make tour reservations in advance. At slower times, you can usually call the same day or simply show up.

BUS TOURS   If you enjoy bus tours, try the one offered by **Gray Line,** 184 Front St. E. (✆ **416/594-3310;** www.grayline.ca). They pass such major sights as the Eaton Centre, City Hall, the University of Toronto, Yorkville, Casa Loma, Chinatown, Harbourfront, and the CN Tower. These tours, which operate daily starting at 10am, cost C$29 (US$20) for adults, C$26 (US$18) for seniors, and C$15 (US$10) for children 5 to 11. Gray Line also offers a daily **hop-on hop-off bus tour** at similar rates.

HARBOR & ISLAND TOURS   **Mariposa Cruise Line** (✆ **800/976-2442** or 416/203-0178; www.mariposacruises.com) operates 1-hour narrated tours of the harborfront and the Toronto islands from mid-May through September. There are five cruises a day, departing between 11am and 4pm, and the cost is C$16 (US$11) for adults, C$14.50 (US$9.85) for seniors and students, and C$11 (US$7.50) for children 4 to 11. Tours leave from Queen's Quay Terminal at 207 Queen's Quay W.

For a real thrill, board the *Kajama,* a three-masted, 50m (164-ft.) schooner, for a 90-minute cruise. The schedule varies, but through July and August there are three tours a day on weekdays and weekends. Prices for the cruise are C$19 (US$13) for adults, C$17 (US$12) for seniors and students, and C$11 (US$7.50) for children. For more information, call the **Great Lakes Schooner Company,** 249 Queens Quay W., Suite 111 (© **800/267-3866** or 416/ 260-6355; www.greatlakesschooner.com).

HELICOPTER TOURS   For an aerial view of the city, contact **National Helicopters,** Toronto City Centre Airport, Toronto ON M5V 1A1 (© **416/ 361-1100;** www.nationalhelicopters.com). Excursions from the Toronto Island Airport cost C$50 (US$34) per person for 7 minutes of aerial sightseeing.

WALKING/BIKING TOURS   Toronto is a city made for walking, and there's no shortage of options for those willing to pound the pavement. **Civitas Cultural Resources** (© **416/966-1550**) offers downtown tours with guides who know their history—and a little local gossip, too. The charge is C$12 (US$8.15) per person; free for children under 12.

A **Taste of the World Neighbourhood Bicycle Tours and Walks** ⊛ (© **416/ 923-6813;** www.torontowalksbikes.com) leads visitors through the nooks and crannies of places like Chinatown, Yorkville, and Rosedale. Walking tours cost C$15 (US$10) for adults, C$13 (US$8.85) for seniors and students, and C$9 (US$6.10) for children under 12. Bike tours cost C$45 (US$31), C$40 (US$27), and C$30 (US$20), respectively; the price includes bike and helmet rental.

During the summer, the **Toronto Historical Board** (© **416/392-6827**) offers free walking tours of several neighborhoods, including Cabbagetown and Rosedale. Call ahead for details. Also during the summer, the **Royal Ontario Museum** (© **416/586-5513**) offers walking tours at 6pm Wednesday and 2pm Sunday in various neighborhoods across Toronto. Most of the walks are free, though a few cost C$5 (US$3.40) per person.

12 Outdoor Activities

Toronto residents love the great outdoors, whatever the time of year. In summer, you'll see people cycling, boating, and hiking; in winter, there's skating, skiing, and snowboarding.

For additional information on facilities in the parks, golf courses, tennis courts, swimming pools, beaches, and picnic areas, call **Toronto Parks and Recreation** (© **416/392-8186;** www.city.toronto.on.ca/parks). Also see "Parks & Gardens," earlier in this chapter.

BEACHES

The Beaches is the neighborhood along Queen Street East from Coxwell Avenue to Victoria Park. It has a charming boardwalk that connects the beaches, starting at **Ashbridge's Bay Park,** which has a sizable marina. **Woodbine Beach** connects to **Kew Gardens Park** and is a favorite with sunbathers and volleyball players. Woodbine also boasts the **Donald D. Summerville Olympic Pool.** Snack bars and trinket sellers line the length of the boardwalk.

The **Toronto Islands** are where you'll find the city's favorite beaches. The ones on **Centre Island,** always the busiest, are favorites with families because of nearby attractions like **Centreville.** The beaches on **Wards Island** are much more secluded. They're connected by the loveliest boardwalk in the city, with masses of fragrant flowers and raspberry bushes along its edges. **Hanlan's Point,** also in the Islands, is Toronto's only nude beach.

Tips Don't Drink the Water!

Situated on Lake Ontario, Toronto boasts several beaches where you can lap up the sun. Just don't lap up the polluted H_2O, even though you'll see many Torontonians doing just that as they swim through the murky waters. Lake Ontario has high counts of *escherichia coli*, a very nasty bacteria that can cause ear, nose, and throat infections, skin rashes, and diarrhea—not exactly the kind of souvenir you were looking for.

BOATING/CANOEING

At the **Harbourside Boating Centre,** 283 Queen's Quay W. (© **416/203-3000**), you can rent sailboats or powerboats and take sailing lessons. Depending on the boat's size, a 3-hour sailboat rental costs at least C$60 (US$41). Powerboats cost C$95 (US$65) and up. The center also offers weeklong and weekend sailing courses.

The **Harbourfront Canoe and Kayak School,** 283A Queens Quay W. (© **416/203-2277**), rents kayaks for C$40 to $50 (US$27–$34) a day (higher rates apply on weekends). Canoes go for C$35 to $45 (US$24–$31). Open daily mid-June to Labour Day, weekdays only spring and fall, weather permitting.

You can also rent canoes, rowboats, and pedal boats on the **Toronto Islands** just south of Centreville.

CROSS-COUNTRY SKIING

Just about every park in Toronto becomes potential cross-country skiing territory as soon as snow falls. Best bets are Sunnybrook Park and Ross Lord Park, both in North York. For more information, call **Toronto Parks and Recreation** (© **416/392-8186;** www.city.toronto.on.ca/parks). Serious skiers interested in day trips to excellent out-of-town sites like Horseshoe Valley can call **Trakkers Cross Country Ski Club** (© **416/763-0173**), which also rents equipment.

CYCLING

With biking trails through most of the city's parks and more than 29km (18 miles) of street bike routes, it's not surprising that Toronto has been acclaimed as one of the best cycling cities in North America. Favorite pathways include the **Martin Goodman Trail** (from the Beaches to the Humber River along the waterfront); the **Lower Don Valley** bike trail (from the east end of the city north to Riverdale Park); **High Park** (with winding trails over 160 hectares/400 acres); and the **Toronto Islands,** where bikers roam free without fear of cars. For advice, call the **Ontario Cycling Association** (© **416/426-7416**) or **Toronto Parks and Recreation** (© **416/392-8186**).

Bike lanes are marked on College/Carlton streets, the Bloor Street Viaduct leading to the Danforth, Beverly/St. George streets, and Davenport Road. The Convention and Visitors Association can supply more detailed information.

There's no shortage of bike-rental options. Renting usually runs about C$12 to $24 (US$8.15–$16) a day. On Centre Island, try **Toronto Island Bicycle Rental** (© **416/203-0009**). In the city, head for **Wheel Excitement,** 5 Rees St., near Harbourfront (© **416/260-9000**); **McBride Cycle,** 180 Queens Quay W., at York Street, on the Harbourfront (© **416/203-5651**); or **High Park Cycle and Sports,** 24 Ronson Dr. (© **416/614-6689**). If you're interested in cycling

---

Finds **Walk/Jog/Cycle in Peace**

One of the best places to walk, jog, or cycle in the city is the sprawling **Mount Pleasant Cemetery** (p. 139). No, I'm not joking! The wide paths of the cemetery are like roads, and there's lots of space for everyone, from athletic types to parents pushing strollers. Locals love this park-like space, which abounds with trees and antique statuary, not just tombstones. It's a lively scene, and it's anything but depressing.

---

with a group, call the **Toronto Bicycling Network** (© 416/766-1985) for information about daily excursions and weekend trips.

FITNESS CENTERS

The **Metro Central YMCA,** 20 Grosvenor St. (© 416/975-9622), has excellent facilities, including a 25m (82 ft.) swimming pool, all kinds of cardiovascular machines, Nautilus equipment, an indoor track, squash and racquetball courts, and aerobics classes. A day pass costs C$20 (US$14). The **University of Toronto Athletic Centre,** 55 Harbord St., at Spadina Avenue (© 416/978-4680), offers similar facilities for the same price.

For yoga aficionados, there's no better place to stretch than the **Yoga Studio,** 344 Bloor St. W. (© 416/923-9366). A 90-minute session costs C$16 (US$11). Incidentally, the ashtanga class has been known to draw visiting celebrities.

GOLF

Toronto is obsessed with golf, as evidenced by its more than 75 public courses within an hour's drive of downtown. Here's information on some of the best.

- **Don Valley,** 4200 Yonge Street south of Highway 401 (© 416/392-2465). Designed by Howard Watson, this is a scenic par-71 course with some challenging elevated tees. The par-3 13th hole is nicknamed the Hallelujah Corner (it takes a miracle to make par). It's a good place to start your kids. Greens fees are C$45 (US$31) from Monday to Thursday, and C$49 (US$33) Friday through Sunday.
- **Humber Valley** (© 416/392-2488), 40 Beattie Avenue at Albion Road. The relatively flat par-70 course is easy to walk, and gets lots of shade from towering trees. The three final holes require major concentration (the 16th and 17th are both par-5s). Greens fees are C$27 to $42 (US$18–$29).
- The **Tam O'Shanter,** at 2481 Birchmount Avenue, north of Sheppard Ave. E. (© 416/392-2547). The par-70 course features links holes and water hazards among its challenges. Greens fees are C$27 to $43 (US$18–$29).
- The **Glen Abbey Golf Club,** 1333 Dorval Drive, Oakville (© 905/844-1800; www.glenabbey.com). The championship course is one of the most famous in Canada. Designed by Jack Nicklaus, the par-73 layout traditionally plays host to the Canadian Open. Greens fees are C$130 (US$88) in early spring and fall, C$235 (US$160) in summer.

Other championship courses of note include the **Lionhead Golf Club** in Brampton (© 905/455-8400). It has two 18-hole par-72 courses; greens fees are C$135 (US$92) for the tougher course, C$125 (US$85) for the easier

Moments **Spa-ctacular**

Maybe you have a kink in your neck you just can't work out. Or perhaps you're just in the mood for pampering. In Toronto, you won't have to look too far. Some of the city's best spas, including the **Still-water at the Park Hyatt** (© 416/924-5471), and the **Elizabeth Milan Hotel Spa at the Fairmont Royal York** (© 416/350-7500), have their own on-site full-service spas for men and women (see chapter 4). Here are two other options:

Estée Lauder Spa: Located in one of Toronto's most luxurious shops is, appropriately enough, one of the city's most luxurious spas. Decorated in minimalist-chic blond wood and glass (and with a seemingly endless number of private treatment rooms), the spa delivers top-notch treatments. One of the most interesting is the Jet Lag facial, which rehydrates the skin; during the facial, "lymphatic leg therapy" reduces puffiness and swelling. While this unusual offering costs C$120 (US$82), most of the spa's services will set you back C$30 to $100 (US$20–$68). Holt Renfrew, 50 Bloor St. W. © 416/960-2909; www.holtrenfrew.com. Subway: Yonge/Bloor.

HealthWinds: This is as serene a setting as you'll find anywhere in the city. Perhaps that's because the spa is in a smaller space than some of its downtown cousins. Standards are extremely high—owner Kailee Kline is president of the Spas Ontario association. Some of the best treatments at HealthWinds take place in the tub, a hydrotherapy bath with 120 water and air jets, all the better to soothe your aching back. Hydrotherapy treatments start at C$55 (US$37). 2401 Yonge St., lower level. © 416/488-9545; www.healthwindsspas.com. Subway: Eglinton.

course. In Markham, the **Angus Glen Golf Club** (© 905/887-5157) has a Doug Carrick–designed par-72 course. The greens fees range from C$120 to $175 (US$82–$119).

HORSEBACK RIDING 🐎

Believe it or not, you can go riding in parkland a mere 15 minutes from downtown. The **Central Don Riding Academy** (© 416/444-4044), in Sunnybrook Park at Eglinton Avenue East and Leslie Street, has 19km (12 miles) of bridle trails. For beginners, there's an indoor ring and an outdoor ring. It's open Monday to Thursday from 1 to 5pm, and weekends from noon to 5pm. Reservations are required. Rates vary depending on the level of instruction; a 1-hour trail ride costs C$30 (US$20). Happy trails!

ICE-SKATING

Nathan Phillips Square in front of City Hall becomes a free ice rink in winter, as does an area at Harbourfront Centre. Rentals are available on-site. More than 25 parks contain artificial rinks (also free), including Grenadier Pond in High Park—a romantic spot, with a bonfire and vendors selling roasted chestnuts. They're open from November to March.

Tips **Skate Till You Drop?**

Let's say you'd like to go skating while your traveling companion wants to hit the shops. If you head to **Hazelton Lanes,** you can both get what you want. A central courtyard doubles as a skating rink. Better yet, the shopping center's Customer Service Centre (✆ **416/968-8600**) offers complimentary skate rentals. It's hard to beat a deal like that.

IN-LINE SKATING

In summer, in-line skaters pack Toronto's streets (and sidewalks). Go with the flow and rent some blades from **Planet Skate,** 2144 Queen St. E. (✆ **416/690-7588**) or **Wheel Excitement** (see "Cycling," above). A 1-day rental runs C$18 to $22 (US$12–$15). Popular sites include the Beaches, Harbourfront, and the Toronto Islands.

JOGGING

Downtown routes might include **Harbourfront** and along the lakefront, or through **Queen's Park** and the University. The **Martin Goodman Trail** runs 20km (12 miles) along the waterfront from the Beaches in the east to the Humber River in the west. It's ideal for jogging, walking, or cycling. It links to the **Tommy Thompson Trail,** which travels the parks from the lakefront along the Humber River. Near the Ontario Science Centre in the Central Don Valley, **Ernest Thompson Seton Park** is also good for jogging. Parking is available at the Thorncliffe Drive and Wilket Creek entrances.

These areas are generally quite safe, but you should take the same precautions you would in any large city.

PARACHUTING

The **Parachute School of Toronto** (✆ **800/361-5867**; www.parachuteschool. com), in Arthur, north of Toronto, will help you get a better understanding of gravity. Going for a dive costs C$225 (US$153) during the summer (the prices drops to C$155/US$105 in winter). After morning instruction, you jump in the afternoon. Reservations aren't required, but I'd recommend calling ahead to make sure the school's plane is sky-bound that day. Geronimo!

ROCK-CLIMBING

The dilemma: indoors or outdoors? Toronto has several climbing gyms, including **Joe Rockhead's,** 29 Fraser Ave. (✆ **416/538-7670**), and the **Toronto Climbing Academy,** 100 Broadview Ave. (✆ **416/406-5900**). You can pick up the finer points of knot-tying and belaying. Both gyms also rent equipment.

For the real thing, you need to head out of town. Weekend excursions to the Elora Gorge are organized through **Humber College** (✆ **416/675-5097**).

SNOWBOARDING

The snowboard craze shows no sign of abating. Popular sites include Earl Bales Park and Centennial Park, which both offer rentals. Call **Toronto Parks and Recreation** (✆ **416/392-8186**) for more information.

SWIMMING

The municipal parks, including High and Rosedale parks, offer a dozen or so outdoor pools (open June–Sept). Several community recreation centers have indoor pools. For **pool information,** call ✆ **416/392-7838**.

Visitors may buy a day pass (C$20/US$14) and use the pools at the **YMCA,** 20 Grosvenor St. (© **416/975-9622**), and the **University of Toronto Athletic Centre,** 55 Harbord St., at Spadina Avenue (© **416/978-4680**).

TENNIS

More than 30 municipal parks have free tennis facilities. The most convenient are the courts in High, Rosedale, and Jonathan Ashridge parks. They are open in summer only. At Eglinton Flats Park, west of Keele Street at Eglinton Avenue, six of the courts can be used in winter. Call City Parks (© **416/392-8186**) for additional information.

13 Spectator Sports

AUTO RACING   The Molson Indy (© **416/872-4639**; www.molsonindy. com) runs at the Exhibition Place Street circuit, usually on the third weekend in July.

BASEBALL   SkyDome, 1 Blue Jays Way, on Front Street beside the CN Tower, is the home of the **Toronto Blue Jays.** For information, contact the Toronto Blue Jays, P.O. Box 7777, Adelaide St., Toronto, ON M5C 2K7 (© **416/341-1000**; www.bluejays.ca). For tickets, which cost C$16 to C$60 (US$11–$41), call © 416/341-1234.

BASKETBALL   Toronto's basketball team, the **Raptors, has generated urban fever. The team's home ground is the **Air Canada Centre,** 40 Bay St., at Lakeshore Boulevard. The NBA schedule runs from October to April. The arena seats 19,500 for basketball. For information, contact the **Raptors Basketball Club,** 40 Bay St. (© **416/815-5600**; www.nba.com/raptors). For tickets, which cost C$25 to $125 (US$17–$85), call **Ticketmaster** (© **416/870-8000**).

FOOTBALL   Remember Kramer on *Seinfeld?* He would only watch Canadian football. Here's your chance to catch a game. **SkyDome, 1 Blue Jays Way, is home to the **Argonauts** of the Canadian Football League. They play between June and November. For information, contact the club at SkyDome, Gate 3, Suite 1300, Toronto, ON M5V 1J3 (© **416/341-5151**; www.argonauts.on.ca). Argos tickets cost C$13 to $48 (US$8.85–$33); call **Ticketmaster** (© **416/ 870-8000**).

GOLF TOURNAMENTS   Canada's national golf tournament, the **Bell Canadian Open, usually takes place at the **Glen Abbey Golf Club** in Oakville, about 40 minutes from the city (© **905/844-1800**). Most years, it runs over the Labour Day weekend.

HOCKEY   While basketball is still in its honeymoon phase in Toronto, hockey is a longtime love. The **Air Canada Centre, 40 Bay St., at Lakeshore Boulevard, is the home of the **Toronto Maple Leafs** (www.toronto mapleleafs.com). Though the arena seats 18,700 for hockey, tickets are not easy to come by, because many are sold by subscription. The rest are available through **Ticketmaster** (© **416/870-8000**); prices are C$25 to $100 (US$17–$68).

HORSE RACING   Thoroughbred racing takes place at **Woodbine Race-track, Rexdale Boulevard and Highway 427, Etobicoke (© **416/675-6110** or 416/675-7223). It's famous for the Queen's Plate (usually contested on the third Sun in June); the Canadian International, a classic turf race (Sept or Oct); and the North America Cup (mid-June). Woodbine also hosts harness racing in spring and fall.

TENNIS TOURNAMENTS   Canada's international tennis championships, the AT&T Rogers Cup (for women) and the Montreal/Toronto Tennis Masters Series (for men), are important stops on the pro tours. They attract stars like Jennifer Capriati, Serena Williams, Pete Sampras, and Andre Agassi to the National Tennis Centre at York University in August. The men's and women's championships alternate cities each year. In 2003, the men play in Montreal and the women in Toronto. For information, call © **416/665-9777** (www.tenniscanada.com).

7

City Strolls

Toronto is one of the best walking cities in the world. I know I'm boasting, but look at the evidence: the patchwork of dynamic ethnic neighborhoods, the impressive architecture, and the many parks. Because the city is such a sprawling place, however, you'll need to pick your route carefully.

The walking tours in this chapter aren't designed to give you an overview. They offer a look at the most colorful, exciting neighborhoods in the city, as well as areas that are packed with sights on almost every corner.

WALKING TOUR 1	CHINATOWN & KENSINGTON MARKET

Start:	Osgoode subway station.
Finish:	Queen's Park subway station.
Time:	At least 2 hours. Depending on how long you want to linger at the Art Gallery of Ontario and at various stops, perhaps as long as 8 hours.
Best Times:	Tuesday to Saturday during the day.
Worst Times:	Sunday, when many of the stores in Kensington Market close, and Monday, when the Art Gallery is closed.

This walk takes you through the oldest of Toronto's several Chinatowns. The original Chinatown was on York Street between King and Queen streets, but skyscrapers replaced it long ago. Although today there are at least four Chinatowns and most Chinese live in the suburbs, the intersection of Dundas Street and Spadina Avenue is still a major shopping and dining area for the Asian community. As a new wave of immigrants has arrived from Southeast Asian countries—Thailand and Vietnam in particular—this old, original Chinatown has taken them in. Today, many businesses are Vietnamese or Thai.

Successive waves of immigration have also changed the face of the nearby Kensington Market. From the turn of the century until the 1950s, it was the heart of the Jewish community. In the 1950s, Portuguese immigrants arrived to work in the food-processing and meatpacking industries and made it their home. In the '60s, a Caribbean presence arrived. Today, traces of all these communities remain in the vibrant life of the market.

From the Osgoode subway station, exit on the northwest corner of Queen Street and University Avenue, and walk west on Queen Street. Turn right onto McCaul Street. If you're interested in crafts, you'll want to stop at 52 McCaul St., on the left side of the street, and visit the:

❶ Prime Gallery
It sells ceramics, jewelry, fabrics, and other art objects crafted by contemporary artisans.

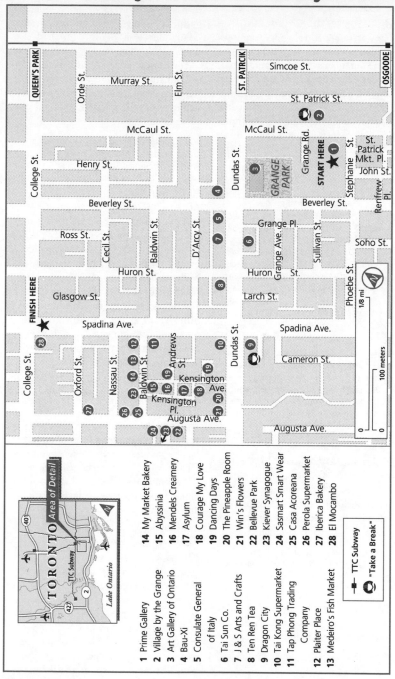

1 Prime Gallery
2 Village by the Grange
3 Art Gallery of Ontario
4 Bau-Xi
5 Consulate General
  of Italy
6 Tai Sun Co.
7 J & S Arts and Crafts
8 Ten Ren Tea
9 Dragon City
10 Tai Kong Supermarket
11 Tap Phong Trading
   Company
12 Plaiter Place
13 Medeiro's Fish Market

14 My Market Bakery
15 Abyssinia
16 Mendels Creamery
17 Asylum
18 Courage My Love
19 Dancing Days
20 The Pineapple Room
21 Win's Flowers
22 Bellevue Park
23 Kiever Synagogue
24 Sasmart Smart Wear
25 Casa Acoreana
26 Perola Supermarket
27 Iberica Bakery
28 El Mocambo

■ TTC Subway
☺ "Take a Break"

On the right is:

❷ Village by the Grange

The apartment and shopping complex consists of a series of courtyards (one even contains a small ice-skating rink). Go into the complex at the southern end and stroll through, emerging from the food market. En route you'll come across some small fashion boutiques and **18 Karat** (*℗* **416/593-1648**), where the proprietors design and create jewelry behind the counter.

TAKE A BREAK
Also in Village by the Grange is one of the city's oldest and most popular Chinese restaurants, **Sun Lok** (*℗* **416/593-8808**). The **Food Market** contains stalls that sell everything—freshly brewed coffee, schnitzels, satay, Japanese noodles, salads, falafel, hot dogs, Chinese food, kebabs, pizza, and fried chicken.

Exit at McCaul Street and turn right to continue walking north. You'll pass the Ontario College of Art on the other side of the street. At Dundas Street, you'll encounter a Henry Moore sculpture, *Large Two Forms,* which describes precisely what it is.

Turn left onto Dundas Street. On the left is the entrance to the:

❸ Art Gallery of Ontario

If you don't want to go in to see the collections, you can browse the gallery stores without paying admission. The wonderful restaurant, **Agora** (see chapter 5), is open for lunch.

Cross to the north side of Dundas Street, opposite the Art Gallery. A worthwhile stop is:

❹ Bau-Xi

This gallery, at 340 Dundas St. W. (*℗* **416/977-0600**), represents modern Canadian artists. From here, continue west along Dundas Street.

At the northwest corner of Dundas and Beverley is the:

❺ Consulate General of Italy

It doesn't look like a government building: The rambling late 19th-century mansion, with its sandy brick, quasi-gothic windows, and wrought-iron decoration, is a beauty. Too bad it doesn't offer tours.

You're now walking into the heart of Chinatown, with its grocery stores, bakeries, bookstalls, and emporiums selling foods, handcrafts, and other items from Asia.

What follows are some of my favorite stops along the stretch of Dundas Street between Beverley Street and Spadina Avenue. On the south or left side as you go west is:

❻ Tai Sun Co.

At nos. 407–409, the supermarket carries dozens of different mushrooms, all clearly labeled in English, as well as fresh Chinese vegetables, meats, fish, and canned goods. **Melewa Bakery,** no. 433, has a wide selection of pastries, like mung-bean and lotus-paste buns. Outside **Kiu Shun Trading,** no. 441, dried fish are on display; inside you'll find numerous varieties of ginseng and such miracle remedies as "Stop Smoking Tea."

On the north side of the street is:

❼ J & S Arts and Crafts

This shop, at no. 430, is a good place to pick up souvenirs, including kimonos and happy coats, kung-fu suits, address books, cushion covers, and all-cotton Chinatown T-shirts. **Kim Moon,** no. 438, is an Asian bakery that features almond cookies, deep-fried taro pastries, and dim sum pork buns.

At the northwest corner of Huron and Dundas streets, is:

❽ Ten Ren Tea

At no. 454, Ten Ren sells all kinds of tea—black, oolong, and so forth—stored in large canisters in the back of the store. Charming small ceramic teapots are priced from C$25 to $75 (US$17–$51). You will probably be asked to sample some tea in a tiny cup. The large variety of gnarled ginseng root on display is also for sale.

Next door, **W Y Trading Co., Inc.,** has a great selection of records, CDs, and tapes—everything from Chinese folk songs and cantatas to current hit albums from Hong Kong and Taiwan. At no. 482A, **Po Chi Tong** is a fun store that sells exotic remedies, like deer-tail extract and liquid-gold ginseng or royal jelly. The best remedy of all time is the "slimming tea." Watch the staff weigh each item out and total the bill with a fast-clicking abacus.

At Spadina Avenue, cross over to the southwest corner to:

❾ Dragon City

The three-level Asian shopping complex at 280 Spadina Ave. is complete with a food court. Here you'll find books, music, clothing, toys, and homeopathic remedies under one roof.

Spadina (pronounced "spa-DYE-na") Avenue is the widest street in the city because the wealthy Baldwin family had a 40m (132-ft.) swath cut through the forest from Queen Street to Bloor Street so that they could view the lake from their new home on top of Spadina Hill. Later, in the early 20th century, Spadina Avenue became Toronto's garment center and the focal point of the city's Jewish community. Although it's still the garment center, with wholesale and discount fashion houses, as well as the fur district (farther south around Adelaide), today it's more Asian than Jewish.

If you enjoy strolling through supermarkets filled with exotic Asian delights, including such fruits as durian in season, visit the:

❿ Tai Kong Supermarket

Look at all the different provisions—chili and fish sauces, fresh meat and fish (including live tilapia in tanks), preserved plums, chrysanthemum tea and other infusions, moon cakes, and large sacks of rice.

TAKE A BREAK
For fine, reasonably priced food, a Chinatown favorite is **Happy Seven,** 358 Spadina Ave. (℃ **416/971-9820;** see chapter 5). If you don't mind lining up, head for the ever-popular **Lee Garden,** 331 Spadina Ave. (℃ **416/593-9524;** see chapter 5). For speedy service, check out **Co Yen,** 334 Spadina Ave. (℃ **416/597-1573**), a Vietnamese takeout spot (there are no seats). Continuing north, cross St. Andrews Street.

⓫ Tap Phong Trading Company

This shop, at 360 Spadina Ave., stocks terrific wicker baskets of all shapes and sizes, as well as woks and ceramic cookware; attractive mortars and pestles; and other household items.

Cross Baldwin Street and you'll come to:

⓬ Plaiter Place

At 384 Spadina Ave., it has a huge selection of finely crafted wicker baskets, birdcages, woven blinds, bamboo steamers, hats, and other fun items. **Fortune Housewares,** no. 388, carries kitchen and household items—including brand names—for at least 20% off prices elsewhere in the city.

Now double back to Baldwin Street. You're heading into the heart of the **Kensington Market** area, which has always reflected the city's waves of immigration. Once it was primarily a Jewish market; later it became a Portuguese neighborhood. Today, it is largely Asian and Caribbean, but there are still many Jewish and Portuguese elements.

As you walk west, you'll find:

⓭ Medeiro's Fish Market, Seven Seas, and Coral Sea

At these and other fish stores on the north side of the street, folks buy their supplies of salt cod.

⓮ My Market Bakery

The merchandise at 172 Baldwin St. (℃ **416/593-6772**) will doubtless lure you in to buy some bread. Focaccia, sourdough—you name it, they have it.

When you reach Kensington Avenue, turn left and you'll find:

⑮ Abyssinia

It specializes in African and West Indian products. You'll also find **Patty King,** which stocks Jamaican breads and other West Indian goods, including roti, bread pudding, and tamarind balls. Several **seafood stores** display a variety of fresh fish and salted cod piled in boxes on the sidewalk; and the **Royal Food Centre** sells a variety of Jamaican specialties, including goat.

⑯ Mendels Creamery

This shop, at no. 72, sells smoked fish, herring, cheeses, and fine dill pickles. Another door down, **Global Cheese,** no. 76, offers an enormous selection at good prices.

As you stroll south along Kensington Avenue and pass Andrews Street, you will find a series of second-hand and vintage clothing stores.

⑰ Asylum

At no. 42 Kensington Ave. (see chapter 8), on the west side of the street, the store has good jeans, leather jackets, and assorted accessories. I once found a silk Anne Klein scarf for C50¢ (US35¢) in one of the bargain bins here.

⑱ Courage My Love

The best spot for cheap but chic vintage clothing (see chapter 8) is at no. 14. It stocks retro gowns and wedding dresses, suits, and accessories, as well as new jewelry and beads for do-it-yourself projects.

⑲ Dancing Days

At no. 17 (on the east side of the street), you'll find party-ready glad rags that will make you look like an extra in *Grease!*

⑳ The Pineapple Room

This shop at no. 2 stocks classic cocktail shakers and other doodads among the clothes.

When you reach Dundas Street, turn right and walk one block to Augusta Avenue. Along the way you pass:

㉑ Win's Flowers

They have gorgeous greenery and blossoms. The jade plants in particular are extraordinarily beautiful.

Turn right on Augusta Avenue; as you walk north, in the center of Denison Square, you'll find:

㉒ Bellevue Park

The houses facing the south edge of the park have cherry trees in front of them; they are a colorful sight in season.

Stroll through the park; at the corner of Bellevue Avenue and Denison Square you'll find:

㉓ Kiever Synagogue

This building at 28 Denison Square was completed in 1927. Architect Benjamin Swartz designed it with Byzantine style in mind. The most striking features outside are the twin domes atop the building; inside, stained-glass windows, brass ornaments, and a gigantic Holy Ark dominate the space. (The Kiever Synagogue was the first specifically Jewish building designated a historic site by the province of Ontario.)

Turn back toward Augusta Avenue and you'll see:

㉔ Sasmart Smart Wear

This discount store has the strangest assortment of goods you'll find anywhere. OshKosh clothing for kids is on display near antique china; a little farther along is kitchen gear (new and used), luggage, and gadgets. It's a weird, cluttered space, but the prices are unbeatable.

Walk north on Augusta to:

㉕ Casa Acoreana

An old-fashioned store at no. 235, it stocks a full range of fresh coffees, as well as great pecans and filberts. Just up the block at no. 214 is the **Alvand Food Mart** (© **416/597-2252**), which specializes in Middle Eastern foods and stocks imported goods from the region.

Just up the street is:

㉖ Perola Supermarket

This store at 247 Augusta Ave. displays cassava and strings of peppers—ancho, arbol, pasilla—hung up to dry and sitting in bins, plus more exotic fruits and herbs.

TAKE A BREAK
If you're in the neighborhood after 5:30pm, a perfect place to stop is La Palette, 256 Augusta Ave. (✆ 416/929-4900; see chapter 5). Enjoy a meal of classic French bistro staples—or tuck into one of the many divine desserts.

Cross Nassau Street to get to:

㉗ Iberica Bakery

The bakery, where you can enjoy coffee and pastries at a handful of tables, is on the east side of the street at 279

Augusta Ave. It represents one of the few remaining traces of the Portuguese presence in the Kensington Market area. Other vestiges are the Portuguese church on Nassau Street and the Portuguese radio station around the corner on Oxford Street.

Turn right onto Oxford Avenue and walk to Spadina Avenue. Turn left and walk 1 block north to reach:

㉘ El Mocambo

At this rock-and-roll landmark, the Rolling Stones played on March 4 and 5, 1977. The neon palms are no longer lit up, as the venue is finito at the moment. But it has gone through many openings and closings over the years, so stay tuned. Now hop on the streetcar that runs east along College Street to the Queen's Park subway station. The southbound train will take you back downtown.

WALKING TOUR 2   HARBOURFRONT

Start:	Union Station.
Finish:	Harbourfront Antique Market.
Time:	At least 2 hours, and possibly a lot more, depending on how entranced you are with the antiques market.
Best Times:	Saturday and Sunday, when the Harbourfront Antique Market is bustling.
Worst Time:	Monday, when the antiques market is closed.

As you start your tour, pause to look at the beaux-arts interior of **Union Station,** which opened in 1927. The hall has a cathedral-like ceiling, and 22 pillars that weigh 70 tons each. From here, either take the LRT to York Quay or walk south along York Street (away from the Fairmont Royal York hotel) to Queen's Quay West. On the way you'll pass the **Air Canada Centre,** home to the Toronto Maple Leafs hockey team and the Toronto Raptors basketball team. The Gardiner Expressway looms overhead, making this a noisy, dark spot.

When you reach the end of the street, you're at Queen's Quay West. Look across to:

❶ Queen's Quay Terminal

This large complex houses more than 100 shops and restaurants. On the third floor is a theater designed for dance performances. Built in 1927 when lake and railroad trade flourished, this eight-story concrete warehouse has been attractively renovated. The light,

airy two-story marketplace has garden courts, skylights, and waterfalls. Condos occupy the floors above.

Although you'll find few bargains here, there are some charming stores on the street level. They include **Rainmakers,** which sells zillions of whimsical umbrellas and parasol hats, plus terrific insulated rainwear, and **Oh Yes Toronto,** which specializes in

Walking Tour: Harbourfront

1 Queen's Quay Terminal
2 Power Plant Contemporary
   Art Gallery
3 York Quay Centre
4 John Quay
5 Radisson Plaza Hotel
   Admiral and Admiralty
   Point Condominiums
6 Maple Leaf Quay
7 Harbourfront Antique
   Market

 "Take a break"

souvenirs and Toronto-centric clothing.

On the upper level, options include the classic **Tilley Endurables,** founded by Torontonian Alex Tilley (who invented the world's most adaptable hat). **First Hand Canadian Crafts** represents more than 200 contemporary

TAKE A BREAK
If you want to sit out and watch the lakefront traffic—boat and human—go for a light meal or a drink at **Spinnakers** (© 416/203-0559), or the **Boathouse Cafe** (© 416/203-6300), on the ground floor of Queen's Quay. **Pearl Harbourfront Chinese Cuisine** (© 416/203-1233) offers more formal dining. The Queen's Quay complex also has a variety of cafes, and food vendors just outside.

folk artists who make both decorative and functional pieces, and **Table of Contents** sells all kinds of kitchen gear.

From Queen's Quay Terminal, walk along the water to the:

2 Power Plant Contemporary Art Gallery

This was indeed a power plant when it was built in 1927. Identifiable by its towering smokestack, the space has been converted to display modern art. The same building houses the Du Maurier Theatre Centre, which presents works in French.

Behind this building, adjacent to Queen's Quay West, is the Tent in the Park, where events take place during the summer season.

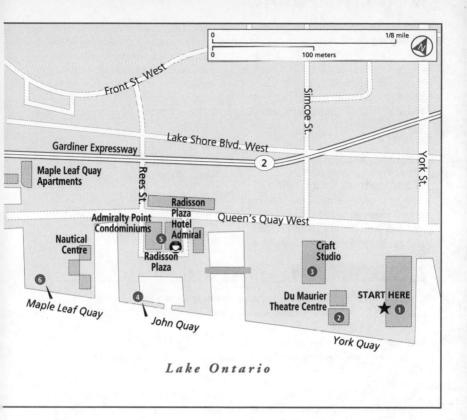

Walk next door to the:

❸ York Quay Centre

A complex converted from a 1940 trucking warehouse, it contains a number of interesting restaurants and galleries. Spend some time in the Craft Studio watching the glassblowers, potters, jewelry makers, and other artisans at work, and browse in the store that sells their work.

On the waterfront side in front of York Quay, there's a pond where kids operate model boats in summer; in winter it turns into an ice-skating rink.

From York Quay, cross the Amsterdam Bridge above Marina 4, checking out the wealth that's bobbing down below. You'll arrive on:

❹ John Quay

The first building you'll come to contains four restaurants, beyond which are the towers of the:

❺ Radisson Plaza Hotel Admiral and Admiralty Point Condominiums

The complex sits across Queen's Quay West from the HarbourPoint Condominiums. The ground level of the Admiralty Point Condos houses a few interesting stores. The **Nautical Mind** sells marine books, photographs, navigational charts, and boating videos; the **Dock Shoppe** overflows with all kinds of sailing gear and fashions.

 TAKE A BREAK
Pop into the **Radisson Plaza Hotel Admiral** (☎ 416/203-3333), 249 Queen's Quay W. It has a couple of dining options (the **Commodore's Dining Room** and the **Gallery Café**, which serves light fare), plus a pleasant terrace if it's a sunny day.

Continue west along Queen's Quay West past:
❻ Maple Leaf Quay
You can stop at the Nautical Centre to sign up for sailing classes first. Continue west and you'll see the Maple Leaf Quay Apartments on your right and the Harbour Terrace Condominiums farther along on your left, on the waterfront.

Next door to the westernmost tower of the Maple Leaf Quay Apartments is the:
❼ Harbourfront Antique Market
A terrific destination, the market houses more than 100 dealers selling fine furniture, jewelry, books, clocks, and Art Deco items. In summer, there are often 150 or more dealers, as the market expands out-of-doors. Of course, there's a lot of junk here, too. On Sunday, an outdoor market features less well-established dealers. The market is open Tuesday through Sunday from 10am to 6pm.

WINDING DOWN
In the Harbourfront Antiques Market, **Sophie's** has great fresh salads, sandwiches, quiches, and desserts. To return to downtown, board the LRT and head back to Union Station.

WALKING TOUR 3 · THE FINANCIAL DISTRICT

Start:	The CN Tower, near the corner of John and Front streets.
Finish:	A Queen Street West watering hole.
Time:	2 to 4 hours.
Best Time:	Weekdays during business hours.
Worst Times:	Weekends, when the stock market is closed and the Financial District is dead.

This is the Wall Street of Toronto, the financial engine that has made Ontario the nation's strongest and wealthiest economy. For more information about some of the major sights mentioned below, see chapter 6.

Start by going up the:
❶ CN Tower
This is the tallest freestanding structure in the world. Although it has become a symbol of the city, the CN Tower drew a great deal of criticism when it was built in 1975. It has since been recognized as an important symbol of a city trying to forge a new identity. Robert Fulford writes about it in *Accidental City:* "In the 1970s [Toronto] was struggling to shake off the dowdy self-image that was part of its heritage as a colonial city. . . . Torontonians were starting to consider, with shy pleasure, the novel idea that their city might be attractive, even enviable. . . . At that happy moment, the tower reinforced local exuberance and asserted the city's claim to even more attention."

However you view it, the most enjoyable thing is the view *from* it.

Once you're back down at the base, exit at the corner of John and Front streets. From here, look to the right along Front Street to see the glistening golden Royal Bank towers (part of the Royal Bank Centre). The CBC Centre stretches along the north side of Front Street for a whole long block. Inside, you can peek at the lobby radio studios and take a nostalgic radio-TV trip in the free museum.

Walk north on John Street (with the CN Tower behind you), cross Wellington Street, and continue up to King Street. Turn right. On the northeast corner, sports fans will want to stop in at **Legends of the Game,** 322 King St. W. (✆ **416/971-8848**).

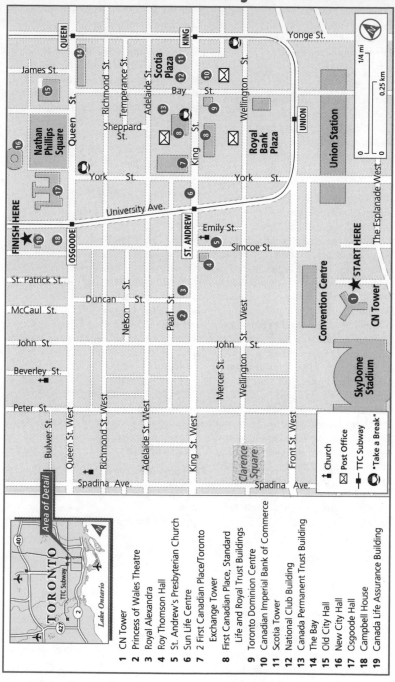

James St.

QUEEN

Queen St.

Richmond St.

Temperance St.

Adelaide St.

KING

Yonge St.

Scotia Plaza

Bay St.

St.

Sheppard St.

King St.

Royal Bank Plaza

UNION

Union Station

Nathan Phillips Square

York St.

York St.

The Esplanade West

FINISH HERE

OSGOODE

University Ave.

ST. ANDREW

Emily St.

Simcoe St.

START HERE

Convention Centre

CN Tower

St. Patrick St.

Duncan St.

Pearl St.

Nelson St.

West St.

John St.

Mercer St.

Wellington St.

SkyDome Stadium

McCaul St.

John St.

Beverley St.

Peter St.

Bulwer St.

Queen St. West

Richmond St. West

Adelaide St. West

King St. West

Front St. West

Clarence Square

Spadina Ave.

Spadina Ave.

✝ Church
☒ Post Office
■ TTC Subway
◗ "Take a Break"

Area of Detail

TORONTO

401

427

2

TTC Subway

Lake Ontario

1 CN Tower
2 Princess of Wales Theatre
3 Royal Alexandra
4 Roy Thomson Hall
5 St. Andrew's Presbyterian Church
6 Sun Life Centre
7 2 First Canadian Place/Toronto Exchange Tower
8 First Canadian Place, Standard Life and Royal Trust Buildings
9 Toronto Dominion Centre
10 Canadian Imperial Bank of Commerce
11 Scotia Tower
12 National Club Building
13 Canada Permanent Trust Building
14 The Bay
15 Old City Hall
16 New City Hall
17 Osgoode Hall
18 Campbell House
19 Canada Life Assurance Building

Doors with baseball-shaped handles open onto an emporium that features the Wall of Fame and every conceivable sports collectible.

Continue walking along the north side of King Street 1 block to:

❷ The Princess of Wales Theatre

Princess Diana opened it in 1993. Constructed for a production of *Miss Saigon,* the theater was the brainchild of impresario Ed Mirvish and his son, David. Try to pop inside for a peek at the 10,000 square feet of murals created by Frank Stella. There's one on the exterior back of the building that's worth walking around to see.

Exit the theater and continue along King Street past a cluster of restaurants owned by Ed Mirvish. (Drop in to one to check out the larger-than-life decor Ed has purchased at antiques closeouts.)

You'll also pass a wall of newspaper clippings about this gutsy Torontonian. Booster and benefactor of the city, he started out in bleak circumstances as owner of a bankrupt store during the Depression. He paid off the debt and launched **Honest Ed's** (see chapter 8), a discount store at Bloor and Bathurst that brought him fame and fortune. He saved the Royal Alex (see below) from demolition, and he and his son have become theater impresarios in Toronto and in London, where Ed outbid Andrew Lloyd Webber in 1982 for the Old Vic.

Cross Duncan Street. Next you'll come to:

❸ The Royal Alexandra

John M. Lyle built this beloved theater in 1906 and 1907 at a cost of C$750,000 (US$510,000). In 1963, it was scheduled for demolition, but Ed Mirvish bought it for C$200,000 (US$136,000) and refurbished it. Named after Queen Alexandra, wife of Edward VII, the magnificent beaux-arts structure is Edwardian down to the last detail. It abounds with gilt and velvet, and green marble lines the entrance foyer.

Across the street from these two theaters stands the new **Metro Hall,** 55 John St., designed by Brisbin Brook Beynon. This building is pretty much a white elephant these days—it was constructed when Toronto had six separate municipal governments and a Metro Council for joint projects and concerns. If you go in, check out the art installations. Free tours (✆ **416/392-8000**) of the first three floors are available, but they're not very interesting.

Also on the south side of the street, at the corner of King and Simcoe streets, is:

❹ Roy Thomson Hall

The hall bears the name of newspaper magnate Lord Thomson of Fleet (a Canadian press baron who wound up taking a seat in the British House of Lords). Built between 1972 and 1982 and designed by Arthur Erickson, the building's exterior looks very space age. Inside, the mirrored effects are dramatic.

Continue walking east on King Street. You'll pass through the heart of the Financial District, surrounded by many towers owned and operated by banks and brokerage, trust, and insurance companies.

On the northeast corner of King and Simcoe rises the first of the towers that make up the Sun Life Centre; on the southeast corner stands:

❺ St. Andrew's Presbyterian Church

The church (1874–75) is a quietly inviting retreat from the city's pace and noise. It was designed by the city's premier architect of the time, W. G. Storm, in an inspired picturesque Scottish Romanesque style. Sun Life paid C$4.3 million (US$2.9 million) for the church's air rights. Continue along King Street to University Avenue.

Opposite, on the northeast corner, is the:

6 Sun Life Centre's second tower

A Sorel Etrog sculpture marks this tower. Farther along the block you'll find another sculpture, *Parent I,* by British sculptor Barbara Hepworth. It's in a courtyard setting, complete with a splashing fountain, at the northwest corner of York and King streets.

On the northeast corner stands:

7 2 First Canadian Place

The north corner of the structure is the **Toronto Exchange Tower,** at the corner of Adelaide and York streets. The Sculptor's Society Gallery, which always has an interesting free show, is in 2 First Canadian Place. Also on the ground floor in the building, stop in to see the fabulous glass sculptures and other glass pieces in the **Sandra Ainsley** gallery (C 416/362-4480).

Continue along King Street past:

8 First Canadian Place

It sits on the north side, and the **Standard Life** and **Royal Trust buildings** (part of the Toronto Dominion Centre) are on the south. At the end of this block, you'll reach Bay Street. The Standard Life building is the work of New York architect Edward Durell Stone with Bregman & Hamann; the marble facing contrasts with the TD Centre, which is black. Again, there are views of the magnificent towers of the Royal Bank Centre from here.

The intersection of Bay and King streets was once considered the geographical center of Toronto's financial power. During the mining booms in the 1920s and 1950s, Bay Street was lined with offices that were filled with commission salesmen peddling stocks to the equivalent of the little old lady from Dubuque. This is the hub that gave Torontonians their reputation as a voracious band of money-grubbing folks. Today it's called Mint Corner because a major bank occupies each corner.

If it's near lunchtime and your stomach is rumbling, this isn't a bad place to:

TAKE A BREAK
Your best bet for a leisurely lunch in this neighborhood is a block south and a block east at **Jump Café and Bar,** 1 Wellington St. W. ((C 416/363-3400; see chapter 5). For a quick snack, seek out one of the casual spots in the concourse of **First Canadian Place.**

Our next stop, at King and Bay streets, is the:

9 Toronto Dominion Centre

Built between 1963 and 1969, the center was designed by Mies van der Rohe in his sleek trademark style. The black steel and dark-bronze-tinted glass tower rises from a gray granite base. Go through the Royal Trust and Toronto Dominion Towers, stopping to browse in the **Toronto Dominion Gallery of Inuit Art,** 79 Wellington St. W. (C 416/982-8473), on the ground floor and mezzanine of the Toronto Dominion Tower. Close to 100 marvelous soapstone sculptures are on display. Exit the TD Centre on Wellington Street and walk right; you'll come to a small staircase that leads to the courtyard behind the Toronto Dominion Bank Tower. Here you'll find a patch of grass that holds half a dozen lazing bronze cows. Artist Joe Fafard's *Pasture* reminds the bankers and stockbrokers that Toronto's wealth derived from other stock, too.

Walk through the Centre to the King Street exit. Exit onto King Street and turn right to continue east. Cross Bay Street. On the south side of King Street, you'll come to the entrance to Commerce Court. Architecture buffs will also want to go into the:

10 Canadian Imperial Bank of Commerce

Visit this building (1929–31) if only to see the massive banking hall—44m (145 ft.) long, 26m (85 ft.) wide, and 20m (65 ft.) high—with its coffered ceiling, gilt moldings, and sculpted friezes. Squirrels, roosters, bees, bears, and figures representing industry, commerce, and Mercury decorate the main entrance. For years, this 34-story building dominated the Toronto skyline. New Yorkers York and Sawyer, with Darling and Pearson, designed it. Note the carved heads on the top of the building depicting courage, observation, foresight, and enterprise. In the early 1970s, I. M. Pei was asked to design a new complex while preserving the old building. He set the new mercury-laminated stainless-steel bank tower back from King Street, creating Commerce Court.

Opposite, on the north side of King Street, note the:

⓫ Scotia Tower

It's a red-granite building, designed by Webb Zerafa Menkes Housden between 1985 and 1988.

Walk back to Bay Street and turn right. You're now going north. At no. 303, on the east side, is the:

⓬ National Club Building

In 1874, the nationalist Canada First Movement, which had started in Ottawa in 1868, became centered in Toronto. It established a weekly, *The Nation,* entered politics (as the Canadian National Association), and founded the National Club, which moved here in 1907. Today, it's a prestigious private club.

Across the street on the west side, at the corner of Bay and Adelaide streets, stands the:

⓭ Canada Permanent Trust Building (1928)

Enter this structure, at 7 King St. E., to view the beautifully worked Art Deco brass and bronze, particularly the elevator doors, which are chased and engraved with foliage and flowers.

Cross Adelaide Street. As you walk up Bay Street, the magnificent Old City Hall is clearly in view. First, on the east side of Bay Street between Richmond and Queen streets, look at—or stop in to:

⓮ The Bay

This is one of Canada's venerable retailers. The Bay, along with its arch-rival, Eaton's, has influenced the development of the downtown areas of most major Canadian cities. (See chapter 8, "Shopping," for listings)

Across Queen Street looms:

⓯ Old City Hall

Its reflection appears dramatically in the Cadillac Fairview Office Tower at the corner of James and Queen streets. This solid, impressive building, designed by Edward James Lennox, was built out of Credit River Valley sandstone. The magnificent Romanesque Revival style shows the obvious influence of H. H. Richardson. Begun in 1885, it opened in 1899, and for years its clock tower was a skyline landmark. Today, the building houses the provincial criminal courts. Go in to see the impressive staircase, columns with decorative capitals, and mosaic floor. The stained-glass window (1898) by Robert McCausland depicts the union of Commerce and Industry watched over by Britannia. Note the carved heads on the exterior entrance pillars—supposedly portraits of political figures and citizens of the period, including the architect.

Exit along Queen Street and turn right. Pause at the intersection of Queen and Bay streets. Bay, Toronto's equivalent of Wall Street, curves at this intersection, offering a good view north and south. Cross Bay Street and you'll find yourself in Nathan Phillips Square, with New City Hall looming above.

⓰ New City Hall

The city's fourth, it was built between 1958 and 1965 in modern sculptural style. It's the symbol of Toronto's postwar dynamism, although not everyone felt that way when it was built. According to Pierre Berton, Frank Lloyd Wright said of it, "You've got a headmarker for a grave and future generations will look at it and say: 'This marks the spot where Toronto fell.'" The truth is quite the opposite—this

Impressions

The real achievement of Toronto is to have remained itself.
    —Jan Morris, *O Canada: Travels in an Unknown Country,* 1992

breathtaking building was the first architectural marker of an evolving metropolis. Finnish architect Viljo Revell won a design competition that drew entries by 510 architects from 42 countries, including I. M. Pei. The building has a great square in front with a fountain and pool; people flock here in summer to relax, and in winter to skate. The square's namesake, Nathan Phillips, was Toronto's first Jewish mayor.

City Hall also has some art worth viewing. Look just inside the entrance for *Metropolis,* which local artist David Partridge fashioned from more than 100,000 common nails. You'll need to stand well back to enjoy the effect. Henry Moore's sculpture *The Archer* stands in front of the building—thanks to Mayor Phil Givens, who raised the money to buy it through public subscription after city authorities refused. The gesture encouraged Moore to bestow a major collection of his works on the Art Gallery of Ontario (see chapter 6). Two curved concrete towers, which house the bureaucracy, flank the Council Chamber. From the air, the whole complex supposedly looks like an eye peering up at the heavens.

TAKE A BREAK For some light refreshment, stop in at one of several dining spots in the **Sheraton Centre,** 123 Queen St. W. They include the pub **Good Queen Bess** (📞 416/361-1000).

From City Hall, walk west along Queen Street. On your right, behind an ornate wrought-iron fence that once kept out the cows, you'll see:

⑰ Osgoode Hall

Since the 1830s, this has been the headquarters of the Law Society of Upper Canada, a professional association. Named after the first chief justice of Upper Canada, the building was constructed in stages. It started with the East Wing (1831–32), then the West Wing (1844–45), and the center block (1856–60). The last, designed by W. G. Storm with a Palladian portico, is the most impressive. Inside is the **Great Library**—34m (112 ft.) long, 12m (40 ft.) wide, and 12m (40 ft.) high—with stucco decoration and a domed ceiling. The Ontario Supreme Court is across Queen Street.

Walk west 1 block to University Avenue. On the northwest corner, you can visit:

⑱ Campbell House

This elegant Georgian residence was home to Sir William Campbell, a Scot who moved to York in 1811 and rose to become chief justice of Upper Canada. A handsome piece of Georgian architecture, it was moved to this location from a few miles farther east.

Stretching northward behind Campbell House, on the northwest side of University Avenue, is the:

⑲ Canada Life Assurance Building

Atop the tower a neon sign provides weather reports—white flashes for snow, red flashes for rain, green beacon for clement weather, red beacon for cloudy weather. If the flashes move upward, the temperature is headed that way, and vice versa.

At University Avenue and Queen Street, you can end the tour by boarding the subway at Osgoode to your next destination. Or continue walking west along Queen Street to explore its many shops and cafes.

WALKING TOUR 4	ST. LAWRENCE & DOWNTOWN EAST

Start: Union Station.
Finish: King subway station.
Time: 2 to 3 hours.
Best Time: Saturday, when the St. Lawrence Market is in full swing.
Worst Time: Sunday, when it's closed.

At one time, this area was at the center of city life. Today it's a little off-center, and yet it has some historic and modern architectural treasures, and a wealth of history in and around the St. Lawrence Market.

Begin at:

① Union Station

Check out the interior of this classical revival beauty, which opened in 1927 as a temple to and for the railroad. The shimmering ceiling, faced with vitrified Guastavino tile, soars 27m (88 ft.) above the 79m (260-ft.) -long hall.

Across the street, at York and Front streets, stands the:

② Fairmont Royal York Hotel

The venerable railroad hotel is a longtime gathering place for Torontonians. It's the home of the famous Imperial Room cabaret and nightclub, which used to be one of Eartha Kitt's favorite venues. The hotel was once the tallest building in Toronto and the largest hotel in the British Commonwealth. Check out the lobby, with its coffered ceiling and opulent furnishings.

As you leave the hotel, turn left and walk east on Front Street. At the corner of Bay and Front streets, look up at the stunning:

③ Royal Bank Plaza

The two triangular gold-sheathed towers rise 41 floors and 26 floors. A 40m-high (130-ft.) atrium joins them, and 150 pounds of gold enhances the mirrored glass. Webb Zerafa Menkes Housden designed the project, which was built between 1973 and 1977.

Cross Bay Street and continue east on Front Street. On the south side of the street is the impressive sweep of **One Front Street,** the main post

office building (okay, not an exciting-sounding sight, but an attractive one).

On the north side of the street is the city's latest financial palace and most impressive architectural triumph, Bell Canada Enterprises':

④ BCE Place

Go inside to view the soaring galleria. Skidmore, Owings, and Merrill, with Bregman & Hamann, designed it in 1993. The twin office towers connect through a huge glass-covered galleria five stories high, spanning the block between Bay and Yonge streets. Designed by artist-architect Santiago Calatrava with Bregman & Hamann, it links the old Midland Bank building to the twin towers.

TAKE A BREAK
For an unusual dining experience, stop in at **BCE Place's Movenpick Marché** (✆ 416/ 366-8986), which turns diners into hunter-gatherers. Rather than waiting for table service, you forage for salads, pastas, and meat dishes at various counters. If you can't bear the thought of chasing down your grub, head across the courtyard to **Acqua** (✆ 416/368-7171) for Italianate dishes. The downstairs food court offers a variety of fast-food and casual dining choices. If you prefer a deli sandwich, head for **Shopsy's,** 33 Yonge St. (✆ 416/365-3333; see chapter 5).

Walking Tour: St. Lawrence & Downtown East

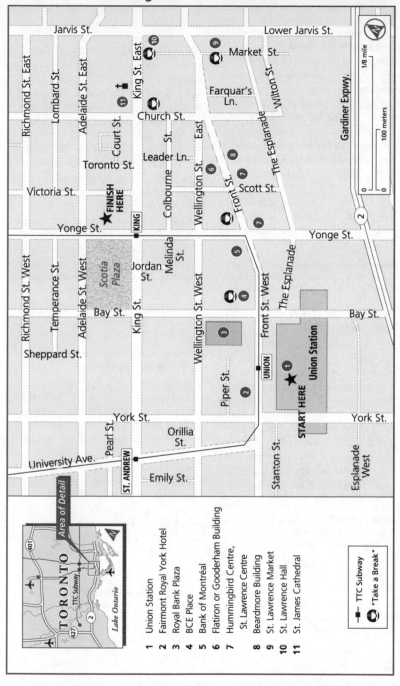

1   Union Station
2   Fairmont Royal York Hotel
3   Royal Bank Plaza
4   BCE Place
5   Bank of Montréal
6   Flatiron or Gooderham Building
7   Hummingbird Centre,
    St. Lawrence Centre
8   Beardmore Building
9   St. Lawrence Market
10 St. Lawrence Hall
11 St. James Cathedral

TTC Subway
"Take a Break"

Back out on Front Street, turn left and continue to the northwest corner of Yonge and Front, stopping to admire the:

❺ Bank of Montréal

The suitably ornate building (1885–86) held the most powerful Canadian bank of the 19th century, a force behind the colonial and federal governments. Inside, the banking hall rises to a beamed coffered ceiling with domed skylights of stained glass. It now houses the Stanley Cup and other hockey trophies, plus the **Hockey Hall of Fame** (p. 137), another example of the city's genius for architectural adaptation. The exterior, embellished with carvings, porthole windows, and a balustrade, is a sight.

From here, you can look ahead along Front Street and see the weird mural by Derek M. Besant that adorns the famous and highly photogenic:

❻ Flatiron or Gooderham Building (1892)

It was built as the headquarters of George Gooderham, who had expanded his distilling business into railroads, insurance, and philanthropy. At one time his liquor business was the biggest in the British Empire, and he was also president of the Bank of Toronto. The five-story building occupies a triangular site, and the western tip (and the windows) is beautifully curved and topped with a semicircular tower. The design is by David Roberts.

At the southwest corner of Yonge and Front streets, you can stop in at:

❼ The Hummingbird Centre

It sits across Scott Street from the **St. Lawrence Centre.** The former is home to the National Ballet of Canada and, at the moment, to the Canadian Opera Company (plans for a new opera house have come to naught).

Continue east along Front Street to the:

❽ Beardmore Building

It's at 35–39 Front St. E. This and the many other cast-iron buildings that line the street were the heart of the late-19th-century warehouse district, close to the lakefront and railheads. Now they hold stores like **Frida Crafts,** which sells imports from Guatemala, India, and Bangladesh, as well as jewelry, bags, candles, and other knickknacks; and **Mountain Equipment Co-op,** stocked with durable outdoor adventure goods. At no. 41–43, note the **Perkins Building,** and at no. 45–49, look for the building with a totally cast-iron facade. The **Nicholas Hoare** bookstore, one of the coziest in the city, is at no. 45.

Continue browsing as you pass Church Street. **Wonderful & Whites,** 83 Front St., features delicate pieces—Victorian linens, lace, pillows, china, and glass. Some of the pieces even have beautiful, colorful patterns. Next door, **Ra** offers an array of Indian and other decorative accents—bedspreads and pillows, along with apparel and jewelry.

Now cross Market Street to the:

❾ St. Lawrence Market

The old market building on the right. holds this great market hall, which was constructed around the city's second city hall (1844–45). The elegant pedimented facade that you see as you stand in the center of the hall was originally the center block of the city hall. Today the market abounds with vendors selling fresh eggs, Mennonite sausage, seafood, meats, cheeses, and baked goods. From Thursday to Saturday in the north building across the street, a farmers' market starts at 5am.

TAKE A BREAK
The most fun place to stop is at one of the stands offering fresh produce in the market itself. Other choices include **Le Papillon,** 16 Church St. (☏ **416/363-0838;** see chapter 5), which features a raft of savory and dessert crepes, and **Hot House Cafe,** 35 Church St. (☏ **416/366-7800).**

Exit the market where you came in. Cross Wellington Street and cut through Market Lane Park and the shops at Market Square, past the north market building. Turn right onto King Street to:

🔟 St. Lawrence Hall

This was the focal point of the community in the mid–19th century. This hall was the site of grand city occasions, political rallies, balls, and entertainment. Frederick Douglass delivered an antislavery lecture; Jenny Lind and Adelina Patti sang in 1851 and 1860, respectively; General Tom Thumb appeared in 1862; and George Brown campaigned for Confederation. William Thomas designed the elegant Palladian-style building, which boasts a domed cupola.

Cross King Street and enter the 19th-century garden. It has a cast-iron drinking fountain for people, horses, and dogs, and flowerbeds filled with seasonal blooms.

If you like, rest on a bench while you admire the handsome proportions of St. Lawrence Hall and listen to the chimes of:

🔟 St. James Cathedral

Adjacent to the garden on the north side of King Street, this is one of my favorite places in Toronto. The beautiful building and its surrounding park make a serene setting to rest and gather one's thoughts—at least for now. A condo developer is hoping to build on the grounds of the park that surrounds St. James. Now *there* goes the neighborhood. Enjoy this beautiful oasis while you still can.

York's first church was built here from 1803 to 1807. Originally a frame building, it was enlarged in 1818 and 1819, and replaced in 1831. The second church burned in 1839. The first cathedral replaced it, only to be destroyed in the great fire of 1849. The present building was begun in 1850 and finished in 1874. It boasts the tallest steeple in Canada. Inside, at the northern end of the east aisle, there's a Tiffany window in memory of William Jarvis, one of Toronto's founding fathers.

St. James' first incumbent was the Rev. George O'Kill Stuart; his successor, John Strachan (pronounced Strawn), later became the first bishop of Toronto. Strachan wielded tremendous temporal as well as spiritual power. For 50 years, until his death in 1867, he was an indomitable spirit. He threatened the Americans with the vengeance of the British Navy after they occupied York (Toronto), defied the British prelates by keeping King's College open over their objections that the charter was too liberal, and dismissed Thomas Jefferson as "a mischief maker." He revered British institutions and abhorred anything Yankee.

From here, you can view one of the early retail buildings that were built when King Street was the main commercial street. **Nos. 129–35** were originally an Army and Navy Store; cast iron, plate glass, and arched windows allowed the shopper to see what was available in the store. Also note nos. 111 and 125. The **Toronto Sculpture Garden,** 115 King St. (✆ **416/485-9658**), is a quiet corner for contemplation.

WINDING DOWN
From St. James, the venerable **Le Royal Meridien King Edward,** 37 King St. E. (✆ 416/863-9700), is only a block away. You can stop for afternoon tea in the lounge, or light fare or lunch in the **Café Victoria.** Both **La Maquette,** 111 King St. E. (✆ 416/366-8191), and **Biagio,** 157 King St. E. (✆ 416/366-4040), have appealing courtyards.

From St. James, go south on Church Street for 1 block and turn right into Colbourne Street. From Colbourne, turn left down Leader Lane to Wellington, where you can enjoy a fine view of the mural on the Flatiron Building and of the rhythmic flow of mansard rooflines along the south side of Front Street.

Turn right and proceed to Yonge Street, then turn right and walk to King Street to catch the subway to your next destination.

8

Shopping

Shopping in Toronto can be a kaleidoscopic experience. The *haute*-est international retailers—like Prada, Chanel, and Gucci—compete for attention with discount emporiums like Honest Ed's. Megastores dominate the landscape, yet boutiques are blossoming. And while foreign chains stake their claim in shopping arcades and malls, they stand shoulder to shoulder with homegrown talent.

The result of this chaos is a cornucopia of shops that fit a wide range of budgets and tastes. The bad news: While window-shopping is a laudable pastime, don't fool yourself that it will stop there. Just don't break the bank.

1 The Shopping Scene

While you may want to check out the impressive array of international retailers, it would be a mistake to overlook the locals. If your passion is fashion, do check out Canadian labels such as Lida Baday, Ross Mayer, Misura by Joeffer Caoc, Linda Lundstrom, Crystal Siemens, and Frette by Michelle Secours, Brian Bailey, Mimi Bizjak, Mercy, and Comrags.

Toronto also has a bustling arts and crafts community, with many galleries, custom jewelers, and artisans. Some of the best buys are on native and Inuit art. Artwork can be imported into the United States duty-free.

Stores usually open at around 10am from Monday to Saturday. Closing hours change depending on the day. From Monday to Wednesday, most stores close at 6pm; on Thursday and Friday, hours run to 8pm or 9pm; on Saturday, closing is quite early, usually around 6pm. Most stores are open on Sunday, though the hours may be restricted—11am or noon to 5pm is not unusual.

Almost every establishment accepts MasterCard and Visa, and a growing number take American Express. Many retailers accept U.S. cash, and the exchange rate tends to be a favorable one, especially downtown in the Eaton Centre area.

2 Great Shopping Areas

BLOOR STREET WEST   This strip of real estate, bordered by Yonge Street to the east and Avenue Road to the west, is where most of the top international names in fashion set up shop. If you're in the mood to see what Karl Lagerfeld is designing or to pick up a glittering bauble from Cartier or Tiffany, this is your hunting ground.

YORKVILLE   A far cry from its days as a hippie hangout and commune in the 1960s, this is now one of Toronto's best known—and most expensive—shopping neighborhoods. Little alleyways crisscross the streets, giving Yorkville a romantic, old-fashioned appeal. The shops here tend to be small boutiques that specialize, say, in beaded handbags or fine handmade papers. Bistros and cafes abound, giving rise to Yorkville's other pastime: people-watching.

Tips **Good to Know: Taxes & Rebates**

The provincial sales tax (PST) is 8%, and the national goods-and-services tax (GST) is 7%. Visitors can apply for a rebate of both when they leave the country. For details, see "Taxes" under "Fast Facts: Toronto," in chapter 3.

QUEEN STREET WEST   Playing down its grittier roots, this area is getting to be as glamorous as its uptown siblings. Queen Street West between University and Spadina avenues is rich with cutting-edge design in both fashion and housewares. Locals complain that this neighborhood isn't what it was before the Gap moved in, but it's still a great stomping ground for fashionistas in need of a fix.

THE EATON CENTRE   Okay, you're short on time, but you still want to fit in all your shopping. Where else can you go but the Eaton Centre? With more than 300 shops, including Browns, Danier, Birks, Nine West, La Vie en Rose, Femme de Carriere, Eddie Bauer, Banana Republic, Mendocino, Laura Secord, and Indigo, you'll be sure to find something.

THE UNDERGROUND CITY   Subterranean Toronto is a hive of shopping activity. While you won't find too many shops down here that don't have an above-ground location, the Underground City is a popular place in winter, and with those whose schedules don't allow them out of the Financial District.

CHINATOWN   It's crowded and noisy, but don't let that put you off. Sure, there's the usual touristy junk, like cheapo plastic toys and jewelry, but the real Chinatown has a lot more to offer, including fine rosewood furniture, exquisite ceramics, and homeopathic herbs. Just don't try driving here: This is traffic purgatory, and best navigated on foot.

3 Shopping A to Z
ANTIQUES
Toronto's antiques scene has exploded. Throw a stone in any direction and you're bound to hit an Edwardian console, or at least a classic Eames chair. For fine antiques, head north from Bloor Street along Avenue Road until you reach Davenport Avenue, or walk north on Yonge Street from the Rosedale subway station to St. Clair Avenue. Another top area is Mount Pleasant Road from St. Clair Avenue to Eglinton Avenue. For less pricey finds, head west on Queen Street to the Bathurst Street area. Merchandise at the Harbourfront Antique Market varies widely in quality and price.

At Home *(Finds*   An inviting, airy room filled with an ever-changing collection of furniture and accessories, including French chairs (often in pairs), fine tables, vintage lamps, and decorative mirrors. 1156 Yonge St. ✆ **416/924-6590.** Subway: Summerhill or Rosedale.

Belle Epoque   If you're feeling pretty and looking for furniture to match, this attic-like shop is worth a look. The furnishings are luxurious, and some pieces would not be out of place at Versailles, gilt and all. Some reproductions mix with the real articles. 1066 Yonge St. ✆ **416/925-0066.** Subway: Rosedale.

Bernardi's Antiques   The tiny showroom is jam-packed with furniture, silver flatware, paintings, bronzes, and carpets. Discontinued Royal Doulton

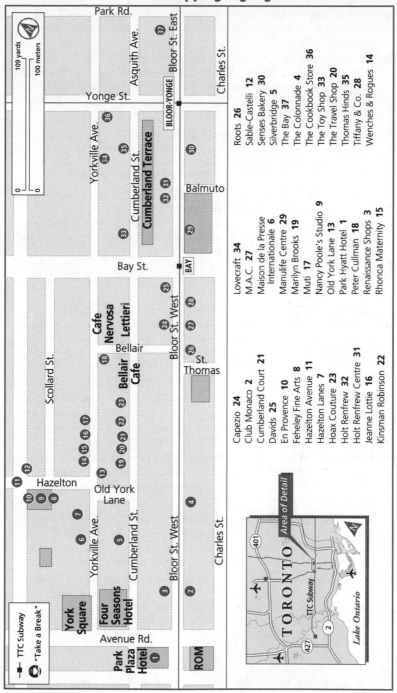

Park Rd.

Asquith Ave.

Yonge St.

BLOOR-YONGE

Bloor St. East

Charles St.

Yorkville Ave.

Cumberland St.

Cumberland Terrace

Balmuto

BAY

Bay St.

Bloor St. West

Bellair

St. Thomas

Scollard St.

Cafe Nervosa Lettieri

Bellair Cafe

Hazelton

Old York Lane

Yorkville Ave.

Cumberland St.

Bloor St. West

Charles St.

York Square

Four Seasons Hotel

Avenue Rd.

Park Plaza Hotel

ROM

- 109 yards
- 100 meters

TTC subway
"Take a Break"

Roots **26**
Sable-Castelli **12**
Senses Bakery **30**
Silverbridge **5**
The Bay **37**
The Colonnade **4**
The Cookbook Store **36**
The Toy Shop **33**
The Travel Shop **20**
Thomas Hinds **35**
Tiffany & Co. **28**
Wenches & Rogues **14**

Lovecraft **34**
M.A.C. **27**
Maison de la Presse Internationale **6**
Manulife Centre **29**
Marilyn Brooks **19**
Muti **17**
Nancy Poole's Studio **9**
Old York Lane **13**
Park Hyatt Hotel **1**
Peter Cullman **18**
Renaissance Shops **3**
Rhonca Maternity **15**

Capezio **24**
Club Monaco **2**
Cumberland Court **21**
Davids **25**
En Provence **10**
Feheley Fine Arts **8**
Hazelton Avenue **11**
Hazelton Lanes **7**
Hoax Couture **23**
Holt Renfrew **32**
Holt Renfrew Centre **31**
Jeanne Lottie **16**
Kinsman Robinson **22**

Area of Detail

TORONTO

Lake Ontario

TTC Subway

figurines are a specialty. 699 Mount Pleasant Rd. (south of Eglinton Ave.). © **416/483-6471.** www.bernardisantiques.com. Subway: Eglinton, then no. 34 bus to Mount Pleasant, and walk 1 block south.

Constantine *(Finds* Every item in this newly renovated shop has been hand-picked by its owner, Rita Tsantis. It's stocked with imposing wood furniture and delicate baubles. Be sure to check out the lighting selection—hand-painted Fortuny lamps are a house specialty—and gilt-trimmed glassware. 1110 Yonge St. © **866/929-1177** or 416/929-1177. Subway: Rosedale.

Decorum Decorative Finds If you're going on an ocean voyage, can you resist a C$2,200 (US$1,500) vintage Louis Vuitton trunk? The wares here range from tables and chaise lounges to oil paintings and old books. All are top priced, but also top of the line. 1210 Yonge St. © 416/966-6829. Subway: Summerhill.

Harbourfront Antique Market Renowned for its top-quality antiques, the market has its share of attic-worthy junk, too. With more than 100 dealers, what else would you expect? The variety is intriguing: furniture, glassware, art, silver, and jewelry dating back just a decade or as much as a century. Throughout the summer, itinerant dealers set up shop outside. Year-round, serious shoppers start early, but if you're looking for a bargain, start bidding just before closing time. The market is open 10am to 6pm Tuesday to Sunday. 390 Queen's Quay W. © **416/ 260-2626.** www.hfam.com. Subway: Union, then LRT to Rees St.

Horsefeathers! If your taste runs to English and French country house styles, this emporium's for you. The 12,000-square-foot space boasts striking wooden pieces in walnut and mahogany that share the spotlight with tapestries and Persian carpets. A new, smaller outlet is at 1212 Yonge St. (© **416/934-1771**). 630 Mount Pleasant Rd. © **416/486-4555.** Subway: Eglinton, then no. 34 bus to Mount Pleasant.

L'Atelier This is about as glamorous as it gets. Napoleon III side tables share space with chrome bar stools and rococo Italian lamps. Many of the price tags hit four digits, but there are lovely accoutrements for as little as C$10 (US$6.80). 1224 Yonge St. © **416/966-0200.** Subway: Summerhill.

Mark McLaine Collection This shop features styles as diverse as Art Deco and chinoiserie (a blend of Asian and French design). Many of the furnishings, carvings, and jewelry are the real McCoy, mixed with some fabulous fakes. Hazelton Lanes, 55 Avenue Rd. © **416/927-7972.** Subway: Bay.

Michel Taschereau Antiques In business since 1955, this attic-like shop is filled with 18th-, 19th-, and early 20th-century pieces from England, France, and North America. There's also a collection of decorative glass objects, ceramics, and folk art. 176 Cumberland St. © **416/923-3020.** Subway: Bay.

Mostly Movables Inc Turn-of-the-century Canadiana and English Jazz Age furnishings fill this shop. The pieces are generally in fine form, and the prices are somewhat lower than those at many Yorkville and Rosedale competitors. 785 Queen St. W. (west of Bathurst St.). © **416/504-4455.** Subway: Osgoode, then any streetcar west to Euclid Ave.

Putti *(Finds* Two generously proportioned rooms hold grand (and grandly priced) European treasures old and new: dining sets, armoires, cushions, and china. A recent addition is the floral department, which features both fresh and dried flowers. *Victoria* magazine has repeatedly featured this shop. 1104 Yonge St. © **416/972-7652.** Subway: Rosedale.

Whim Antiques   The store is aptly named—whimsical it is. In business since 1973, it's filled with beautiful baubles, silverware, and decorative *objets,* and walking through it feels rather like being let loose in great-grandma's attic. 561 Mount Pleasant Rd. © 416/481-4474. Subway: St. Clair, then Mount Pleasant bus to Belsize Ave.

Zig Zag   This shop carries a mélange of styles, but the specialty is early Modernist pieces. The names to watch out for are Eames, Saarinen, Arne Jacobsen, and Warren Platner. There are some bargains, with excellent pieces in the C$200 to $400 (US$136–$272) range, with a few stellar finds that run as high as C$3,500 (US$2,380). 1107 Queen St. E. © 416/778-6495. Subway: Queen, then any streetcar east to Pape Ave.

ART

Bau-Xi   After viewing the masterworks at the Art Gallery of Ontario, you can head across the street and buy your own. Founded in 1965, Bau-Xi features contemporary works by artists from across the country. 340 Dundas St. W. © 416/977-0600. Subway: St. Patrick.

Bay of Spirits Gallery   Here you'll find works by native Indians from across Canada. Most of the collection focuses on the art of the Pacific Northwest, including totem poles, masks, prints, and jewelry. 156 Front St. W. © 416/971-5190. Subway: Union.

Eskimo Art Gallery   This award-winning gallery has the largest collection of Inuit sculpture in Toronto. At any given time, it shows more than 500 pieces, with prices ranging from C$16 to $22,000 (US$11–$14,960). 12 Queens' Quay W. (opposite Westin Harbour Castle). © 800/800-2008 or 416/366-3000. Subway: Union, then LRT to Queen's Quay.

Feheley Fine Arts   The Feheleys have been personally selecting every piece in their gallery for over 40 years, making this one of the most individualized collections of early and contemporary Inuit art anywhere. 14 Hazelton Ave. © 416/323-1373. Subway: Bay.

Gallery Moos   German native Walter Moos has been a fixture on the Toronto art scene for 30 years. His gallery features top Canadian artists as well as international figures. 622 Richmond St. W. © 416/504-5445. Subway: Osgoode, then any streetcar west to Bathurst St., and walk 1 block south.

Jane Corkin Gallery   Most items here are historical and contemporary photographs from around the world. They include works by Cylla von Tiedemann, Irving Penn, and Herb Ritts. There is also a small collection of modernist painting and sculpture. 179 John St. © 416/979-1980. Subway: Osgoode.

Kinsman Robinson Galleries   The two stories of this Yorkville gallery display 20th-century figurative paintings, sculpture, and drawings. Artists represented include Stanley Cosgrove, Robert Katz, Esther Wertheimer, and Donald Liardi. Native Canadians Robert Davidson and Norval Morrisseau also exhibit their work here. There are a few paperworks by Zuniga, Braque, and Chagall, among others. 108 Cumberland St. © 800/895-4278 or 416/964-2374. Subway: Bay.

Nancy Poole's Studio   This intimate gallery of painting and sculpture has been in business for three decades. Most of the art is contemporary, much of it Canadian in origin. The gallery launches solo exhibitions every three weeks. 16 Hazelton Ave. © 416/964-9050. Subway: Bay.

Olga Korper Gallery   Established in 1973, this gallery houses contemporary Canadian and international works. Artists represented include Averbuch, John

Brown, Sankawa, and the estate of Louis Comtois. 17 Morrow Ave. (off Dundas St. W.).
© 416/538-8220. Subway: Dundas West.

Ontario College of Art & Design Gallery *Finds* If you're interested in the work of an emerging generation of artists, check out the ongoing exhibitions at the OCAD. Students display sculpture, photography, painting, and multimedia installations. 115 McCaul St., 3rd floor © 416/977-6000, ext. 262. Subway: St. Patrick.

Sable-Castelli This highly regarded gallery has been in business for more than 25 years. It represents contemporary American and Canadian artists, including heavy hitters like Warhol and Oldenburg. 33 Hazelton Ave. © 416/961-0011. Subway: Bay.

Sandra Ainsley Specializing in glass sculpture, this renowned gallery represents more than 50 artists from across North America, including Dale Chihuly, Jon Kuhn, Peter Powning, Tom Scoon, Susan Edgerley, and David Bennett. The one-of-a-kind pieces have big price tags, but there are also some affordable items, such as paperweights, vases, and jewelry. Toronto Exchange Tower, 130 King St. W. © 416/362-4480. Subway: St. Andrew.

Stephen Bulger Gallery This gallery displays contemporary Canadian and international photography; some of the artists represented include Diana Shearwood, Volker Seding, Lida Moser, and Vincenzo Pietropaolo. 700 Queen St. W. (west of Bathurst St.). © 416/504-0575. Subway: Osgoode, then any streetcar west to Palmerston Ave.

Susan Hobbs Gallery This small gallery, in an unprepossessing warehouse far from the Yorkville crowd, is a major player in Canadian contemporary art. Hobbs represents 11 of Toronto's best artists, including Ian Carr-Harris, Shirley Wiitasalo, Robin Collyer, and Sandra Meigs. 137 Tecumseth St. (at Queen St.) © 416/504-3699. Subway: Osgoode, then any streetcar west to Tecumseth St.

Ydessa Hendeles Art Foundation This is one of the most interesting contemporary art collections in the city. Hendeles features installations by international artists. Works on display include paintings, photography, and multimedia projects. 778 King St. W. © 416/603-2227. Subway: St. Andrew, then any streetcar west to Bathurst St.

AUDIO-VISUAL & ELECTRONIC GOODS

Bay-Bloor Radio This 13,000-square-foot store carries all the latest and greatest audio equipment, from portable units to in-home theater systems. Manulife Centre, 55 Bloor St. W. © 416/967-1122. Subway: Bay.

Canadian Tire This is handyman heaven. The endless aisles overflow with gadgets for home, yard, office, car, and any place in between. This is where I head as Father's Day approaches. 839 Yonge St. © 416/925-9592. www.canadiantire.com. Subway: Yonge/Bloor.

Henry's *Finds* This bi-level shop deals in analog and digital photography. The first floor has electronic equipment, darkroom supplies, and a photo processing lab. Upstairs, there's a wide selection of secondhand cameras and gear. 119 Church St. © 416/868-0872. Subway: Queen.

SpyTech James Bond wannabes, welcome. Entering Spy Tech is like having a free pass to Q's lab. Looking for a gadget to modify your telephone voice or a spook-worthy camera? You'll find it all here, though the price tags do get a little steep—all the way up to C$100,000 (US$68,000) for a bulletproof car. 2028 Yonge St. © 416/482-8588. Subway: Davisville.

BOOKS

Another Man's Poison This shop boasts an international collection of books about graphic arts, interior design, and architecture. Anything you can't find on the shelves can be special ordered. There's also a substantial selection of out-of-print titles. 29 McCaul St. (just north of Queen St.). ℂ 416/593-6451. Subway: Osgoode.

Atticus Books Bookworms can while away hours in this crowded shop filled with secondhand scholarly tomes. It stocks many volumes of philosophy, psychology, and psychoanalysis. Antiquarian books and illuminated manuscripts are at the back of the store. 84 Harbord St. ℂ 416/922-6045. Subway: Spadina, then walk south.

Ballenford Books on Architecture Interior designers, whether amateur or pro, will love this well-arranged store. The books cover everything from antique furniture to architectural theory, from urban design to landscaping. The shop also displays sketches and drawings by local architects. 600 Markham St. (south of Bloor St. W.) ℂ 416/588-0800. Subway: Bathurst.

Bob Miller Book Room When I was a student at the University of Toronto, I would come into this academic bookstore looking for one text and end up browsing for ages. It stocks mainly literary fiction, humanities, and social sciences. Works in translation are carefully selected. 180 Bloor St. W., lower concourse. ℂ 416/922-3557. Subway: St. George.

Book City All the books here are new, and many are discounted by 10% to 30%. There is also a good assortment of international magazines. Book City also has branches at 1430 Yonge St. (ℂ **416/961-1228**), 1950 Queen St. E. (ℂ **416/698-1444**), and 348 Danforth Ave. (ℂ **416/469-9997**). 501 Bloor St. W. ℂ 416/961-4496. Subway: Bathurst.

Chapters While the Chapters bookstores are now owned and operated by Indigo (see below), they retain their own unique charm. Eminently browse-worthy and well-stocked, Chapters boasts comfy chairs, a Starbucks cafe, and a host of free special events. Celebrity authors Sophia Loren and Sarah, Duchess of York, had their Toronto engagements here. There's another Chapters store at 142 John St. (ℂ **416/595-7349**). The stores are open late, usually until 10 or 11pm on weeknights and midnight on weekends. 110 Bloor St. W. ℂ 416/920-9299. Subway: Bay.

The Cookbook Store I call it food porn: lush, gooey close-ups of scallop ceviche and tiramisu. This store specializes in the kind of book that makes a gourmet's heart go pitter-patter. There are also tomes about wine, health, and restaurants. 850 Yonge St. ℂ 416/920-2665. Subway: Yonge/Bloor.

David Mason This charming used-book store is straight out of Dickens. It stocks many travel books, and a number of first editions of Canadian, American, and British works. The collections of 19th- and 20th-century literature are vast. 342 Queen St. W. ℂ 416/598-1015. Subway: Osgoode.

Glad Day Bookshop This was the first gay-oriented bookstore in Canada, and it remains one of the best. The shelves hold a sizable collection of gay and lesbian fiction, biography, and history books, and the offerings have expanded to include magazines, CDs, videos, calendars, posters, and cards. 598A Yonge St., 2nd floor. ℂ 877/783-3725 or 416/961-4161. Subway: Wellesley.

Shopping Highlights: Queen Street West

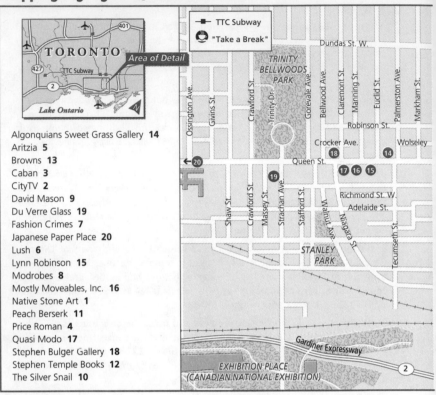

Algonquians Sweet Grass Gallery **14**
Aritzia **5**
Browns **13**
Caban **3**
CityTV **2**
David Mason **9**
Du Verre Glass **19**
Fashion Crimes **7**
Japanese Paper Place **20**
Lush **6**
Lynn Robinson **15**
Modrobes **8**
Mostly Moveables, Inc. **16**
Native Stone Art **1**
Peach Berserk **11**
Price Roman **4**
Quasi Modo **17**
Stephen Bulger Gallery **18**
Stephen Temple Books **12**
The Silver Snail **10**

Indigo Books Music & More This Canadian-owned chain boasts an excellent selection of books, magazines, and videotapes. It has tables and chairs to encourage browsing, a cafe, and helpful staff. Best of all, there are special events (author visits, live performances, even seminars) almost daily. There are also events for kids. The store is a favorite with night owls—it's open until 11pm or midnight every day. There are branches at the Eaton Centre (✆ **416/591-3622**) and at 2300 Yonge St., at Eglinton Avenue (✆ **416/544-0049**). Manulife Centre, 55 Bloor St. W. ✆ **416/925-3536.** www.indigo.ca. Subway: Yonge/Bloor or Bay.

Mabel's Fables *Finds* This charming shop is stocked with every book a child could possibly want—and a lot more. Offerings are grouped by age, going up to early adolescence. On weekends there are author visits and other special events. 662 Mount Pleasant. ✆ **416/322-0438.** Eglinton, then no. 34 bus to Mount Pleasant, and walk 2 blocks south.

Nicholas Hoare This shop has the cozy feel of an English library, with hardwood floors, plush couches, and a fireplace. There's an extensive selection of Canadian and international fiction, as well as heavyweight art tomes and children's books. 45 Front St. E. ✆ **416/777-2665.** Subway: Union.

Open Air Books & Maps This shop caters to nature lovers and ecology buffs. It carries a vast assortment of travel guidebooks and maps. 25 Toronto St. ✆ **416/363-0719.** Subway: King.

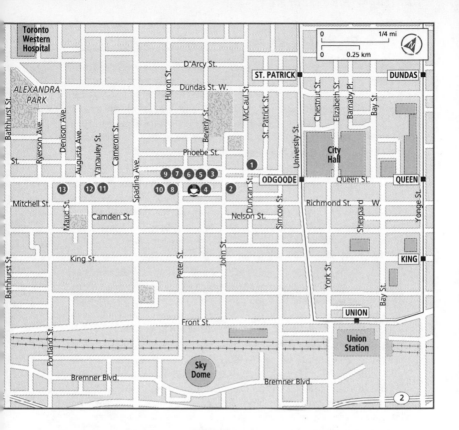

Seekers Books New and old books about Eastern religion, mysticism, meditation, and the occult mix on the shelves. The focus is definitely New Age, but you'll find general-interest fiction and nonfiction, too. 509 Bloor St. W. ℂ **416/925-1982.** Subway: Bathurst.

The Silver Snail Remember those comic books you read as a kid? Well, they're all here, with adult-oriented comics like the *Sandman* series. You'll see a sizable section of imported editions, and posters and movie memorabilia, too. 367 Queen St. W. ℂ **416/593-0889.** Subway: Osgoode.

Steven Temple Books If you're looking for a rare first edition of a 19th- or 20th-century literary work in English, be sure to visit this shop, which is open by appointment only. It also carries secondhand books about a variety of subjects. 489 Queen St. W., 2nd floor. ℂ **416/703-9908.** Subway: Osgoode, then any streetcar west.

The World's Biggest Bookstore The debate about whether the World's Biggest is *really* the world's biggest rages on. Either way, the 27km (17 miles) of bookshelves do contain a good selection. Browsing is welcome, but the bright, bright lights are headache-inducing after a while. There are also software, video, and magazine departments. 20 Edward St. ℂ **416/977-7009.** Subway: Dundas.

CHINA, SILVER & GLASS
Du Verre Glass The store name is a bit of a misnomer. Gorgeous glassworks are on display, but they share this airy, open space with ceramics, wood and

Value The Best Bargains

Maybe you can't get something for nothing . . . but you can score some pretty fab finds on the cheap in Toronto. It's a treasure hunt of sorts, and the spoils are anything but certain, but when you find that perfect piece marked down to next-to-nothing, well, that just makes it all worthwhile. Many Toronto retailers, including luxurious Holt Renfrew, have their own outlet shops. Here's my own little black book of favorite foraging grounds. Happy hunting!

Dixie Outlet Mall   Ten minutes from Pearson International Airport is the answer to bargain-shoppers' prayers. It's hard to beat the Dixie Outlet Mall for number of bargains per square foot. There are more than 120 outlet shops here, including Femme de Carriere and chocolatier Laura Secord, so you're bound to find something. 1250 S. Service Rd., Mississauga. © 905/278-7492. Gardiner Expressway/Queen Elizabeth Way (QEW) west to Dixie Rd. exit. Turn left, follow Dixie Rd. south to S. Service Rd.

Grreat Stuff   There's an awful lot of men's clothes packed into this small retail space, but if you're not troubled by claustrophobia, dig in for some amazing deals. Business casual is this shop's mainstay, though there are grreat prices on Italian silk ties and brand-name suits. 870 Queen St. W. © 416/533-7680. Subway: Osgoode, then streetcar west to Shaw St.

Holt Renfrew Last Call   It might not be the most organized store you've laid eyes on, but what it lacks in tidiness it makes up for in bargains. The racks are laden with brands such as Donna Karan, Prada, and Versace, marked down to one-half to one-fifth of what they would normally cost. There have been rumors of Kate Spade handbags on sale here, but I have yet to arrive in time. May you have better luck. 370 Steeles Ave. W. © 905/886-7444. Subway: Finch, then Steeles West bus.

Honest Ed's World Famous Shopping Centre (Finds)   Ed's is a Toronto institution, framed with flashing red and yellow lights both outdoors *and* indoors. "Don't just stand there, buy something!" blurts out one brazen sign. This idiosyncratic store has a deal on everything from housewares to carpets, from clothing to sundries. Crazy-making as shopping here can be, the bargains are unbeatable—but be warned, the queues are, too. 581 Bloor St. W. © 416/537-2111. Subway: Bathurst.

wrought-iron furniture, lamps, and candlesticks. 188 Strachan Ave. © 416/593-0182. Subway: Osgoode, then any streetcar west.

Muti   Murano glass designs and cheery ceramics from Italy dominate this store. Look a little closer and you'll find a few French tapestries and tablecloths, too. 88 Yorkville Ave. © 416/969-0253. Subway: Bay.

William Ashley (Finds)   The last word in luxe, whether it be fine china, crystal, or silver. All of the top manufacturers are represented, including Waterford, Baccarat, Christofle, Wedgewood, and Lenox. Even if you're not in a buying mood, the detailed displays are fascinating. Manulife Centre, 55 Bloor St. W. © 416/964-2900. Subway: Bay.

Marilyn's   Here's a rare thing: knockdown prices paired with attentive service. The specialty is Canadian fashions for women, from sportswear to glamorous gowns. There are also in-store seminars about fashion-forward topics like traveling with just one suitcase. 130 Spadina Ave. ℭ 416/504-6777. Subway: Spadina, then LRT to Queen St. W.

Paris Samples   This store snaps up designers' samples and marks them down 20% to 75%. The clothes range from wool pants to velvet dresses to micro-miniskirts. *One caveat:* The sizes are all under 14, and many clothes come only in the smallest sizes. 101 Yorkville Ave. ℭ 416/926-0656. Subway: Bay.

The Shoe Company   This is every foot fetishist's dream: great shoes for men and women from Unisa, Nine West, and others, marked down to unbeatable prices. There are lots of funky styles that won't be stylish for long, but it won't hurt your pocketbook to splurge. There are outlets around the city, including First Canadian Place. 711 Yonge St. ℭ 416/923-8388. Subway: Yonge/Bloor.

Tom's Place   After more than 40 years in business, Tom's Place looks sharper than ever. While the shop devotes an entire floor to women's wear, the best buys are in the men's department: You'll find brand-name merchandise by the likes of Armani and Valentino. Suits that cost C$495 to $1,800 (US$337–$1,224) elsewhere ring up for C$299 to $850 (US$203–$578) here. Tom's Place stocks sizes from 36 short to 50 tall. 190 Baldwin St. ℭ 416/596-0297. Subway: Spadina, then LRT to Baldwin St.

Winner's   This northern outpost of the U.S.-owned T.J. Maxx chain offers great deals on clothes for men and women (think Jones New York, Tommy Hilfiger, and Earl Jeans), and top-name togs for the kiddies. There's also an ever-changing selection of housewares, cookware, linens, toiletries, and toys. The new 40,000-square-foot outlet at College Park is always packed, but its large, airy space is filled with deals. College Park. ℭ 416/598-8800; Subway: College. The smaller but longstanding location in the Fashion District is another good bet. 57 Spadina Ave. ℭ 416/585-2052. Subway: Spadina, then LRT to King St. W.

CIGARS & TOBACCO

Thomas Hinds   This is Havana heaven for the stogie set. Thomas Hinds carries a wide range of Cuban cigars and cigarillos, as well as pipes and the other smoking accouterments. Upstairs there's a lounge and humidor. 8 Cumberland St. ℭ 416/927-7703. Subway: Yonge/Bloor.

CRAFTS

The Algonquians Sweet Grass Gallery   Ojibway-owned and -operated, this shop specializes in exquisite Native Canadian arts and crafts. The collection includes porcupine-quill jewelry, soapstone sculpture, Iroquois masks, prints, antique spearheads, and moccasins. 668 Queen St. W. ℭ 416/703-1336. Subway: Osgoode, then any streetcar west.

Arctic Canada   Here you'll find a wide range of arts and crafts, from soap-stone carvings to jewelry and clothing, all hailing from the Arctic Circle. There's another branch at Pearson International Airport, Terminal 2 (② **905/678-6064**). 207 Queen's Quay W. ② **416/203-7889**. Subway: Union, then LRT to Queen's Quay.

Arts on King   This 10,000-square-foot complex consists of boutiques selling original art, folk crafts, and furniture. Connected to it is the Wagner Rosenbaum Gallery, which exhibits work by new and established Toronto artists every month. 169 King St. E. ② **416/777-9617**. Subway: King.

Art Zone   Sisters Jane and Kathryn Irwin own and operate this gallery-like space. Their main medium is stained glass, and their style is colorful and mod-ern. They also carry a limited number of glass gift items, including bowls, trays, and sculptural objects. 592 Markham St. (south of Bloor St. W.). ② **416/534-1892**. Subway: Bathurst.

Five Potters Studio   Phone ahead for an appointment, and you're free to watch the ceramic artists—all women—at work. The pieces on display vary from functional to sculptural items. Prices range from C$15 to $300 (US$10–$204). 131A Pears Ave. ② **416/924-6992**. Subway: St. George.

Frida   Arts and crafts from Africa, Southeast Asia, and Latin America share space in this bi-level shop. It offers an assortment of colorful woven mats, clothes, carved statuettes, jewelry, and candelabras. 39 Front St. E. ② **416/366-3169**. Subway: Union.

Lynn Robinson   Robinson herself creates many of the bronze and raku (Japanese earthenware) objects on display. In addition to the sculpture and glass, wood, and clay pieces, you'll see objects by five jewelers working with precious metals. Visitors are often treated to the sight of a potter working near the entrance. 709 Queen St. W. ② **416/703-2467**. Subway: Osgoode, then any streetcar west to Bathurst St.

Native Stone Art   This shop houses the creations of native Indian artisans from across North America. There are Mohawk and Iroquois carvings, Cree moccasins, and Navajo, Zuni, and Hopi jewelry. The quality is very high. 2 McCaul St. (at Queen St. W.). ② **416/593-0924**. Subway: Osgoode.

DEPARTMENT STORES

Eatons   If you visited Toronto before 2000, you'll remember the gorgeous Eaton's department store, which anchored the Eaton Centre complex. Owned and operated by the Toronto-based Eaton family for more than a century, it closed in 1999. Sears Canada bought the Eatons name (minus the apostrophe) and opened this department store in its place. Sadly, the new store has been a money-loser from the get-go, and Sears is now planning to close Eatons and open a Sears store in its place. Eaton Centre. ② **416/343-2111**. Subway: Dundas.

Holt Renfrew   Designers such as Donna Karan, Christian Lacroix, and Yves St. Laurent figure in Holt Renfrew's four levels of merchandise. The basement connects with an underground mall, and features a gourmet food department and a cafe. Holt Renfrew Centre, 50 Bloor St. W. ② **416/922-2333**. Subway: Yonge/Bloor.

The Hudson's Bay Company   Started as a fur-trading business when the first French-speaking settlers came to Canada, the Bay boasts excellent mid-range selections of clothing and housewares. It schedules weekend sales almost every week, though shoppers should be warned that winning the staff's attention requires patience. There are several locations around the city, with the best being

176 Yonge St. (at Queen St.). ℭ **416/861-9111.** Subway: Queen. Another good one is at 2 Bloor St. E. (at Yonge St.). ℭ **416/972-3333.** Subway: Yonge/Bloor.

FASHION

Let's get this out of the way first: Toronto has all of the requisite big-name European boutiques along Bloor Street West between Yonge Street and Avenue Road. You'll find **Louis Vuitton** at no. 110, **Gucci** at no. 130, and **Chanel, Prada,** and **Hermès** bundled together at The Colonnade shopping arcade at no. 131. The listings below focus primarily on shops that are unique to Toronto (with just a couple of exceptions). Also see the listings under "Shoes" and "Vintage Clothing," later in this chapter.

CHILDREN'S

A Joaninha   The name means "ladybug" in Portuguese, and this small shop in Little Italy boasts a gorgeous selection of European-imported kidswear. 764 College St. ℭ **416/533-9356.** Subway: Queen's Park, then streetcar west to Ossington.

Kids Cats & Dogs   Not just for kids—the shop carries its signature T-shirts, pajamas, and sweats in sizes from infant to adult. Everything, including knapsacks and comforters, sports a cat or dog motif. 508 Eglinton Ave. W. ℭ **416/484-1844.** Subway: Eglinton.

Lovechild   A favorite with tiny tots who are already developing fashion savvy, Lovechild offers a selection of groovy clothes in a rainbow of colors. 2523 Yonge St. ℭ **416/486-4746.** Subway: Eglinton.

Misdemeanors   Located just across the street from Pat Chorley's shop for grown-ups, Fashion Crimes (see below), Misdemeanors stocks the stuff that little girls' dreams are made of. In addition to gossamer gowns, there's a selection of flower-power home accents. 322½ Queen St. W. ℭ **416/351-8758.** Subway: Osgoode.

MEN'S & WOMEN'S

Club Monaco   This is Club Monaco's flagship store in Toronto. It's an airy, high-ceilinged space filled with casual wear and sportswear, with a smattering of work-ready clothes. It also has its own accessories and makeup lines. There are 19 other outlets around the city, including 403 Queen St. W. (ℭ **416/979-5633**). 157 Bloor St. W. ℭ **416/591-8837.** www.clubmonaco.com. Subway: Museum.

Hoax Couture   The corset-topped dresses on display in the front window bring a *Moulin Rouge* cancan show to mind, but the shop's owners, Chris Tyrell and Jim Searle, design dramatic, playful clothes for men and women. 114 Cumberland St. ℭ **416/929-4629.** Subway: Bay.

Irish Shop   If you're yearning for the Emerald Isle, you'll welcome the sight of lace shawls, linens, sweaters, and Celtic music, books, and giftware. There's also a selection of linen suits by Dublin designer Paul Costelloe. 150 Bloor St. W. ℭ **416/922-9400.** Subway: Bay.

Modrobes   Renowned for its comfy, casual clothing, Canadian-owned Modrobes got its start when its founder, Steven Debus, was still attending the university. Debus designed "exam pants"—trousers so comfy you could spend a day writing exams in them without your bum going numb. Today the store's offerings include T-shirts, jackets, and hats. 239 Queen St. W. ℭ **416/597-9560.** www.modrobes.com. Subway: Osgoode.

Old Navy   The Gap's little brother hit Toronto like a hurricane when it opened in 2001. There are no longer queues to get into the store, but it remains incredibly popular—a fact that's an enduring mystery to me. Sure, the prices are reasonable, but the store is cramped and chaotic, and the product selection is much smaller than at its U.S. counterparts. Unless you've never been to an Old Navy outlet before, steer clear. Eaton Centre. ✆ 416/593-2551. Subway: Dundas.

Roots This is one Canadian retailer that seems to be universally loved. The clothes are casual, from hooded sweats to fleece jackets, and there's a good selection of leather footwear. Don't overlook the tykes' department, which has the same stuff in tiny sizes. Other locations include the Eaton Centre (✆ **416/593-9640**). 95A Bloor St. W. ✆ **416/323-9512**. www.roots.ca. Subway: Bay.

Sim & Jones Shop owners Pui Sim and Alarice Jones design clothes that move easily between a "smart casual" office environment and the smart chic of the latest bistro. The women's clothes are available in sizes 6 to 16. 388 College Street. ✆ **416/920-2573**. Subway: Queen's Park, then streetcar to Borden St.

TNT Man/TNT Woman *(Finds)* The acronym stands for "The New Trend," and this small chain offers just that, with fashions from Betsey Johnson and Plein Sud for les femmes, and Diesel and Iceberg Jean for les hommes. There are also locations uptown at 368 and 388 Eglinton Avenue. Hazelton Lanes, 55 Avenue Rd. ✆ **416/975-1960** (men's shop) and **416/975-1810** (women's shop). Subway: Bay.

Wenches & Rogues *(Finds)* This upscale shop carries the latest and greatest in Canadian design for men and women. Featured labels include Misura by Joeffer Caoc, as well as up-and-coming talent from around the country. 610 Queen St. W. ✆ **416/536-2172**. Subway: Osgoode, then streetcar west to Bathurst.

Zara This Spanish retailer is renowned for transferring the latest looks into affordable fashions less than a month after they appear on the runway. This bi-level shop has a women's department at street level; the equally stylish men's shop is on the lower concourse. 50 Bloor St. W. ✆ **416/916-2401**. Subway: Bay.

MEN'S

Alan Cherry In addition to Cherry's own line of European-made clothes, this shop carries top-notch designer menswear. The clearance center at the back boasts some serious markdowns. Hazelton Lanes, 55 Avenue Rd. ✆ **416/923-9558**. Subway: Bay.

Boomer *(Finds)* Ever wonder where the Barenaked Ladies or Moist get the glad rags they wear in their videos? Look no farther than Boomer, a hip shop that stocks staples like Hugo Boss and Cinque, and well as the latest from Swedish trendsetter J. Linderberg. 309 Queen St. W. ✆ **416/598-0013**. Subway: Osgoode.

Decibel This trendy shop is a terrific spot to pick up the latest and greatest in casualwear. Labels range from well-known brands like Kenneth Cole to up-and-comers like Psycho Cowboy or Pusch (from Denmark and Calgary, respectively). 200 Queen St. W. ✆ **416/506-9648**. Subway: Osgoode.

Harry Rosen Designed like a mini department store, Harry Rosen carries the crème de la crème of menswear designers, including Hugo Boss, Brioni, and Versace. There's also a good selection of work-worthy footwear, and a famous "Great Wall of Shirts." 82 Bloor St. W. ✆ **416/972-0556**. Subway: Bay.

Moores There's something for everyone at this spacious shop. Most of the suits, sport coats, and dress pants are Canadian-made, and international designers like Oscar de la Renta are represented, too. Sizes run from extra short to extra tall and oversize. The prices tend to be reasonable, and bargains abound. 100 Yonge St. ✆ **416/363-5442**. Subway: King.

Rotman Hat Shop and Haberdasher   In business for more than 45 years, this shop is a reminder of Spadina's original Jewish community. Rotman's boasts a selection of top-quality headgear, including fedoras, tam-o'-shanters, and cool Kangol caps. 345 Spadina Ave. ⓒ 416/977-2806. Subway: Spadina, then LRT to Baldwin St.

Thomas K.T. Chui   Established three decades ago, Chui's shop looks unremarkable from the street. Inside, however, you'll immediately see why he has such a following among the famous. The quality can't be beat, which is why a custom-made suit costs C$1,000 (US$680) and up, up, up. 754 Broadview Ave. ⓒ 416/465-8538. Subway: Broadview.

WOMEN'S

Andrew's   Smaller than nearby Holt Renfrew, this department store nonetheless stocks a competing collection of European sportswear, formal dresses, lingerie, and cosmetics. Hazelton Lanes, 55 Avenue Rd. ⓒ 416/969-9991. Subway: Bay.

Aritzia   This Vancouver retailer now has an outpost on Queen West. The clothes are a mix of the house label, Talullah Babaton, and trendy lines such as Parasuco and the hard-to-find French label Kookai. 280 Queen St. W. ⓒ 416/977-9919. Subway: Osgoode.

Fashion Crimes   If Misdemeanors (see above) was a playground for little princesses, then Fashion Crimes is the stomping ground for their fairy godmothers. The glamorous dresses, designed by shop owner Pam Chorley, are a tribute to playful femininity. 395 Queen St. W. ⓒ 416/592-9001. Subway: Osgoode.

Femme de Carriere   For a dose of Quebecois savoir-faire, look no further than this elegant emporium. While the name translates into "career woman," the offerings range from shapely suits to evening-appropriate dresses and chic separates. Eaton Centre. ⓒ 416/595-0951. Subway: Queen.

Fresh Baked Goods *(Finds*   No, this *isn't* a bakery. Owner Laura Jean "the knitting queen" features a line of flirty knitwear made of cotton, mohair, wool, or lace. This is a favorite haunt of the celebrity set—stars like Neve Campbell drop by when they're in town. The staff is friendly and incredibly helpful—if you like a sweater but not its buttons, they will sew on different ones from their sizeable collection free of charge. They also do custom orders. 274 Augusta Ave. ⓒ 416/966-0123. www.freshbakedgoods.com. Subway: Spadina, then LRT to Baldwin St., and walk 2 blocks west.

F/X   The significance of the name is clear from the start: This is dressing for dramatic effect. Funkier pieces from the prêt-à-porter collections of Vivienne Westwood and Anna Sui are at the back of the store. There are also cutting-edge shoes and boots, a makeup collection, and candy. 152 Spadina Ave. ⓒ 416/703-5595. Subway: Spadina, then LRT to Queen St. W.

Jeanne Lottie *(Finds*   Can you make a fashion statement with a handbag? Canadian designer Jane Ip thinks so. Purses for all occasions, from zebra-patterned boxy bags for day to glittering sequin-encrusted numbers for a night out, fill her boutique. Prices are surprisingly low, with most offerings in the C$50 to $80 (US$34–$54) range. 106 Yorkville Ave. ⓒ 416/975-5115. Subway: Bay.

Linda Lundstrom   Lundstrom has been designing women's clothing since the early 1970s. Her distinctive brand of sportswear incorporates native Canadian art and themes. The famous La Parka coat is still a best-seller. 136 Cumberland St. ⓒ 416/927-9009. Subway: Bay.

Marilyn Brooks   Still going strong after almost four decades of designing, Brooks displays her own easy-fitting creations alongside the clothes of budding Canadian couturiers. 132 Cumberland St. ℂ **416/961-5050.** Subway: Bay.

Maxi Boutique   Homegrown talent takes center stage here, with designs from Lida Baday, Ross Mayer, and Misura by Joeffer Caoc. There's a full complement of suits, separates, and eveningwear. 575 Danforth Ave. ℂ **416/461-6686.** Subway: Pape.

Peach Berserk   Toronto designer (and local legend) Kingi Carpenter creates dramatically printed silk separates, dresses and coats. But don't look for demure florals—prints range from bold martini glasses to the ironic "Do I Look Fat in This?" logo. 507 Queen St. W. ℂ **416/504-1711.** Subway: Osgoode, then streetcar west to Spadina.

Price Roman   The husband-and-wife team of Derek Price and Tess Roman produces sleek, tailored clothes with a sultry edge. They are rightly famous for their special occasion dresses. 267 Queen St. W. ℂ **416/979-7363.** Subway: Osgoode.

Rhonda Maternity   For the last of the red-hot mamas, there's this glamorous boutique. The stylish suits, sweater sets, and sportswear are this store's exclusive designs. 110 Cumberland St. ℂ **416/921-3116.** Subway: Bay.

Suitables   Silk, glorious silk, is the mainstay of this popular shop. In addition to blouses in a variety of colors, there are hand-painted vests, sweaters, jerseys, and jackets, many of them Canadian-made. The store also stocks some contemporary costume jewelry. 26 Bellair St. ℂ **800/561-2548** or **416/203-0655.** Subway: Bay.

FOOD

The Big Carrot   Who says health food can't be fun? This large-scale emporium stocks everything from organic produce to vitamins to all-natural beauty potions. Stop in at the cafe for a vegetarian snack or light meal. 348 Danforth Ave. ℂ **416/466-2129.** Subway: Chester.

The Bonnie Stern School   Crammed to the rafters with cooking accoutrements (such as stovetop grills) and exotic books, this store also features the raw ingredients you need to produce fine cuisine. It carries top-notch olive oil, balsamic vinegar, Asian sauces, and candied flower petals. If you take a course or seminar, you get a 10% discount on everything you buy. 6 Erskine Ave. ℂ **416/484-4810.** Subway: Eglinton.

Global Cheese Shoppe   Cheese, glorious cheese. More than 150 varieties are available, from mild boccocini to the greenest of Gorgonzola, and the staff is generous with samples. 76 Kensington Ave. ℂ **416/593-9251.** Subway: Spadina, then LRT to Baldwin Ave.

House of Tea   Visitors to this shop can drink in the heady scent of more than 150 loose teas. And the selection of cups, mugs, and tea caddies runs from chic to comical. 1017 Yonge St. ℂ **416/922-1226.** Subway: Rosedale.

Senses   The food here is delicate, exquisite, and priced accordingly. There are counters of terrines and patés, caviar, pastries, and chocolates, as well as shelves filled with bottled Hong Kong sauces and boxed Dean & Deluca spices. 15 Bloor St. W. ℂ **416/961-0055.** Subway: Yonge/Bloor.

Simone Marie Belgian Chocolate   All of the rich truffles, colorful almond dragées, and fruit jellies in this shop are flown in from Belgium. If you're going to splurge, you may as well do it in style. 126A Cumberland St. ℂ **416/968-7777.** Subway: Bay.

Sugar Mountain Confectionery   Remember Pez, candy necklaces, and lollipop rings? Sugar Mountain carries the tooth-aching sweets of youth, several of which have been elevated to cult status. Teens are drawn to this store, but the biggest customers are nostalgic boomers. 320 Richmond St. W. ⓒ 416/204-9544. Subway: Osgoode.

GIFTS & MORE

Down East Gifts and Gallery   If your travels won't take you any farther east than Toronto, drop in on this shop to check out the folk art of the Atlantic provinces. The carvings, prints, and knickknacks are whimsical and charming. 508 Bathurst St. ⓒ 416/925-1642. Subway: Bathurst.

French Country *(Finds*   Owner Viola Jull spent several years living in France, and she re-creates a Parisian atmosphere in her shop. Many items are unique, including painted lampshades, antique silver, and framed prints. There are also a few gourmet food products and hand-milled soaps. 6 Roxborough St. W. ⓒ 416/944-2204. Subway: Rosedale.

Ice   This small store is a big lure for visiting celebs. Do the Bliss Spa and Philosophy skin care lines draw them in? Maybe it's the eye-catching T-shirts or the fab costume jewelry. 163 Cumberland St. ⓒ 416/964-6751. Subway: Bay.

Japanese Paper Place   The Japanese have elevated paper-making to an art form. In addition to being popular with artists, this shop has all the boxes, papers, and handmade cards you could ever need to create exquisite gift-wrappings. Better yet, it also stocks instruction books! 887 Queen St. W. ⓒ 416/703-0089. Subway: Osgoode, then any streetcar west to Ossington Ave.

Legends of the Game   This collectibles store, just 2 blocks north of Sky-Dome, houses memorabilia of Babe Ruth, Wayne Gretzky, Muhammad Ali, and Michael Jordan, among others. There are trading cards, team jerseys, and other souvenirs. 322A King St. W. ⓒ 416/971-8848. Subway: St. Andrew.

Oh Yes, Toronto   Looking for souvenirs for the folks back home? Oh Yes, Toronto stocks no end of Hogtown knickknacks, as well as quality T-shirts and sweatshirts. There's another outlet at Queen's Quay West (ⓒ **416/203-0607**). Eaton Centre. ⓒ 416/593-6749. Subway: Dundas or Queen.

Pencraft   If you take your writing implements seriously—and cringe at the thought of a disposable ballpoint—check out this small store. It carries top-of-the-line pens from Mont Blanc and Waterman, as well as secondhand fountain pens. 159 Yonge St. ⓒ 416/364-8977. Subway: Dundas or Queen.

HEALTH & BEAUTY

Elizabeth Milan Hotel Day Spa   Even if you don't have time for the spa, you will appreciate the well-stocked shop in its foyer. Elizabeth Milan carries one of the widest arrays of imported beauty products I've ever seen, including Dermologica, Yonka, Gehwol, and the perennial favorite from France, Decleor. Fairmont Royal York, 100 Front St. W. ⓒ 416/350-7500. Subway: Union.

Lush   This clever U.K. emporium looks like a gourmet grocery store. The heady scent of perfumes is the giveaway. Lush stocks a selection of fizzy bath bombs, skin lotions and potions, and aromatherapy-oriented items. All products are sold by weight. 312 Queen St. W. ⓒ 416/599-5874. Subway: Osgoode.

M.A.C. *(Finds*   This makeup line used to be a trade secret among models and actors, though the word has been out for a while. (The company was founded in Toronto and is now owned by Estée Lauder.) M.A.C.'s flagship store is perpetually packed, especially on weekends, but if you call ahead you can schedule an appointment for a makeup lesson. The C$25 (US$17) charge is entirely redeemable in product. In addition to cosmetics, the store carries skin- and hair-care supplies. 89 Bloor St. W. ℭ **416/929-7555.** Subway: Bay.

Noah's   This is a mecca for health nuts. Noah's boasts aisle after aisle of vitamins and dietary supplements, organic foods and "natural" candies, skin care and bath products, and books and periodicals. The staff is well informed and helpful. There's a smaller but more centrally located outlet at 667 Yonge St. (at Bloor), ℭ **416-969-0220.** 322 Bloor St. W. ℭ **416/968-7930.** Subway: Spadina.

Thompson's Homeopathic Supplies   This is just like an old-fashioned apothecary, with endless rows of potions behind a wooden counter. It has a homeopathic remedy for everything from the common cold to dermatitis to conjunctivitis. The staff is friendly and knowledgeable. 844 Yonge St. ℭ **416/922-2300.** Subway: Yonge/Bloor.

HOUSEWARES & FURNISHINGS

The Art Shoppe   This is one of the prettiest stores in the city, with top-notch furniture arranged into suites of rooms. A wide range of styles is on display, from gilty baroque to streamlined Art Deco. The price tags are high, but the store is well worth browsing. 2131 Yonge St. ℭ **416/487-3211.** Subway: Eglinton.

Caban *(Finds*   Club Monaco's foray into the world of home décor has been a slam-dunk. This bi-level ode to loft living features clean-lined furnishings, table settings and accessories—all for reasonable prices. 262 Queen St. W. ℭ **416/596-0386.** www.caban.com. Subway: Osgoode.

Elte Carpet & Home   With 130,000 square feet of showroom space, Elte has room for a lot more than rugs. This megastore is divided into boutiques where big names like Ralph Lauren and Calvin Klein flog their home-design lines. History-spanning reproductions abound, and there are a few antiques finds, too. 80 Ronald Ave. (just west of Dufferin St.). ℭ **416/785-7885.** Subway: Eglinton W., then any west-bound bus to Ronald Ave.

En Provence   Anyone who has been carried away by reading about the south of France—think of Peter Mayle's *A Year in Provence*—will feel right at home here. It stocks brightly colored dinnerware, printed bed linens, and wrought-iron furniture. 20 Hazelton Ave. ℭ **416/975-9400.** Subway: Bay.

Kitchen Stuff Plus   This housewares shop sells brand-name goods from the likes of Umbra at discount prices. It offers a good selection of picture frames, wine racks, area rugs, candles, painted ceramics, and kitchen accessories. 703 Yonge St. ℭ **416/944-2718.** Subway: Yonge/Bloor.

Nestings   This terrific shop delivers comfort and style in equal measure. Many of the items, from ornate iron kettles to tassel-trimmed ottomans, hark back to a more glamorous age. There's also **Nestings Kids** at 418 Eglinton Ave. (ℭ **416/322-0511;** Subway: Eglinton, then walk west to Avenue Rd.). 1609 Bayview Ave. ℭ **416/932-3704.** Subway: Eglinton, then no. 34 bus to Bayview.

Quasi-Modo Modern Furniture   With offerings for both home and office, this shop showcases some of the best of streamlined 20th-century design. Many of the items are European imports, like the tables and chairs by Sweden's Bruno Mathsson; other furnishings are from lines such as Knoll, Kartell, and Flou. 789 Queen St. W. ℭ **416/366-8370.** Subway: Osgoode.

Tap Phong Trading Co. *Finds* If you have only a few minutes in Chinatown, spend them here. You'll find beautiful hand-painted ceramics, earthenware, decorative items, kitchen utensils, and small appliances. Best of all, just about everything is inexpensive and of reliable quality. 360 Spadina Ave. ✆ 416/977-6364. Subway: Spadina, then LRT to Baldwin St.

UpCountry This Canadian company made its reputation with upscale Arts & Crafts and Mission-style home furnishings. The offerings at its flagship Toronto shop have expanded to include modern and contemporary furniture as well as vintage metal pieces. The sizable selection of decorative touches includes globes and pottery, and now inhabits a separate location at 16 Eastern Ave. (at Trinity St.), ✆ **416/367-3906.** 214 King St. E. ✆ **416/777-1700.** www.upcountry.ca. Subway: King.

JEWELRY

Birks This Canadian institution, founded in 1879, is synonymous with top quality. Among the silver, crystal, and china is an extensive selection of top-quality jewelry, including exquisite pearls and knockout diamond engagement rings (the diamonds themselves were mined in northern Canada). There's even a children's section, filled with keepsake gifts like Royal Doulton Bunnykins china and whimsical picture frames by Nova Scotia's Seagull Pewter. My personal favorite is the showcase of antique estate jewelry. There's a smaller branch at the Eaton Centre (✆ **416/979-9311**). Manulife Centre, 55 Bloor St. W. ✆ **416/922-2266.** Subway: Bay.

Experimetal Some of proprietor Anne Sportun's sterling silver, gold, and platinum creations have won design awards. She will also fashion custom engagement and wedding bands. Also on display are pieces by other North American jewelers. 588 Markham St. (south of Bloor St. W.). ✆ **416/538-3313.** Subway: Bathurst.

Mink *Finds* A gangster-speak, a "mink" is a sexy woman—exactly the type who would love the fabulous fakes at this boutique. Many of the necklaces, bracelets, and rings are Canadian-designed, but a few are Euro imports 550 College St. ✆ **416/929-9214.** Subway: Queen's Park, then streetcar west to Euclid Ave.

Peter Cullman Cullman, who recently celebrated his 40th year as a goldsmith, studied and apprenticed in Europe, but his designs also show the influence of his travels to Africa and Mexico. You can watch him create his unique mini-masterpieces in his shop. Cumberland Court, 99 Yorkville Ave. ✆ **416/964-2196.** Subway: Bay.

Royal de Versailles Jewellers This European-style shop carries an eye-catching assortment of pearls, gold, and platinum. The designs range from classic to funkier, playful styles. There are also watches by the likes of Piaget, Cartier, Rolex, and TagHeuer, as well as a Bulgari boutique. 101 Bloor St. W. ✆ **416/967-7201.** Subway: Bay.

Silverbridge Most of the necklaces, bracelets, rings, and earrings here are fashioned of silver, and the sensibility is modern. Most of the designs are the work of Costin Lazar, and they are produced in Toronto; Lazar will also take on custom work. There are also a few pieces in 18-karat gold and platinum, as well as watches by Georg Jensen and Ole Mathiesen. 162 Cumberland St. ✆ **416/923-2591.** Subway: Bay.

Tiffany & Co. Diamonds are still a girl's best friend at this Art Deco–style shop. Precious gems and designs by Elsa Peretti and Paloma Picasso are on the first level; the second floor holds silver jewelry, stationery, and housewares. 85 Bloor St. W. ℂ **416/921-3900.** Subway: Bay.

LEATHER GOODS

Danier This Canadian chain carries suede and leather coats, suits, pants, and skirts at reasonable prices. Not-uncommon sales knock the prices down 20% to 50%. Eaton Centre. ℂ **416/598-1159.** Subway: Queen.

Taschen! Exclusive designer handbags, luggage, wallets, and other accessories are mainstays here. Many are European imports, and quality is high. 162 Cumberland St. ℂ **416/961-3185.** Subway: Bay.

LINGERIE

La Senza This Montreal-based chain carries inexpensive but eye-catching bra-and-panty sets and naughty-looking nighties. There are also plush unisex robes and patterned boxers. An assortment of slippers, candles, bath mousse, and picture frames rounds out the offerings. Holt Renfrew Centre, 50 Bloor St. W. ℂ **416/972-1079.** Subway: Yonge/Bloor.

La Vie en Rose You'll find quite the eclectic collection of undies here, from sensible cotton briefs to maribou-trimmed teddies, retro PJs to up-to-the-minute cleavage enhancers. The items at the front of the store are inexpensive; the farther back you go, the pricier it gets. Eaton Centre. ℂ **416/595-0898.** Subway: Queen.

MAGAZINES & INTERNATIONAL NEWSPAPERS

Great Canadian News Company This small shop has a great selection, with more than 2,000 magazines filling its shelves, but not a comfortable place for a lengthy browse. BCE Place, 30 Yonge St. (at Front St.). ℂ **416/363-2242.** Subway: Union.

Maison de la Presse Internationale Although this store fills up fast on weekends, drawing expats and locals alike, it's still a great place to while away an hour. The many international magazines and newspapers are as current as you'll find. 124 Yorkville Ave. ℂ **416/928-2328.** Subway: Bay.

MALLS & SHOPPING CENTERS

Atrium on Bay This two-level complex has more than 60 shops selling clothing, jewelry, furniture, and more. Bay and Dundas sts. ℂ **416/980-2801.** Subway: Dundas.

College Park This shopping center has been under renovation forever, but some new sections are now complete, including the giant new Winner's store (see "The Best Bargains," p. 178). 444 Yonge St. ℂ **416/597-1221.** Subway: College.

Eaton Centre It's odd that one of urban Toronto's main attractions is a mall—but, oh, what a mall. More than 300 shops and restaurants spread over four levels in the Eaton Centre, which takes up 2 entire city blocks. 220 Yonge St. ℂ **416/598-2322.** Subway: Dundas or Queen.

First Canadian Place A piece of the labyrinth of the underground city, this complex houses 120 shops and restaurants. It also stages free noontime events each week, with performances as diverse as Opera Atelier's Handel recital and the dancing monks of the Tibetan Drikung Monastery. There are also ongoing art exhibitions. King and Bay sts. ℂ **416/862-8138.** Subway: King.

Hazelton Lanes A byword for elegance and extravagance, Hazelton is a two-level complex with about 90 shops, though it is currently under renovation.

Tips **Same Time Next Year**

In addition to the post-holiday sales at most shops, there are some don't-miss special sales that locals have penned into their calendars. Sale locations are often scattered around the city, so call each store for details and exact dates.

- **MAY:** The **Fashion Design Council of Canada** hosts a clearance sale of top-name Canadian designer wear at the Design Exchange, 234 Bay St. © **416/977-6184.**

- **JULY:** Many retailers host semi-annual sales that cut prices by as much as 50%. Some of the best are at the **Art Shoppe,** 2131 Yonge St., © **416/487-3211** (p. 186); **Holt Renfrew,** 50 Bloor St. W., © **416/ 922-2333** (p. 180); and **Elte Carpet & Home,** 80 Ronald Ave., © **416/ 785-7885** (p. 186).

- **OCTOBER:** The **Old Clothing Show & Sale** should really be called the New *and* Old Clothing Show, because there's almost as much new clothing here as there is vintage wear. Exhibition Place. © **416/ 410-1310.**

- **NOVEMBER:** Fine china and crystal retailer **William Ashley** (p. 178) annual warehouse sale is one of the season's most eagerly antici- pated events; call © **416/964-2900** for information. The **One-of-a- Kind Craft Show & Sale** brings about 400 craft artists under one roof at Exhibition Place, and the prices are often better than you'll find in shops; call © **416/960-3680.** The **Fashion Design Council of Canada** hosts another designer clearance sale this month, in case you missed the one in May (see above).

The charming courtyard at the center transforms into a skating rink in winter. 55 Avenue Rd. © **416/968-8602.** Subway: Bay.

Holt Renfrew Centre   Anchored by the chic Holt Renfrew department store, this small underground concourse is more down to earth. It connects with the Manulife Centre and the Hudson's Bay Centre. 50 Bloor St. W. © **416/923-2255.** Sub- way: Yonge/Bloor.

Manulife Centre   More than 50 posh shops—including William Ashley, Indigo Books Music & More, and a top-notch LCBO outlet—occupy this complex. The Manulife connects to the Holt Renfrew Centre underground. 55 Bloor St. W. © **416/923-9525.** Subway: Bay.

Queen's Quay Terminal   This is waterfront shopping at its best, with more than 30 shops and cafes. Queen's Quay caters to tourists—you'll find some unique items, but the prices tend to be moderate to high. 207 Queen's Quay W. © **416/203-0510.** Subway: Union, then LRT to Queen's Quay.

Royal Bank Plaza   Part of Toronto's underground city, the Royal Bank Plaza connects to Union Station and to the Royal York Hotel. Its 60-plus outlets include a variety of shops, two full-service restaurants, and a food court. The building above it is worth a look, too. Bay and Front sts. © **416/974-5570.** Subway: Union.

Scarborough Town Centre   This is a megamall to rival the Eaton Centre; if you're staying on the city's eastern fringe, you can't miss it. It has more than 200 shops, including branches similar to those at the Eaton Centre. Hwy. 401 and McCowan Ave. ✆ 416/296-0296. Subway: Scarborough Town Centre.

Village by the Grange   Cheek-by-jowl to the Art Gallery of Ontario, the Grange contains more than 40 shops. Its International Food Market has decent Middle Eastern and Asian selections. 122 St. Patrick St. ✆ 416/598-1414. Subway: St. Patrick.

MARKETS

Kensington Market   This neighborhood has changed dramatically in the past 40 years. Originally a Jewish community, it now borders on Chinatown. It contains several Asian herbalists and grocers, as well as West Indian and Middle Eastern shops. Kensington Avenue has the greatest concentration of vintage clothing stores in the city. For a full description, see "Walking Tour: Chinatown & Kensington Market," in chapter 7. Along Baldwin, Kensington, and Augusta aves. No phone. Subway: Spadina, then LRT to Baldwin St. or Dundas St. W.

St. Lawrence Market   This market is a local favorite for fresh produce, and it even draws people who live a good distance away. Hours are Tuesday to Thursday from 9am to 7pm, Friday from 8am to 8pm, and Saturday from 5am (when the farmers arrive) to 5pm. See chapter 6 for a complete description. 92 Front St. E. ✆ 416/392-7219. Subway: Union.

MUSIC

HMV   This is the flagship Toronto store of the British chain. (You'll find smaller outlets throughout the city.) The selection of pop, rock, jazz, and classical music is large. Best of all, you can listen to a CD before you buy it. 333 Yonge St. ✆ 416/596-0333. Subway: Dundas.

The Music Store   On the Toronto Symphony Orchestra's home turf, this attractive shop includes several TSO CDs in its collection of classical and choral music. Roy Thomson Hall, 60 Simcoe St. ✆ 416/593-4822. Subway: St. Andrew.

Sam the Record Man   I, like most Torontonians, still have a soft spot for Sam's, though it is but a shadow of its former glory. The store—beloved by Canadian artists like Joni Mitchell, Rush, Liona Boyd, and the Guess Who because it has always promoted homegrown talent—has gone through rough times of late, and large sections of the store now lie empty. 347 Yonge St. ✆ 416/977-4650. Subway: Dundas.

SEX TOYS

Lovecraft   Believe it or not, Lovecraft—which marks its 31st anniversary in 2003—is downright wholesome. Sure, there are the requisite bad-girl (and -boy) lingerie and toys, but much of the shop stocks joke gifts, T-shirts with suggestive slogans, and an impressive collection of erotic literature (no porn mags). The staff is friendly and the atmosphere playful. 27 Yorkville Ave. ✆ 877/923-7331 or 416/923-7331. Subway: Bay.

SHOES

Browns   To treat your feet to fabulous footwear by Manolo Blahnik, Prada, or Ferragamo, beat a path to this newly renovated shop for men and women. There's also a selection of leather handbags. Browns has several branches around the city. Eaton Centre. ✆ 416/979-9270. Subway: Queen.

Capezio Whether you're looking for the perfect pair of ballet slippers or an up-to-the-minute design from Steve Madden or Guess, you'll find it here. All the shoes and other leather goods are for women. 70 Bloor St. W. ✆ 416/920-1006. Subway: Bay.

David's For serious shoppers only. This high-end store stocks elegant footwear for men and women—from Bruno Magli, Bally, and Sonia Rykiel, as well as the store's own collection—but prices are accordingly steep. 66 Bloor St. W. ✆ 416/920-1000. Subway: Bay.

Mephisto These shoes are made for walking—particularly because they're made from all natural materials. Devotees of this shop, now in its third decade, swear that it's impossible to wear out Mephisto footwear. 1177 Yonge St. ✆ 416/968-7026. Subway: Summerhill.

Petit Pied For especially tiny tootsies, check out this elegant shop. Petit Pied carries children's shoes for newborns to adolescents. Many of the brands are European, including Minibel and Elefanten, but there are also sporty designs from Nike and Reebok. 890 Yonge St. ✆ 416/963-5925. Subway: Rosedale.

TOYS

George's Trains Everything the young (or young at heart) could want to spruce up a model train set is here, including tracks, stations, and scenic backdrops. There are wooden trains as well as train kits. 510 Mount Pleasant Rd. ✆ 416/489-9783. Subway: Davisville, then no. 11 or 28 bus to Mount Pleasant, and walk one block north.

Just Bears The name tells you all you need to know about this upscale shop. Anything that isn't a teddy has a bear motif. 29 Bellair St. ✆ 416/928-5963. Subway: Bay.

Kidding Awound *Finds* Wind-up gadgets are the specialty here—there are hundreds to choose from. There are also some antique toys (which you won't let the kids near) and gag gifts. 91 Cumberland St. ✆ 416/926-8996. Subway: Bay.

The Little Dollhouse Company This toy store isn't really for kids. It's beloved by adults in search of miniature tea services and wicker furniture. It also sells nine different dollhouse kits, from a stately Victorian mansion to a ranch bungalow. 617 Mt. Pleasant Rd. ✆ 416/489-7180. Subway: Eglinton, then no. 34 bus east to Mount Pleasant, and walk 2 blocks south.

Science City Kids and adults alike will love this tiny store filled with games, puzzles, models, kits, and books—all related to science. Whether your interest is astronomy, biology, chemistry, archaeology, or physics, you'll find something here. Holt Renfrew Centre, 50 Bloor St. W. ✆ 416/968-2627. Subway: Yonge/Bloor.

Top Banana Fun for kids—and their parents. The toys range from Thomas the Tank Engine to Stomp Rockets. There are also games and books galore. 639 Mount Pleasant Rd. ✆ 416/440-0111. Subway: Eglinton, then no. 34 bus east to Mount Pleasant, and walk 2 blocks south.

The Toy Shop This double-decker shop carries toys, many of them educational, from around the world. It also stocks a good selection of books, games, and videos. 62 Cumberland St. ✆ 416/961-4870. Subway: Bay.

TRAVEL GOODS

The Travel Stop If an item is made in travel size, The Travel Stop stocks it. Offerings include steamers and hair dryers, travel guides, and luggage. There's also a travel agency at the back of the store. 130 Cumberland St. ✆ 416/961-6088. Subway: Bay.

VINTAGE CLOTHING

Asylum Secondhand jeans and vintage dresses line the racks in this Kensington Market stalwart. Bargains turn up in odd places, like the Anne Klein scarf at the bottom of a C$1 (US68¢) bin. There's also an assortment of toys and candy. 42 Kensington Ave. ℂ 416/595-7199. Subway: Spadina, then LRT to Baldwin St.

Brava *(Finds* This shop is a favorite among local stylists, who pick up everything from cashmere sweaters to evening wraps for ladies, and printed shirts to golf pants for gents. 483 Queen St. W. ℂ 416/504-8742. Subway: Osgoode, then streetcar west to Spadina.

Courage My Love With its mix of vintage clothing and new silver jewelry, Courage is a Kensington Market favorite. Dresses run from '50s velvet numbers to '70s polyester, and almost everything costs less than C$25 (US$17). There's also a good selection of tweedy jackets and starchy white shirts. The owners' cat makes an occasional furtive appearance. 14 Kensington Ave. ℂ 416/979-1992. Subway: Spadina, then LRT to Dundas St. W.

Divine Decadence *(Finds* Owner Carmelita Blondet has a unique line on vintage clothes: She imports them from her native Peru. Chic Peruvians had previously brought these glad rags in from Europe, so it's not unusual to find great French couture. The price tags are uniformly high, but so is the quality. 136 Cumberland St. ℂ 416/324-9759. Subway: Bay.

Ex-Toggery This is a consignment shop with outlets around the city. Items don't last long, particularly because the price drops every week. Scour the racks for designer names like Versace and Donna Karan. There are also a variety of vintage items on display, from clothing to accessories. 115 Merton St. ℂ 416/488-5393. Subway: Davisville.

Preloved *(Finds* The clothes here really are one-of-a-kind: the shop's owners breathe new life into cast-off jeans and T-shirts by adding unique details like vintage lace. The roster of celeb fans includes Alanis Morissette. 613 Queen St. W. ℂ 416/504-8704. Subway: Osgoode, then streetcar west to Bathurst.

WINE

In Ontario, Liquor Control Board of Ontario (LCBO) outlets and small boutiques at upscale grocery stores sell wine; no alcohol is sold at convenience stores. The best deals are on locally produced wines—especially the dessert-sweet ice wine, which has won awards the world over. There are LCBO outlets all over the city, and prices are the same at all of them. The loveliest shop is at the **Manulife Centre,** 55 Bloor St. W. (ℂ 416/925-5266). Other locations are at 20 Bloor St. E. (ℂ 416/368-0521); the **Eaton Centre** (ℂ 416/979-9978); and **Union Station** (ℂ 416/925-9644).

Vintages stores have a different name, but they're still LCBO outlets. Check out the one at **Hazelton Lanes** (ℂ 416/924-9463) and at **Queen's Quay** (ℂ 416/864-6777).

9

Toronto After Dark

Toronto may not have a reputation for being a city that never sleeps, but it does have a vital and varied nightlife scene. It's a mecca for top-notch theater—you can sometimes see Broadway shows before they reach Broadway. The Toronto Symphony Orchestra is world renowned, and the city's many dance and music venues host the crème de la crème of international performers. Some of the best entertainment is in Toronto's comedy clubs, which have served as training grounds for stars such as Jim Carrey, Mike Myers, Dan Aykroyd, and John Candy.

The nightclub scene moves at a frenetic pace. Cigar and martini bars are still popular, though lower-key pool bars are in vogue, too.

MAKING PLANS For listings of local performances and events, check out *Where Toronto* and *Toronto Life* (www.torontolife.com), as well as *The Globe & Mail* (www.globeandmail.

com), the *Toronto Star* (www.thestar. com), and the *National Post* (www. nationalpost.com). For up-to-the-minute lists of hot-ticket events, check out the free weeklies *Now* and *Eye,* available around town in newspaper boxes, and at bars, cafes, and bookstores. The city website **www.toronto. com** also boasts lengthy lists of performances. Events of particular interest to the gay and lesbian community are listed in *Xtra!* (www.xtra.ca), another free weekly available in newspaper boxes and many bookstores.

GETTING TICKETS For almost any theater, music, or dance event, you can buy tickets from **Ticketmaster** (© 416/870-8000; www.ticket master.ca). There's a service charge on every ticket (not just every order) sold over the phone. To avoid the charge, head to a ticket center. They're scattered throughout the city; call the information line for the lengthy list of locations.

1 The Performing Arts

Toronto's arts scene offers something for everyone year-round. The city's arts institutions are widely renowned, and many top-notch international performers pass through town.

THEATER

While it may seem that Toronto favors big-budget musicals—*The Lion King* and *Mamma Mia!* both made a big splash—there are many excellent smaller companies, too. Many of the smaller troupes have no permanent performance space, so they move from venue to venue.

The best time to capture the flavor of Toronto's theater life is during the **Fringe Festival** (© 416/534-5919; fringeto@interlog.com), usually held for 10 days starting in early July. In July and August, try to catch the **Dream in High**

Downtown After Dark

ARTS & ENTERTAINMENT
Air Canada Centre **50**
Buddies in Bad Times Theatre **25**
CanStage **60**
Cinematheque Ontario **3**
Elgin & Winter Garden Theatre **38**
Factory Theatre **13**
Glenn Gould Studio **49**
Hummingbird Centre/
  St. Lawrence Centre **53**
Laugh Resort **18**
La Cage Dinner Theatre **36**
Maple Leaf Gardens **26**
Massey Hall **40**
Pantages Theatre **37**
Premiere Dance Theatre **52**
Princess of Wales Theatre **46**
Roy Thomson Hall **48**
Royal Alexandra Theatre **47**
Second City **22**
St. James's Cathedral **56**
St. Patrick's Church **35**
Theatre Passe Muraille **4**
Young People's Theatre **58**

MUSIC, BARS & CLUBS
Al Frisco's **12**
Amsterdam **14**
BamBoo **10**
Bar 501 **31**
The Barn/The Stables **27**
Bauhaus **24**
The Bishop Belcher **11**
Byzantium **28**
Cameron House **7**
C'est What? **57**
Churchill's Cigar &
  Wine Bar **45**
Consort Bar **55**
Crews/Tango **32**
Crocodile Rock **44**
Easy & the Fifth **41**
El Mocambo **2**
Horseshoe Tavern **8**
Kit Kat Bar **20**
Left Bank **6**
Library Bar **51**
Limelight **43**
Milano **19**
Mint et Menthe **16**
Montreal Bistro and Jazz Club **59**

NASA **5**
Phoenix Concert Theatre **34**
The Rivoli **9**
Sailor **29**
Slack Alice **33**
Sneaky Dee's **1**
Temple **17**
Top O' the Senator **39**

Vines **54**
Vineyards Wine Bar
  & Bistro **21**
Wayne Gretzky's/
  Oasis **23**
Wheat Sheaf Tavern **15**
Woody's **30**
Yuk Yuk's Supper Club **42**

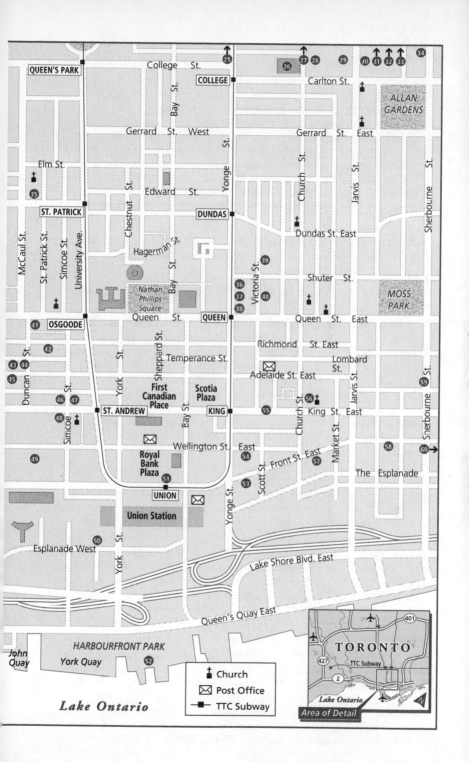

Church

Post Office

TTC Subway

QUEEN'S PARK

College St.

COLLEGE

Carlton St.

ALLAN GARDENS

Bay St.

Gerrard St. West

Gerrard St. East

Yonge St.

Church St.

Jarvis St.

Sherbourne St.

Elm St.

Edward St.

35

ST. PATRICK

DUNDAS

Dundas St. East

McCaul St.

St. Patrick St.

Simcoe St.

University Ave.

Chestnut St.

Hagerman St.

Bay St.

Victoria St.

39

Shuter St.

MOSS PARK

Nathan Phillips Square

36

37

40

41

OSGOODE

Queen St.

QUEEN

38

Queen St. East

42

Richmond St. East

43 44

Sheppard St.

Temperance St.

Lombard St.

45

Duncan St.

York St.

Adelaide St. East

Jarvis St.

59

Sherbourne St.

46 47

First Canadian Place

Scotia Plaza

56

48

Simcoe St.

ST. ANDREW

Bay St.

KING

55

King St. East

Market St.

49

Royal Bank Plaza

Wellington St. East

54

58

60

51

UNION

53

Scott St.

Front St. East

57

The Esplanade

Union Station

Yonge St.

Esplanade West

50

York St.

Lake Shore Blvd. East

Queen's Quay East

John Quay

HARBOURFRONT PARK

York Quay

52

Lake Ontario

† Church

⊠ Post Office

— TTC Subway

TORONTO

401

427

2

TTC Subway

Lake Ontario

Area of Detail

Value **Discount Tickets**

Want to take in a show, but don't want to spend a bundle on it? Drop by the T.O. Tix booth (© **416/536-6468**, ext. 40), which sells half-price day-of-performance tickets. It accepts cash and credit cards; all sales are final. T.O. Tix is open Tuesday to Friday from noon to 7:30pm and Saturday from noon to 6pm; the booth is closed Sunday and Monday (tickets for performances on those days are sold on Sat). The booth has been moved around the Yonge and Dundas area several times, and its latest home is in the Dundas Mall Corridor of the Eaton Centre; the easiest access to the booth is from Dundas Street.

Park (© **416/368-3110**). It mounts stunning productions of Shakespearean or Canadian plays from the CanStage company in an outdoor setting.

LANDMARK THEATERS
The following major theaters all offer guided tours, usually for C$5 (US$3.40) or less; call ahead for schedules.

The Elgin and Winter Garden Theatres   These landmark theaters first opened their doors in 1913, and today they vie with the Royal Alex and the Princess of Wales Theatre for major shows and attention. Recent productions have included *The Full Monty.* Both book concerts and opera performances, and are favorite venues of the Toronto International Film Festival.

Both the Elgin and the Winter Garden have been restored to their original gilded glory at a cost of C$29 million (US$19.8 million). They are the only double-decker theaters in Toronto. The downstairs Elgin is larger, seating 1,500 and featuring a lavish domed ceiling and gilded decoration on the boxes and proscenium. Hand-painted frescoes adorn the striking interior of the 1,000-seat Winter Garden. Suspended from its ceiling and lit with lanterns are more than 5,000 branches of beech leaves, which have been preserved, painted, and fireproofed. Both theaters offer everything from Broadway musicals and dramas to concerts and opera performances. 189 Yonge St. © **416/872-5555** for tickets, 416/314-2901 for tour info. Tickets C$20–$85 (US$14–$58). Subway: Queen.

Pantages Theatre   The Pantages is one of the theaters adversely affected by the collapse of the Livent production company; at the moment, the space is virtually empty. Livent had restored the glorious, glamorous building, which opened in 1920, to the tune of C$18 million (US$12.2 million). Originally a silent film house and vaudeville theater, the 2,250-seat Pantages was resurrected as a home for the splashy Andrew Lloyd Webber show *The Phantom of the Opera;* more recently, shows such as *Fosse* have played here. 244 Victoria St. © **416/872-2222.** Tickets C$51–$92.50 (US$35–$63). Subway: Dundas.

Princess of Wales Theatre   This spectacular 2,000-seat state-of-the-art facility was built for the production of *Miss Saigon,* with a stage large enough to accommodate the landing of the helicopter in that production. Currently it is home of *The Lion King.* Frank Stella, who painted 10,000 square feet of colorful murals, decorated the exterior and interior walls. People in wheelchairs have access to all levels of the theater (not the norm in Toronto). 300 King St. W. © **416/872-1212.** www.onstagenow.com. Tickets C$21–$116 (US$14–$79). Subway: St. Andrew.

Royal Alexandra Theatre   When shows from Broadway migrate north, they usually head for the Royal Alex. Subscription buyers often snap up tickets, so your best bet is to call or write ahead (260 King St. W., Toronto, ON M5V 1H9). Recent favorites have included *Mamma Mia!,* the ABBA-inspired musical, which will continue into 2002.

The 1,495-seat Royal Alex is a magnificent spectacle. Constructed in 1907, it owes its current health to discount-store czar and impresario Ed Mirvish, who refurbished it (as well as the surrounding area) in the 1960s. Inside it's a riot of plush reds, gold brocade, and baroque ornamentation. Avoid the second balcony and the seats "under the circle," which don't have the greatest sight lines. 260 King St. W. ℂ 800/461-3333 for tickets, or 416/872-1212. www.onstagenow.com. Tickets C$26–$94 (US$18–$64). Subway: St. Andrew.

St. Lawrence Centre for the Arts   For three decades the St. Lawrence Centre has presented top-notch theater, music, and dance performances. The Bluma Appel Theatre is home to the CanStage company, and the smaller Jane Mallet Theatre features the Toronto Operetta Theatre Company, among others. This is a popular spot for lectures, too. 27 Front St. E. ℂ 800/708-6754 or 416/366-7723. www.stlc.com. Tickets C$20–$70 (US$14–$48). Mon night pay what you can. Senior and student discounts may be available 30 min. before performance. Subway: Union.

Toronto Centre for the Arts   Built in 1993, this gigantic complex is home to the North York Symphony and the Amadeus Choir. It contains several performance venues. The 1,850-seat Apotex Theatre has featured award-winning musicals such as *Sunset Boulevard* and *Ragtime;* the 1,025-seat George Weston Recital Hall books music events. There are a 250-seat studio theater and an art gallery. Since the collapse of theater giant Livent, the Toronto Centre (formerly the Ford Centre for the Performing Arts) has been sadly underused. 5040 Yonge St. ℂ 416/733-9388. www.tocentre.com. Tickets C$15–$75 (US$10–$51). Subway: North York Centre.

THEATER COMPANIES & SMALLER THEATERS

Buddies in Bad Times Theatre   This gay, or queer (as the company prefers to be called), theater company produces radical new Canadian works that celebrate difference, and blur as well as reinvent the boundaries between gay and straight, gay and lesbian, male and female. American Sky Gilbert has built its cutting-edge reputation. 12 Alexander St. ℂ 416/975-8555. www.buddiesinbadtimes theatre.com. Tickets C$12–$25 (US$8.15–$17). Subway: Wellesley.

CanStage   The CanStage company performs an eclectic variety of Canadian and international plays. Recent productions included *The Shape of Things* by Neil LaBute (who wrote *In the Company of Men*), and Pulitzer Prize-winner Carol Shield's *Larry's Party.* The St. Lawrence Centre seats 500 to 600; the Berkeley Theatre is a more avant-garde, intimate space.

CanStage also presents open-air summer theater—traditionally Shakespeare—in High Park. It's known as the **Dream in High Park.** The company plans to

⎛*Tips* **Farther Afield**

Don't forget that two major theater festivals—the **Shaw Festival** in Niagara-on-the-Lake and the **Stratford Festival** in Stratford—are only an hour or two away. See chapter 10 for details.

focus more on Canadian-written works in the near future. Performing at the Berkeley Theatre, 26 Berkeley St., and St. Lawrence Centre, 27 Front St. E. ℭ 416/368-3110. www. canstage.com. Tickets C$20–$69 (US$14–$47). Mon night pay what you can. Senior and student discounts may be available 30 min. before performance. Subway: Union for St. Lawrence Centre. King, then any streetcar east to Berkeley St. for Berkeley Theatre.

Factory Theatre Since it opened in 1970, the Factory Theatre has focused on presenting Canadian plays, from political dramas to over-the-top comedies. Performances showcase up-and-coming scribes as well as established playwrights. George F. Walker started his career at the Factory, and the clown duo Mump and Smoot appears occasionally. 125 Bathurst St. ℭ 416/504-9971. www. factorytheatre.ca. Tickets C$10–$30 (US$6.80–$20). Subway: St. Andrew, then any streetcar west.

Lorraine Kimsa Theatre for Young People Toronto's such a theater town that even tiny tots (and the rest of the family) get their own performance center. The always-enjoyable Lorraine Kimsa Theatre (formerly known as the Young Peoples Theatre) mounts whimsical productions such as *Jacob Two-Two's First Spy Case* (a musical by the late Mordecai Richler), and children's classics such as *Pinocchio* and *The Miracle Worker.* The theater company is committed to diversity in its programming and in its artists. 165 Front St. E. ℭ 416/862-2222. www. lktyp.ca. Tickets C$14–$28 (US$9.50–$19). Subway: Union.

Native Earth Performing Arts Theatre This small company is dedicated to performing works that express and dramatize the native Canadian experience. Playwright Thomson Highway, who authored *Dry Lips Oughta Move to Kapuskasing,* was one of the company's founders. 720 Bathurst St. ℭ 416/531-1402. Tickets C$10–$20 (US$6.80–$14). Subway: Bathurst.

Tarragon Theatre The Tarragon Theatre opened in 1971. It produces original works by such famous Canadian literary figures as Michel Tremblay, Michael Ondaatje, and Judith Thompson, and an occasional classic or off-Broadway play. It's a small, intimate theater. 30 Bridgman Ave. (near Dupont and Bathurst sts.). ℭ 416/531-1827, or 416/536-5018 for administration. www.tarragontheatre.com. Tickets C$15–$30 (US$10–$20). Sun pay what you can. Subway: Bathurst.

Theatre Passe Muraille This theater started in the late 1960s, when a pool of actors began experimenting and improvising original Canadian material. It continues to produce innovative, provocative theater by such contemporary Canadian playwrights as John Mighton, Daniel David Moses, and Wajdi Mouawad. There are two stages—the Mainspace seats 220, the more intimate Backspace 70. 16 Ryerson Ave. ℭ 416/504-7529. www.passemuraille.on.ca. Tickets C$14–$28 (US$9.50–$19) Subway: Osgoode, then any streetcar west to Bathurst.

Toronto Truck Theatre The Toronto Truck Theatre is the home of Agatha Christie's *The Mousetrap,* now in its 27th year. It's Canada's longest-running show—and it shows no signs of losing steam. 94 Belmont St. ℭ 416/922-0084. Tickets C$15–$25 (US$10–$17). Subway: Rosedale.

DINNER THEATER

Famous People Players Dinner Theatre This group mounts unique, visually fantastic "black light" shows. Famous People Players is renowned not just for the quality of its shows, but also for bringing out the creative potential in disabled performers. The price of the show includes a four-course dinner and backstage tour. 110 Sudbury St. ℭ 888-453-3385 or 416/532-1137. www.fpp.org. Dinner and show

C$40 (US$27) adults, seniors and youths, C$27 (US$18) children under 13. Subway: Osgoode, then any streetcar west.

La Cage Dinner Theatre   For the best in campy impersonations, head to La Cage. Buddy Holly, Roy Orbison, and Elvis may never have performed together, but their mimics get along famously here. 278 Yonge St. ℭ 416/364-5200. Dinner and show C$39–$44 (US$27–$30); show only C$24–$28 (US$16–$19). Subway: Dundas.

Medieval Times Dinner & Tournament   Milord and Milady welcome you to their castle, where you'll be brought a cutlery-free meal by "serving wenches," view knights on horseback, and witness medieval games in the company of 1,000 of your closest friends. Adults may have trouble getting into the spirit of things, but it's always a hit with kids. Exhibition Place. ℭ 416/260-1234. www.MedievalTimes.com. Tickets C$55 (US$37) adults, C$37 (US$25) children 12 and under. Subway: Bathurst, then Bathurst streetcar south to Exhibition Place (last stop).

Mysteriously Yours   After 12 years at the Royal York, the show has gone uptown. The action at this interactive whodunit gets under way around dessert time. Actors are scattered at tables around the room, and guests try to solve the crime with the aid of a detective who leads the investigation. 2026 Yonge St. ℭ 800-668-3323 or 416/486-7469. www.mysteriouslyyours.com. Dinner and show C$48–$75 (US$33–$51); show only C$35–$45 (US$24–$31). Subway: Davisville.

MAJOR CONCERT HALLS & AUDITORIUMS

In addition to the Elgin and Winter Garden Theatres, the Toronto Centre for the Arts, and the St. Lawrence Centre, these are the city's top performance venues.

Glenn Gould Studio   This 340-seat radio concert hall offers chamber, jazz, and spoken-word performances. Its name celebrates the great, eccentric Toronto pianist whose life was cut short by a stroke in 1982. 250 Front St. W. ℭ 416/205-5555. www.glenngouldstudio.cbc.ca. Tickets C$20–$75 (US$14–$51). Subway: Union.

Hummingbird Centre for the Performing Arts   If you visited Toronto before 1997, you might remember this as the O'Keefe Centre. It became famous in 1974 when Mikhail Baryshnikov defected after performing here. Since then, Hummingbird Communications has invested in renovations and refurbishing. This 3,223-seat center is still the home of the National Ballet of Canada; the Canadian Opera Company also performs here, though it has been trying to find another home. 1 Front St. E. ℭ 416/872-2262. www.hummingbirdcentre.com. Tickets C$40–$125 (US$27–$85). Subway: Union.

Massey Hall   This landmark building is one of Canada's premier music venues. The 2,800 seats aren't the most comfortable, but the flawless acoustics will make you stop squirming. The music performances run from classical to pop to rock to jazz, with recent stops by the likes of Diana Krall, Jewel, Prince, and Pink. This is also a popular stop for lectures. 178 Victoria St. ℭ 416/593-4822. www.masseyhall.com. Tickets C$25–$100 (US$17–$68). Subway: King.

Premiere Dance Theatre   This hall, specifically designed for dance performances, is where you can catch Toronto's leading contemporary dance companies. Toronto Dance Theatre, Dancemakers, and the Danny Grossman Dance Company perform here. Queen's Quay Terminal, 207 Queen's Quay W. ℭ 416/973-4000. www.harbourfront.on.ca. Tickets C$30–$95 (US$20–$65). Subway: Union, then LRT to York Quay.

Roy Thomson Hall This stunning concert hall is home to the Toronto Symphony Orchestra, which performs here from September to June, and to the Toronto Mendelssohn Choir. Since it opened in 1982, it has also played host to an array of international musical artists, including Cecilia Bartoli, Ray Charles, Ravi Shankar, and Aretha Franklin. The hall was designed to give the audience a feeling of unusual intimacy with the performers—none of the 2,812 seats is more than 33m (107 ft.) from the stage. The hall closed for five months in 2002 for an extensive acoustic enhancement project that also increased the size of the stage. 60 Simcoe St. (C) 416/593-4822. www.roythomson.com. Tickets C$25–$120 (US$17–$82). Subway: St. Andrew.

CLASSICAL MUSIC & OPERA

In addition to the major musical venues mentioned above, visitors can check to see what's playing at churches around town. Possibilities include **Trinity-St. Paul's,** 427 Bloor St. W. ((C) **416/964-6337**), the home of the Toronto Consort, performers of early music; **St. Patrick's,** Dundas and McCaul streets ((C) **416/483-0559**); and **St. James' Cathedral,** King Street East and Jarvis Street, where the Orpheus Choir sings. The **University of Toronto** ((C) **416/ 978-3744** for the box office) offers a full range of instrumental and choral concerts and recitals in Walter Hall and the Macmillan Theatre. It's also worth checking out who's performing at the **Royal Conservatory of Music,** 273 Bloor St. W. ((C) **416/408-2825**).

If you're a fan of new music, look out for the **Sonic Boom concert series** ((C) **416/944-3100**), which produces new opera and other contemporary music.

Canadian Opera Company Canada's largest opera company, the sixth largest in North America, dates to 1950. It stages six operas at the Hummingbird Centre from September to April. Recent productions include *Salome* and *Boris Godunov.* 227 Front St. E. (C) 416/872-2262 or 416/363-6671. www.coc.ca. Tickets C$38–$135 (US$26–$92). Subway: Union.

Tafelmusik Baroque Orchestra This internationally acclaimed group plays baroque compositions by the likes of Handel, Bach, and Mozart on authentic period instruments. Visiting musicians frequently join the 19 permanent performers. It gives a series of concerts at **Trinity/St. Paul's United Church,** 47 Bloor St. W., and stages other performances in Massey Hall and the Toronto Centre for the Arts (see above). 427 Bloor St. W. (C) 416/964-6337. www.tafelmusik.org. Tickets C$20–$55 (US$14–$37). Subway: Yonge/Bloor for Trinity/St. Paul's; King for Massey Hall; North York Centre for Toronto Centre for the Arts.

Toronto Mendelssohn Choir This world-renowned group first performed in Massey Hall in 1895; it now calls Roy Thomson Hall home. Its repertoire ranges from Verdi's *Requiem,* Bach's *St. Matthew Passion,* and Handel's *Messiah* to the soundtrack of *Schindler's List.* In 2002, its schedule included performances of Orff's *Carmina Burana.* 60 Simcoe St. (C) 416/598-0422. www.tmchoir.org. Tickets C$25–$50 (US$17–$34). Subway: St. Andrew.

Toronto Symphony Orchestra The symphony performs at Roy Thomson Hall from September to June. Its repertoire ranges from classics to jazzy Broadway tunes to new Canadian works. In June and July, the symphony puts on free concerts at outdoor venues throughout the city. 60 Simcoe St. (C) 416/593-4828. www.tso.on.ca. Tickets C$15–$75 (US$10–$51). Subway: St. Andrew.

POP & ROCK MUSIC VENUES

Everyone comes to Toronto—even Madonna, who ran into some trouble with the obscenity police a while back. Tickets are available through **Ticketmaster** (© **416/870-8000**). In addition to the previously mentioned **Hummingbird Centre** and **Massey Hall,** these are the major pop and rock music venues.

Kingswood Music Theatre   From May through September, Kingswood's open-air theater plays host to diverse, top-notch talent. Don Henley, the Beach Boys, the Scorpions, Barry Manilow, and Public Enemy have all played here. The bandshell is covered, but the lawn seats aren't—so beware in bad weather. Paramount Canada's Wonderland, 9580 Jane St., Vaughn. © 905/832-8131. Subway: Yorkdale or York Mills, then GO Express Bus to Wonderland. By car: Take Yonge St. north to Hwy. 401 and go west to Hwy. 400. Go north on Hwy. 400 to Rutherford Rd. exit and follow signs. From the north, exit at Major Mackenzie.

Maple Leaf Gardens   The good old Gardens just haven't been the same since the Leafs left. Nonetheless, this is a popular site for rock concerts. Don't expect cushy seats, but the sight lines are generally good. The exceptions are gray seats and green seats that bracket the stage (sections 94–97 and 76–77); avoid these if you care about seeing the show. 60 Carlton St. © 416/977-1641. Subway: College.

Molson Amphitheatre   This is a favorite summer spot because you can listen to music by the side of Lake Ontario. Most of the seating is on the lawn, and it's usually dirt cheap. Ontario Place, 955 Lakeshore Blvd. W. © 416/314-9900. Subway: Bathurst, then Bathurst streetcar south to Exhibition Place (last stop).

SkyDome   The biggest venue in the city, SkyDome is where the biggest acts usually play. Ticket prices frequently rise into the stratosphere. This venue is about as intimate as a parking lot. If you're seated in the 400 (Upper SkyBox) or 500 (SkyDeck) levels, you'll be watching the show on the JumboTron, unless you bring your binoculars. And remember to steer clear of the seats next to the JumboTron, or you won't see anything at all. 1 Blue Jays Way. © 416/341-3663. www.skydome.com. Subway: Union.

DANCE

Dancemakers   Artistic director Serge Bennathan's nine-person company has gained international recognition for its provocative mix of stylized physical movement and theater. One of the best-known works in its repertoire is *Sable/Sand,* which won a Dora Award for choreography. Performing at Premiere Dance Theater, Queen's Quay Terminal, 207 Queen's Quay W. © 416/973-4000. Office: 927 Dupont St. © 416/535-8880. www.dancemakers.org. Tickets C$20–$35 (US$14–$24).

Danny Grossman Dance Company   The choreography of this local dance favorite is noted for its athleticism, theatricality, humor, and passionate social vision. The company performs both new works and revivals of modern-dance classics. Refreshing, fun, and exuberant. Performing at Premiere Dance Theater, Queen's Quay Terminal, 207 Queen's Quay W. © 416/973-4000. Office: 511 Bloor St. W. © 416/408-4543 or 416/531-5268. www.dgdance.org. Tickets C$22–$38 (US$15–$26).

National Ballet of Canada   Perhaps the most beloved and famous of Toronto's cultural icons is the National Ballet of Canada. English ballerina Celia Franca launched the company in Toronto in 1951, and served as director, principal dancer, choreographer, and teacher. Over the years, the company has achieved great renown.

The company performs at the Hummingbird Centre in the fall, winter, and spring; tours internationally; and makes summer appearances before enormous crowds at the open theater at Ontario Place. Its repertoire includes the classics and works by Glen Tetley (*Alice*), Sir Frederick Ashton, and Jerome Robbins. James Kudelka, who has created *The Miraculous Mandarin, The Actress,* and *Spring Awakening,* was appointed artist-in-residence in 1991. Performing at Hummingbird Centre for the Performing Arts, 1 Front St. E. ℂ **416/872-2262,** and Ontario Place, 955 Lakeshore Blvd. W. Office: 157 King St. E. ℂ 416/366-4846. www.national.ballet.ca. Tickets C$26–$114 (US$18–$78).

Toronto Dance Theatre   The city's leading contemporary dance company burst onto the scene in 1972, bringing an inventive spirit and original Canadian dance to the stage. Director Christopher House joined in 1979 and has contributed more than 35 new works to the repertoire, including *Severe Clear* and the critically acclaimed *Nest.* Performing at Premiere Dance Theatre, Queen's Quay Terminal, 207 Queen's Quay W. ℂ **416/973-4000.** Office: 80 Winchester St. www.tdt.org. Tickets C$17–$37.50 (US$12–$26).

2 The Club & Music Scene

COMEDY CLUBS

Toronto must be one heck of a funny place. That would explain why a disproportionate number of comedians, including Jim Carrey and Mike Myers, hail from here. This is one true Toronto experience you shouldn't miss.

The Laugh Resort   If you get your kicks from incisive humor with occasional dashes of social commentary, this is your place. Gilbert Gottfried, Paula Poundstone, Ray Romano, and George Wallace have performed here. Most of the acts are stand-up solos, though there are sometimes inspired improvs, too. At the Holiday Inn on King, 370 King St. W. ℂ **416/364-5233.** Tickets C$7–$18 (US$4.75–$12). Subway: St. Andrew.

The Rivoli   While the Riv is well known for its music performances and poetry readings, the Monday night ALT.COMedy Lounge is its biggest draw. It features local and visiting stand-ups, and is best known as the place where the Kids in the Hall got their start. Shows take place in the intimate 125-seat back room. See chapter 5 for a restaurant review. 332 Queen St. W. ℂ **416/597-0794.** Pay what you can admission. Subway: Osgoode.

Second City   This was where Mike Myers, otherwise known as Austin Powers, received his formal—and improvisational—comic training. Over the years, the legendary Second City has nurtured the likes of John Candy,

---

Tips Good to Know: Nightlife

The drinking age in Ontario is 19, and most establishments enforce the law. Expect long queues on Friday and Saturday after 10pm at clubs in the downtown core. Bars and pubs that serve drinks only are open Monday to Saturday from 11am to 2am. Establishments that also serve food are open Sunday, too. If you're out at closing time, you'll find the subway shut down, but special late-night buses run along Yonge and Bloor streets. Major routes on streets such as College, Queen, and King operate all night. To find out what's on, see "Making Plans," earlier in this chapter.

Impressions

Toronto is known as Toronto the Good, because of its alleged piety. My guess is that there's more polygamy in Toronto than Baghdad, only it's not called that in Toronto.

—Austin F. Cross, *Cross Roads* (1936)

Dan Aykroyd, Bill Murray, Martin Short, Andrea Martin, and Eugene Levy. It continues to turn out talented young actors. The scenes are always funny and topical, though the outrageous post-show improvs usually get the biggest belly laughs. Next door is the **Tim Simms Playhouse** (© 416/343-0022), an intimate space that features fledgling local stand-up talent. 56 Blue Jays Way. © 800/263-4485 or 416/343-0011. www.secondcity.com. Dinner and show from C$35 (US$24); show only C$13–$25 (US$8.85–$17). Reservations required. Subway: St. Andrew.

Yuk Yuk's Superclub   Yuk Yuk's is Canada's original home of stand-up comedy. Comic Mark Breslin founded the place in 1976, inspired by New York's Catch a Rising Star and Los Angeles's Comedy Store. Some famous alumni include Jim Carrey, Harland Williams, Howie Mandel, and Norm MacDonald. Other headliners have included Jerry Seinfeld, Robin Williams, and Sandra Bernhard. Monday is new talent night, and Tuesday is all improv. There's another Yuk Yuk's in **Mississauga,** not far from Pearson International Airport (© 905/434-4985). 224 Richmond St. W. © 416/967-6425. www.yukyuks.com. Dinner and show from C$25 (US$16); show only C$5–C$15 (US$3.40–$10). Subway: Osgoode.

COUNTRY, FOLK, ROCK & REGGAE

The BamBoo   Colorful confusion reigns here. The granddaddy of Toronto's reggae scene, the 'Boo also books calypso, salsa, jazz, soul, and R&B. Tables set for dinner surround the teensy dance floor, and the menu is as diverse as the music. Pad Thai, barbecued burgers, and jerk chicken are top choices. Forget quiet conversation, even if you score a seat on the rooftop patio—you're here for the music. 312 Queen St. W. © 416/593-5771 (staffed 10am–5pm). Cover C$5–$10 (US$3.40–$6.80). Subway: Osgoode.

C'est What?   About as cozy as the basement of a historic warehouse can be, this casual spot attracts young and old alike. It offers 28 draught beers and a broad selection of single malts. Half pub and half performance space, C'est What? has played host to the likes of Jewel, the Barenaked Ladies, and Rufus Wainwright before they hit the big time. If the nightly acoustic music doesn't suit, check out the abundant board games. 67 Front St. E. © 416/867-9499. www.cestwhat.com. Cover C$2–$10 (US$1.35–$6.80). Subway: Union.

El Mocambo   This rock-and-roll institution was where the Rolling Stones rocked in the '70s, Elvis Costello jammed in the '80s, and Liz Phair mesmerized in the '90s. It has played peekaboo in recent years—it regularly closes and reopens. At the moment its usual Spadina Avenue digs have shut down, but the head of El Mocambo Productions has declared that the El Mo' is alive and well at the Tequila Lounge. In other words . . . El Mocambo is dead. Long live El Mocambo! At the Tequila Lounge, 794 Bathurst Ave. (at Bloor St. W.) © 416/536-0346. Cover C$5–$15 (US$3.40–$10). Subway: Bathurst.

The Horseshoe Tavern   This old, traditional venue has showcased the sounds of the decades: blues in the '60s, punk in the '70s, New Wave in the '80s, and everything from ska to rockabilly to Celtic to alternative rock in the '90s. It's the place that launched Blue Rodeo, the Tragically Hip, the Band, and Prairie Oyster, and staged the Toronto debuts of the Police and Hootie & the Blowfish. It attracts a cross section of 20- to 40-year-olds. 368 Queen St. W. ✆ **416/598-4753.** No cover; cover from C$10 (US$6.80) for special concerts. Subway: Osgoode.

Lee's Palace Versailles this ain't. Still, that hasn't deterred the crème de la crème of the alternative music scene. The Red Hot Chili Peppers, the Tragically Hip, and Alanis have performed here. Despite the graffiti grunge, Lee's does boast the best sight lines in town. The audience is young and rarely tires of slam-dancing in the mosh pit in front of the stage. 529 Bloor St. W. ✆ **416/532-1598.** Cover C$10 (US$6.80) or less. Subway: Bathurst.

The Rivoli Currently this is the club for an eclectic mix of performances, including grunge, blues, rock, jazz, comedy, and poetry reading. Holly Cole launched her career here, Tori Amos made her Toronto debut in the back room, and the Kids in the Hall still consider it home (see "Comedy Clubs," above). Shows begin at 8pm and continue until 2am. People dance if they're inspired. Upstairs, there's a billiards room and espresso bar. 332 Queen St. W. ✆ **416/597-0794.** Cover C$5–$15 (US$3.40–$10). Subway: Osgoode.

JAZZ, RHYTHM & BLUES

Toronto knows how to jazz things up. The best time to hear jazz is in late June during the 11-day **Du Maurier Downtown Jazz Festival** (✆ **416/363-8717** for information, or 416/973-3000 for tickets). Legendary international artists perform traditional and fusion jazz, blues, and gospel at 50 venues around town. In addition to the clubs listed below, the **BamBoo** (see "Country, Folk, Rock & Reggae," above) also offers some of the hottest jazz in town. Check out www.JazzInToronto.com for the latest listings.

Montreal Bistro and Jazz Club Here's a great two-for-one deal. Top per-formers like Oscar Peterson (still performing after his stroke in 1993), Molly Johnson, Ray McShann, and George Shearling perform in a small room lit by rose-tinted lamps; the neighboring room (see chapter 5) is a Quebecois eatery that features *tourtière* and smoked-meat sandwiches. 65 Sherbourne St. ✆ **416/363-0179.** www.montrealbistro.com. Cover C$8–$20 (US$5.45–$14). Subway: King, then any street-car east to Sherbourne St.

Reservoir Lounge This perennial favorite is a modern-day speakeasy. The cramped space—it seats only 100—is below street level, and feels intimate rather than claustrophobic. Live jazz, whether Dixieland, New Orleans, or swing, belts out six nights a week. The epicenter for the swing dance craze in Toronto, this is still the place to watch glam hepcats groove. 52 Wellington St. E. ✆ **416/955-0887.** www.reservoirlounge.com. Cover C$5–$7 (US$3.40–$4.75). Subway: King.

Rex Jazz and Blues Bar This watering hole has been drawing jazz fans since it first opened in 1951. Admittedly the décor hasn't changed much since the old days, but the sounds you'll find here are cutting edge. The Rex lures top local and international talent; Tuesday is the weekly jam night. 194 Queen St. W. ✆ **416/598-2475.** Cover up to C$8 (US$5.45). Subway: Osgoode.

Southern Po Boys This new restaurant and club bills itself as the "Mardi Gras of the North." The menu is strictly rich Southern fare, and the sounds are bluesy and soulful. 159 Augusta St. ✆ **416/993-6768.** Cover C$2–$5 (US$1.35–$3.40). Sub-way: Spadina, then LRT south to Dundas.

Top O' the Senator   Upstairs from the Torch Bistro (see review in chapter 5) and the Senator Diner, this is one of the classiest jazz joints in town. Top performers, such as vocalist Molly Johnson and sax goddess Jane Bunnett, have graced the long, narrow space. Leathery couches and banquettes add to the lounge-lizard ambiance. For those who still care, the third-floor humidor has a premium collection of Cuban smokes. 249 Victoria St. ℂ 416/364-7517. www.the senator.com. Cover C$10–$20 (US$6.80–$14). Subway: Dundas.

DANCE CLUBS

Dance clubs come and go at an alarming pace—the hottest spot can close or turn into a decidedly unhip place almost overnight—so keep in mind that some of the spots listed below may have disappeared or changed entirely by the time you visit. Some things stay constant, though. One is that, with few exceptions, everyone lines up to get into a club—so don't get the idea that charming the bouncer will get you in faster. Most clubs don't have much of a dress code, though "no jeans" rules are not uncommon. I have indicated what the current scene looks like, but it will almost certainly change, so be sure to call ahead. The club listings in the free weekly *Now* are consistently the best.

Several primarily gay and lesbian clubs attract a sizable hetero contingent; one notable destination is **El Convento Rico** (see "The Gay & Lesbian Scene," later in this chapter).

Bauhaus   The unfinished metal-and-rivet decor gives this space an industrial feel. A young PVC-clad crowd dances to R&B and soul on the first floor, and to house and hip-hop on the second. 31 Mercer St. ℂ 416/977-9813. www.bauhaus nightclub.com. Cover C$10–$15 (US$6.80–$10). Subway: St. Andrew.

Berlin   As sophisticated and soigné as it tries to be—it has a smashing dining room and Tuesday-night salsa lessons—Berlin is best known as an upscale meat market. A perennial favorite in the Young and Eligible—oops, Yonge and Eglinton—neighborhood, the crowd is a little older (late 20s to mid-40s) than at most of the downtown clubs. As the club's cheesy but memorable ad goes, this is where "man meets woman, not boy meets girl." Consider yourself warned. 2335 Yonge St. ℂ 416/489-7777. Cover C$10 (US$6.80). Subway: Eglinton.

Crocodile Rock   Casual and laid-back, without any trace of attitude, this place spins '80s dance sounds for the 25- to 40-year-old crowd, which includes a sprinkling of suits from Bay Street. Eclectic sounds and scene, and pool tables, too. Best of all, there's a new rooftop patio. 240 Adelaide St. W. ℂ 416/599-9751. www.crocrock.ca. Cover C$5 (US$3.40). Subway: St. Andrew.

The Docks   This vast waterfront party is a complex that books live entertainers like James Brown, Blue Rodeo, and the Pointer Sisters. The dance club boasts more than a dozen bars, the latest in lighting, and other party effects. Thursday night is foam fun (that is, beer). There's a restaurant and a full raft of sports facilities, too. Open Tuesday to Sunday. 11 Polson St. (off Cherry St.). ℂ 416/461-DOCKS. Subway: Union, then taxi (about C$7/US$4.75) to Lakeshore Blvd. E. and Cherry St.

Easy & the Fifth   This is the place to come if you're looking for a sophisticated crowd. The music is less frenzied, and you might even manage a conversation. The dance area is a loft-like space. In the back, there's a cigar bar furnished with Oriental rugs and comfortable armchairs, plus two pool tables. The dress code in effect is "smart casual" (collared shirts, no jeans or caps). 225 Richmond St. W. ℂ 416/979-3000. Cover C$10–$14 (US$6.80–$9.50). Subway: Osgoode.

Indian Motorcycle Café and Lounge   It's got a bar, pool tables, and a dance floor—who could ask for anything more? When the 20- and 30-something patrons tire of dancing to R&B and rock, they take refuge on one of the several comfy couches in the bar. 355 King St. W. (*C*) 416/593-6996. No cover. Subway: St. Andrew.

Limelight   The Limelight's first floor is for dancing, the second for pool, and the third for lounging in the "Greek Room." Wednesday is progressive; alternative and retro sounds play on weekends. The crowd is predominantly 18- to 25-year-olds, mostly from the suburbs. No jeans. 250 Adelaide St. W. (*C*) 416/593-6126. Cover C$5–$10 (US$3.40–$6.80). Subway: St. Andrew.

Meow   Definitely not for mousy types, this hot spot is for cats who want to roar. The scene is frenetic, with dressed-to-kill 20-somethings dancing to house, R&B, and dance music while laser and light shows play. Don't forget to look up—at the girls suspended from the ceiling on swings. Bad kitty! 1926 Lake Shore Blvd. W. (*C*) 416/604-1513. Cover C$12 (US$8.15). Subway: Union, then taxi (about C$7/US$4.75) west.

NASA   Space cadets, unite: house music plays in a "Jetsons"-like futuristic space. The crowd here is too young to have seen *2001: A Space Odyssey* the first time around, but video screens offer glimpses. If you think a theme bar sounds like fun, this is your place; if you've been there and done that, go elsewhere. 609 Queen St. W. (*C*) 416/504-8356. Subway: Osgoode.

Phoenix Concert Theatre   One of the oldest dance halls in Toronto, the Phoenix attracts an all-ages, all-races crowd that includes straights and gays. As a rock venue, it showcases such artists as Screaming Headless Torsos and Patti Smith. On the weekends, it gets the crowds dancing with a mixture of retro, Latin, alternative, and funk. Thursday is gay night. 410 Sherbourne St. (*C*) 416/323-1251. Cover C$5–$15 (US$3.40–$10). Subway: College, then any streetcar east to Sherbourne St.

Sneaky Dee's   Pool tables and Mexican food complement alternative rock spun by a DJ in the club upstairs until 1:30am. Downstairs, the bar is open until 3am on weekdays, 5am on weekends. 431 College St. (*C*) 416/603-3090. No cover. Subway: Queen's Park, then any streetcar west to Bathurst St.

Temple   Don't let the leering gargoyles that perch on the roof put you off—this pleasure palace is a haunt for hip 20-somethings. While the religious icons get tired fast (like we haven't seen neon crosses before . . . please!), the music, which veers from house to Latin, inspires devotion. 469 King St. W. (*C*) 416/598-4050. Cover C$5–$10 (US$3.40–$6.80). Subway: St. Andrew.

3 The Bar Scene

The current night scene encompasses a flock of attractive bistros with billiard tables. You can enjoy cocktails, a reasonably priced meal, and a game of billiards in comfortable, aesthetically pleasing surroundings. The cigar bar is still in vogue, and most clubs have a humidor for the stogie set. Unlike dance clubs, the bars and lounges in Toronto are a pretty stable bunch.

BARS & LOUNGES

Al Frisco's   This is one of the few Toronto bars with its own microbrewery. Upstairs, people crowd around the pool tables or jam the dance floor, moving to retro sounds. Downstairs, cozy fireplaces enhance the gathering-spot atmosphere. The food is Mediterranean—pizza, pasta, salads, and antipasti.

After Dark: Chinatown to Bloor Street

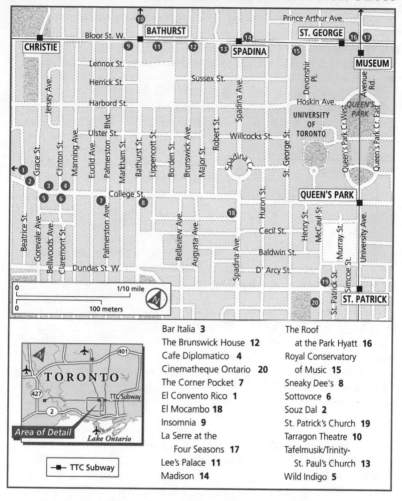

Bar Italia **3**
The Brunswick House **12**
Cafe Diplomatico **4**
Cinematheque Ontario **20**
The Corner Pocket **7**
El Convento Rico **1**
El Mocambo **18**
Insomnia **9**
La Serre at the
    Four Seasons **17**
Lee's Palace **11**
Madison **14**

The Roof
    at the Park Hyatt **16**
Royal Conservatory
    of Music **15**
Sneaky Dee's **8**
Sottovoce **6**
Souz Dal **2**
St. Patrick's Church **19**
Tarragon Theatre **10**
Tafelmusik/Trinity-
    St. Paul's Church **13**
Wild Indigo **5**

In summer, a mix of tourists, suits, and casual professionals in their late 20s and beyond jams the extra-large patio. 133 John St. ℂ **416/595-8201**. Subway: Osgoode.

Kit Kat Bar and Grill   If you're interested in something a little more sophisticated than the usual bar scene, the Kit Kat is your place. The bar area is charmingly old-fashioned, albeit a little cramped. The selection of cocktails and fine wines is strictly for grownups. 297 King St. W. ℂ **416/977-4461**. Subway: St. Andrew.

Left Bank   An over-25 crowd gathers in the lower-level bar at this restaurant. It's especially inviting in winter, when the fire warms folks playing billiards or lolling on the comfortable banquettes. 567 Queen St. W. ℂ **416/504-1626**. Subway: Osgoode, then any streetcar west to Bathurst.

Madison   Madison has to be one of the city's most popular gathering places, with people (many of them students) jamming every floor and terrace. The newest development is the billiard room, with 10 tables. Everyone in the friendly crowd seems to know everyone else. 14 Madison Ave. ✆ 416/927-1722. Subway: Spadina.

Milano Up front there's a bar, and beyond it stand several billiard tables. The dining area is off to the side. In summer, French doors open to the street, making for a pleasant Parisian atmosphere. The bistro-style food includes pizza, pasta, and sandwiches. 325 King St. W. ✆ 416/599-9909. Subway: St. Andrew.

Mint et Menthe Strictly for the been-there-done-that types, this lounge serves up excellent cocktails to a 30-something crowd. The setting is a little on the antiseptic side—white walls, white floors, white furniture—but the sexy music and communal couches give this bar some heat. 325 King St. W. ✆ 416/599-9909. Subway: St. Andrew.

> ### Impressions
> *Returning to Toronto was like finding a Jaguar parked in front of the vicarage and the padre inside with a pitcher of vodka martinis reading* Lolita.
> —Maclean's magazine, January 1959

Panorama From this 51st-floor perch above Bloor and Bay, visitors can see north and south for 241km (150 miles)—at least on a clear day. Go for the lit skyline and the Latin ambiance (check out the Rio carnival mural) and music. The seating is comfortable, and more than a dozen types of cigars are available. Arrive early if you want a window seat. In the Manulife Centre, 55 Bloor St. W. ✆ 416/967-0000. Subway: Bloor/Yonge.

The Pilot This watering hole dates to the early years of the Second World War. Regulars who go way back mix with a suited-up after-work crowd. It's an unpretentious place with pool tables and a wonderful rooftop patio. 22 Cumberland St. ✆ 416/923-5716. Subway: Yonge/Bloor.

The Real Jerk The original Real Jerk became so popular that it moved to this larger space. The hip crowd digs the hot background music, the lively ambiance, and the moderately priced, super-spiced Caribbean food—jerk chicken, curries, shrimp Creole, rotis, and patties. 709 Queen St. E. ✆ 416/463-6055. www.therealjerk. com. Reservations only for parties of 8 or more. Subway: Queen, then any streetcar east.

Shark City Forget *Jaws*—the sharks here sport well-cut suits and smoke Havanas. When not busy striking a pose, the young, hip crowd shoots some pool at the basement tables. There's also a restaurant with basic pizza and pasta offerings, and a small patio. 117 Eglinton Ave. E. ✆ 416/488-7899. Subway: Eglinton.

Smokeless Joe This is Toronto's only smoke-free bar. It stocks more than 175 brews from around the globe; offerings hail from Scotland, Belgium, Singapore, and Poland, not to mention many homegrown options. There's also a patio that, uniquely in the city, remains staunchly nicotine-free. 125 John St. ✆ 416/591-2221. Subway: St. Andrew.

Souz Dal Located in Little Italy, Souz Dal stands out. It's dark and intimate, painted deep purple and mustard, and decorated in exotic Moroccan fashion. Kilims adorn the walls; the bar is fashioned out of copper. Candles light the small, trellised patio. There's a great selection of martinis and margaritas, as well as tropical drinks, like the Havana (rum, guava juice, and lime). Thursday is acid-jazz night. 636 College St. ✆ 416/537-1883. Subway: Queen's Park, then any streetcar west to Grace St.

Cueing Up

It's not hard to find a bar or a restaurant with a token pool table—it's a must-have accessory in some quarters—but real shark shops aren't so easy to come by. If you have a serious pool habit, try one of the following clubs.

Academy of Spherical Arts: Okay, maybe this isn't your typical pool hall, but it has a great pedigree: The 5,000-square-foot space used to house billiard manufacturer Brunswick. Now it looks more like a turn-of-the-century gentlemen's club (there are even a few antique pool tables). This is a popular celebrity-sighting spot, and the likes of Kevin Bacon, Minnie Driver, Dennis Hopper, and Lennox Lewis have been known to drop by. (Because the Academy hosts private parties, always call before setting out to make sure it's open.) 38 Hanna St. **416/ 532-2782.** Subway: St. Andrew, then streetcar west along King St. to Atlantic Ave. and walk one block south.

Bar Italia & Billiards: Downstairs, a young, trendy, good-looking crowd quaffs drinks or coffee and snacks on Italian sandwiches. Upstairs, guys and gals gather 'round the six pool tables. This scene is strictly for the flirtatious—serious game-players should go elsewhere. 582 College St. **416/535-3621.** Subway: Queen's Park, then any streetcar west to Clinton St.

Charlotte Room: *Billiards Digest* has called the Charlotte Room one of the 10 best billiard rooms in North America. It feels like an old-boys' club. In addition to the 10 tables, there's a pub-grub menu and, on occasion, live jazz music. 19 Charlotte St. **416/598-2882.** Subway: St. Andrew.

The Corner Pocket: Smack-dab in the middle of trendy Little Italy, there's the Corner Pocket. Unpretentious and low-key, the hall has 17 billiard tables (and one foosball table, in case you're interested). The big-screen television is always tuned to sports. 722 College St. **416/ 928-3540.** Subway: Queen's Park, then any streetcar west to Crawford St.

Wayne Gretzky's   Hockey fans will want to visit this shrine to the Great One, who hails from the nearby town of Brantford. Several cases display memorabilia—photos, uniforms, and equipment. They trace Gretzky's rise from the junior leagues in Sault Ste. Marie, through his professional debut with the Indianapolis Racers, to his career in the NHL. Forget the food, unless you simply have to say that you dined at *his* place. Better to have a drink at the long bar or head upstairs to the rooftop Oasis patio, with a fine view of the CN Tower. 99 Blue Jays Way. 416/979-PUCK. www.gretzkys.com. Subway: St. Andrew or Union.

Wild Indigo   This intimate Little Italy bar has a small, atmospheric patio in the back. It attracts a youngish, intellectual crowd and features a DJ on weekends. 607 College St. 416/536-8797. Subway: Queen's Park, then any streetcar west to Clinton St.

Hotel Bars

Just as some of the best restaurants in the city are in hotels, so are some of the most charming watering holes. While I'm all for heading out and experiencing what a city has to offer, don't overlook these options in your home away from home.

Accents: This romantic wine bar offers many selections by the glass. The lighting is flattering, and a pianist provides jazz background music throughout the evening. Given how popular the Sutton Place is with the Hollywood glitterati, it's no surprise to see stars pass through the bar. At the Sutton Place Hotel, 955 Bay St. ✆ **416/924-9221.** Subway: Museum or Wellesley.

The Consort Bar: This is a wonderfully clubby, old-fashioned bar. Not only does it boast comfortable wing chairs, but also its 2.5m-high (8-ft.) windows onto the street afford excellent people watching. The suited-up crowd is generally more corporate than romantic—with some sweet exceptions. At Le Royal Meridien King Edward, 37 King St. E. ✆ **416/863-9700.** Subway: King.

La Serre: This piano bar offers a full range of single malts and martinis, and welcomes cigar aficionados. Located at street level, it's a great place to people-watch along Yorkville Avenue. One caveat: The live piano music refuses to remain in the background. It's so noisy that I find it impossible to talk—but the suits don't seem to mind. At the Four Seasons Hotel Toronto, 21 Avenue Rd. ✆ **416/964-0411.** Subway: Bay.

The Library Bar: This small, wood-paneled bar is the best place in the city to order a top-quality martini, which is served in a generous "fishbowl" glass. The crowd seems wholly business-minded. It's a pity, because the old-fashioned room speaks of retro romance. At the Fairmont Royal York, 100 Front St. W. ✆ **416/863-6333.** Subway: Union.

The Roof: Author Mordecai Richler called this the only civilized spot in Toronto. It's an old literary haunt, with comfortable couches in front of a fireplace, and excellent drinks. The walls sport caricatures of members of Canada's literary establishment. The James Bond martini—vodka with a drop of lillet—is my personal favorite. The view from the outdoor terrace is one of the best in the city. At the Park Hyatt Toronto. 4 Avenue Rd. ✆ **416/924-5471.** Subway: Museum or Bay.

PUBS & TAVERNS

Allen's   Allen's sports a great bar that offers more than 80 beer selections and 164 single malts. Guinness is the drink of choice on Tuesday and Saturday nights, when folks reel and jig to the Celtic-Irish entertainment. 143 Danforth Ave. ✆ **416/463-3086.** Subway: Broadview.

The Amsterdam   This brewpub is a beer-drinker's heaven, serving more than 200 labels as well as 30 types on draft. By 8pm the tables in the back are filled, and the long bar is jammed. In summer the patio is fun, too. 600 King St. W. (at Portland St.). ✆ **416/504-6882.** Subway: St. Andrew, then streetcar west.

The Bishop and the Belcher   This British-style pub offers 14 drafts on tap and a decent selection of single malts. The classic pub fare includes bangers and mash, shepherd's pie, and a ploughman's lunch. 361 Queen St. W. ℭ **416/591-2352.** Subway: Osgoode.

The Brunswick House   This cavernous room, affectionately known as the Brunny House, is a favorite with University of Toronto students. Waiters carry trays of frothy suds between the Formica tables. Impromptu dancing to background music and pool and shuffleboard playing drown out the sound of at least 2 of the large-screen TVs, if not the other 18. This is an inexpensive place to down some beer. Upstairs, there's live-broadcast thoroughbred and harness racing from international tracks, including Hong Kong. 481 Bloor St. W. ℭ **416/964-2242.** Subway: Spadina or Bathurst.

Cameron House   Old and new hippies hang in the front room, with its rococo bar. Local bands try out in the back room. On Sunday, the Cameron serves an amazingly good brunch. 408 Queen St. W. ℭ **416/703-0811.** Subway: Osgoode.

Dora Keogh Irish Pub   Created by the same crew that devised the perennially popular Allen's, Dora Keogh is an unusually elegant pub. The evening brings music, with local fiddlers and vocalists strutting their stuff; famous fiddler Natalie McMaster has been known to join in, as have various members of the Irish group the Chieftains. 141 Danforth Ave. ℭ **416/778-1804.** Subway: Broadview.

The Rebel House   The youngish crowd here dresses in designer sportswear. This neighborhood pub draws them in with its impressive selection of microbrews and reasonably priced grub. 1068 Yonge St. ℭ **416/927-0704.** Subway: Rosedale.

The Unicorn   This Celtic pub is named for the Irish Rovers song. Along with the usual pub staples, there's Irish stew and a great list of imported dark ales. It's a fun, relaxed place to unwind. 175 Eglinton Ave. E. ℭ **416/482-0115.** Subway: Eglinton.

Wheat Sheaf Tavern   Designated a historic landmark, this is the city's oldest tavern—it's been in operation since 1849. For fans, eight screens show great moments in sports. The jukebox features 1,200 choices, and there are two pool tables and an outdoor patio. 667 King St. W. ℭ **416/504-9912.** Subway: St. Andrew, then any streetcar west to Bathurst St.

WINE BARS

Centro   Upstairs is the gorgeous dining room (see review in chapter 5); downstairs is the upscale wine bar. A well-dressed crowd drops by for the convivial atmosphere, the gourmet pizzas and pastas, and the extensive selection of wines, which includes more than 600 varieties from around the globe. 2472 Yonge St. ℭ **416/483-2211.** Subway: Eglinton.

Sottovoce   The name (which translates as "very softly") must be an in joke, because the decibel level here is outrageous. This wine bar is still a great find, not least because it serves truly inspired focaccia sandwiches and salads. 595 College St. ℭ **416/536-4564.** Subway: Queen's Park, then any streetcar west to Clinton St.

Vines   Vines provides a pleasant atmosphere in which to sample a glass of champagne or any one of 40 wines. Accompaniments include salads, cheeses, and light meals, served with fresh French sticks (mini baguettes). 38 Wellington St. E. ℭ **416/861-9920.** Subway: King.

4 The Gay & Lesbian Scene

Toronto's large, active gay and lesbian community has created a varied nightlife scene. At some nightspots, such as the **Phoenix Concert Theatre,** one night a week is gay night (in this case, Thurs). See "Dance Clubs," earlier in this chapter.

Bar 501   This bar is popular with gay men for its Sunday evening drag shows, which often attract crowds that watch from the sidewalk through the large front window. There's also Saturday afternoon bingo with the infamous Sister Bedelia. 501 Church St. ℂ 416/944-3272. Subway: Wellesley.

The Barn/The Stables   This is one of the city's oldest gay bars. The male-only crowd keeps the second-story dance floor jammed. There are afternoon underwear parties on Sunday, and sex videos, too. The favored look is denim with occasional ranch-style allusions (you'll see a few spurs). There's also an on-site leather shop selling fetish gear and clothing. 418 Church St. ℂ 416/977-4702. Subway: College.

Byzantium   An attractive bar-restaurant, Byzantium attracts an affable gay and straight crowd for cocktails followed by dinner in the adjacent dining room. This is a comfortable, relaxed space, and the cooking is top-notch. 499 Church St. ℂ 416/922-3859. Subway: Wellesley.

Crews/Tango   Located in a renovated Victorian house, this two-in-one club boasts a large outdoor patio. Crews is a gay bar for men, and it known for its pubby atmosphere and its drag shows, which start at 11pm on Wednesday through Sunday. The adjoining Tango bar draws a lesbian crowd. It hosts Tuesday- and Thursday-night karaoke; on Friday and Saturday nights, the women head for the dance floor. 508 Church St. ℂ 416/972-1662. Subway: Wellesley.

El Convento Rico   The Latin beat beckons one and all—straight, gay, and otherwise—to this lively club. If you don't know how to samba, you can pick up the basics at the Friday- and Sunday-night dance lessons, but if you don't learn, no one on the jam-packed dance floor will notice. There's a substantial hetero contingent that comes out just to watch the fabulous drag queens. 750 College St. ℂ 416/588-7800. www.elconventorico.com. Cover C$5 ($3.40) or less. Subway: Queen's Park, then streetcar west.

Pope Joan   This is the city's most popular lesbian bar. It has a pool table and a game room furnished with old, cozy couches downstairs, and a restaurant and dance area upstairs. On Saturday, there's a hearty buffet brunch. In summer, the fenced-in patio is the place to cool off. A group called the Drag Kings performs occasionally. 547 Parliament St. (at Winchester St.). ℂ 416/925-6662. Subway: Wellesley, then any streetcar east to Parliament St., and walk 2 blocks south.

Sailor   This bar is attached to Woody's (see below), but has a livelier atmosphere; unlike Woody's, you won't see many women here. Every Thursday there's a Best Chest competition, and on Sunday the draw is the drag show. In the evening, a DJ spins an assortment of dance and alternative tunes. 465 Church St. ℂ 416/972-0887. Subway: Wellesley.

Slack Alice   This incredibly popular bar draws a gay and lesbian crowd, with more than a few straights. The menu features home-style comfort food; on weekend evenings, a DJ gets the crowd on its feet. 562 Church St. ℂ 416/969-8742. Subway: Wellesley.

Woody's   A friendly, popular local bar, Woody's attracts mainly men but welcomes women; the crowd is a mix of gay and hetero. It's a popular meeting spot, especially for weekend brunch. 467 Church St. (south of Wellesley St.). $\mathcal{C}$ 416/972-0887. www.woodystoronto.com. Subway: Wellesley.

5 Cinemas & Movie Houses

There is no shortage of movie theaters—in fact, monster megaplexes are the rage at the moment. The largest theaters are at the Eaton Centre, St. Lawrence Market Square, and Yonge and Eglinton. Cinemas with a mere pair of screens can be found at the Sheraton Centre, Bloor and Yonge, and Yonge and St. Clair. Check *Now, Eye,* or one of the newspapers for listings.

Carlton Cinemas   Home to the subtitled set, the Carlton plays films—many of them superb—that frequently don't see the light of day anywhere else. Many of the offerings originate in France, Italy, Russia, or China; there's also a smattering of independent North American films. Buy tickets early on weekends. 20 Carlton St. $\mathcal{C}$ 416/964-2463. Tickets C$10 (US$6.80). Tues discounts. Subway: College.

Cinematheque Ontario   This organization shows the best in contemporary cinema. The programs include directors' retrospectives, plus new films from France, Germany, Japan, Bulgaria, and other countries that you won't find in the first-run theaters around town. Screenings at Art Gallery of Ontario, 317 Dundas St. W. (between McCaul and Beverley sts.). Office: 2 Carlton St. $\mathcal{C}$ 416/967-7371 or 416/923-3456 (box office). Tickets C$8 (US$5.45) adults, C$4.25 (US$2.90) seniors and students.

6 Coffeehouses

While Starbucks has certainly staked out territory in Toronto, the Canadian chain the **Second Cup** is holding its ground. It offers a full range of flavored coffees and espresso varieties, plus cakes, muffins, croissants, and gift items. Another chain, **Timothy's,** invites you to pour your own selection from about 10 varieties. My favorite coffeehouses are all independents, though.

Cafe Diplomatico   One of the oldest cafes in Toronto, this Little Italy gem has mosaic marble floors, wrought-iron chairs, and an extra-large sidewalk patio. Many longtime area residents get their caffeine fix here in the morning; the patio attracts a trendier crowd. 594 College St. $\mathcal{C}$ 416/534-4637. Subway: Queen's Park.

Daily Express Café   Near the student ghetto in the Annex neighborhood, this lively cafe draws most of its crowd from the nearby University of Toronto. 280 Bloor St. W. $\mathcal{C}$ 416/944-3225. Subway: St. George.

Future Bakery   This rambling cafe attracts an artsy crowd with fine breads and a selection of coffees. Would-be writers scribble away in well-lit corners. 483 Bloor St. W. $\mathcal{C}$ 416/922-5875. Subway: Spadina.

Gypsy Co-op   Coffee is not the only king here. Many teas and herbal infusions (for everything from stress to colds and flu) are available, as are super-rich brownies. 815 Queen St. W. $\mathcal{C}$ 416/703-5069. Subway: Osgoode, then any streetcar west.

Lettieri   The house rule is that after 7 minutes, a pot of coffee is no longer fresh. This place takes the bean seriously. In addition to the wide range of coffees, there are focaccia sandwiches, tarts, cookies, and pastries. 94 Cumberland St. $\mathcal{C}$ 416/515-8764. Subway: Bay.

Sweet Treats: Toronto's Dessert Cafes

Nightlife doesn't have to mean high culture, barhopping, or anything in between. It doesn't even mean you have to stop eating. Here are some of the city's most agreeable places to satisfy a sweet tooth and do some people watching.

Demetre Caffe: In the heart of Greektown on the Danforth, Demetre is known for its Old World ambiance as well as its sweets: Belgian waffles, oversized sundaes, cakes, tortes, and baklava. It's popular at all hours of the evening with a casual crowd, and on weekends it draws families. Closing time is midnight Sunday through Thursday, and 3am Friday and Saturday. 400 Danforth Ave. (C) **416/778-6654.** Subway: Broadview.

Desserts by Phipps: The cafe serves salads and sandwiches, but what really draw the crowds are the decadent desserts. Cappuccino chiffon cake is a direct hit, as are the moist but not gooey apple confections. 420 Eglinton Ave. W. (C) **416/481-9111.** Subway: Eglinton.

Dufflet Pastries: On menus around town, you'll sometimes see mention of "desserts by Dufflet." *Divine* is the word that best applies to these confections. Owner Dufflet Rosenberg bakes some of the most delectable tortes, tarts, and pastries in the city. The problem is deciding where to start. Chocolate raspberry truffle? Cappuccino dacquoise? Your call. There are a few selections for people with gluten or nut allergies, and the cafe also serves light fare. 787 Queen St. W. (C) **416/504-2870.** www.dufflet.com. Subway: Osgoode, then any streetcar west to Euclid Ave.

Greg's Ice Cream: One taste of Greg's homemade ice cream will turn you into an addict. (I should know—I've been one for years.) Different flavors are available each day, and the staff is generous about handing out samples. It's hard for me to pick one favorite flavor, but the roasted marshmallow would definitely be up there. 200 Bloor St. W. (C) **416/961-4734.** Subway: Museum or St. George.

Just Desserts: This cafe stays open practically around the clock on weekends for those in need of a sugar fix. Around 40 desserts are available—as many as 12 different cheesecakes, 10 or so pies, plus an array of gâteaux, tortes, and meringues. All cost around C$6 (US$4.10). 555 Yonge St. (at Wellesley). (C) **416/963-8089.** Subway: Wellesley.

Sicilian Ice Cream Company: This old-fashioned ice cream parlor is Toronto's top purveyor of Italian *gelati*. The wonderful patio is open in the summer. 712 College St. (C) **416/531-7716.** Subway: Queen's Park, then streetcar west.

10

Side Trips from Toronto

Here's a classic good news/bad news situation: Some of the greatest attractions in this region are within a 2-hour drive of Toronto. They're easily accessible, which is a good thing, but if you're trying to shoehorn all of the sights into a short stay . . . you've got some serious choices to make. This chapter describes the big three—Niagara-on-the-Lake, Niagara Falls, and Stratford—as well as the less well-known city of Hamilton.

For information about the areas surrounding Toronto, contact **Tourism Ontario** (© **800/ONTARIO** or 416/314-0944; www.travelinx.com), or visit the travel center in the Eaton Centre on Level 1 at Yonge and Dundas streets. It's open Monday to Friday from 10am to 9pm, Saturday from 9:30am to 6pm, and Sunday from noon to 5pm.

1 Stratford ✦

145km (90 miles) NW of Toronto

The Stratford Festival was born in 1953 when director Tyrone Guthrie lured Alec Guinness to perform. The festival has become one of the most famous in North America, and it has put this scenic town on the map. While visitors will notice the Avon River and other sights named in honor of the Bard, they may not realize that Stratford has another claim to fame. It's home to one of Canada's best cooking schools, which makes dining at many of the spots in town a delight.

ESSENTIALS

VISITOR INFORMATION For first-rate visitor information, go to the **Information Centre** (© **519/273-3352**) by the river on York Street at Erie. From May to early November, it's open Sunday to Wednesday from 9am to 5pm, and Thursday to Saturday from 9am to 8pm. At other times, contact **Tourism Stratford,** 47 Downie St., Stratford, ON N5A 1W7 (© **800/561-SWAN** or 519/271-5140; www.city.stratford.on.ca).

GETTING THERE Driving from Toronto, take Highway 401 west to Interchange 278 at Kitchener. Follow Highway 8 west onto Highway 7/8 to Stratford.

Amtrak and **VIA Rail** (© **416/366-8411**) operate several trains daily along the Toronto–Kitchener–Stratford route. Call © **800/361-1235** in Canada or **800/USA-RAIL** in the United States.

THE STRATFORD FESTIVAL ✦

On July 13, 1953, *Richard III,* starring Alec Guinness, was staged in a huge tent. From that modest start, Stratford's artistic directors have built on the radical, but faithfully classic, base established by Tyrone Guthrie to create a repertory theater with a glowing international reputation.

⌐Tips A Helpful Planning Tool

Each week **Outside Toronto** (www.outsidetoronto.com) suggests things to see and do within a 2-hour drive of the city: antiques shows, farmers' markets, recreational events. The "Places to Go" section directs you to museums, festivals, and charming little towns. The site provides maps, too.

Stratford has four theaters. The **Festival Theatre,** 55 Queen St., in Queen's Park, has a dynamic thrust stage (a modern re-creation of an Elizabethan stage). The recently renovated **Avon Theatre,** 99 Downie St., has a classic proscenium. The **Tom Patterson Theatre,** Lakeside Drive, is an intimate 500-seat theater. The newest venue—the **Studio Theatre**—opened its doors in July 2002; the 278-seat space will be used for new and experimental works.

World famous for its Shakespearean productions, the festival also offers classic and modern theatrical masterpieces. Recent productions have included *My Fair Lady, The Threepenny Opera,* and *The Scarlet Pimpernel.* Offerings from the Bard have included *Romeo and Juliet, Richard III,* and *King Lear.* Among the company's famous alumni are Dame Maggie Smith, Sir Alec Guinness, Sir Peter Ustinov, Alan Bates, Christopher Plummer, Irene Worth, and Julie Harris. Present company members include Tom McCamus, Cynthia Dale, Colm Feore, and Lucy Peacock.

In addition to attending plays, visitors may enjoy the "Celebrated Writers Series," which features renowned authors (some of whom have penned works performed at the Stratford Festival). The list of speakers has included Michael Ondaatje, Joyce Carol Oates, and Rohinton Mistry. All lectures take place on Sunday mornings at the Tom Patterson Theatre, and they cost C$24 (US$16) per person; tickets are available from the box office.

The season usually begins in May and continues through October, with performances Tuesday to Sunday nights and matinees on Wednesday, Saturday, and Sunday. Ticket prices range from C$39 to $100 (US$27–$68), with special prices for students and seniors. For tickets, call ⓒ **800/567-1600;** visit www. stratfordfestival.ca; or write to the Stratford Festival, P.O. Box 520, Stratford, ON N5A 6V2. Tickets are also available in the United States and Canada at Ticketmaster outlets. The box office opens for mail and fax orders in late January; telephone and in-person sales begin in late February.

EXPLORING THE TOWN

Stratford has a wealth of attractions that complement the theater offerings. It's a compact town, easily negotiable on foot. Within sight of the Festival Theatre, **Queen's Park** has picnic spots beneath tall shade trees and by the Avon River. There are also some superb dining and good shopping prospects.

Past the Orr Dam and the 90-year-old stone bridge, through a rustic gate, lies a very special park, the **Shakespearean Garden.** In the formal English garden, where a sundial measures the hours, you can relax and contemplate the herb and flower beds and the tranquil river lagoon, and muse on a bust of Shakespeare by Toronto sculptor Cleeve Horne.

If you turn right onto Romeo Street North from highways 7 and 8 as you come into Stratford, you'll find the **Gallery/Stratford,** 54 Romeo St. (ⓒ **519/ 271-5271;** www.gallerystratford.on.ca). It's in a historic building on the fringes

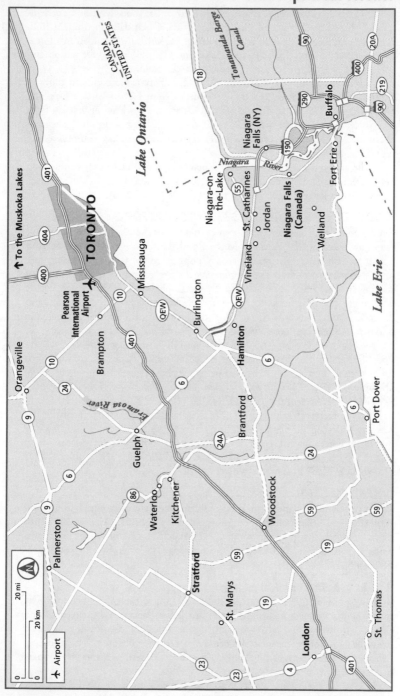

of Confederation Park. Since it opened in 1967, it has mounted fine Canadian-focused shows, often oriented to the theater arts. Open daily in summer from 9am to 6pm; Tuesday to Sunday from 10am to 4pm off-season. Admission is approximately C$10 (US$6.80) for adults, and C$8 (US$5.45) for seniors and students 12 and up (prices vary because of special exhibits).

Stratford is a historic town, dating to 1832. Ninety-minute **guided tours of early Stratford** take place Monday to Saturday from July to Labour Day, and on Saturday in May, June, September and October. They leave at 9:30am from the visitors' booth by the river, and cost C$3 (US$2) per person (call ahead to confirm). Another option is the self-guided tour; Tourism Stratford sells a map for C$1 (US60¢).

Paddleboat and canoe rentals are available at the **Boathouse,** behind and below the information booth. It's open daily from 9am until dark in summer. Contact **Avon Boat Rentals,** 20 York St. (© **519/271-7739**).

A COUPLE OF EXCURSIONS FROM STRATFORD
Only half an hour or so away, the twin cities of **Kitchener** and **Waterloo** have two drawing cards: the **Farmer's Market** and the famous 9-day **Oktoberfest.** The cities still have a German-majority population (of German descent, and often German speaking), and many citizens are Mennonites. On Saturday starting at 6am, you can sample shoofly pie, apple butter, kochcase, and other Mennonite specialties at the market in the Market Square complex, at Duke and Frederick streets in Kitchener. For additional information, contact the **Kitchener–Waterloo Area Visitors and Convention Bureau,** 2848 King St. E., Kitchener, ON N2A 1A5 (© **519/748-0800;** www.kw-visitor.on.ca). It's open from 9am to 5pm weekdays only in winter, daily in summer. For Oktoberfest information, check out www.oktoberfest.ca; or write **K-W Oktoberfest,** P.O. Box 1053, 17 Benton St., Kitchener, ON N2G 4G1 (© **888/294-HANS** or 519/570-HANS).

Eight kilometers (5 miles) north of Kitchener is the town of **St. Jacobs.** It has close to 100 shops in venues such as a converted mill, silo, and other factory buildings. For those interested in learning more about the Amish-Mennonite way of life, the **Meetingplace,** 33 King St. (© **519/664-3518**), shows a short film about it (daily in summer, weekends only in winter).

WHERE TO STAY
When you book your theater tickets, you can book your accommodations at no extra charge. Options range from guest homes for as little as C$40 (US$27) to first-class hotels charging more than C$125 (US$85). Call or write the **Festival Theatre Box Office,** P.O. Box 520, Stratford, ON N5A 6V2 (© **800/567-1600** or 519/273-1600).

HOTELS & MOTELS
Bentley's   This inn enjoys an excellent location at the center of town. The soundproof rooms are luxurious duplex suites with efficiency kitchens. Period English furnishings and attractive drawings, paintings, and costume designs on the walls make for a pleasant ambience. Five units have skylights. The adjoining British-style pub, also called Bentley's, is popular with festival actors (see "Where to Dine," below).

99 Ontario St., Stratford, ON N5A 3H1. © **519/271-1121.** 13 units. Apr–Nov C$150 (US$102) double; Nov–June C$90 (US$61) double. Extra person C$20 (US$14). AE, DC, MC, V. **Amenities:** Pub. *In room:* A/C, TV, kitchen with fridge and coffeemaker, hair dryer.

Stratford

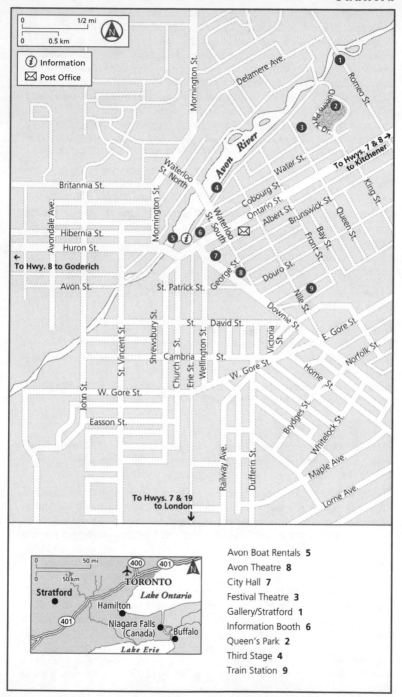

Festival Inn   The Festival Inn sits outside town off highways 7 and 8, on 8 hectares (20 acres) of landscaped grounds. The place has an Old English air, with stucco walls, Tudor-style beams, and high-backed red settees in the lobby. Tudor style prevails throughout the large, motel-style rooms. All have wall-to-wall carpeting, matching bedspreads, and floor-to-ceiling drapes, and reproductions of old masters on the walls. Some units have charming bay windows with sheer curtains, and all rooms in the main building, north wing, and annex have refrigerators. The indoor pool has an outdoor patio.

1144 Ontario St. (P.O. Box 811), Stratford, ON N5A 6W1. © 519/273-1150. Fax 519/273-2111. www. festivalinnstratford.com. 182 units. C$140–$200 (US$95–$136) double. Extra person C$10 (US$6.80). Winter discounts (about 30%) available. AE, DC, MC, V. **Amenities:** Dining room; coffee shop; indoor pool; Jacuzzi; sauna. *In room:* A/C, TV, mini fridge, coffeemaker.

The Queen's Inn   The Queen's Inn occupies the best location in Stratford—it's right in the town center. The historic building is about a century and a half old, but the guest rooms have a fresh look every year, after the owners use the winter months for refurbishing. The English-style Boar's Head Pub is on the premises.

161 Ontario St., Stratford, ON N5A 3H3. © 800/461-6450 or 519/271-1400. Fax 519/271-7373. www. queensinnstratford.ca. 31 units. May–Nov 15 C$105–$130 (US$71–$88) double, C$165–$190 (US$112–$129) suite; Nov 16–Apr C$65 (US$44) double, from C$85 (US$58) suite. AE, DC, MC, V. Free parking. Pets accepted. **Amenities:** Restaurant; pub; business center; limited room service; babysitting; same-day dry-cleaning. *In room:* A/C, TV, hair dryer.

23 Albert Place   Around the corner from the Avon Theatre, the Albert Place has large rooms with high ceilings. Furnishings are simple and modern. Some units have separate sitting rooms. Rates include coffee, tea, and doughnuts served in the lobby in the early morning.

23 Albert St., Stratford, ON N5A 3K2. © 519/273-5800. Fax 519/273-5008. 34 units. C$95–$105 (US$65–$71) double; C$115 (US$78) minisuite; from C$140 (US$95) suite. MC, V. **Amenities:** Restaurant; dry cleaning. *In room:* A/C, TV.

A PICK OF THE BED & BREAKFASTS

For more information on the bed-and-breakfast scene, write to **Tourism Stratford,** P.O. Box 818, 88 Wellington St., Stratford, ON N5A 6W1 (© **519/ 271-5140**). It's open from 9am to 5pm Monday to Friday.

Acrylic Dreams   As its name suggests, the recently renovated and refurbished Acrylic Dreams has a fun, modern atmosphere, thanks to its artist owners. Cottage-style antiques furnish most of the house, but the living room is done in new wave style, with transparent acrylic furniture. Upstairs, a suite decorated in Provençal colors has a separate sitting room with TV and refrigerator. On the ground floor, two doubles share a refrigerator. The full breakfast varies, but might include peaches, peach yogurt, and homemade scones and preserves with ingredients from the garden (but no meat—the owners are vegetarians). There's a phone for guests' use. Co-owner Karen Zamara offers in-room reflexology treatments; guests are also welcome to attend yoga classes at her downtown studio (C$12/US$8.15 per class).

66 Bay St., Stratford, ON N5A 4K6. © and fax **519/271-7874**. www.bbcanada.com/3718.html. 4 units. C$90–$130 (US$58–$83) double; C$135 (US$92) suite. 3rd person in suite C$25 (US$16). Rates include full breakfast. 2-night minimum on weekends. No credit cards. **Amenities:** In-room massage. *In room:* A/C, no phone.

Ambercroft   This inviting 1878 home in a quiet downtown area is convenient to the theaters and restaurants. The quirky, angular rooms are country cozy, and were refurbished last year. There's a comfy front parlor, a small TV room, and front and rear porches. Guests have the use of a refrigerator. The extended continental breakfast includes seasonal fruits, cereals, homemade baked goods, and more. No smoking.

129 Brunswick St., Stratford, ON N5A 3L9. ⓒ 519/271-5644. Fax 519/272-0156. www.bbcanada.com/2482. html. 4 units. C$95–$135 (US$65–$92) double. Rates include full breakfast. MC, V. *In room:* A/C, hair dryer, no phone.

Avonview Manor   In a 1916 Edwardian house on a quiet street, Avonview Manor offers attractive individually furnished rooms. Three have queen-size beds; the suite contains four singles, a sitting room, and a private bath. Breakfast is served in a bright dining room that overlooks the garden. Guests have the use of a kitchen. The living room is very comfortable, particularly in winter, when guests can cozy up in front of the stone fireplace. Smoking is allowed only on the porch. There's also an in-ground pool and Jacuzzi.

63 Avon St., Stratford, ON N5A 5N5. ⓒ 519/273-4603. www.bbcanada.com/avonview. 4 units (3 with private bathroom). C$90–$110 (US$61–$85) double; C$120–$160 (US$82–$109) suite. Rates include full breakfast. No credit cards; personal checks accepted. **Amenities:** Outdoor pool; Jacuzzi; sauna. *In room:* A/C; no phone.

Deacon House ⓐ   This is a great location, within walking distance of everything. Dianna Hrysko and Mary Allen have restored Deacon House, a shingle-style structure built in 1907. Rooms are decorated in country style, with iron-and-brass beds, quilts, pine hutches, oak rockers, and rope-style rugs. The comfortable living room holds a fireplace, TV, wingback chairs, and a sofa. The main-floor guest kitchen is a welcome convenience, as is the second-floor sitting and reading room. The entire house is nonsmoking, but allergy suffers should know that there are pets in the house.

101 Brunswick St., Stratford, ON N5A 3L9. ⓒ 877/825-6374 or 519/273-2052. Fax 519/273-3784. www.bbcanada.com/1152.html. 6 units. C$110–$132 (US$75–$90) double. Extra person C$35 (US$24). Rates include full breakfast. Off-season packages available. MC, V. Free parking. *In room:* A/C, hair dryer, no phone.

Woods Villa   This handsome 1870 house is home to Ken Vinen, who collects and restores the Wurlitzers, Victrolas, and player pianos throughout the house. The large drawing room contains six—and they all work. Five rooms have fireplaces, and the handsome suite boasts a canopy bed. Rooms are large and offer excellent value. Morning coffee is delivered to your room, followed by breakfast prepared to order and served in the dining room. There's an attractively landscaped outdoor pool and terrace.

62 John St. N., Stratford, ON N5A 6K7. ⓒ 519/271-4576. www.woodsvilla.orc.ca. 6 units. C$145–$230 (US$99–$145) double. Rates include full breakfast. MC, V. **Amenities:** Outdoor pool. *In room:* A/C, TV, hair dryer, iron.

A NEARBY PLACE TO STAY & DINE

Langdon Hall ⓐⓐ   This elegant house stands at the head of a curving, tree-lined drive. Eugene Langdon Wilks, a great-grandson of John Jacob Astor, completed it in 1902. It remained in the family until 1987, when its transformation into a small country-house hotel began. Today, its Langdon Hall is a Relais & Chateaux property, and its 81 hectares (200 acres) of lawns, gardens, and woodlands make for an ideal retreat. The main house, of red brick with classical pediment and Palladian-style windows, has a beautiful symmetry. Throughout, the emphasis is on comfort rather than grandiosity. The luxurious on-site spa offers a complete range of treatments. Most rooms surround the cloister garden. Each is individually decorated; most have fireplaces. The furnishings consist of handsome antique reproductions, mahogany wardrobes, ginger-jar porcelain lamps, and armchairs upholstered with luxurious fabrics.

The light, airy **dining room** serves fine regional cuisine. Main courses run C$22 to $30 (US$15–$20). Tea is served on the verandah, and there's a bar.

RR #3, Cambridge, ON N3H 4R8. © 800/268-1898 or 519/740-2100. Fax 519/740-8161. www.langdon hall.ca. 49 units. C$259–$699 (US$176–$475) double. Rates include full breakfast. Spa packages from C$180 (US$122). AE, DC, MC, V. Free parking. From Hwy. 401, take Exit 275 south, turn right onto Blair Rd., follow signs. Pets accepted. **Amenities:** Dining room; bar; outdoor pool; outdoor tennis court; exercise room; spa; Jacuzzi; sauna; croquet lawn; billiard room; cross-country ski trails; concierge; business center; 24-hr. room service; babysitting; dry cleaning. *In room:* A/C, TV, dataport, coffeemaker, hair dryer, iron.

WHERE TO DINE
VERY EXPENSIVE

The Church 🌟🌟 CONTINENTAL   The Church is simply stunning. The organ pipes and the altar of the 1873 structure are intact, along with the vaulted roof, carved woodwork, and stained-glass windows. You can sit in the nave or the side aisles and dine to appropriate sounds—usually Bach. Fresh flowers and elegant table settings further enhance the experience.

In summer, there's a special four-course fixed-price dinner menu and an after-theater menu. Appetizers might include asparagus served hot with black morels in their juices, white wine, and cream; or sauté of duck foie gras with leeks and citron, mango, and ginger sauce. Among the selection of eight or so entrees, you might find Canadian caribou with port and blackberry sauce, cabbage braised in cream with shallots and glazed chestnuts, or lobster salad with green beans, new potatoes, and truffles scented with caraway. Desserts are equally exciting—try charlotte of white chocolate mousse with summer fruit and dark chocolate sauce.

To dine here during the festival, make reservations in March or April when you buy your tickets. In the off-season, call ahead; hours vary. The upstairs Belfry Bar is a popular pre- and post-theater gathering place.

70 Brunswick St. (at Waterloo St.). © 519/273-3424. www.churchrestaurant.com. Reservations strongly recommended. Fixed-price dinner (summer only) C$59–$73 (US$40–$50); main courses C$33–$46 (US$22–$31). AE, DC, MC, V. Tues–Sat 11:30am–1am, Sun 11:30am–11pm. Off-season hours vary. Call for Mon hours during special events.

MODERATE

Bentley's CANADIAN/ENGLISH   Bentley's is *the* local watering hole, and a favorite theater company gathering spot. The popular pastime is darts, but you can also watch TV. In summer you can sit on the garden terrace and enjoy the light fare—grilled shrimp, burgers, gourmet pizza, fish-and-chips, shepherd's pie, and pasta dishes. The dinner menu features more substantial fare, including lamb curry, sirloin steak, and salmon baked in white wine with peppercorn-dill butter. The bar offers 16 drafts on tap.

99 Ontario St. © 519/271-1121. Reservations not accepted. Main courses C$8–$14 (US$5.45–$9.50). AE, DC, MC, V. Daily 11:30am–1am.

Keystone Alley Cafe 🌟 CONTINENTAL   The food here is better than the fare at some pricier competitors. Theater actors often stop in for lunch—perhaps a sandwich, like the maple-grilled chicken and avocado club, or a main dish like cornmeal-crusted Mediterranean tart. At dinner, entrees range from breast of Muscovy duck with stir-fried Asian vegetables and egg noodles in honey-ginger sauce, to escalopes of calf's liver accompanied by garlic potato puree and creamed Savoy cabbage with bacon. The short wine list is reasonably priced.

34 Brunswick St. ✆ **519/271-5645.** www.keystonealley.com. Reservations recommended. Main courses C$17–C$26.50 (US$12–$18). AE, DC, MC, V. Mon–Sat 11:30am–2:30pm; Tues–Sat 5–9pm.

The Old Prune ✿ CONTINENTAL   Two charming, whimsical women— Marion Isherwood and Eleanor Kane—run the Prune. In a lovely Edwardian home, it has three dining rooms and an enclosed garden patio. Former Montrealers, the proprietors demonstrate Quebec flair in both decor and menu. Marion's inspired paintings grace the walls.

Chef Bryan Steele selects the freshest local ingredients, many from the region's organic farmers, and prepares them simply to reveal their abundant flavor. Appetizers might include outstanding house-smoked salmon with lobster potato salad topped with Sevruga caviar, or refreshing tomato consommé with saffron and sea scallops. Among the main courses, you might find Perth County pork loin grilled with tamari and honey glaze and served with shiitake mushrooms, pickled cucumbers, and sunflower sprouts; steamed bass in Napa cabbage with curry broth and lime leaves; or rack of Ontario lamb with smoky tomatillo- chipotle pepper sauce. Desserts, such as rhubarb strawberry Napoleon with vanilla mousse, are always inspired. The Old Prune is also lovely for lunch or a late supper.

151 Albert St. ✆ **519/271-5052.** Reservations required. 3-course fixed-price dinner C$53 (US$36); main courses C$7–$12 (US$4.75–$8.15) at lunch, C$7–$14 (US$4.75–$9.50) at dinner. AE, MC, V. Wed–Sun 11:30am–1:30pm; Tues–Sat 5–9pm, Sun 5–7pm. After-theater menu Fri–Sat from 9pm. Call for winter hours.

Rundles ✿ INTERNATIONAL   Rundles provides a premier dining experi- ence in a serene dining room overlooking the river. Proprietor Jim Morris eats, sleeps, thinks, and dreams food, and chef Neil Baxter delivers the exciting, exquisite cuisine to the table. The fixed-price dinner offers palate-pleasing flavor combinations. Appetizers might include shaved fennel, arugula, artichoke, and Parmesan salad or warm seared Quebec foie gras. Among the five main dishes might be poached Atlantic salmon garnished with Jerusalem artichokes, wilted arugula, and yellow peppers in a light carrot sauce, or pink roast rib-eye of lamb with ratatouille and rosemary aioli. My dessert choice would be glazed lemon tart and orange sorbet, but hot mango tart with pineapple sorbet is also a dream.

9 Cobourg St. ✆ **519/271-6442.** Reservations required. 3-course fixed-price dinner C$59 (US$40). AE, DC, MC, V. Apr–Oct Wed and Sat–Sun 11:30am–1:30pm; Tues 5–7pm, Wed–Sat 5–8:30pm, Sun 5–7pm. Closed Nov–Mar, Mon year-round.

INEXPENSIVE
Let Them Eat Cake LIGHT FARE   Let Them Eat Cake is great for breakfast (bagels and scones) and lunch (soups, salads, sandwiches, quiche, and chicken potpie), but best of all for dessert. It offers 15 to 20, including pecan pie, orange Bavarian cream, lemon bars, carrot cake, Black Forest cake, and chocolate cheesecake.

82 Wellington St. ✆ **519/273-4774.** www.letthemeatcake.on.ca. Reservations not accepted. Lunch items less than C$10 (US$6.80); desserts C$1–$4 (US70¢–$2.70). V. Apr–Oct Mon 7:30am–4pm, Tues–Sat 7:30am 12:30am, Sun 9am–6pm; Nov–Mar Mon–Sat 7:30am–4pm, Sun 9am–4pm.

York Street Kitchen ECLECTIC   This small restaurant is a fun, funky spot that serves reasonably priced, high-quality food. You can come here for break- fast burritos and other morning fare, and for lunch sandwiches, which you build yourself by choosing from a list of fillings. In the evenings, expect to find comfort foods like meatloaf and mashed potatoes or barbecued chicken and ribs.

41 York St. ℭ **519/273-7041.** Reservations not accepted. Main courses C$8–$13 (US$5.45–$8.85). AE, V. Daily Apr to early Oct 8am–8pm, mid-Oct to Mar 8am–3pm. Closed Dec 24–Jan 5.

2 Niagara-on-the-Lake

130km (80 miles) SE of Toronto

Only 1½ hours from Toronto, Niagara-on-the-Lake is one of the best-preserved and prettiest 19th-century villages in North America. Handsome clapboard and brick period houses border the tree-lined streets. It's the setting for one of Canada's most famous events, the **Shaw Festival.** The town is the jewel of the **Ontario wine region.**

ESSENTIALS

VISITOR INFORMATION The **Niagara-on-the-Lake Chamber of Commerce,** 153 King St. (P.O. Box 1043), Niagara-on-the-Lake, ON L0S 1J0 (ℭ **905/468-4263;** www.niagara-on-the-lake.com/visit.html), provides information and can help you find accommodations at one of the 120 local bed-and-breakfasts. It's open Monday to Friday from 9am to 5pm, and Saturday and Sunday from 10am to 5pm.

GETTING THERE Niagara-on-the-Lake is best seen by **car.** From Toronto, take the Queen Elizabeth Way (signs read QEW) to Niagara via Hamilton and St. Catharines, and exit at Highway 55. The trip takes about 1½ hours.

Amtrak and **VIA** (ℭ **416/366-8411**) operate **trains** between Toronto and New York, but they go only as far as St. Catharines and Niagara Falls. Call ℭ **800/361-1235** in Canada or **800/USA-RAIL** in the United States. From either place, you'll need to rent a car. Rental outlets in St. Catharines include **National Tilden,** 162 Church St. (ℭ **905/682-8611**), and **Hertz,** 404 Ontario St. (ℭ **905/682-8695**). In Niagara Falls, **National Tilden** is at 4523 Drummond Rd. (ℭ **905/374-6700**).

THE SHAW FESTIVAL

The Shaw celebrates the dramatic and comedic works of George Bernard Shaw and his contemporaries. From April through October, the festival offers a dozen plays in the historic Court House, the exquisite Festival Theatre, and the Royal George Theatre. Some recent performances have included *Hay Fever, The House of Bernarda Alba, Chaplin,* and Shaw's *Caesar and Cleopatra.*

Free chamber concerts take place Sunday at 11am. Chats introduce performances on Friday evenings in July and August, and question-and-answer sessions follow Tuesday evening performances.

The Shaw announces its festival program in mid-January. Tickets are difficult to obtain on short notice, so book in advance. Prices range from C$26 to $75 (US$18–$51). For more information, contact the **Shaw Festival,** P.O. Box 774, Niagara-on-the-Lake, ON L0S 1J0 (ℭ **800/511-7429** or 905/468-2172; www.shawfest.com).

EXPLORING THE TOWN

Niagara-on-the-Lake is small, and most of its attractions are along one main street, making it easy to explore on foot.

Fort George National Historic Park ⚑ It's easy to imagine taking shelter behind Fort George's stockade fence and watching for the enemy from across the river—even though today there are only condominiums on the opposite riverbank.

Niagara-on-the-Lake

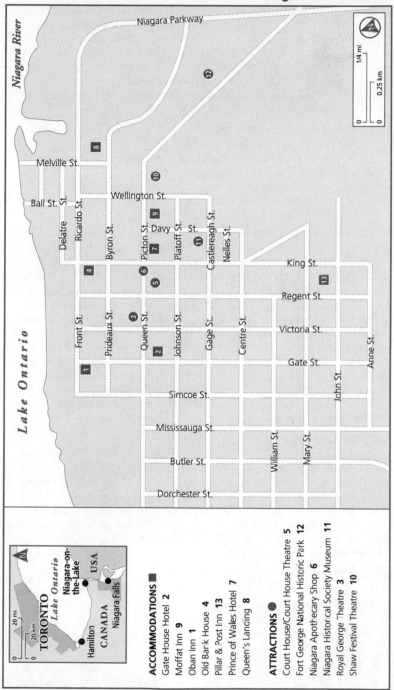

Niagara River

Niagara Parkway

Lake Ontario

Melville St.

Ball St. St.

Wellington St.

Delatre

Ricardo St.

Byron St.

Picton St.

Davy St.

Platoff St.

Castlereagh St.

Nelles St.

King St.

Regent St.

Victoria St.

Gate St.

Front St.

Prideaux St.

Queen St.

Johnson St.

Gage St.

Centre St.

John St.

Anne St.

Simcoe St.

Mississauga St.

William St.

Mary St.

Butler St.

Dorchester St.

1/4 mi
0.25 km

TORONTO

Lake Ontario

Niagara-on-the-Lake

USA

CANADA

Hamilton

Niagara Falls

20 mi
20 km

ACCOMMODATIONS
Gate House Hotel 2
Moffat Inn 9
Oban Inn 1
Old Bark House 4
Pillar & Post Inn 13
Prince of Wales Hotel 7
Queen's Landing 8

ATTRACTIONS ●
Court House/Court House Theatre 5
Fort George National Historic Park 12
Niagara Apothecary Shop 6
Niagara Historical Society Museum 11
Royal George Theatre 3
Shaw Festival Theatre 10

225

The fort played a key role in the War of 1812, before the Americans invaded and destroyed it in May 1813. Although rebuilt by 1815, it was abandoned in 1828 and not reconstructed until the 1930s. You can view the guard room (with its hard plank beds), the officers' quarters, the enlisted men's quarters, and the sentry posts. The self-guided tour includes interpretive films. Those who believe in ghosts, take note: The fort is one of Ontario's favorite "haunted" sites.

Niagara Pkwy. ℂ **905/468-6614.** Admission C$6 (US$4.10) adults, C$5 (US$3.40) seniors, C$4 (US$2.70) children 6–16, free for children under 6; C$20 ($14) family. Apr 1–Oct 31 Daily 10am–5pm.

Niagara Historical Society Museum   More than 20,000 artifacts pertaining to local history make up this collection. They include many possessions of United Empire Loyalists who first settled the area at the end of the American Revolution.

43 Castlereagh St. (at Davy). ℂ **905/468-3912.** Admission C$6 (US$4.10) adults, C$4 (US$2.70) seniors, C$3 (US$2.05) students, C$1 (US70¢) children 5–12. May–Oct daily 10am–5pm; Mar–Apr and Nov–Dec daily 1–5pm; Jan–Feb Sat–Sun 1–5pm.

A NOSTALGIC SHOPPING STROLL

A stroll along the town's main artery, Queen Street, will take you by some entertaining, albeit touristy, shops. The **Niagara Apothecary Shop,** at no. 5 (ℂ **905/468-3845**), dates to 1866. Gold-leaf script marks its original black-walnut counters and the contents of the drawers, and the original glass and ceramic apothecary ware is on display. **Loyalist Village,** no. 12 (ℂ **905/468-7331**), stocks Canadian clothes and crafts, including Inuit art, native Canadian decoys, and sheepskins. **Maple Leaf Fudge,** no. 14 (ℂ **905/468-2211**), offers more than 20 varieties that you can watch being made on marble slabs. At no. 16 is a charming toy store, the **Owl and the Pussycat** (ℂ **905/468-3081**). At no. 35 is **Greaves Jam** (ℂ **905/468-7331**), run by fourth-generation jam makers. The **Shaw Shop** (ℂ **800/511-7429**), no. 79, next to the Royal George Theatre, carries GBS memorabilia and more. There's also a Dansk outlet and several galleries selling contemporary Canadian and other ethnic crafts.

JET-BOATING THRILLS

Jet boat excursions leave from the dock across from 61 Melville St. at the King George III Inn. Don a rain suit, poncho, and life jacket, and climb aboard. The boat takes you out onto the Niagara River for a trip along the stone-walled canyon to the whirlpool downriver. The ride starts slow but gets into turbulent water. Trips, which operate from May to October, last an hour and cost C$52 (US$35) for adults, and C$42 (US$29) for children 13 and under. Reservations are required. Call the **Whirlpool Jet Boat Company** (ℂ **888/438-4444** or 905/468-4800; www.whirlpooljet.com).

WHERE TO STAY

In summer, hotel space is in high demand, but don't despair if you're having trouble nailing down a room. Contact the Chamber of Commerce, which provides an accommodations-reservations service.

IN TOWN
Expensive

Gate House Hotel   Unlike many of the Canadiana-influenced lodgings in town, the Gate House Hotel is decorated in cool, clean-lined Milanese style. Guest rooms have a marbleized look, accented with ultramodern black lamps, block marble tables, leatherette couches, and bathrooms with sleek Italian

Touring Niagara-on-the-Lake Wineries

Visiting a local winery is one of the loveliest (and tastiest) ways to pass an hour or two in this region. For maps of the area and information about vintners, contact the **Wine Council of Ontario**, 110 Hanover Dr., Suite B-205, St. Catharines, ON L2W 1A4 (© 888/5-WINERY or 905/ 684-8070; www.wineroute.com). The wineries listed below are close to the town of Niagara-on-the-Lake. Tours are free. Prices for tastings vary with the winery and the wine you're sampling, and usually run C$3 to $10 (US$2.05–$6.80).

Take Highway 55 (Niagara Stone Rd.) out of Niagara-on-the-Lake, and you'll come to **Hillebrand Estates Winery** (© 905/468-7123; www. hillebrand.com), just outside Virgil. It's open year-round, plays host to a variety of special events (including a weekend concert series), and even offers bicycle tours. Hillebrand's Vineyard Café, with views of both the barrel-filled cellar and the Niagara Escarpment, is a delightful spot for lunch or dinner. Winery tours start on the hour daily from 10am to 6pm.

If you turn off Highway 55 and go down York Road, you'll reach **Château des Charmes,** west of St. Davids (© 905/262-5202; www. chateaudescharmes.com). The winery was built to resemble a French manor house, and its architecture is unique in the region. One-hour tours are given daily. Open from 10am to 6pm year-round.

To reach the **Konzelmann Winery,** 1096 Lakeshore Road (© 905/ 935-2866; www.konzelmannwines.com), take Mary Street out of Niagara-on-the-Lake. This vintner is famous for its award-winning ice wines. It offers tours from May to late September, Monday to Saturday.

fixtures. The effect is quite glamorous. Ristorante Giardino, one of the best places to dine in town, is in the hotel.

142 Queen St. (P.O. Box 1364), Niagara-on-the-Lake, ON L0S 1J0. © 905/468-3263. www.gatehouse-niagara.com. 10 units. C$170–$185 (US$116–$126) double. AE, MC, V. **Amenities:** Restaurant; concierge. *In room:* A/C, TV, hair dryer.

Oban Inn ✿ In a prime location overlooking the lake, the Oban Inn is the place to stay. It's in a charming white Victorian house with a green dormer-style roof and windows, plus a large verandah. (The house is a re-creation of the original 1824 structure, which burned down in 1992.) The gorgeous gardens are the source of the bouquets throughout the house. Downstairs is a piano bar with leather Windsor-style chairs and a fireplace.

Each of the comfortable rooms is unique. They are furnished with antique reproductions—corn-husk four-poster beds with candlewick spreads, ginger-jar lamps, and club-style sofas. It's all very homey and old-fashioned. Note that the inn no longer allows pets in the rooms.

160 Front St. (at Gate St.), Niagara-on-the-Lake, ON L0S 1J0. © 888/669-5566 or 905/468-2165. www. vintageinns.com. 25 units. C$170 (US$116) standard double, C$290 (US$197) double with lake view. Winter packages available. AE, DC, DISC, MC, V. Free parking. **Amenities:** Piano bar (dinner main courses C$21–$27/US$14–$18); lounge and sunroom; access to nearby health club; bike rental; babysitting. *In room:* A/C, TV, dataport, hair dryer, iron.

Pillar & Post Inn   The discreetly elegant Pillar & Post is a couple of blocks from the madding crowds on Queen Street. In recent years it has been transformed into one of the most sophisticated accommodations in town, complete with a spa that offers the latest in deluxe treatments and a Japanese-style warm mineral-spring pool, complete with cascading waterfall (spa packages are available). The light, airy lobby boasts a fireplace, lush plantings, and comfortable seating. The style is classic Canadiana: The spacious rooms all contain old-fashioned furniture, Windsor-style chairs, a pine cabinet (with a color TV tucked inside), and historical engravings. In the back, there's a secluded pool. Some rooms facing the outdoor pool on the ground level have bay windows and window boxes.

48 John St. (at King St.), Niagara-on-the-Lake, ON L0S 1J0. ℭ 888/669-5566 or 905/468-2123. Fax 905/468-1472. www.vintageinns.com. 123 units. C$225–$365 (US$153–$248) double; C$305–$445 (US$169–$303) suite. Extra person C$50 (US$34). AE, DC, MC, V. Free parking. Pets accepted for C$35 (US$24) per day extra charge. **Amenities:** 2 dining rooms (main courses C$17–$30/US$12–$20); well-stocked wine bar; indoor pool; outdoor pool; spa (treatments from C$45/US$31); Jacuzzi; sauna; bike rental; children's programs; concierge; business center; dry cleaning. *In room:* A/C, TV, dataport, minibar, hair dryer, safe.

Prince of Wales Hotel ⟨★★⟩   The Prince of Wales is the most luxurious hotel in the district. This place has it all: a central location across from the lovely gardens of Simcoe Park; full recreational facilities, including an indoor pool; lounges, bars, and restaurants; and attractive rooms, beautifully decorated with antiques or reproductions. It has a lively atmosphere yet retains the elegance and charm of a Victorian inn. Bathrooms have bidets, and most rooms have minibars. The hotel's original section was built in 1864; in 1999, the hotel was renovated and restored to its original glory.

6 Picton St., Niagara-on-the-Lake, ON L0S 1J0. ℭ 888/669-5566 or 905/468-3246. Fax 905/468-5521. www.vintageinns.com. 108 units. From C$260 (US$177) double. Extra person C$75 (US$51). Packages available. AE, DC, DISC, MC, V. Pets accepted for C$35 (US$24) per night extra charge. **Amenities:** Dining room (main courses C$18–$28/US$12–$19); cafe; bar; lounge; indoor pool; fitness center with aerobics classes; spa; Jacuzzi; bike rental; concierge; business center; 24-hr. room service; massage; dry cleaning. *In room:* A/C, TV, dataport, minibar, hair dryer, iron.

Queen's Landing Inn   Overlooking the river and within walking distance of the theaters, the Queen's Landing Inn is a modern, Georgian-style mansion. Half the rooms have fireplaces, and 32 contain fireplaces and Jacuzzis. The spacious rooms are comfortably furnished with half-canopy or brass beds, wingback chairs, and large desks. This hotel attracts a business-oriented crowd, in part because of its excellent conference facilities, which include 20 meeting rooms.

155 Byron St., at Melville St., (P.O. Box 1180), Niagara-on-the Lake, ON L0S 1J0. ℭ 888/669-5566 or 905/468-2195. www.vintageinns.com. 144 units. C$170 (US$116) double; C$275–$310 (US$187–$211) double with fireplace; from C$420 (US$286) double with fireplace and Jacuzzi. AE, DC, DISC, MC, V. Free parking. **Amenities:** Dining room (dinner main courses C$24–$36/US$16–$25); lounge; indoor pool; exercise room; Jacuzzi; sauna; bike rental; concierge; business center; room service (7am–11pm); babysitting; dry cleaning. *In room:* A/C, TV, dataport, minibar, hair dryer, iron, safe.

White Oaks Conference Resort & Spa   Not far from Niagara-on-the-Lake, White Oaks is a sports enthusiast's paradise. In 2000, the resort added a full-service luxury spa, which has become one of its main attractions. It's entirely possible to arrive here, be caught in a flurry of athletic activity all weekend, and not set foot outside the resort. The rooms are as good as the facilities, with oak furniture, vanity sinks, and niceties like a phone in the bathroom. Suites have brick fireplaces, marble-top desks, Jacuzzis (some heart-shaped), and bidets.

The long list of spa treatments for men and women includes facials, massages, body wraps, and manicures. Some of the less orthodox therapies include reiki (a Japanese massage to "align your energy field"), and Danse de la Mains, a massage choreographed to music and performed by two therapists.

Taylor Rd., Niagara-on-the-Lake, ON L0S 1J0. ℂ 800/263-5766 or 905/688-2550. Fax 905/688-2220. www. whiteoaksresort.com. 90 units. July–Aug C$160–$190 (US$109–$129) double; C$185–$260 (US$126–$177) suite. Off-season discounts available. AE, DC, MC, V. From QEW, exit at Glendale Ave. **Amenities:** Restaurant–wine bar; outdoor terrace cafe; cafe and coffee shop; eight indoor tennis courts; five squash courts; two racquetball courts; Nautilus room; personal trainers; spa; sauna; bike rental; concierge; business center; massage; day-care center with professional staff; tanning beds. *In room:* A/C, TV, dataport, hair dryer.

Moderate
Moffat Inn   This is a fine choice in a convenient location. Most rooms contain brass-framed beds and furnishings in traditional-style wood, wicker, and bamboo. Each has a teakettle and supplies. Eight rooms have fireplaces. Free coffee is available in the lobby. Smoking is allowed at the bar only.

60 Picton St. (at Queen St.), Niagara-on-the-Lake, ON L0S 1J0. ℂ 905/468-4116. www.moffatinn.com. 22 units. Apr 15–Oct and late Dec C$89–$159 (US$61–$108) double; Nov to mid-Dec and Jan–Apr 14 C$69–$149 (US$47–$101) double. AE, MC, V. **Amenities:** Restaurant; bar; access to nearby health club. *In room:* A/C, TV, dataport, coffeemaker, hair dryer.

The Old Bank House   Beautifully situated down by the river, this two-story Georgian was built in 1817 as the first branch of the Bank of Canada. All of the guest rooms and bathrooms were refurbished and redecorated in 2001. Several tastefully decorated units have private entrances; one is the charming Garden Room, which also has a private trellised deck. Eight units have a refrigerator and coffee or tea supplies. The most expensive suite accommodates four in two bedrooms. The extraordinarily comfortable sitting room (open to all guests) holds a fireplace and eclectic antique pieces.

10 Front St. (P.O. Box 1708), Niagara-on-the-Lake, ON L0S 1J0. ℂ 877-468-7136 or 905/468-7136; www.oldbankhouse.com. 9 units. C$125–$195 (US$85–$133) double; C$230 (US$156) 2-bedroom suite. Rates include breakfast. AE, MC, V. **Amenities:** Jacuzzi. *In room:* A/C, no phone.

ALONG THE WINE ROAD
Inn on the Twenty   In the village of Jordan, about 30km (18 miles) from Niagara-on-the-Lake, this modern accommodation consists entirely of handsome suites. Each has an elegantly furnished living room with a fireplace, and a Jacuzzi in the bathroom. Seven are duplexes—one of them, the deluxe loft, has two double beds on its second level—and three are single-level suites with high ceilings. The inn's eatery, On the Twenty Restaurant & Wine Bar, is across the street (see "Along the Wine Road" under "Where to Dine," below).

3845 Main St., Jordan, ON L0R 1S0. ℂ 800/701-8074 or 905/562-5336. www.innonthetwenty.com. 31 units. C$175–$315 (US$119–$214) double. AE, DC, MC, V. From QEW, take Jordan Rd. exit south; at first intersection, turn right onto 4th Ave., then right onto Main St. **Amenities:** Restaurant; nearby golf course; exercise room; concierge. *In room:* A/C, TV, dataport, coffeemaker, hair dryer, iron.

WHERE TO DINE
IN TOWN
In addition to the listings below, don't forget the dining rooms at the **Pillar & Post, Queen's Landing,** and the **Prince of Wales,** all listed above.

The stylish **Shaw Cafe and Wine Bar,** 92 Queen St. (ℂ **905/468-4772**), serves lunch and light meals, and has a patio. The **Epicurean,** 84 Queen St. (ℂ **905/468-3408**), offers hearty soups, quiches, sandwiches, and other fine dishes in a sunny Provence-inspired dining room. Service is cafeteria style. Half a block off Queen Street, the **Angel Inn,** 224 Regent St. (© **905/468-3411**), is a delightfully authentic English pub. For an inexpensive down-home breakfast, go to the **Stagecoach Family Restaurant,** 45 Queen St. (© **905/468-3133**). It also serves basic family fare, such as burgers, fries, and meatloaf, but doesn't accept credit cards. **Niagara Home Bakery,** 66 Queen St. (© **905/468-3431**), is the place to stop for chocolate-date squares, cherry squares, croissants, cookies, and individual quiches.

The Buttery CANADIAN/ENGLISH/CONTINENTAL   The Buttery has been a dining landmark for years. At its weekend Henry VIII feasts, "serving wenches" bring food and wine while "jongleurs" and "musickers" entertain. The meal consists of "four removes"—courses involving broth, chicken, roast lamb, roast pig, sherry trifle, syllabub, and cheese, all washed down with a goodly amount of wine, ale, and mead.

The tavern menu features spareribs, 8-ounce New York strip, shrimp in garlic sauce, and such English pub fare as lamb curry and steak, kidney, and mushroom pie. On the dinner menu, I highly recommend rack of lamb or shrimp curry. Finish with mud pie or Grand Marnier chocolate cheesecake. You can take home fresh baked goods—pies, strudels, dumplings, cream puffs, or scones.

19 Queen St. © **905/468-2564.** Reservations strongly recommended; required for Henry VIII feast. Henry VIII feast C$49 (US$33); tavern main courses (available Tues–Sun 11am–5pm, all day Mon) C$8–$15 (US$5.45–$10); dinner main courses C$14–$22 (US$9.50–$15). MC, V. Apr–Nov daily 11am–11pm; Nov–Mar Sun–Thurs 11am–7:30pm. Afternoon tea year-round daily 2–5pm.

Fans Court CHINESE   This comfortable spot, decorated with fans, cushioned bamboo chairs, and round tables spread with golden tablecloths, serves some of the best food in town. In summer, there's outdoor dining in the courtyard. The cuisine is primarily Cantonese and Sichuan. The menu includes Singapore beef, moo shu pork, Sichuan scallops, and lemon chicken.

135 Queen St. © **905/468-4511.** Reservations recommended. Main courses C$13–$20 (US$8.85–$14). AE, MC, V. Tues–Sun noon–9pm.

Ristorante Giardino ✰ NORTHERN ITALIAN   On the ground floor of the Gate House Hotel is this sleek, ultramodern restaurant, with a gleaming marble-top bar and brass accents throughout. The food is Northern Italian with fresh American accents. Main courses might include baked salmon seasoned with olive paste and tomato concasse, veal tenderloin marinated with garlic and rosemary, and braised pheasant in juniper-berry-and-vegetable sauce. There are several pasta dishes, plus such appealing appetizers as medallions of langostine garnished with orange and fennel salad. Desserts include a fine tiramisu, and panna cotta with seasonal berries.

In the Gate House Hotel, 142 Queen St. © **905/468-3263.** www.gatehouse-niagara.com. Main courses C$25–$40 (US$17–$27). AE, MC, V. May–Sept daily 11:30am–2:30pm and 5–10pm; Oct–Apr daily 5:30–9pm.

IN NEARBY VIRGIL, ST. CATHARINES & WELLAND

Café Garibaldi ✰ ITALIAN   This relaxed spot is a favorite among locals. It serves Italian staples such as zuppa di pesce and veal scalloppine; homemade lasagna is the most requested dish. The wine list features the local vintners' goods and some fine bottles from Italy.

375 St. Paul St., St. Catharines. © **905/988-9033.** Reservations recommended for dinner. Main courses C$13–$27 (US$8.85–$18). AE, DC, MC, V. Tues–Sat 11:30am–2:30pm and 5–10pm. From QEW, exit at Ontario St., follow DOWNTOWN sign to St. Paul St. and turn left.

Hennepin's CONTEMPORARY   The region's first tapas bar, Hennepin's still stands out. The dining rooms display the works of local artists. The specialty of the house is Mediterranean- and Asian-inspired tapas—coconut shrimp, olive stuffed meatballs, chicken satay, samosas—which are served all day. At dinner, starters always include such temptations as escargots in Pernod, and pan-seared game paté with blueberry kirsch sauce. Game and serious meats dominate the main courses—venison bordelaise, liver in chausseur sauce, steak, and pork tenderloin with portobello calvados sauce. The desserts are seriously rich—try the death by chocolate cake. The wine list is extensive; 28 selections are available by the glass.

1486 Niagara Stone Rd. (Hwy. 55), at Creek Rd., Virgil. (℃) 905/468-1555. Tapas C$4–$8 (US$2.70–$5.45); main courses C$15–$28 (US$10–$19). AE, MC, V. Sun–Wed 11:30am–9pm, Fri–Sat 11:30am–11pm. From QEW, exit at York Rd., turn left, follow to Niagara Stone Rd., turn right.

Iseya ⊛ JAPANESE   Chef Yasutoshi Hachoitori has had a virtual monopoly since he opened this eatery: Iseya is one of the region's few traditional Japanese restaurants. The restaurant attracts locals as well as out-of-towners. It serves fresh sushi and sashimi as well as teriyaki, tempura, and sukiyaki dishes. The classic Japanese cuisine doesn't offer a lot of surprises, but everything is beautifully done.

22 James St. (between St. Paul and King sts.), St. Catharines. (℃) 905/688-1141. Reservations recommended for dinner. Main courses C$12–$27 (US$8.15–$18). AE, MC, V. Mon–Fri 11:30am–2:30pm; Mon–Sat 5–11pm. From QEW, exit at St. Paul St., turn right, follow to St. James St., turn right.

Rinderlin's CONTINENTAL   An intimate town-house restaurant, Rinderlin's has evolved from a traditional French restaurant to one with a continental flair. On the dinner menu, you might find sautéed shrimps and scallops in medium-hot curry sauce on a bed of basmati rice; roast pork tenderloin with honey-mustard-bacon sauce; herb polenta with grilled bell pepper, eggplant and zucchini; and local venison with wild mushrooms and game sauce. There are also several vegetarian options. Desserts are seasonal—one favorite is the white chocolate torte flavored with brandy and served with raspberry sauce.

24 Burgar St., Welland. (℃) 905/735-4411. Reservations recommended. Main courses C$21–$30 (US$14–$20). AE, DC, MC, V. Mon–Fri 11:30am–1:30pm; daily 6–8pm. From QEW, take Hwy. 406 to Burgar St. exit, turn left.

Wellington Court Restaurant CONTINENTAL   In an Edwardian town house with a flower trellis, the dining rooms here sport contemporary decor with modern lithographs and photographs. The menu features daily specials along with such items as beef tenderloin in shallot-and-red-wine reduction, roasted breast of chicken on gingered plum preserves, and grilled sea bass with cranberry vinaigrette.

11 Wellington St., St. Catharines. (℃) 905/682-5518. Reservations recommended. Main courses C$20–$28 (US$14–$19). MC, V. Tues–Sat 11:30am–2:30pm and 5–9:30pm. From QEW, exit at St. Paul St., turn right, follow to Wellington Ave., turn left.

ALONG THE WINE ROAD

Hillebrand's Vineyard Café ⊛ CONTINENTAL   This dining room is light and airy, and its floor-to-ceiling windows offer views over the vineyards to the distant Niagara Escarpment, or of wine cellars bulging with oak barrels. The food is excellent. The seasonal menu might feature such dishes as poached Arctic char with shellfish ragout, or prosciutto-wrapped pheasant breast atop linguine tossed with mushrooms, roasted eggplant, and shallot. The starters are equally luxurious. Try roasted three-peppercorn pear served warm with salad greens, pine nuts, and Parmesan slivers, or spiced goat cheese and grilled portobello "sandwich" with walnuts and endive. My favorite among the irresistible desserts is chocolate tortellini.

Hwy. 55, between Niagara-on-the-Lake and Virgil. ℂ 905/468-7123. www.hillebrand.com. Main courses C$24–$35 (US$16–$24). AE, MC, V. Daily 11:30am–11pm (closes earlier in winter).

On the Twenty Restaurant & Wine Bar CANADIAN   This restaurant is a favorite among foodies. The gold-painted dining rooms cast a warm glow. The cuisine features ingredients from many producers, giving On the Twenty a small-town feel. Naturally, there's an extensive selection of Ontario wines, including some wonderful ice wines to accompany such desserts as lemon tart and fruit cobbler. Inn on the Twenty Restaurant is associated with the Vintner's Inn, across the street (see "Along the Wine Road" under "Where to Stay," above).

At Cave Spring Cellars, 3836 Main St., Jordan. ℂ 905/562-7313. www.innonthetwenty.com. Reservations recommended. Main courses C$22–$40 (US$15–$27). AE, DC, MC, V. Daily 11:30am–3pm and 5–10pm.

Vineland Estates ☆ CONTINENTAL   This inspired eatery serves some of the most innovative food along the wine trail. On warm days you can dine on a deck under a spreading tree, or stay in the airy dining room. Start with a plate of seasoned mussels in a ginger broth. Follow with a Canadian Angus tenderloin with a risotto of truffles and morel mushrooms, or go for pan-seared sweetbreads with a celeriac and potato mash and confit of mushrooms glazed with ice wine. For dessert, there's a wonderful tasting plate of Canadian farm cheeses, including Abbey St. Benoit blue Ermite.

3620 Moyer Rd., Vineland. ℂ 888/846-3526 or 905/562-7088. www.vineland.com. Reservations recommended. Main courses C$20–$40 (US$14–$27). AE, MC, V. Daily noon–2:30pm and 5:30–9pm.

3 Niagara Falls

160km (100 miles) SE of Toronto

Niagara Falls was for decades the region's honeymoon capital. I say this in an attempt to explain its endless motels—each with at least one suite that has a heart-shaped pink bed. Today, it is better known for its casino, amusement parks, and wax museums. Nonetheless, nothing can steal the thunder of the falls. (Well, almost nothing—longtime locals fondly reminisce about Marilyn Monroe's coming here to film *Niagara* in 1953.) If the tacky commercial side starts to grate on your nerves, get out of town by driving along the Niagara Parkway. With its endless parks and gardens, it's an oasis for nature-lovers. (See "Along the Niagara Parkway," below.)

ESSENTIALS

VISITOR INFORMATION   Contact the **Niagara Falls Canada Visitor and Convention Bureau,** 5433 Victoria Ave., Niagara Falls, ON L2G 3L1 (ℂ **905/ 356-6061;** www.nfcvb.com), or the **Niagara Parks Commission,** Box 150, 7400 Portage Rd. S., Niagara Falls, ON L2E 6T2 (ℂ **905/356-2241;** www. niagaraparks.com).

   Summer information centers are open daily from 9am to 6pm at Table Rock House, Maid of the Mist Plaza, Rapids View parking lot, and Niagara-on-the-Lake.

GETTING THERE   If you're driving from Toronto, take the Queen Elizabeth Way (signs read QEW) to Niagara. The trip takes 1½ to 1¾ hours.

Niagara Falls

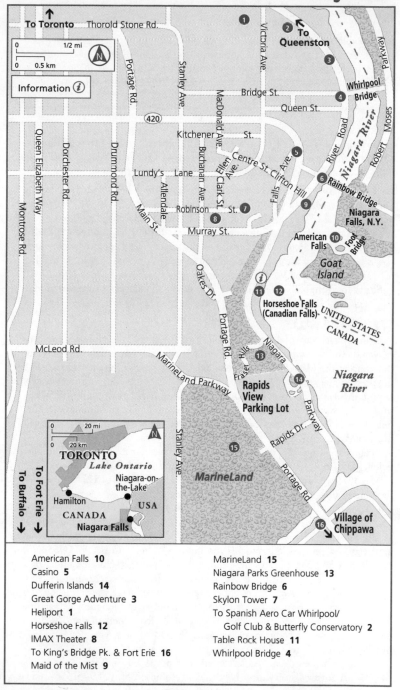

American Falls **10**
Casino **5**
Dufferin Islands **14**
Great Gorge Adventure **3**
Heliport **1**
Horseshoe Falls **12**
IMAX Theater **8**
To King's Bridge Pk. & Fort Erie **16**
Maid of the Mist **9**

MarineLand **15**
Niagara Parks Greenhouse **13**
Rainbow Bridge **6**
Skylon Tower **7**
To Spanish Aero Car Whirlpool/
    Golf Club & Butterfly Conservatory **2**
Table Rock House **11**
Whirlpool Bridge **4**

Value **A Money-Saving Pass**

The **Explorer's Passport Plus** includes admission to Journey Behind the Falls, Great Gorge Adventure, and the Butterfly Conservatory, plus all-day transportation aboard the People Movers. It's available at information booths for C$24 (US$16) for adults, and C$12 (US$8.15) for children ages 6 to 12.

Amtrak and **VIA Rail** (© 416/366-8411) operate trains between Toronto and New York, stopping in St. Catharines and Niagara Falls. Call © 800/361-1235 in Canada or © 800/USA-RAIL in the United States.

GETTING AROUND   The best way to get around is aboard the **Niagara Parks People Movers** (© 905/357-9340). They cost C$5.50 (US$3.70) for adults, and C$2.75 (US$1.90) for children 6 to 12. Parking at Rapid View, several kilometers from the falls, is free. Preferred Parking (overlooking the falls) costs C$9.75 (US$6.65) with no in-out privileges. The People Mover, which serves both parking areas, is an attraction in itself. It travels in a loop, making nine stops from Rapid View to the Spanish Aero Car, from 8am to 10pm.

Shuttles to the falls operate from downtown and Lundy's Lane; an all-day pass costs C$7 (US$4.75) for adults, and C$4 (US$2.70) for children 6 to 12.

SEEING THE FALLS

You simply can't do anything else before you've seen the falls, the seventh natural wonder of the world. The most exciting way to do that is from the decks of the **Maid of the Mist** *฿฿*, 5920 River Rd. (© 905/358-5781; www.maidofthe mist.com). The sturdy boat takes you right in—through the turbulent waters around the American Falls, past the Rock of Ages, and to the foot of the Horseshoe Falls, where 34.5 million Imperial gallons of water tumble over the 54m-high (176-ft.) cataract each minute. You'll get wet, and your glasses will mist, but that won't detract from the thrill.

Boats leave from the dock on the parkway just down from the Rainbow Bridge. Trips operate daily from mid-May to mid-October. Fares are C$12.25 (US$8.35) for adults, and C$7.50 (US$5.10) for children 6 to 12, free for children under 6.

Go down under the falls using the elevator at Table Rock House, which drops you 46m (150 ft.) through solid rock to the tunnels and viewing portals of the **Journey Behind the Falls** (© 905/354-1551). You'll receive—and appreciate—a yellow biodegradable mackintosh. Admission is C$7 (US$4.75) for adults, C$3.50 (US$2.40) for children 6 to 12, free for children under 6.

To view the falls from a spectacular angle, take a 12-minute spin (C$195/US$133 for two) in a chopper over the whole Niagara area. Helicopters leave from the heliport, adjacent to the whirlpool at the junction of Victoria Avenue and Niagara Parkway. They operate daily from 9am to dusk, weather permitting. Contact **Niagara Helicopters,** 3731 Victoria Ave. (© 905/357-5672; www.niagarahelicopters.com).

You can ride the external glass-fronted elevators 159m (520 ft.) to the top of the **Skylon Tower Observation Deck,** 5200 Robinson St. (© 905/356-2651; www.skylon.com). The observation deck is open daily from 8am to midnight from June to Labour Day; hours vary in other seasons, so call ahead. Adults pay

C$8.50 (US$5.80), seniors C$7.50 (US$5.10), children 6 to 12 C$4.50 (US$3.05), free for children under 6.

For a thrilling introduction to Niagara Falls, stop by the **IMAX Theater,** 6170 Buchanan Ave. (© **905/358-3611**). You can view the raging, swirling waters in *Niagara: Miracles, Myths, and Magic,* shown on a six-story-high screen. Admission is C$8 (US$5.45) for adults, C$7 (US$4.75) for seniors and children 12 to 18, C$5.50 (US$3.75) for children 5 to 11, free for children under 5.

The falls are also exciting in winter, when the ice bridge and other formations are quite remarkable.

ALONG THE NIAGARA PARKWAY 🗘

Whatever you think of the tourist-oriented town, you can't help but love the Niagara Parkway, on the Canadian side of the falls. Unlike the American side, it abounds with natural wonders, including vast expanses of parkland. The 56km (35-mile) parkway, with a bike path, makes a refreshing respite from the neon glow that envelops the town both day and night.

You can drive all the way from Niagara Falls to Niagara-on-the-Lake on the parkway, taking in attractions en route. The first diversion you'll come to is the **Great Gorge Adventure,** 4330 River Rd. (© **905/374-1221**). The scenic boardwalk runs beside the raging white waters of the Great Gorge Rapids. Stroll along and wonder how it must have felt to challenge this mighty torrent, where the river rushes through the narrow channel at an average speed of 35kmph (22 mph). Admission is C$5.75 (US$3.90) for adults, C$2.90 (US$2) for children 6 to 12, free for kids under 6.

Nearly 1km (a half mile) farther north, you'll arrive at the **Niagara Spanish Aero Car** (© **905/354-5711**), a red-and-yellow cable-car contraption that whisks you on a 1,097m (3,600-ft.) jaunt between two points in Canada. High above the whirlpool, you'll enjoy excellent views of the surrounding landscape. Admission is C$6 (US$4.10) for adults, C$3 (US$2.05) for children 6 to 12, free for kids under 6. Open daily May to the third Sunday in October. Hours are from 9am to 6pm in May, 9am to 8pm in June, 9am to 9pm in July and August, 10am to 7:30pm in September, and 9am to 5pm in October.

At **Ride Niagara,** 5755 River Rd. (© **905/374-7433;** www.rideniagara. com), you can experience the falls without risking your life. Before going "over" the falls in the computerized motion simulator, you'll see a short video showing some of the weirder contraptions folks have devised for the journey. Then you take an elevator down to the simulator. Admission is C$9 (US$6.10) for adults, C$4.50 (US$3.05) for children 5 to 13, free for 3- and 4-year-olds. Children under 3 aren't admitted. Open daily year-round; summer hours are from 9:15am to 10:30pm.

(Moments The Falls by Night

Don't miss seeing the falls after dark. Twenty-two xenon gas spotlights, each producing 250 million candlepower of light, illuminate them in shades of rose pink, red magenta, amber, blue, and green. Call © **800/ 563-2557** (in the U.S.) or 905-356-6061 for schedules. The show starts around 5pm in winter, 8:30pm in spring and fall, and 9pm in summer. In addition, from July to early September, free fireworks start at 10pm every Friday.

After passing the Whirlpool Golf Club, stop at the **School of Horticulture** (© 905/356-8119) for a free view of the vast gardens and a look at the Floral Clock, which contains 25,000 plants in its 12m-diameter (40-ft.) face. The new **Butterfly Conservatory** is also in the gardens. In this lush tropical setting, more than 2,000 butterflies (50 international species) float and flutter among such nectar-producing flowers as lantanas and pentas. The large bright blue luminescent Morpho butterflies from Central and South America are particularly gorgeous. Interpretive programs and other presentations take place in the auditorium and two smaller theaters. The native butterfly garden outside attracts the more familiar swallowtails, fritillaries, and painted ladies. The school opens at 9am daily. It closes at 8pm in May and June; 9pm in July and August; 6pm in March, April, September, and October; and 5pm from November through February. It's closed December 25. Admission is C$8.50 (US$5.80) for adults, C$4 (US$2.70) for children 6 to 12, free for children under 6.

From here you can drive to **Queenston Heights Park,** site of a famous War of 1812 battle, and take a walking tour of the battlefield. Picnic or play tennis (for C$6/US$4.10 per hour) in the shaded arbor before moving to the **Laura Secord Homestead,** Partition Street, Queenston (© 905/262-4851). This heroic woman threaded enemy lines to alert British authorities to a surprise attack by American soldiers during the War of 1812. Her home contains a fine collection of Upper Canada furniture from the period, plus artifacts recovered from an archaeological dig. Stop at the candy shop and ice-cream parlor. Tours run every half hour. Admission is C$2 (US$1.35). Open from late May to Labour Day, daily from 10am to 6pm.

Also worth viewing just off the parkway in Queenston is the **Samuel Weir Collection and Library of Art,** R.R. #1, Niagara-on-the-Lake (© 905/262-4510). The small personal collection is displayed as it was originally, when Samuel Weir occupied the house. Weir (1898–1981), a lawyer from London, Ontario, was an enthusiastic collector of Canadian, American, and European art as well as rare books. Open from Victoria Day to Canadian Thanksgiving (U.S. Columbus Day), Wednesday to Saturday from 11am to 5pm, and Sunday from 1 to 5pm. Admission is free.

From here, the parkway continues into Niagara-on-the-Lake. You'll see fruit farms, like **Kurtz Orchards** (© 905/468-2937), and wineries such as the **Inniskillin Winery,** Line 3, Service Road 66 (© 905/468-3554 or 905/468-2187). Inniskillin is open daily from 10am to 6pm from June to October, and Monday to Saturday from 10am to 5pm November to May. The self-guided free tour has 20 stops that explain the winemaking process. A free guided tour, daily in summer and Saturday only in winter, begins at 2:30pm.

The next stop between Niagara Falls and Niagara-on-the-Lake is the Georgian-style **McFarland House,** 15927 Niagara River Pkwy. (© 905/468-3322). Built in 1800, it was home to John McFarland, "His Majesty's Boat Builder" to George III. It's open daily late May through June from noon to 5pm, and July to Labour Day from 11am to 6pm. Admission is C$4 (US$2.70) for adults, and C$2 (US$1.35) for children. The last tour starts 30 minutes before closing.

A trip south from Niagara Falls along the parkway will take you by the Table Rock complex to the old-fashioned **Park Greenhouse.** The free attraction is a pleasant place to make a stop. It's open daily from 9:30am to 7pm in July and August, and from 9:30am to 4:15pm September to June.

Farther along are the **Dufferin Islands.** The children can swim, rent a paddleboat, and explore the surrounding woodland areas while you play a round of golf on the illuminated 9-hole par-3 course. Open from the second Sunday in April to the last Sunday in October.

A little farther on, stop for a picnic in **King's Bridge Park** and stroll along the beaches. Continue to **Historic Fort Erie,** 350 Lakeshore Rd., Fort Erie (© **905/871-0540**). It's a reconstruction of the fort that was seized by the Americans in July 1814, besieged later by the British, and finally blown up as the Americans retreated across the river to Buffalo. Guards in period costume stand sentry duty, fire the cannons, and demonstrate drill and musket practice. Open from 10am to 6pm daily from the first Saturday in May to mid-September, and weekends only to Canadian Thanksgiving (U.S. Columbus Day). Admission is C$6.50 (US$4.40) for adults, C$4 (US$2.70) for children 6 to 16, free for kids under 6.

MORE NIAGARA FALLS ATTRACTIONS

The biggest crowds aren't here for the falls; they head to **Casino Niagara,** 5705 Falls Ave. (© **905/374-3598**). The monolithic complex features 123 gambling tables that offer blackjack, roulette, baccarat, several different pokers, plus 3,000 slot and video poker machines. The casino contains five restaurants, including the Hard Rock Cafe, seven lounges, and several shops. It's open 24 hours a day, 365 days a year.

A don't-miss spot for families is **Marineland** *(★*, 7657 Portage Rd. (© **905/ 356-9565;** www.marinelandcanada.com). At the aquarium-theater, King Waldorf, the walrus mascot, presides over performances by killer whales, dolphins, and sea lions. Friendship Cove, a 4.5-million-gallon breeding and observation tank, lets the little ones see killer whales up close. Another aquarium features displays of freshwater fish. At the small wildlife display, kids enjoy petting and feeding the deer and seeing bears and Canadian elk.

Marineland also has theme-park rides, including a roller coaster, Tivoli wheel, and Dragon Boat rides, and a fully equipped playground. The big thriller is Dragon Mountain, a roller coaster that loops, double-loops, and spirals through 305m (1,000 ft.) of tunnels. There are three restaurants, or you can picnic.

In summer, admission is C$30 (US$20) for adults, C$26 (US$18) for children 5 to 9 and seniors, free for children under 5. Off-season discounts are available. Open daily July and August from 9am to 6pm; mid-April to mid-May and September to mid-October from 10am to 4pm; and mid-May to June from 10am to 5pm. Closed November to April. Rides open in late May and close the first Monday in October. In town, drive south on Stanley Street and follow the signs; from the QEW, take the McCleod Rd. exit.

WHERE TO STAY

Every other sign in Niagara Falls advertises a motel. In summer, rates go up and down according to the traffic, and some proprietors will not even quote rates ahead of time. You can secure a reasonably priced room if you're lucky enough to arrive on a "down night," but with the casino in town, that's becoming rare. Still, always request a lower rate and see what happens.

EXPENSIVE

Brock Plaza Hotel   For an unmarred view of the falls, try the Brock Plaza, which has entertained honeymooners and sightseers since 1929. It has a certain air of splendor, with a huge chandelier and marble walls in the lobby. About 150 of the rooms face the falls. City-view rooms are slightly smaller and less expensive.

5685 Falls Ave., Niagara Falls, ON L2E 6W7. © **800/263-7135** or 905/374-4444; www.niagarafallshotels. com. 233 units. Mid-June to Sept C$159–$519 (US$108–$353) double; Oct–Dec and Apr to mid-June C$99–$369 (US$67–$251) double; Jan–Mar C$80–$369 (US$54–$251) double. Children under 18 stay free in parents' room. Extra person C$10 (US$6.80). Packages available. AE, DC, DISC, MC, V. Parking C$6 (US$4.10) Sun–Thurs, C$8 (US$5.45) Fri–Sat. **Amenities:** Restaurant; bar; cafe; indoor pool; Jacuzzi; sauna; concierge; tour desk; shopping arcade; limited room service; dry cleaning. *In room:* A/C, TV, hair dryer.

Sheraton on the Falls Hotel
A hotel to consider if you're looking for a room with a view—many units have balconies. There are also several Jacuzzi suites, and a few bi-level suites. Each unit has individual climate control. The hotel is adjacent to Casino Niagara. It offers 1- and 2-night packages that include meals.

5875 Falls Ave., Niagara Falls, ON L2E 6W7. © **888/229-9961** or 905/374-4445. Fax 905/371-8349. www. niagarafallshotels.com. 670 units. June to early Oct C$199–$999 (US$135–$679) double; mid-Oct to Apr C$119–$999 (US$81–$679) double; May C$159–$999 (US$108–$679) double. Extra person C$10 (US$6.80). Children under 18 stay free in parents' room. Packages available. AE, DC, DISC, MC, V. Valet parking C$16 (US$11), self-parking C$8 (US$5.45). **Amenities:** 2 restaurants, including penthouse dining room with buf-fet menus and nightly live band in season; indoor pool; health club; spa; concierge; tour desk; shopping arcade; limited room service; dry cleaning. *In room:* A/C, TV with pay movies, hair dryer.

MODERATE

The Americana
The Americana is one of the nicer moderately priced motels on this strip. It sits on 10 hectares (25 acres), with a pleasant picnic area and two swimming pools. The large rooms are well appointed and have generously proportioned bathrooms with vanity sinks. Some suites contain Jacuzzis and fireplaces.

8444 Lundy's Lane, Niagara Falls, ON L2H 1H4. © **800/263-3508** or 905/356-8444. Fax 905/356-8576. www.americananiagara.com. 120 units. Late June to Aug C$99–$229 (US$67–$156) double; Sept to mid-June C$59–$129 (US$40–$88) double. Extra person C$10 (US$6.80). AE, DISC, MC, V. Free parking. **Ameni-ties:** Dining room; lounge; coffee shop; indoor pool; outdoor pool; tennis court; squash court; spa; Jacuzzi; sauna; children's center; concierge; tour desk; shopping arcade; limited room service; in-room massage; babysitting; dry cleaning. *In room:* A/C, TV, hair dryer.

Holiday Inn by the Falls
In a prime location right behind the Skylon Tower, this hotel lies only minutes from the falls. It's *not* part of the international chain—the owner had the name first and refuses to sell it. Rooms are large, with ample closet space, an additional vanity sink, and modern furnishings. Most units have balconies, and there are two swimming pools.

5339 Murray St. (at Buchanan), Niagara Falls, ON L2G 2J3. © **905/356-1333.** 122 units. Late June to Labour Day C$125–$195 (US$85–$133) double; spring and fall C$75–$155 (US$51–$105) double; winter C$64–$109 (US$44–$74) double. Extra person C$10 (US$6.80); rollaway C$10 (US$6.80); crib C$5 (US$3.40). AE, DC, DISC, MC, V. Free parking. **Amenities:** Restaurant (steakhouse, pizzeria, and bar); lounge; indoor lap pool; outdoor heated pool; exercise room. *In room:* A/C, TV.

Michael's Inn
At this four-story white building overlooking the Niagara River Gorge, the large rooms are nicely decorated and have modern conven-iences. Many are Jacuzzi-theme rooms, like the Garden of Paradise or Scarlett O'Hara room (with a heart-shaped Jacuzzi). Luxurious amenities include a skylit indoor swimming pool, sauna, and fitness center.

5599 River Rd., Niagara Falls, ON L2E 3H3. © **800/263-9390** or 905/354-2727. Fax 905/374-7706. www. michaelsinn.com. 130 units. June–Sept 15 C$98–$208 (US$67–$141) double; Sept 16–May C$59–$178

(US$40–$121) double. AE, DC, MC, V. Free parking. **Amenities:** Restaurant; lounge; indoor pool; fitness center; sauna; game room; tour desk; babysitting; limited room service. *In room:* A/C, TV, dataport, hair dryer iron.

INEXPENSIVE
Nelson Motel   For budget accommodations, try the Nelson Motel, run by John and Dawn Pavlakovich. The lodgings have character, especially the family units—each has a double bedroom and an adjoining twin-bedded room for the kids. Regular units have modern furniture. Singles have a shower only. All units face the fenced-in pool and neatly trimmed lawn. The Nelson Motel is a short drive from the falls, overlooking the Niagara River.

10655 Niagara River Pkwy., Niagara Falls, ON L2E 6S6. ☎ 905/295-4754. 25 units. June 16–Sept 12 C$60–$100 (US$41–$68) double; mid-Mar to June 15 and Sept 13 to mid-Nov C$45–$55 (US$31–$44) double. Closed mid-Nov to mid-Mar. Rollaway or crib C$10–$20 (US$6.80–$14). MC, V. Free parking. **Amenities:** Outdoor pool. *In room:* A/C, TV, no phone.

The Skyline Inn   Right by Casino Niagara, behind the Skyline and the Sheraton hotels, the Village Inn has unusually large rooms. Some suites measure 700 square feet and contain a bedroom with two double beds and a living room. Because of its proximity to the casino, it's a popular choice with people who want to spend some time gambling.

5685 Falls Ave., Niagara Falls, ON L2E 6W7. ☎ 800/263-7135 or 905/374-4444. www.niagarafallshotels. com. 205 units. Mid-June to Oct C$79–$249 (US$54–$169) double; Nov to mid-June C$59–$179 (US$40–$122) double. Packages available. AE, DC, DISC, MC, V. Parking C$4 (US$2.70). **Amenities:** Restaurant; indoor pool; tour desk; shopping arcade. *In room:* A/C, TV.

A PLACE TO STAY IN NEARBY QUEENSTON
South Landing Inn ☆   The original section of Queenston's South Landing Inn was built in the 1800s. Today it has five attractive rooms with early Canadian furnishings, including four-poster beds. Other rooms are across the street in the modern annex. There's a distant view of the river from the original inn's balcony. In the original building, you'll also find a cozy dining room, with red-gingham-covered tables, that serves breakfast (C$5/US$3.40), lunch, and dinner.

Corner of Kent and Front sts. (P.O. Box 269), Queenston, ON L0S 1L0. ☎ 905/262-4634. Fax 905/262-4639. 23 units. Mid-Apr to Oct C$95–$125 (US$65–$85) double; Nov to mid-Apr C$65–$75 (US$44–$51) double. AE, MC, V. Free parking. Follow Niagara Pkwy. to Queenston; turn right at Kent St. **Amenities:** Dining room. *In room:* A/C, TV, hair dryer.

WHERE TO DINE
Niagara Falls has never been a culinary hotbed, though you can find standard fare at decent prices. If you want to dine well, reserve a table at one of the dining rooms in the wine-country towns of Jordan, Virgil, or Vineland (see listings earlier in this chapter).

Alternatives in Niagara Falls include the **Pinnacle,** 6732 Oakes Dr. (☎ **905/ 356-1501**), which offers a Canadian and continental menu and a remarkable view from the top of the Minolta Tower. There's also a vista from atop the 159m (520-ft.) tower at the **Skylon Tower Restaurants,** 5200 Robinson St. (☎ **905/ 356-2651**, ext. 259). The Summit Suite dining room serves reasonably priced breakfast, lunch, and dinner buffets; the Revolving Restaurant features pricier continental fare for lunch and dinner.

EXPENSIVE

Casa d'Oro ITALIAN   Don't be intimidated by the wealth of kitsch—gilt busts of Caesar, Venetian-style lamps, statues of Roman gladiators, and murals of Roman and Venetian scenes. Start with clams casino or *brodetto Antonio* (a giant crouton topped with poached eggs, floating on savory broth, accompanied by grated cheese). Follow with specialties like saltimbocca alla romana or sole basilica (flavored with lime juice, paprika, and basil). Finish with a selection from the dessert wagon, or spoil yourself with cherries jubilee or bananas flambé.

5875 Victoria Ave. (℃ 877/296-1178 or 905/356-5646; www.thecasadoro.com. Reservations recommended. Main courses C$16–$40 (US$11–$27). AE, DC, DISC, MC, V. Mon–Fri 11:30am–10pm, Sat 4–11pm, Sun 11:30am–10pm.

MODERATE

Betty's Restaurant & Tavern *(Value)* CANADIAN   Betty's is a local favorite for hearty food at fair prices. It's a family dining room where the staff will attempt to stuff you to the gills with massive platters of fish-and-chips, roast beef, and seafood. All include soup or juice, vegetable, and potato. There are burgers and sandwiches, too. It's all but impossible to save room for the enormous portions of home-baked pies. Breakfast and lunch also offer good budget eating.

8921 Sodom Rd. (℃ 905/295-4436. www.bettysrestaurant.com. Reservations only for groups of 8 or more. Main courses C$8–$16 (US$5.45–$11). AE, MC, V. Daily 8am–8pm.

Happy Wanderer GERMAN   Warm hospitality reigns at the chalet-style Happy Wanderer, which offers a full selection of schnitzels, wursts, and other German specialties. Beer steins and game trophies adorn the walls. At lunch there are omelets, cold platters, sandwiches, and burgers. Dinner might start with goulash soup and proceed with bratwurst, knockwurst, rauchwurst (served with sauerkraut and potato salad), or a Wiener schnitzel, Holstein, or jaeger. All entrees include potatoes, salad, and rye bread. Desserts include, naturally, Black Forest cake and apple strudel.

6405 Stanley Ave. (℃ 905/354-9825. Reservations not accepted. Main courses C$10–$26 (US$6.80–$18). AE, MC, V. Daily 9am–11pm.

NIAGARA PARKWAY COMMISSION RESTAURANTS

The Niagara Parkway Commission has commandeered the most spectacular scenic spots, where it operates reasonably priced dining outlets. They serve traditional family-style food at lunch and dinner, and do not accept reservations. **Table Rock Restaurant** (℃ 905/354-3631) and **Victoria Park Restaurant** (℃ 905/356-2217), on the parkway right by the falls, are both pleasant, if crowded. **Diner on the Green** (℃ 905/356-7221) is also on the parkway, at the Whirlpool Golf Course near Queenston. It's very plain. Queenston Heights offers the best dining experience.

Queenston Heights Restaurant CANADIAN   The star of the Niagara Parkway Commission's eateries stands dramatically atop Queenston Heights. Set in the park among firs, cypresses, silver birches, and maples, the open-air balcony affords a magnificent view of the lower Niagara River and the rich fruit-growing land through which it flows. Or you can sit under the cathedral ceiling in a room where the flue of the stone fireplace reaches to the roof. Dinner options might include fillet of Atlantic salmon with Riesling-chive hollandaise, prime rib, or grilled pork with apples and cider–Dijon mustard sauce. Afternoon tea is served from 3 to 5pm in the summer. If nothing else, go for a drink on the deck and enjoy the terrific view.

14276 Niagara Pkwy. © **905/262-4274.** Reservations recommended. Main courses C$21–$30 (US$14–$20). AE, MC, V. Daily 11:30am–3pm; Sun–Fri 5–9pm, Sat 5–10pm. Closed Jan to mid-Mar.

4 Hamilton

75km (47 miles) SW of Toronto

On a landlocked harbor spanned at its entrance by the Burlington Skyway's dramatic sweep, Hamilton has long been nicknamed "Steeltown" for its industrial roots. Since the early 1990s however, Hamilton has been making a name for itself with its ever-expanding list of attractions. It takes less than an hour to drive here from Toronto, and it's well worth a day trip for the whole family.

ESSENTIALS

VISITOR INFORMATION   The Hamilton Tourist Information Centre has been relocated to 1 James St. S., 8th Floor, Hamilton, ON L8P 4R5 (© **800/ 263-8590** or 905/546-2666; www.city.hamilton.on.ca). It has a wealth of information about what to see and do, as well as where to dine and sleep. Its year-round hours run from Monday through Friday, 9am to 5pm.

GETTING THERE   Hamilton is easy to get to by car. From Toronto, take the Queen Elizabeth Way (signs read QEW) to Hamilton. The drive will take about an hour.

   GO (Government of Ontario) Transit is a commuter train that connects Toronto and Hamilton. Call © **800/438-6646** or 416/869-3200 for information. The **John C. Munro Hamilton International Airport** (© **905/679-8359;** www.yhm.com) has long been popular with cargo carriers and is now a hub for WestJet.

WHAT TO SEE & DO

Hamilton's downtown core is best explored on foot, though you may want a car to visit attractions in the outlying areas.

Canadian Warplane Heritage Museum   This interactive museum charts the course of Canadian aviation from the beginning of World War II to the present. Visitors can climb into the cockpits of WWII trainer crafts or a CF-100 jet fighter. The most popular attractions are the flight simulators, which allow aspiring pilots to test their flight skills. There are also short documentary films, photographs, and other memorabilia. The aircraft on display include rarities like the Avro Lancaster bomber and the deHavilland Vampire fighter jet. The collection also includes a variety of military and transport craft.

9280 Airport Rd. (at the John C. Munro Hamilton International Airport), Mount Hope. © **877/347-3359** or 905/670-3347. www.warplane.com. Admission C$10 (US$6.80) adults, C$8 (US$5.45) seniors and youths 8–18; free for children 7 and under; family admission for 2 adults and 2 youths is C$30 (US$20). Fri–Wed 9am–5pm, Thurs 9am–8pm.

Dundurn Castle   The castle affords a glimpse of the opulent life as it was lived in this part of southern Ontario in the mid–19th century. Sir Allan Napier Mac-Nab, prime minister of the United Provinces of Canada in the mid-1850s and a founder of the Great Western Railway built it between 1832 and 1835; Queen Victoria knighted him for the part he played in the Rebellion of 1837. The 35-plus-room mansion has been restored and furnished in the style of 1855. The gray stucco exterior, with its classical Greek portico, is impressive enough, but inside, from the formal dining rooms to Lady MacNab's boudoir, the furnishings are rich. The museum contains a fascinating collection of Victoriana. In December, the castle is decorated splendidly for a Victorian Christmas.

Dundurn Park, York Blvd. ℭ **905/546-2872.** Admission C$7 (US$4.75) adults, C$6 (US$4.10) seniors, C$5.50 (US$3.75) students, and C$3 (US$2.05) children 6–14; free for children 5 and under. Victoria Day to Labour Day, daily 10am–4:30pm; the rest of the year, Tues–Sun noon–4pm (closed Jan 1, Dec 25, and Dec 26).

Royal Botanical Gardens ⟨✿⟩   Situated just north of the city, the Royal Botanical Gardens spreads over 1,214 glorious hectares (3,000 acres). The Rock Garden features spring bulbs in May, summer flowers in June to September, and chrysanthemums in October. The Laking Garden blazes during June and July with irises, peonies, and lilies. The arboretum fills with the heady scent of lilac from the end of May to early June, and the exquisite color bursts of rhododendrons and azaleas thereafter. The Centennial Rose Garden is at its best late June to mid-September.

The gardens hosts many festivals during the year, including the Mediterranean Food & Wine Festival in February, the popular Ontario Garden Show in early April, the Tulip Festival in May, the Rose Society Show in June, and the Japanese Flower Society Show in September.

Should you work up an appetite while strolling the grounds, there are several on-site dining options, including the Gardens Café, which is open year-round, and the Rock Garden Tea House or the Turner Pavilion (both open throughout the summer).

680 Plains Rd. W., Burlington ℭ **905/527-1158.** www.rbg.ca. Admission C$8 (US$5.45) adults, C$6.50 (US$4.40) for students 13–17 and for seniors, C$2.50 (US$1.70) for kids 5–12, free for children 4 and under. Daily 9:30am–dusk.

African Lion Safari ⟨✿⟩   Just a half-hour drive northwest of Hamilton, you'll find a mirror image of a traditional zoo: at the African Lion Safari, visitors remain caged in their cars or in a tour bus while the animals roam wild and free. The 300-hectare (750-acre) wildlife park contains rhino, cheetah, lion, tiger, giraffe, zebra, vultures, and many other species. In addition to the safari, the cost of admission covers other attractions like the cruise aboard the African Queen, during which a tour guide will take you around the lake and point out local inhabitants like spider monkeys, crested macaques, and ring-tailed lemurs. There's also a train that will take you through a forest populated by snapping turtles, among other wildlife.

The park has three baby Asian elephants: Samson, Albert, and George. And the elephant bathing event, which occurs daily, will particularly fascinate the kids. There's also a Pets' Corner filled with frisky otters and pot-bellied pigs. There are several play areas for children as well, including the Misumu Bay water park (bring bathing suits!).

Safari Rd, Cambridge. ℭ **800/461-WILD** or 519/623-2620. www.lionsafari.com. Admission C$23 (US$16) adults and youths, C$19 (US$13) seniors, and C$17 (US$12) children 3–12; free for children 2 and under. Late June to Labour Day, daily 10am–5:30pm; late Apr to mid-June and from early Sept to early Oct, daily 9am–4pm; closed mid-Oct to mid-Apr.

WHERE TO STAY

Because Hamilton is so close to Toronto, it's easy to make a day trip here and back, rather than pulling up stakes and spending the night here. However, if you do want to stay in the area, several well-known chains have hotels here, including **Sheraton** (ℭ **800/514-7101** or 905/529-5515) and **Howard Johnson** (ℭ **800/263-8558** or 905/546-8111).

Hamilton

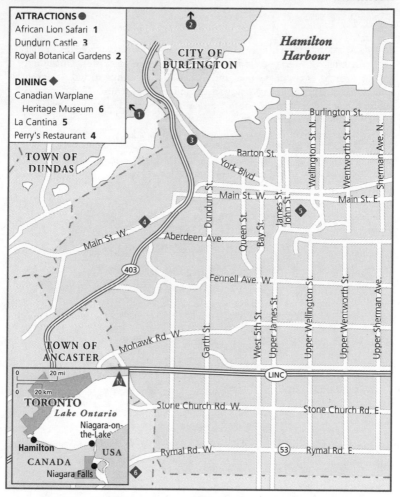

WHERE TO DINE

The suggested restaurants in St. Catharine's and Welland, such as Café Garibaldi, Iseya, and Rinderlin's, are just a short drive away from Hamilton. However, Hamilton has a few restaurants worth checking out, too.

La Cantina ⟨£⟩   This is really two restaurants in one: there's a formal dining room, which serves up elegant plates like veal scaloppini in a dry Marsala sauce, and seared ostrich medallions cooked with Pinot Noir; equally elegant pasta plates include rotini with ham and peppers in a vodka sauce. Then there's the casual pizzeria, which serves up more than 20 varieties of pizza, ranging from the traditional Quattro Stagione (four seasons) with prosciutto, artichokes, olives and mozzarella, to the unusual Gamberi, which is topped with shrimp, smoked, salmon, olives, eggplant, and pesto. This is a very popular spot, so try to make a reservation or arrive early, especially at lunch. If you're very lucky, you might just secure a seat in the restaurant's garden patio.

60 Walnut St. S. ⓒ **905/521-8989.** Reservations recommended. Main courses C$10–$26 (US$6.80–$18). AE, MC, V.

Perry's Restaurant This casual family-style restaurant has a large menu that has something for everyone. It borrows from a range of cuisines, including Italian, French, Mexican, Greek, and American. Offerings include chicken souvlaki, rack of ribs, hearty sandwiches, and fish and chips. There are also lighter options such as salads, soups, and chicken fingers. There's a sunny patio at the front of the restaurant, too.

1088 Main St. W. ⓒ **905/527-3779.** Main courses C$6–$13 (US$4.10–$8.85). MC, V. Daily 11:30am–1am.

Appendix A:
Toronto in Depth

In less than 300 years, Toronto has grown from a trading post to a vibrant international capital. Read on to get a sense of how it happened.

1 History 101

FROM FUR TRADING POST TO MUDDY YORK

As in most cities, the influences of geography, trade, and communications shaped Toronto and its history. Although the city today possesses a downtown core, it also sprawls across a large area—a gift of geography, for there are no physical barriers to stop it. When European settlement began, the broad plain rising from Lake Ontario to an inland ridge of hills (around today's St. Clair Ave.), and stretching between the Don River in the east and the Humber in the west, made the location ideal.

Native Canadians had long stopped here—at the entrance to the Toronto Trail, a short route between the Lower and Upper lakes. In 1615, French fur trader Etienne Brûleé was the first European to travel the trail. It wasn't until 1720 that the French established the first trading post, known as Fort Toronto, to intercept the furs that were being taken across Lake Ontario to New York State by English rivals. Fort Rouille, built on the site of today's CNE grounds, replaced the trading post in 1751. When the 1763 Treaty of Paris ended the Anglo-French War after the fall of Quebec, French rule in North America effectively ended, and the city's French antecedents were all but forgotten.

Only 32km (20 miles) across the lake from the United States, Toronto has always been affected by what happens south of the border. When the

Dateline

- **1615** Etienne Brûleé travels the Toronto Trail. "Toronto" is derived from a Huron term for "place of meeting."
- **1720** France establishes post at Toronto.
- **1751** French build Fort Rouille.
- **1759** Fort Rouille burned during British conquest.
- **1763** Treaty of Paris effectively ends French rule in Canada.
- **1787** Lord Dorchester, British governor of Quebec, purchases land from Scarborough to Etobicoke from the Mississauga tribe.
- **1793** Governor of Upper Canada, Col. John Simcoe, arrives and names settlement York. It becomes capital of Upper Canada.
- **1796** Yonge Street laid out, a 53km (33-mile) oxcart trail.
- **1812–15** War of 1812, between United States and England, uses Canada as a battleground. In 1813, Americans invade, blow up Fort York, and burn Parliament buildings. In 1814, U.S. troops are driven out of Canada.
- **1820s** Immigration of Nonconformists and Irish Catholics fosters reform politics.
- **1828** Erie Canal extended to Oswego on Lake Ontario.
- **1830s** Orange Order becomes prominent influence in politics.
- **1832–34** Cholera epidemics.
- **1834** City named Toronto; City Council replaces magistrates; William Lyon Mackenzie becomes first mayor.

continues

American Revolution established a powerful, potentially hostile new nation, Toronto's location became strategically more important, or so it seemed to John Graves Simcoe. He was lieutenant governor of the newly formed province of Upper Canada, which had been established in 1791 to administer the frontiers—from Kingston and Quinte's Isle to Windsor and beyond—settled largely by Loyalists fleeing the Revolution. To Simcoe, Toronto was more defensible than Fort Niagara and a natural arsenal for Lake Ontario, which also afforded easy access to Lake Huron and the interior.

The governor had already purchased a vast tract of land from the Mississauga tribe for the paltry sum of £1,700 (US$2,600), plus blankets, guns, rum, and tobacco. In 1793, Lieutenant Governor Simcoe, his wife, Elizabeth, and the Queen's Rangers arrived. Simcoe ordered a garrison built, renamed the settlement York, and laid it out in a 10-block rectangle around King, Front, George, Duke, and Berkeley streets. Beyond stretched a series of 100-acre lots from Queen to Bloor, which were granted to mollify government officials, who resented having to move to the mosquito-plagued, marshy outpost. Its muddiness was prodigious, and in fact a story is told of a fellow who saw a hat lying in the middle of a street, went to pick it up, and found the head of a live man submerged below it! In 3 short years a small hamlet had grown, and Simcoe had laid out Yonge Street—then a 53km (33-mile) oxcart trail. Four years later the first Parliament meeting confirmed York as the capital of Upper Canada.

FROM MUDDY YORK TO THE FAMILY COMPACT The officials were a more demanding and finicky lot than the sturdy frontier farmers, and businesses sprang up to serve them. By 1812, the population had

- 1837 Former mayor Mackenzie leads rebellion sparked by economic downturn.
- 1840s–50s Mass Irish immigration.
- 1841 Act of Union establishes the United Province of Canada, with Kingston as ruling seat; Toronto loses status as a capital.
- 1843 The university, King's College, opens.
- 1844 City Hall built. George Brown founds the *Globe*.
- 1849 Great fire destroys much of city. Anglican King's College converts to secular University of Toronto.
- 1851 Population 30,000 (33% Irish). Anglican Trinity College founded. St. Lawrence Hall built.
- 1852 Toronto Stock Exchange opens. Grand Trunk Railroad charted, linking Quebec, Montreal, Toronto, Guelph, and Sarnia.
- 1853 St. James Cathedral completed.
- 1858 Storm creates the Toronto Islands.
- 1861 Horse-powered street railway runs along Yonge to Yorkville.
- 1867 Canadian Confederation; Toronto becomes capital of new province of Ontario.
- 1868 Canada First movement begins.
- 1869 Eaton's department store opens.
- 1871 Population 56,000.
- 1872 Simpson's department store opens.
- 1876 John Ross Robertson starts *Evening Telegram,* which wields influence for next 90 years.
- 1886 Provincial parliament buildings erected in Queen's Park.
- 1893 First Stanley Cup played.
- 1896 *Maclean's* newsmagazine started.
- 1901 Population 208,000.
- 1903 The dramatic short film *Hiawatha* is the first movie made in Canada.
- 1904 Great Fire burns much of downtown.
- 1906 First autos produced by Canada Cycle and Motor Company. Toronto Symphony founded.
- 1907 Bell strike broken. Royal Alexandra opens. The Lord's Day Act forbids all public activity except churchgoing on Sunday.

grown to 703 and included a brewer-baker, blacksmith, watchmaker, chair-maker, apothecary, hatter, and tailor.

During the War of 1812, despite initial victories at Queenston and Detroit, Canada was under siege. In April 1813, 14 ships carrying 1,700 American troops invaded York, blew up the incomplete fort, burned the Parliament buildings, and carried off the mace (which was not returned until 1934). The British general burned a 30-gun warship, the *Sir Isaac Brock,* which was under construction, and retreated, leaving young John Strachan to negotiate the capitulation. This event did much to reinforce the town's pro-British, anti-American attitude—a feeling that persists to some extent to this day. In retaliation for the burning of Fort York, some Canadians went to Washington and torched the American president's residence. (The Americans later white-washed it to hide the charred wood—hence, the White House.)

A conservative pro-British outlook permeated the official political oligarchy that dominated York, a group dubbed the Family Compact. Many of the names on street signs, subway stops, and maps derive from this august group of early government officers and their families. Among them were William Jarvis, a New England Loyalist who became provincial secretary; John Beverley Robinson, son of a Virginia Loyalist, who became attorney general at age 22 and later chief justice of Upper Canada; and Scottish-educated Dr. John Strachan, a schoolmaster who became an Anglican rector and, eventually, the most powerful figure in York. Anglo-Irish Dr. William Warren Baldwin, doctor, lawyer, architect, judge, and parliamentarian, laid out Spadina Avenue as a thoroughfare leading to his country house; the Boultons were prominent lawyers, judges, and politicians—Judge D'Arcy

- **1909** Florence Nightingale Graham drops out of nursing school in Toronto, changes her name to Elizabeth Arden, and founds the first cosmetics empire.
- **1911** Founding members of the Group of Seven meet at the Toronto Arts and Letters Club.
- **1912** Garment workers' strike broken. Royal Ontario Museum founded.
- **1914** New Union Station built.
- **1914–18** World War 1; 70,000 Torontonians enlist, and 13,000 die.
- **1920** The Art Gallery of Toronto mounts the first Group of Seven exhibit.
- **1921** Population 521,893.
- **1922** University of Toronto researchers Frederick Banting and Charles Best discover insulin.
- **1923** Dr. Banting is awarded the Nobel Prize in medicine. Parliament passes the Chinese Exclusion Act. Ernest Hemingway moves to Toronto to become a reporter for the *Star.*
- **1930s** Depression; thousands go on relief.
- **1931** Maple Leaf Gardens built as home base for the Maple Leafs.
- **1938** Toronto native Joseph Shuster creates Superman.
- **1939** Canada enters World War II; thousands of troops leave from Union Station.
- **1940–45** Toronto functions as war supplier.
- **1947** Cocktail lounges approved.
- **1950** Sunday sports allowed.
- **1951** Population 31% foreign-born.
- **1954** Metro created; Toronto becomes a model for urban consolidation. Toronto native Marilyn Bell, 16, becomes first person to swim across Lake Ontario. In October, Hurricane Hazel kills 83 people in Toronto.
- **1959** York University, Toronto's second major institution of higher education, opens.
- **1960** Movies are shown in Toronto on Sunday for the first time.
- **1961** Population 42% foreign-born.
- **1963** Ryerson Polytechnic University founded.

continues

Boulton built a mansion, the Grange, which later became the core of the art museum and still stands today.

These men, extremely conscious of rank, were conformist, conservative, pro-British, Tory, and Anglican. Their power was broken only later in the 19th century, as a larger and more diverse population gave reformers a chance to challenge their control. But even today, their influence lingers in the corporate world, where a handful of companies and individuals control 80% of the companies on the Toronto Stock Exchange.

THE EARLY 1800s—CANAL, RAILROAD & IMMIGRATION

The changes that eventually diluted their control began in the early 19th century. During the 1820s, 1830s, and 1840s, immigrants—Irish Protestants and Catholics, Scots, Presbyterians, Methodists, and other Nonconformists—poured in to settle the frontier farmlands. By 1832 York had become the largest urban community in the province, with a population of 1,600. Already well established commercially as a supply center, York enjoyed another boost when the Erie Canal was extended to Oswego on Lake Ontario, giving it direct access to New York, and the Welland Canal was built across the Niagara Peninsula, allowing access to Lake Erie and points beyond. In 1834 the city was incorporated and York became Toronto, a city bounded by Parliament Street to the east, Bathurst to the west, the lakefront to the south, and 400 yards north of the current Queen Street (then called Lot) to the north. Outside this area—west to Dufferin Street, east to the Don River, and north to Bloor Street—lay the "liberties," out of which the city would later carve new wards. North of Bloor, local brewer Joseph Bloor and Sheriff Jarvis were already drawing up plans for the village of Yorkville.

- **1965** New City Hall at Nathan Phillips Square is unveiled. Canada and the United States sign the Autopact, creating boom times in Toronto and nearby Oshawa.
- **1966** U.S. draft dodgers start fleeing to Canada; many settle in Toronto.
- **1970s** Influx of immigration from Asia, Africa, India, Pakistan, the Caribbean, and Latin America.
- **1974** Mikhail Baryshnikov defects from the USSR during a trip to Toronto.
- **1975** Toronto International Film Festival founded. CN Tower becomes the world's tallest freestanding structure.
- **1980s** Creation and expansion of the Greater Toronto area, including nearby cities of Hamilton and Oshawa.
- **1981** Population 3,898,933.
- **1984** City's 150th anniversary.
- **1989** SkyDome opens, drawing wide criticism of its C$570 million (US$388 million) cost.
- **1992** Residents of Toronto Islands win 40-year struggle to retain their homes. Blue Jays win World Series for the first time.
- **1993** Blue Jays repeat as World Series champions.
- **1995** Progressive Conservative Government elected.
- **1996** Population 4,263,757. *Fortune* magazine names Toronto best city in the world to live and work in. University of Toronto professor John Polanyi wins Nobel Prize in Chemistry.
- **1997** Protests in Queen's Park target social-service cuts and the passage of Bill 103, creating a megacity.
- **1998** Toronto becomes a megacity anyway.
- **1999** Researchers at McMaster University in Hamilton discover unusual characteristics of Einstein's brain. The new Air Canada Centre becomes home to the Maple Leafs and the Raptors.
- **2001** Toronto loses its bid to host the 2008 Olympics to Beijing.
- **2002** Toronto hosts the first World Youth Day ever held in Canada; the event includes a visit by Pope John Paul II.

As more immigrants arrived, the population grew more diverse, and demands arose for democracy and reform. Among the reformers were such leaders as Francis Collins, who launched the radical paper *Canadian Freeman* in 1825; lawyer William Draper; and, perhaps most famous of all, fiery William Lyon Mackenzie, who was elected Toronto's first mayor in 1834.

Mackenzie had started his *Colonial Advocate* to crusade against the narrow-minded Family Compact, calling for reform and challenging their power to such an extent that some of them dumped his presses into the lake. By 1837, Mackenzie, undaunted, was calling for open rebellion.

A severe depression, financial turmoil, and the failure of some banks all contributed to the 1837 Rebellion, one of the most dramatic events in the city's history. On December 5, the rebels, a scruffy bunch of about 700, gathered at Montgomery's Tavern outside the city (near modern-day Eglinton Ave.). Led by Mackenzie on a white mare, they marched on the city. Two days later the city's militia, called out by Sheriff Jarvis, scattered the rebels at Carlton Street. Both sides then turned and ran. Reinforcements arrived, pursued the rebels, and bombarded the tavern with cannonballs. Mackenzie fled to the United States, and two other leaders—Lount and Matthews—were hanged. Their graves are in the Necropolis cemetery.

Between 1834 and 1884 the foundations of an industrial city were laid: Toronto gained water works, gas, and public transportation. Many municipal facilities were built, including a city hall, the Royal Lyceum Theatre (1848) on King near Bay, the Toronto Stock Exchange (1852), St. Lawrence Hall (1851), an asylum, and a jail.

During the 1850s the building of the railroads accelerated the economic pace. By 1860, Toronto was at the center of a railroad web. It became the trading hub for lumber and grain imports and exports. Merchant empires were founded, railroad magnates emerged, and institutions like the Bank of Toronto were established.

Despite its growth and wealth, Toronto still lagged behind Montreal, which had twice Toronto's population in 1861. But Toronto increasingly took advantage of its superior links to the south, and that edge eventually helped it overtake its rival. Under the Confederation of 1867, the city was guaranteed another advantage: As the capital of the newly created Ontario, Toronto, in effect, controlled the minerals and timber of the north.

During this mid-Victorian period the growth of a more diverse population continued. In 1847, Irish famine victims began flooding into Toronto, and by 1851 and 1852 the Irish-born were the city's largest single ethnic group. While many of them were Ulster Protestants who did not threaten the Anglo-Protestant ascendancy, the newcomers were not always welcomed—a pattern that repeated whenever a new immigrant group threatened to change the shape and order of society. As the gap between the number of Anglicans and Catholics closed, sectarian tensions increased, and the old-country Orange and Green conflicts flared into mob violence.

LATE- & HIGH-VICTORIAN TORONTO   Between 1871 and 1891 the city's population more than tripled, shooting from 56,000 to 181,000. The burgeoning urban market helped spawn two great Toronto retailers—Timothy Eaton and Robert Simpson—who moved to Toronto from Ontario towns to open stores at Queen and Yonge streets in 1869 and 1872, respectively. Eaton developed his reputation on fixed prices, cash sales only, and promises of refunds

if the customer wasn't satisfied—all unique gambits at the time. Simpson copied Eaton and competed by providing better service, such as two telephones to take orders instead of one. Both enterprises developed into full-fledged department stores, and both entered the mail-order business, conquering the country with their catalogs.

The business of the city was business, and amassing wealth was the pastime of such figures as Henry Pellatt, stockbroker, president of the Electrical Development Company, and builder of Casa Loma; E. B. Osler; George Albertus Cox; and A. R. Ames. Although these men were self-made entrepreneurs, not Family Compact officials, they formed a traditional socially conservative elite, linked by money, taste, investments, and religious affiliation. And they were staunchly British. They and the rest of the citizens celebrated the Queen's Jubilee in 1897 with gusto, and gave Toronto boys a rousing send-off to fight in the Boer War in 1899. The prominent businessmen also had a fondness for clubs—the Albany Club for the Conservatives, and the National Club for the Liberals. As in England, their sports clubs (notably the Royal Yacht Club, the Toronto Cricket Club, the Toronto Golf Club, and the Lawn Tennis Club) carried a certain cachet.

The boom spurred new commercial and residential construction. Projects included the first steel-frame building—the Board of Trade Building (1889)—at Yonge and Front—George Gooderham's Romanesque-style mansion (1890) at St. George and Bloor (now the York Club), the provincial parliament buildings in Queen's Park (1886–92), and the city hall (1899) at Queen and Bay. Public transit improved, and by 1891 the city had 109km (68 miles) of tracks for horse-drawn cars. Electric lights, telephones, and electric streetcars appeared in the 1890s.

FROM 1900 TO 1933   Between 1901 and 1921 the population more than doubled, climbing from 208,000 to 521,893. The economy continued to expand, fueled by the lumber, mining, wholesale, and agricultural machinery industries, and after 1911 by hydroelectric power. Toronto began to seriously challenge Montreal. Much of the new wealth went into construction, and three marvelous buildings from this era can still be seen today: the Horticultural Building at the Exhibition Grounds (1907), the King Edward Hotel (1903), and Union Station (1914–19). Most of the earlier wooden structures had been destroyed in the Great Fire of 1904, which wiped out 5.6 hectares (14 acres) of downtown.

The booming economy and its factories attracted a wave of new immigrants—mostly Italians and Jews from Russia and Eastern Europe—who settled in the city's emerging ethnic enclaves. By 1912, Kensington Market was well established, and the garment center and Jewish community were firmly ensconced around King and Spadina. Little Italy clustered around College and Grace. By 1911 more than 30,000 Torontonians were foreign-born, and the slow march to change the English character of the city had begun.

It was still a city of churches worthy of the name "Toronto the Good," with a population of staunch religious conservatives, who barely voted for Sunday streetcar service in 1897 and in 1912 banned tobogganing on Sunday. As late as 1936, 30 men were arrested at the lakeshore resort of Sunnyside because they exposed their chests—even though the temperature was 105°F! In 1947, cocktail lounges were approved, but it wasn't until 1950 that playing sports on Sunday became legal.

Increased industrialization brought social problems, largely concentrated in Cabbagetown and the Ward, a large area that stretched west of Yonge and north of Queen. Here, poor people lived in crowded, wretched conditions: Housing was inadequate, health conditions poor, and rag-picking or sweatshop labor the only employment.

As industry grew, unionism also increased, but the movement, as in the United States, failed to organize politically. Two major strikes—at Bell in 1907 and in the garment industry in 1912—were easily broken.

The larger, wealthier city also became an intellectual and cultural magnet. Artists like Charles Jefferys, J. H. MacDonald, Arthur Lismer, Tom Thomson, Lawren Harris, Frederick Varley, and A. Y. Jackson, most associated with the Group of Seven, set up studios in Toronto. Their first group show opened in 1920. Toronto also became the English-language publishing center of the nation, and national magazines like *Maclean's* (1896) and *Saturday Night* were launched. The Art Gallery of Ontario, the Royal Ontario Museum, the Toronto Symphony Orchestra, and the Royal Alexandra Theatre all opened before 1914.

Women advanced, too, at the turn of the century. In 1880, Emily Jennings Stowe became the first Canadian woman authorized to practice medicine. In 1886, the university admitted women. Clara Brett Martin was the first woman admitted to the law courts. The women's suffrage movement gained strength, led by Dr. Stowe, Flora McDonald Denison, and the Women's Christian Temperance Union.

During World War I, Toronto sent 70,000 men to the trenches; about 13,000 were killed. At home, the war had a great impact economically and socially: Toronto became Canada's chief aviation center; factories, shipyards, and power facilities expanded to meet the needs of war; and women entered the workforce in great numbers.

After the war the city took on much more of the aspect and tone that characterize it today. Automobiles appeared on the streets—the Canadian Cycle and Motor Company had begun manufacturing them in 1906 (the first parking ticket was given in 1908), and one or two skyscrapers appeared. Although 80% of the population was of British origin, ethnic enclaves were clearly defined.

The 1920s roared along, fueled by a mining boom that saw Bay Street turned into a veritable gold-rush alley where everyone was pushing something hot. The Great Depression followed, inflicting 30% unemployment in 1933. The only distraction from its bleakness was the opening of Maple Leaf Gardens in 1931. Besides being an ice-hockey center, it also was host to large protest rallies during the Depression, and later such diverse entities as the Jehovah's Witnesses, Billy Graham, the Ringling Bros. Circus, and the Metropolitan Opera.

As in the United States, hostility toward new immigrants was rife during the '20s. It reached a peak in 1923, when the Chinese Exclusion Act was passed, banning Chinese immigration. In the 1930s antagonism toward Jews intensified. Signs such as NO JEWS, NIGGERS, OR DOGS were posted occasionally at Balmy and Kew beaches. In August 1933, the display of a swastika at Christie Pits caused a battle between Nazis and Jews.

AFTER WORLD WAR II   In 1939 Torontonians again rallied to the British cause, sending thousands to fight in Europe. At home, plants turned out fighter bombers and Bren guns, and people endured rationing—one bottle of liquor a month, and limited supplies of sugar and other staples—while they listened to the war-front news delivered by Lorne Greene.

Toronto Today

The past several years have been a tumultuous time for Toronto. The merger of its separate municipalities, rapid population growth, and provincial government budget slashing have all had a serious impact on the life of the city. It has also been a boom time, with construction of new arts and sports facilities, and a burgeoning dining and enter- tainment scene. Toronto is still the city of choice for arriving immi- grants: 300,000 Hong Kong émigrés have joined Toronto's Chinese community, and there have been influxes from Somalia, Eastern Europe, India, Pakistan, and Central America. Neighborhoods around town preserve these cultures. While their influence is strong in many areas, it is perhaps most visible to a short-term visitor in the city's diverse dining options and in Toronto's many cultural festivals.

FAREWELL 2008, HELLO 2012   Toronto made a Herculean effort to convince the International Olympic Committee that it would make the perfect host city for the 2008 Games, but it lost out to Beijing. Local gossip has it that Toronto is being "strongly encouraged" to go after the 2012 Games. In the meantime, local government is considering implementing some of the terrific plans that were drawn up to win over the IOC. Development along the waterfront is likely to proceed.

FIGHT CLUB   The bid for the 2008 Games led the municipal and provincial governments to put up a united front, but the smiles and handshakes were short-lived. (It wasn't that long ago that Toronto's mayor, Mel Lastman, compared the province's Minister of Labour to an "organ grinder's monkey".) The provincial government is a sore spot with Torontonians for many reasons, but most of all for its tendency to ride roughshod over the city. In January 1998, the six interdependent cities that made up Metro Toronto amalgamated into one megacity. The merger was anything but voluntary—two-thirds of the citizenry voted against it in a referendum—and the result was pandemonium: Services and standards had varied from municipality to municipality, and creating a common denominator was no mean feat. (unfortu- nately the lowest common denominator seems to have won out). As you'll undoubtedly discover in conversation with locals, this is a pet peeve with the majority of Toronto's citizens.

TROUBLE ON THE HOME FRONT   Toronto has few friends in the provincial government (perhaps because its citizens vote against it whenever given the opportunity). In addition to forcing the megacity merger through, the Conservative provincial government (or "Tories") cut social spending and reclaimed the land it was supposed to sell to the city for its new opera house. The most frequent complaint heard in Toronto is that the city's municipal taxes aren't reinvested in its infrastructure, but end up being funneled to less populous parts of the province. Funding hasn't even been guaranteed yet for the much- needed subway line under Sheppard Avenue; it is expected to be up and running in a limited capacity, but its future is uncertain.

Already prosperous by World War II, Toronto continued to expand during the 1940s. The suburbs alone added more than 200,000 to the population between 1940 and 1953. By the 1950s, the urban area had grown so large, disputes between city and suburbs were so frequent, and the need for social and other services was so great that an effective administrative solution was needed. In 1953, the Metro Council, composed of equal numbers of representatives from the city and the suburbs, was established.

Toronto became a major city in the 1950s, with Metro providing a structure for planning and growth. The Yonge subway opened, and a network of highways was constructed. It linked the city to the affluent suburbs. Don Mills, the first new town, was built between 1952 and 1962; Yorkdale Center, a mammoth shopping center, followed in 1964. American companies began locating branch plants in the area, fueling much of the growth.

The city also began to loosen up. While the old social elite (still traditionally educated at Upper Canada College, Ridley, and Trinity College) continued to dominate the boardrooms, politics, at least, had become more accessible and fluid. In 1954, Nathan Phillips became the first Jewish mayor, signifying how greatly the population had changed from the days when immigrants were primarily British, American, or French. In 1947, the Chinese Exclusion Act of 1923 was repealed, opening the door to relatives of Toronto's then-small Chinese community. After 1950, the door swung open further. Germans and Italians were allowed to enter, adding to the communities that were already established; then, under pressure from the United Nations, Poles, Ukrainians, Central European and Russian Jews, Yugoslavs, Estonians, Latvians, and other East Europeans poured in. Most arrived at Union Station, having journeyed from the ports of Halifax, Quebec City, and Montreal. At the beginning of the 1950s, the foreign-born were 31% of the population; by 1961, they were 42%, and the number of people claiming British descent had fallen from 73% to 59%. The 1960s brought an even richer mix of people—Portuguese, Greeks, West Indians, South Asians, Chinese, Vietnamese, and Chilean refugees—changing the city's character forever.

In the 1960s, the focus shifted from the suburbs to the city. People moved back downtown, renovating the handsome brick Victorians so characteristic of today's downtown. Yorkville emerged briefly as the hippie capital—the Haight-Ashbury of Canada. Gordon Lightfoot and Joni Mitchell sang in the coffeehouses, and antiwar protests took over the streets. Perhaps the failure of the experimental, alternative Rochdale College in 1968 marked the demise of that era. By the mid-1970s Yorkville had been transformed into a village of elegant boutiques and galleries and high-rent restaurants, and the funky village had moved to Queen Street West.

In the 1970s, Toronto became the fastest-growing city in North America. For years the city had competed with Montreal for first-city status, and now the separatist issue and the election of the Parti Quebecois in 1976 hastened Toronto's dash to the tape. It overtook Montreal as a financial center, boasting more corporate headquarters. Its stock market was more important, and it remained the country's prime publishing center. A dramatically different city hall opened in 1965, a symbol of the city's equally new dynamism. Toronto also began reclaiming its waterfront, with the development of Harbourfront. The city's new power and wealth came alive in new skyscrapers and civic buildings—the Toronto Dominion, the 72-story First Canadian Place, Royal Bank Plaza,

Roy Thomson Hall, the Eaton Centre, the CN Tower—all of which transformed the 1930s skyline into an urban landscape worthy of world attention.

Unlike the rapid building of highways and other structures completed in the 1950s, these developments were achieved with some balance and attention to the city's heritage. From the late '60s to the early '80s, citizens fought to ensure that the city's heritage was saved and that development was not allowed to continue as wildly as it had in the '50s. The best examples of the reform movement's success were the stopping of the proposed Spadina Expressway in 1971 and the fight against several urban renewal plans.

During the 1970s, the provincial government also helped develop attractions that would polish Toronto's patina and lure visitors: Ontario Place in 1971, Harbourfront in 1972, and the Metro Zoo and the Ontario Science Centre in 1974. Government financing also supported the arts and helped turn Toronto from a city with four theaters in 1965 to one boasting more than 40 today.

The city's growth has continued, with the 1989 opening of SkyDome, the first stadium in the world with a fully retractable roof, and the Air Canada Centre stadium in 1999. Construction of commercial and residential buildings continues to boom. A new subway line is being tunneled under Sheppard Avenue, and an extension of the Bloor-Danforth line is under consideration (the plan would take the subway all the way to the airport). In 2001, Toronto made a strong but unsuccessful bid to host the 2008 Olympics. Beijing won out, but planners remain interested in putting some of the proposals into place, particularly those that would revitalize the long-neglected waterfront area.

2 Famous Torontonians

Margaret Atwood (b. 1939)   Author, literary critic and poet. Atwood is best known for her futuristic novel *The Handmaid's Tale,* which was made into a Hollywood film. Perhaps Canada's most famous literary star—her books have been translated into more than 20 languages, and there's a university in Sweden that teaches a course just in the use of comedy in her novels—Atwood's oeuvre includes *The Edible Woman, The Robber Bride,* and *Alias Grace.*

Sir Frederick Banting (1891–1941)   Nobel laureate, scientist and artist. Banting was a renaissance man in his day. He was the co-discoverer of insulin at the University of Toronto; in 1923 he was awarded the Nobel Prize for his lifesaving research. Banting also distinguished himself as a captain in the Army Medical Corps in World War I and, later in life, as an artist.

John Candy (1950–1994)   Actor and comedian. The well-loved funnyman and Toronto native got his start in comedy with the local Second City troupe, playing a succession of crazy characters on *SCTV.* In Hollywood he made a succession of popular films that included *Only the Lonely, Uncle Buck,* and *Planes, Trains and Automobiles.* He was also a co-owner of the Toronto Argonauts football team.

Jim Carrey (b. 1962)   Actor and comedian. Before he became a $20-million man in Hollywood with movies like *The Mask, Ace Ventura: Pet Detective, Dumb and Dumber, The Truman Show,* and *The Majestic,* Carrey lit up the stage at local comedy clubs.

David Cronenberg (b. 1943)   Filmmaker, director and screenwriter. Cronenberg knows how to shock audiences—witness his 1996 film *Crash,* which explored violent injury fetishes and won the Jury Prize at the Cannes film

Festival. His eerie body of work includes *The Fly, The Dead Zone, Dead Ringers, Naked Lunch,* and *eXistenZ.*

Atom Egoyan (b. 1960)   Filmmaker and director. His films—including *Exotica, The Sweet Hereafter,* and *Felicia's Journey*—have been critical successes. Born in Cairo and raised in western Canada, Egoyan originally came to Toronto to study at the University of Toronto. He and his wife, actress Arsinee Khanjian, still call it home.

Barbara Gowdy (b. 1950)   Author and editor. Born in Windsor, Ontario, Gowdy moved to Toronto with her family at the age of four. She worked as an editor at the local publishing house of Lester & Orpen Dennys in the 1970s, but her greatest successes have been as an author. Her critically acclaimed novels include *We So Seldom Look On Love* and *The White Bone.*

Norman Jewison (b. 1926)   Academy Award-winning filmmaker and director. What award or honor hasn't Jewison won? With a raft of Oscars and Emmys, as well as an Order of Canada, Jewison is one of the most important filmmakers of our time. His films include *Fiddler on the Roof, The Cincinnati Kid, Jesus Christ Superstar, Agnes of God,* and *Moonstruck.* In 1986 the Toronto native established the Canadian Centre for Film Studies in his hometown.

Edward Lennox (1854–1933)   Architect. Lennox is responsible for designing much of the face that Toronto presents to the world. His legacy includes Old City Hall, Casa Loma, the King Edward Hotel, and the West Wing of Queen's Park, the seat of the Ontario legislature.

Marshall McLuhan (1911–80)   Media theorist and critic. The man who is best known for coining the phrases "the medium is the message" and "the global village" was a professor of English and the director of the Centre for Culture and Technology at the University of Toronto. His seminal works include *The Gutenberg Galaxy, Understanding Media,* and *War and Peace in the Global Village.*

Agnes McPhail (1890–1954)   Activist and politician. McPhail became the first woman Member of Parliament when she was elected to the House of Commons in 1921. She proposed Canada's first pay equity legislation, encouraged reform of the penal system, and served on the League of Nations, the precursor to the United Nations.

Lorne Michaels (b. 1944)   Writer and producer. Ever wonder why *Saturday Night Live* featured so many Canadian performers? That had more than a little to do with the fact that the show's creator was born and raised in Toronto. Michaels has also produced SNL alumni movies such as *Wayne's World* and *Black Sheep,* as well as the acclaimed *Kids in the Hall* television show.

Lucy Maud Montgomery (1874–1942)   Author. Her most famous creation, *Anne of Green Gables,* was set in Prince Edward Island, Montgomery's own birthplace. But most of her Anne books—and all of her *Emily of New Moon* series— were written after she settled in Ontario, first in Uxbridge and then in Toronto.

Mike Myers (b. 1963)   Actor, comedian, screenwriter. Myers became a celebrity when he starred on *Saturday Night Live* from 1989 to 1994 playing a series of characters that included metalhead rocker Wayne Campbell and German aesthete Dieter. On the big screen, Myers has struck gold writing and starring in films like *Wayne's World* and *Austin Powers* (and their respective sequels).

Michael Ondaatje (b. 1943)   Author, editor and poet. Ondaatje's name will forever be linked to his novel *The English Patient,* which was adapted into an

Oscar-winning film. Born in Sri Lanka, Ondaatje has taught at Toronto's York University since 1971. His acclaimed body of work includes *Running in the Family, In the Skin of a Lion,* and *Anil's Ghost.*

Lester B. Pearson (1897–1972)   Prime Minister, Nobel laureate and international statesman. Born, raised and educated in Toronto, Pearson's career as a diplomat took him to London and to Washington. He was a strong proponent of an alliance of Western powers, and his proposals formed part of the groundwork for the creation of NATO. In 1957 he was awarded the Nobel Prize for creating the United Nations emergency force in the Suez Canal crisis. He was elected Prime Minister in 1963, and held that position until he retired in 1968. But he continued his work on the world stage, establishing the United Nations peacekeeping forces.

Mary Pickford (1893–1979)   Actress, Academy Award winner, and film studio founder. Known in the Jazz Age as "America's Sweetheart," Pickford was born and raised in Toronto. While she made some memorable films, including *Little Lord Fauntleroy* and *Coquette,* her most important role was of movie magnate: in 1919, Pickford, her husband Douglas Fairbanks and Charlie Chaplin founded the United Artists film studio.

Christopher Plummer (b. 1927)   Acclaimed actor. He might be best remembered as the dashing Baron Von Trapp from *The Sound of Music,* but this versatile actor has played everyone from Sherlock Holmes to a renegade Klingon captain. Born in Toronto, the Shakespearean-trained Plummer has returned to his roots many times at the Stratford Festival in Ontario.

John Polanyi (b. 1929)   Nobel laureate and chemist. Polanyi, a University of Toronto professor, was award the Nobel Prize in Chemistry in 1996 for his use of chemiluminescence of molecules to highlight energy relationships in chemical reactions. Sound confusing? The fruit of his research has been the creation of vibrational and chemical lasers, the most powerful sources of infrared radiation currently known.

Joe Shuster (1914–92)   Creator of Superman. Poor Joe Shuster—if only he and his co-creator Jerome Siegel had known what a success their cartoon character would be one day, they wouldn't have sold the rights to D.C. Comics for a pittance in 1940. Shuster had been a newspaper boy for the Toronto Star, and in the early Superman strips, Clark Kent worked for the *Daily Star* (later rechristened as the *Daily Planet*). Toronto purportedly served as the model for the city of Metropolis.

Michael Snow (b. 1929)   Sculptor, painter and filmmaker. While galleries like New York's Museum of Modern Art and Paris's Musée d'Art Moderne feature Snow's installations, Toronto residents can appreciate the public works of art he created for his hometown, including the flock of fiberglass geese at the Eaton Centre and the sculpted caricatures of sports fans at SkyDome. Other notable works include his series of "Walking Women" paintings, and his acclaimed art film *Wavelength.*

Appendix B:
Useful Toll-Free Numbers
& Websites

AIRLINES

Aer Lingus
☏ 01/886-8888 in the U.K.
☏ 800/474-7424 in the U.S.
www.aerlingus.com

Aeroméxico
☏ 800/237-6639 in the U.S.
www.aeromexico.com

Air Canada
☏ 888/247-2262 in the U.S.
☏ 08705/247-226 in the U.K.
☏ 9286-8900 in Australia
☏ 379-3371 in New Zealand
www.aircanada.ca

Air New Zealand
☏ 0800/737-767 in New Zealand
☏ 800/262-1234 in the U.S.
www.airnewzealand.com

Air Transat
☏ 877/872-6728 in the U.S.
www.airtransat.com

Alitalia
☏ 8488-65642 in Italy
☏ 0870/544-8259 in the U.K.
☏ 800/361-8336 in the U.S.
www.alitalia.com

American Airlines
☏ 800/433-7300 in the U.S.
www.aa.com

America West Airlines
☏ 800/235-9292 in the U.S.
www.americawest.com

British Airways
☏ 0845/773-3377 in the U.K.
☏ 800/247-9297 in the U.S.
www.britishairways.com

Continental Airlines
☏ 800/525-0280 in the U.S.
www.continental.com

Delta Air Lines
☏ 800/221-1212 in the U.S.
www.delta.com

KLM Royal Dutch Airlines
☏ 020/4747-747 in the Netherlands
☏ 08705/074-074 in the U.K.
☏ 800/225-2525 in the U.S.
www.klm.com

Lufthansa
☏ 01803/803-803 in Germany
☏ 0845/773-7747 in the U.K.
☏ 800/645-3880 in the U.S.
www.lufthansa.com

Mexicana Airlines
☏ 54-48-09-90 in Mexico
☏ 800/531-2721 in the U.S.
☏ 020/8492-0000 in the U.K.
www.mexicana.com

Northwest Airlines
☏ 800/225-2525 in the U.S.
www.nwa.com

Qantas
☏ 02/9691-3636 in Australia
☏ 800/227-4500 in the U.S.
www.qantas.com

SAS Scandinavian Airlines
☏ 0845/6072-7727 in the U.K.
☏ 800/221-2350 in the U.S.
www.scandinavian.net

Singapore Airlines
☏ 0870/608-8886 in the U.K.
☏ 800/387-0038 in the U.S.
www.singaporeair.com

South African Airways
© 021/254-610 in South Africa
© 800/722-9675 in the U.S.
www.saa.co.za

United Airlines
© 800/241-6522 in the U.S.
www.united.com

US Airways
© 800/428-4322 in the U.S.
www.usairways.com

Virgin Atlantic Airways
© 0293/747-747 in the U.K.
© 800/862-8621 in the U.S.
www.virgin-atlantic.com

CAR-RENTAL AGENCIES

Alamo
© 800/327-9633
www.goalamo.com

Avis
© 800/331-1212
www.avis.com

Budget
© 800/527-0700
www.budget.com

Dollar
© 800/800-4000
www.dollar.com

Enterprise
© 800/325-8007
www.enterprise.com

Hertz
© 800/654-3131
www.hertz.com

National
© 800/CAR-RENT
www.nationalcar.com

Thrifty
© 800/367-2277
www.thrifty.com

MAJOR HOTEL & MOTEL CHAINS

Best Western International
© 800/528-1234
www.bestwestern.com

Choice Hotels International
© 800/4-CHOICE
www.choicehotels.com

Courtyard by Marriott
© 800/321-2211
www.courtyard.com

Days Inn
© 800/325-2525
www.daysinn.com

Doubletree Hotels
© 800/222-TREE
www.doubletree.com

Hilton Hotels
© 800/HILTONS
www.hilton.com

Holiday Inn
© 800/HOLIDAY
www.basshotels.com

Howard Johnson
© 800/654-2000
www.hojo.com

Hyatt Hotels & Resorts
© 800/228-9000
www.hyatt.com

InterContinental Hotels & Resorts
© 888/567-8725
www.intercontinental.com

ITT Sheraton
© 800/325-3535
www.starwood.com

La Quinta Motor Inns
© 800/531-5900
www.laquinta.com

Marriott Hotels
© 800/228-9290
www.marriott.com

Motel 6
© 800/4-MOTEL6
www.motel6.com

Radisson Hotels International
© 800/333-3333
www.radisson.com

Ramada Inns
© 800/2-RAMADA
www.ramada.com

Sheraton Hotels & Resorts
© 800/325-3535
www.sheraton.com

Super 8 Motels
© 800/800-8000
www.super8.com

Travelodge
© 800/255-3050
www.travelodgc.com

Vagabond Inns
© 800/522-1555
www.vagabondinn.com

Westin Hotels & Resorts
© 800/937-8461
www.westin.com

Wyndham Hotels & Resorts
© 800/822-4200
www.wyndham.com

Index

See also Accommodations and Restaurant indexes, below.

RESTAURANTS

Frommer's® Complete Travel Guides

Alaska
Alaska Cruises & Ports of Call
Amsterdam
Argentina & Chile
Arizona
Atlanta
Australia
Austria
Bahamas
Barcelona, Madrid & Seville
Beijing
Belgium, Holland & Luxembourg
Bermuda
Boston
Brazil
British Columbia & the Canadian Rockies
Budapest & the Best of Hungary
California
Canada
Cancún, Cozumel & the Yucatán
Cape Cod, Nantucket & Martha's Vineyard
Caribbean
Caribbean Cruises & Ports of Call
Caribbean Ports of Call
Carolinas & Georgia
Chicago
China
Colorado
Costa Rica
Denmark
Denver, Boulder & Colorado Springs
England
Europe
European Cruises & Ports of Call
Florida
France
Germany
Great Britain
Greece
Greek Islands
Hawaii
Hong Kong
Honolulu, Waikiki & Oahu
Ireland
Israel
Italy
Jamaica
Japan
Las Vegas
London
Los Angeles
Maryland & Delaware
Maui
Mexico
Montana & Wyoming
Montréal & Québec City
Munich & the Bavarian Alps
Nashville & Memphis
Nepal
New England
New Mexico
New Orleans
New York City
New Zealand
Northern Italy
Nova Scotia, New Brunswick & Prince Edward Island
Oregon
Paris
Philadelphia & the Amish Country
Portugal
Prague & the Best of the Czech Republic
Provence & the Riviera
Puerto Rico
Rome
San Antonio & Austin
San Diego
San Francisco
Santa Fe, Taos & Albuquerque
Scandinavia
Scotland
Seattle & Portland
Shanghai
Singapore & Malaysia
South Africa
South America
South Florida
South Pacific
Southeast Asia
Spain
Sweden
Switzerland
Texas
Thailand
Tokyo
Toronto
Tuscany & Umbria
USA
Utah
Vancouver & Victoria
Vermont, New Hampshire & Maine
Vienna & the Danube Valley
Virgin Islands
Virginia
Walt Disney World® & Orlando
Washington, D.C.
Washington State

Frommer's® Dollar-a-Day Guides

Australia from $50 a Day
California from $70 a Day
Caribbean from $70 a Day
England from $75 a Day
Europe from $70 a Day
Florida from $70 a Day
Hawaii from $80 a Day
Ireland from $60 a Day
Italy from $70 a Day
London from $85 a Day
New York from $90 a Day
Paris from $80 a Day
San Francisco from $70 a Day
Washington, D.C. from $80 a Day

Frommer's® Portable Guides

Acapulco, Ixtapa & Zihuatanejo
Amsterdam
Aruba
Australia's Great Barrier Reef
Bahamas
Berlin
Big Island of Hawaii
Boston
California Wine Country
Cancún
Charleston & Savannah
Chicago
Disneyland®
Dublin
Florence
Frankfurt
Hong Kong
Houston
Las Vegas
London
Los Angeles
Los Cabos & Baja
Maine Coast
Maui
Miami
New Orleans
New York City
Paris
Phoenix & Scottsdale
Portland
Puerto Rico
Puerto Vallarta, Manzanillo & Guadalajara
Rio de Janeiro
San Diego
San Francisco
Seattle
Sydney
Tampa & St. Petersburg
Vancouver
Venice
Virgin Islands
Washington, D.C.

Frommer's® National Park Guides

Banff & Jasper
Family Vacations in the National Parks
Grand Canyon
National Parks of the American West
Rocky Mountain
Yellowstone & Grand Teton
Yosemite & Sequoia/ Kings Canyon
Zion & Bryce Canyon

FROMMER'S® MEMORABLE WALKS

Chicago	New York	San Francisco
London	Paris	Washington, D.C.

FROMMER'S® GREAT OUTDOOR GUIDES

Arizona & New Mexico	Northern California	Vermont & New Hampshire
New England	Southern New England	

SUZY GERSHMAN'S BORN TO SHOP GUIDES

Born to Shop: France	Born to Shop: Italy	Born to Shop: New York
Born to Shop: Hong Kong, Shanghai & Beijing	Born to Shop: London	Born to Shop: Paris

FROMMER'S® IRREVERENT GUIDES

Amsterdam	Los Angeles	San Francisco
Boston	Manhattan	Seattle & Portland
Chicago	New Orleans	Vancouver
Las Vegas	Paris	Walt Disney World®
London	Rome	Washington, D.C.

FROMMER'S® BEST-LOVED DRIVING TOURS

Britain	Germany	Northern Italy
California	Ireland	Scotland
Florida	Italy	Spain
France	New England	Tuscany & Umbria

HANGING OUT™ GUIDES

Hanging Out in England	Hanging Out in France	Hanging Out in Italy
Hanging Out in Europe	Hanging Out in Ireland	Hanging Out in Spain

THE UNOFFICIAL GUIDES®

Bed & Breakfasts and Country Inns in:	Southwest & South Central Plains	Mid-Atlantic with Kids
California	U.S.A.	Mini Las Vegas
Great Lakes States	Beyond Disney	Mini-Mickey
Mid-Atlantic	Branson, Missouri	New England and New York with Kids
New England	California with Kids	
Northwest	Chicago	New Orleans
Rockies	Cruises	New York City
Southeast	Disneyland®	Paris
Southwest	Florida with Kids	San Francisco
Best RV & Tent Campgrounds in:	Golf Vacations in the Eastern U.S.	Skiing in the West
California & the West	Great Smoky & Blue Ridge Region	Southeast with Kids
Florida & the Southeast	Inside Disney	Walt Disney World®
Great Lakes States	Hawaii	Walt Disney World® for Grown-ups
Mid-Atlantic	Las Vegas	Walt Disney World® with Kids
Northeast	London	Washington, D.C.
Northwest & Central Plains		World's Best Diving Vacations

SPECIAL-INTEREST TITLES

Frommer's Adventure Guide to Australia & New Zealand	Frommer's Italy's Best Bed & Breakfasts and Country Inns
Frommer's Adventure Guide to Central America	Frommer's New York City with Kids
Frommer's Adventure Guide to India & Pakistan	Frommer's Ottawa with Kids
Frommer's Adventure Guide to South America	Frommer's Road Atlas Britain
Frommer's Adventure Guide to Southeast Asia	Frommer's Road Atlas Europe
Frommer's Adventure Guide to Southern Africa	Frommer's Road Atlas France
Frommer's Britain's Best Bed & Breakfasts and Country Inns	Frommer's Toronto with Kids
Frommer's Caribbean Hideaways	Frommer's Vancouver with Kids
Frommer's Exploring America by RV	Frommer's Washington, D.C., with Kids
Frommer's Fly Safe, Fly Smart	Israel Past & Present
Frommer's France's Best Bed & Breakfasts and Country Inns	The New York Times' Guide to Unforgettable Weekends
Frommer's Gay & Lesbian Europe	Places Rated Almanac
	Retirement Places Rated

Booked seat 6A, open return.

Rented red 4-wheel drive.

Reserved cabin, no running water.

Discovered space.

With over 700 airlines, 50,000 hotels, 50 rental car companies and 5,000 cruise and vacation packages, you can create the perfect get-away for you. Choose the car, the room, even the ground you walk on.

Travelocity.com
A Sabre Company
Go Virtually Anywhere.

You Need A Vacation.

700 Airlines, 50,000 Hotels, 50 Rental Car Companies, And A Million Ways To Save Money.

Travelocity.com
A Sabre Company
Go Virtually Anywhere.